Dynamics under Uncertainty

Dynamics under Uncertainty: Modeling Simulation and Complexity

Editors

Dragan Pamucar
Dragan Marinkovic
Samarjit Kar

MDPI • Basel • Beijing • Wuhan • Barcelona • Belgrade • Manchester • Tokyo • Cluj • Tianjin

Editors
Dragan Pamucar
Military academy, Department
of Logistics
University of Defence in
Belgrade
Belgrade
Serbia

Dragan Marinkovic
Faculty of Mechanical
Engineering and Transport
Systems
Technische Universitaet Berlin
Berlin
Germany

Samarjit Kar
Department of Mathematics
National Institute of Technology
Durgapur
India

Editorial Office
MDPI
St. Alban-Anlage 66
4052 Basel, Switzerland

This is a reprint of articles from the Special Issue published online in the open access journal *Mathematics* (ISSN 2227-7390) (available at: www.mdpi.com/journal/mathematics/special_issues/Dynamics_Uncertainty_Modeling_Simulation_Complexity).

For citation purposes, cite each article independently as indicated on the article page online and as indicated below:

LastName, A.A.; LastName, B.B.; LastName, C.C. Article Title. *Journal Name* **Year**, *Volume Number*, Page Range.

ISBN 978-3-0365-1576-2 (Hbk)
ISBN 978-3-0365-1575-5 (PDF)

© 2021 by the authors. Articles in this book are Open Access and distributed under the Creative Commons Attribution (CC BY) license, which allows users to download, copy and build upon published articles, as long as the author and publisher are properly credited, which ensures maximum dissemination and a wider impact of our publications.

The book as a whole is distributed by MDPI under the terms and conditions of the Creative Commons license CC BY-NC-ND.

Contents

About the Editors vii

Preface to "Dynamics under Uncertainty: Modeling Simulation and Complexity" ix

Dragan Pamučar, Dragan Marinković and Samarjit Kar
Dynamics under Uncertainty: Modeling Simulation and Complexity
Reprinted from: *Mathematics* 2021, 9, 1416, doi:10.3390/math9121416 1

Jose L. Salmeron and Antonio Ruiz-Celma
Synthetic Emotions for Empathic Building
Reprinted from: *Mathematics* 2021, 9, 701, doi:10.3390/math9070701 5

Aleksandar Aleksić, Slobodan Nedeljković, Mihailo Jovanović, Miloš Ranđelović, Marko Vuković, Vladica Stojanović, Radovan Radovanović, Milan Ranđelović and Dragan Ranđelović
Prediction of Important Factors for Bleeding in Liver Cirrhosis Disease Using Ensemble Data Mining Approach
Reprinted from: *Mathematics* 2020, 8, 1887, doi:10.3390/math8111887 17

Alptekin Ulutaş, Darjan Karabasevic, Gabrijela Popovic, Dragisa Stanujkic, Phong Thanh Nguyen and Çağatay Karaköy
Development of a Novel Integrated CCSD-ITARA-MARCOS Decision-Making Approach for Stackers Selection in a Logistics System
Reprinted from: *Mathematics* 2020, 8, 1672, doi:10.3390/math8101672 39

Dragan Pamučar, Fatih Ecer, Goran Cirovic and Melfi A. Arlasheedi
Application of Improved Best Worst Method (BWM) in Real-World Problems
Reprinted from: *Mathematics* 2020, 8, 1342, doi:10.3390/math8081342 55

Ali Hamzenejad, Saeid Jafarzadeh Ghoushchi, Vahid Baradaran and Abbas Mardani
A Robust Algorithm for Classification and Diagnosis of Brain Disease Using Local Linear Approximation and Generalized Autoregressive Conditional Heteroscedasticity Model
Reprinted from: *Mathematics* 2020, 8, 1268, doi:10.3390/math8081268 75

Mališa Žižović, Dragan Pamučar, Miloljub Albijanić, Prasenjit Chatterjee and Ivan Pribićević
Eliminating Rank Reversal Problem Using a New Multi-Attribute Model—The RAFSI Method
Reprinted from: *Mathematics* 2020, 8, 1015, doi:10.3390/math8061015 95

Ivan Pribićević, Suzana Doljanica, Oliver Momčilović, Dillip Kumar Das, Dragan Pamučar and Željko Stević
Novel Extension of DEMATEL Method by Trapezoidal Fuzzy Numbers and D Numbers for Management of Decision-Making Processes
Reprinted from: *Mathematics* 2020, 8, 812, doi:10.3390/math8050812 111

Li Li and Fucheng Liao
Preview Control for MIMO Discrete-Time System with Parameter Uncertainty
Reprinted from: *Mathematics* 2020, 8, 756, doi:10.3390/math8050756 127

Mališa Žižović, Dragan Pamučar, Goran Ćirović, Miodrag M. Žižović and Boža D. Miljković
A Model for Determining Weight Coefficients by Forming a Non-Decreasing Series at Criteria Significance Levels (NDSL)
Reprinted from: *Mathematics* 2020, 8, 745, doi:10.3390/math8050745 147

Chao Fu, Guojin Feng, Jiaojiao Ma, Kuan Lu, Yongfeng Yang and Fengshou Gu
Predicting the Dynamic Response of Dual-Rotor System Subject to Interval Parametric Uncertainties Based on the Non-Intrusive Metamodel
Reprinted from: *Mathematics* **2020**, *8*, 736, doi:10.3390/math8050736 . . . . **165**

Miomir Stanković, Željko Stević, Dillip Kumar Das, Marko Subotić and Dragan Pamučar
A New Fuzzy MARCOS Method for Road Traffic Risk Analysis
Reprinted from: *Mathematics* **2020**, *8*, 457, doi:10.3390/math8030457 . . . . **181**

About the Editors

Dragan Pamucar

Dr. Dragan Pamucar is an Associate Professor at the University of Defence in Belgrade, Department of Logistics, Serbia. Dr. Pamucar received a Ph.D. in Applied Mathematics, with a specialization in Multi-criteria modeling and soft computing techniques, from the University of Defence in Belgrade, Serbia in 2013 and an MSc degree from the Faculty of Transport and Traffic Engineering in Belgrade, 2009. His research interests are in the field of computational intelligence, multi-criteria decision-making problems, Neuro-fuzzy systems, fuzzy, rough and intuitionistic fuzzy set theory, and neutrosophic theory. Application areas include a wide range of logistics, management, and engineering problems.

Dragan Marinkovic

Dr. Dragan Marinkovic is a Full Professor at TU Berlin, Department of Structural Analysis, Germany. Dr. Marinkovic received Ph.D. and M.Sc. degrees from the University in Nis, Serbia. His research interest are in the fields of computational intelligence, multi-criteria decision-making problems, neuro-fuzzy systems, finite element analysis, nanomaterials, nanotechnology, materials science, modeling, mathematical modeling, experimentation, ansys, and labview. Application areas include a wide range of logistics and engineering problems.

Samarjit Kar

Dr. Samarjit Kar is a Professor at the National Institute of Technology Durgapur, West Bengal, India. His research interests are in the fields of computational intelligence, multi-criteria decision-making problems, neuro-fuzzy systems, fuzzy, rough and intuitionistic fuzzy set theory, and neutrosophic theory. Application areas include a wide range of logistics, management, and engineering problems.

Preface to "Dynamics under Uncertainty: Modeling Simulation and Complexity"

Dear Colleagues,

The dynamics of systems have proven to be very powerful tools in understanding the behavior of the different natural phenomena throughout the last two centuries. However, the attributes of natural systems are observed to deviate from their classical state due to the effect of different types of uncertainties. Actually, randomness and impreciseness are the two major sources of uncertainties in natural systems. Randomness is modeled by different stochastic processes, and impreciseness could be modeled by fuzzy sets, rough sets, Dempster–Shafer theory, etc.

Generally, symmetry, asymmetry, and antisymmetry are basic characteristics of binary relations used when modeling dynamical systems. Moreover, the notion of symmetry appeared in many articles about fuzzy sets, rough sets, Dempster–Shafer theory, etc. which are employed in the dynamical systems. Hence, the behavior of dynamical systems with uncertain variables, parameters, and functions has attracted academic attention in the recent past. Similarly, the study of the dynamics manifested in complex networks, or an interaction network of individuals, became popular in the last few decades. The study of collective dynamics in complex interaction networks has been proven to be useful to understand collective dynamic phenomena such as the emergence of cooperation between rational agents, synchronization of signal, like a flashlight or fireflies, rumor spreading, or conscious forming in a social network. Different methods of statistical mechanics are also successfully applied to study such complex systems and to understand the emergence of different collective behavior. When randomness and imprecision coexist in a system, the system is called a hybrid uncertain system. In such a system, the overall uncertainty is an aggregation of both types of uncertainties. However, in the context of modeling the behavior of complex natural systems, it is extremely important to analyze the effect of appropriate uncertainty to understand the predictability of different phenomena. Examples of such uncertain dynamical systems can be found in different levels of the universe ranging from the interaction of quantum particles to the complex interaction of biochemical molecules, such as signaling in the brain, or even complex social interactions like forming opinions.

Potential topics included but not limited to the following:

- Stochastic dynamics, SPDE

- Random dynamical systems

- Rough path analysis, random matrix

- Uncertain dynamics, fuzzy dynamics, rough dynamics

- Network analysis of complex dynamics

- Hybrid uncertainty analysis

- Simulation and complexity of dynamics under uncertainty

Dragan Pamucar, Dragan Marinkovic, Samarjit Kar
Editors

Editorial

Dynamics under Uncertainty: Modeling Simulation and Complexity

Dragan Pamučar [1,*], Dragan Marinković [2] and Samarjit Kar [3]

1. Department of Logistics, Military Academy, University of Defense in Belgrade, 11000 Belgrade, Serbia
2. Faculty of Mechanical Engineering and Transport Systems, Technische Universitaet Berlin, 10623 Berlin, Germany; dragan.marinkovic@tu-berlin.de
3. Department of Mathematics, National Institute of Technology, Durgapur 713209, India; samarjit.kar@maths.nitdgp.ac.in

* Correspondence: dpamucar@gmail.com; Tel.: +38-111-360-3188

Citation: Pamučar, D.; Marinković, D.; Kar, S. Dynamics under Uncertainty: Modeling Simulation and Complexity. *Mathematics* 2021, 9, 1416. https://doi.org/10.3390/math9121416

Received: 11 June 2021
Accepted: 16 June 2021
Published: 18 June 2021

Publisher's Note: MDPI stays neutral with regard to jurisdictional claims in published maps and institutional affiliations.

Copyright: © 2021 by the authors. Licensee MDPI, Basel, Switzerland. This article is an open access article distributed under the terms and conditions of the Creative Commons Attribution (CC BY) license (https://creativecommons.org/licenses/by/4.0/).

This issue contains the successful invited submissions [1–11] to a Special Issue of *Mathematics* on the subject area of "Dynamics under Uncertainty: Modeling Simulation and Complexity".

The dynamics of systems have proven to be very powerful tools in understanding the behavior of different natural phenomena throughout the last two centuries. However, the attributes of natural systems are observed to deviate from their classical state due to the effects of different types of uncertainties. In actuality, randomness and impreciseness are the two major sources of uncertainties in natural systems. Randomness is modeled by different stochastic processes, and impreciseness could be modeled by fuzzy sets, rough sets, the Dempster–Shafer theory, etc.

Hence, the behavior of dynamical systems with uncertain variables, parameters, and functions has attracted academic attention in the recent past. Similarly, the study of the dynamics manifested in complex networks, or an interaction network of individuals, has become popular in the last few decades. The study of collective dynamics in complex interaction networks has been proven to be useful in understanding collective dynamic phenomena such as the emergence of cooperation between rational agents, synchronization of signals as seen in a flashlight or fireflies, rumor spreading, or conscious forming of a social network, etc. Different methods of statistical mechanics are also successfully applied to the study such complex systems and to understand the emergence of different collective behaviors. When randomness and imprecision coexist in a system, the system is called a hybrid uncertain system. In such a system, the overall uncertainty is an aggregation of both types of uncertainties. However, in the context of modeling the behavior of complex natural systems, it is extremely important to analyze the effect of the appropriate uncertainty to understand the predictability of different phenomena. An example of such uncertain dynamical systems could be sited in different levels of the universe, ranging from the interaction of quantum particles to the complex interaction of biochemical molecules, such as signaling in the brain, or even in complex social interactions, such as while forming opinions.

This Special Issue includes the most important forecasting techniques applied to the modeling simulation and complexity in dynamic systems, such as, fuzzy multi-criteria techniques, artificial intelligence, the Dempster–Shafer approach, and heuristics.

Response to our call had the following statistics, Figure 1.

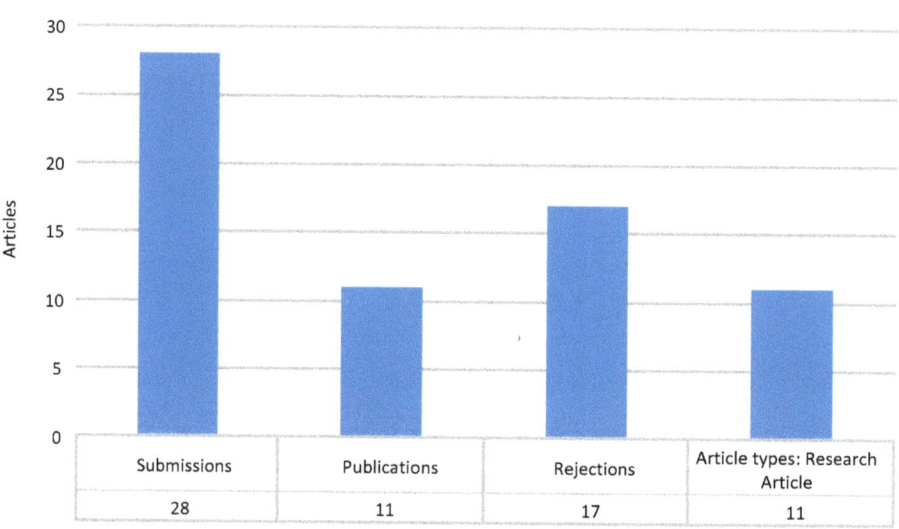

Figure 1. Special Issue statistics.

The geographical distribution of the authors (published papers) is presented in Table 1.

Table 1. Publications by country.

Countries	Countries
Serbia	7
Bosnia and Herzegovina	2
China	2
South Africa	2
Turkey	2
Vietnam	2
Chile	1
India	1
Saudi Arabia	1
Spain	1
Iran	1
UK	1

Published submissions are related to road traffic risk analysis [1], dual-rotor systems [2], multi-criteria decision making [3,5,6,8,9], MIMO discrete-time systems [4], the classification and diagnosis of brain disease [7], data mining [10], and empathic building [11].

This Special Issue presents 11 models, which are briefly presented in the next section. Stanković et al. [1] proposed fuzzy Measurement Alternatives and Ranking according to the COmpromise Solution (fuzzy MARCOS) method for road traffic risk analysis. In addition, they used the fuzzy PIvot Pairwise RElative Criteria Importance Assessment—the fuzzy PIPRECIA method— to determine the weights of the criteria on the basis of which road network sections were evaluated. Fu et al. [2] investigated the non-probabilistic steady-state dynamics of a dual-rotor system with parametric uncertainties under two-frequency excitations. Žižović et al. [3] presented a new method for determining weight coefficients by forming a non-decreasing series at criteria significance levels (the NDSL method). Li et al. [4] investigated the problems of state feedback and the static output feedback preview controller for uncertain discrete-time multiple-input multiple-output systems based on the parameter-dependent Lyapunov function and the linear matrix inequality technique. Pribićević et al. [5] developed a new multi-criteria methodology that enables the objective processing of fuzzy linguistic information in the pairwise comparison of criteria, and they called it the fuzzy DEMATEL-D method. Žižović et al. [6] presented a new MADM method in their research called RAFSI (Ranking of Alternatives through Functional mapping of criterion sub-intervals into a Single Interval), which successfully eliminates the rank reversal problem. Hamzenejad et al. [7] introduced a new robust algorithm using three methods for the classification of brain disease: (1) the Wavelet-Generalized Autoregressive Conditional Heteroscedasticity-K-Nearest Neighbor method; (2) the Wavelet-GARCH-KNN method; and (3) the Wavelet Local Linear Approximation. Pamučar et al. [8] presented an improved Best Worst Method for determining criteria weights in multi-criteria decision making. Ulutaş et al. [9] proposed a multiple-criteria decision-making approach for the selection of the optimal equipment for performing logistics activity. For defining the objective weights of the criteria, they applied the correlation coefficient and the standard deviation, and for the final ranking of the alternatives, they utilized the MARCOS method. Aleksić et al. [10] developed a prediction model that determines the most important factors for bleeding in liver cirrhosis. Salmeron and Ruiz-Celma [11] proposed an artificial intelligence-based approach to detect synthetic emotions based on Thayer's emotional model and Fuzzy Cognitive Maps.

We found the submissions and selections of papers for this issue very inspiring and rewarding. We also thank the editorial staff and reviewers for their efforts and help during the process.

Author Contributions: Conceptualization, D.P., D.M. and S.K.; methodology, D.P. and D.M.; formal analysis, S.K.; investigation, D.P.; supervision, D.M. and D.P. All authors have read and agreed to the published version of the manuscript.

Funding: This research received no external funding.

Conflicts of Interest: The authors declare no conflict of interest.

References

1. Stanković, M.; Stević, Ž.; Das, D.; Subotić, M.; Pamučar, D. A New Fuzzy MARCOS Method for Road Traffic Risk Analysis. *Mathematics* **2020**, *8*, 457. [CrossRef]
2. Fu, C.; Feng, G.; Ma, J.; Lu, K.; Yang, Y.; Gu, F. Predicting the Dynamic Response of Dual-Rotor System Subject to Interval Parametric Uncertainties Based on the Non-Intrusive Metamodel. *Mathematics* **2020**, *8*, 736. [CrossRef]
3. Žižović, M.; Pamučar, D.; Ćirović, G.; Žižović, M.; Miljković, B. A Model for Determining Weight Coefficients by Forming a Non-Decreasing Series at Criteria Significance Levels (NDSL). *Mathematics* **2020**, *8*, 745. [CrossRef]
4. Li, L.; Liao, F. Preview Control for MIMO Discrete-Time System with Parameter Uncertainty. *Mathematics* **2020**, *8*, 756. [CrossRef]
5. Pribićević, I.; Doljanica, S.; Momčilović, O.; Das, D.; Pamučar, D.; Stević, Ž. Novel Extension of DEMATEL Method by Trapezoidal Fuzzy Numbers and D Numbers for Management of Decision-Making Processes. *Mathematics* **2020**, *8*, 812. [CrossRef]
6. Žižović, M.; Pamučar, D.; Albijanić, M.; Chatterjee, P.; Pribićević, I. Eliminating Rank Reversal Problem Using a New Multi-Attribute Model—The RAFSI Method. *Mathematics* **2020**, *8*, 1015. [CrossRef]
7. Hamzenejad, A.; Jafarzadeh Ghoushchi, S.; Baradaran, V.; Mardani, A. A Robust Algorithm for Classification and Diagnosis of Brain Disease Using Local Linear Approximation and Generalized Autoregressive Conditional Heteroscedasticity Model. *Mathematics* **2020**, *8*, 1268. [CrossRef]
8. Pamučar, D.; Ecer, F.; Cirovic, G.; Arlasheedi, M. Application of Improved Best Worst Method (BWM) in Real-World Problems. *Mathematics* **2020**, *8*, 1342. [CrossRef]
9. Ulutaş, A.; Karabasevic, D.; Popovic, G.; Stanujkic, D.; Nguyen, P.; Karaköy, Ç. Development of a Novel Integrated CCSD-ITARA-MARCOS Decision-Making Approach for Stackers Selection in a Logistics System. *Mathematics* **2020**, *8*, 1672. [CrossRef]
10. Aleksić, A.; Nedeljković, S.; Jovanović, M.; Ranđelović, M.; Vuković, M.; Stojanović, V.; Radovanović, R.; Ranđelović, M.; Ranđelović, D. Prediction of Important Factors for Bleeding in Liver Cirrhosis Disease Using Ensemble Data Mining Approach. *Mathematics* **2020**, *8*, 1887. [CrossRef]
11. Salmeron, J.; Ruiz-Celma, A. Synthetic Emotions for Empathic Building. *Mathematics* **2021**, *9*, 701. [CrossRef]

Article

Synthetic Emotions for Empathic Building

Jose L. Salmeron [1,2,*] and Antonio Ruiz-Celma [3]

1. Data Science Lab, Universidad Pablo de Olavide, Ctra. de Utrera km. 1, 41013 Sevilla, Spain
2. Universidad Autónoma de Chile, 5 Poniente, 1670 Talca, Chile
3. Universidad de Extremadura, Avda. de Elvas s/n, 06006 Badajoz, Spain; aruiz@unex.es
* Correspondence: salmeron@upo.es

Abstract: Empathic buildings are intelligent ones that aim to measure and execute the best user experience. A smoother and intuitive environment leads to a better mood. The system gathers data from sensors that measure things like air quality, occupancy, noise and analyse it for the better experience of the users. This research proposes an artificial intelligence-based approach to detect synthetic emotions based on Thayer's emotional model and Fuzzy Cognitive Maps. This emotional model is based on a biopsychological approach to the analysis of the humans' emotional state. In this research, Fuzzy Grey Cognitive Maps are used, which are an extension of the fuzzy cognitive maps using the grey systems theory to model uncertainty. Fuzzy Cognitive Grey Maps (FGCMs) have become a very valuable theory for modeling high-uncertainty systems when small and incomplete discrete data sets are available. This research includes experiments with a couple of synthetic case studies for testing this proposal. This proposal provides an innovative way for simulating synthetic emotions and designing an empathic building.

Keywords: empathic building; fuzzy grey cognitive maps; Thayer's emotion model; artificial emotions; affective computing

Citation: Salmeron, J.L; Ruiz-Celma, A. Synthetics Emotions for Empathic Buildings. *Mathematics* **2021**, *9*, 701. https://doi.org/10.3390/math9070701

Academic Editor: Dragan Pamucar

Received: 16 December 2020
Accepted: 12 March 2021
Published: 24 March 2021

Publisher's Note: MDPI stays neutral with regard to jurisdictional claims in published maps and institutional affiliations.

Copyright: © 2021 by the authors. Licensee MDPI, Basel, Switzerland. This article is an open access article distributed under the terms and conditions of the Creative Commons Attribution (CC BY) license (https://creativecommons.org/licenses/by/4.0/).

1. Introduction

Autonomous systems have been designed to interact with one or more targets in an environment primarily without human intervention [1,2]. Some systems are capable of operating in an environment with high-level objectives and others that do not require any human involvement [3,4]. The complexity of this type of system with a high degree of autonomy makes the result of their interaction with the environment uncertain and it is not possible to ensure the desired behavior [5]. For this reason, approaches such as Off-Line Reinforcement Learning arise, which train agents in a controlled environment.

Regardless of the technique used for the design of autonomous systems, usually highly specialized tasks may require the inclusion of affective behaviors to improve their performance [6]. The role of emotions in human reasoning, daily activities, and decision-making is really critical. In other words, emotions have a huge impact on human intelligence. If their emotions are not working properly, then human beings will not make decisions properly. Therefore, there is a strong interrelation between embedding emotions in systems and making systems that include intelligence. Artificial emotion is an emerging research subject and aims to make machines have artificial emotions [7].

According to [8], affective forecasting studies have shown that people are biased in making both random and systematic errors when anticipating their own future emotional states. Because of the divergence between experienced and anticipated reactions, it is worth examining artificial intelligence methods to avoid these problems.

Empathic building is an intelligent building that aims to measure and execute the best user experience. A smoother and intuitive environment lead to a better mood. The system gathers the relevant data from IoT sensors that measure things like air quality, occupancy, noise and analyze it for the better experience of the users.

The main contribution of this paper is to propose Fuzzy Cognitive Grey Maps (FGCMs) as an innovative technique to predict artificial emotions in systems with a certain degree of autonomy in complex environments with high uncertainty. In addition, the dynamic analysis mapping of the FGCM uses Thayer's model of emotion within an emotional space. They define the categories of emotions in a matrix with four quadrants. This proposal translates said matrix to a two-dimensional Cartesian coordinate according to its valence and excitation.

The remainder of the paper is organized as follows. Section 2 presents the theoretical background. Section 3 shows the FGCMs fundamentals. Section 4 describe the methodological proposal. The next section details the experimental approach with two case studies and conclusions are finally shown.

2. Theoretical Background

Affective Computing seeks to bring computers and effective humans closer together. Affective computing tries to assign systems the human-like capabilities of emotions' observation, interpretation and generation [9]. As the authors explained previously, emotions have a huge impact on human physical states, beliefs, motivations, activities, decisions, and even wishes. An appropriate balance of emotions makes human beings having flexibility and creativity in solving problem [10].

Affective computing focuses on the recognition and processing of human emotions. Emotion processing is useful for analyzing human reactions, eliciting behavioral intentions, and generating reasonable responses from systems. Over the last years emotions' research has become a multi-disciplinary research field with a growing interest [11]. Moreover, emotions play a fundamental role in human-machine interaction. The simulation or automatic detection of emotional states aims to improve the interaction between humans and machines. Therefore, such simulation or detection would allow systems to perform alternative operating paths in accordance with current human emotions.

It could be worthy in a lot of real-life applications as a fear-type emotion recognition for audio-based surveillance systems [12], real-life emotion detection within a medical emergency call centre [13], semi-automatic diagnosis of psychiatric diseases [14] detection of children's emotional states in a conversational computer games [15], and so on.

On the other hand, relevant advances were made in speech synthesis as well [16]. Biosignals (e.g.: electrocardiogram (ECG or EKG), electroencephalogram (EEG), electromyogram (EMG) and electrooculogram (EOG) and so on), face and body images are options to detect emotional states [17,18]. However, those kinds of methods are more invasive, and so complex for applying in a lot of real applications [11]. This research proposes a non-invasive soft computing-based method for simulating emotions in real-world applications.

So far, there are a lot of emotion-based theories, such as the OCC model [19] and Thayer's emotion model. The OCC model comprises a classification of twenty-two emotion kinds within a hierarchy. The hierarchy includes three branches, namely emotions concerning the consequences of events, actions of agents, and aspects of objects. The emotions identified in the OCC model are the following: joy, hope, relief, pride and gratitude, like distress, fear, disappointment, remorse, anger and dislike [20].

Furthermore, some branches mix to form a set of composed emotions, specifically emotions concerning consequences of events. According to the OCC model, all emotions can be grouped in terms of the event that provokes each emotion. Scenarios that drive emotions can be folded into three kinds. The first scenario's kind that drives emotions is the consequences of events. The second kind of scenario that generates emotions is the actions of the agents. The third one that provokes emotions is the appearance of objects.

Thayer's emotional model is the affective framework that supports this research. Next, the fundamentals of that model are shown.

2.1. Thayer's Emotion Model

Thayer's model [21] is based on mood analysis as a biopsychological concept [22]. Thayer considers mood as an affective state highly related to psychophysiological and biochemical elements. Moreover, individual cognitive actions and casual events perform a critical role in its sudden understanding.

Thayer's emotion model is frequently used to avoid the ambiguity of adjectives [23]. Thayer's model organizes the major categories of emotions in a matrix according to their arousal (how calming versus exciting) and valence (how negative versus positive). The emotion categories can be separated into the four quadrants of the common two-dimensional cartesian coordinate system (Figure 1), valence (x), excitement (y). The origin models the lack of emotions.

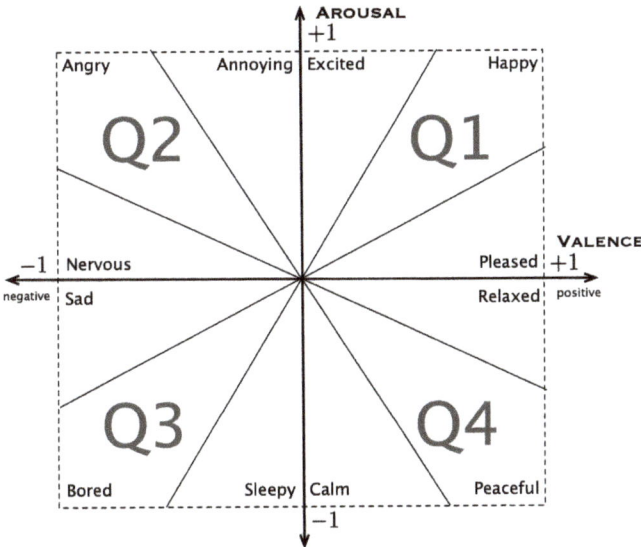

Figure 1. Emotional model.

Three emotions are located in each quadrant. The first quadrant (valence and positive arousal) is made up of emotions: excited, happy and excited. The second quadrant (negative valence and positive arousal) includes the emotions annoying, angry, and nervous. The third quadrant emotions (valence and negative arousal) are sadness, boredom, and sleepiness. Finally, the last quadrant (positive valence and negative arousal) contains the emotions calm, peace and relaxation. According to this, the emotional space is made up of twelve emotions.

The distance to the origin reflects the intensity of the emotion. Emotions closer to the source are less intense, while those further away from the source represent more intense emotions.

2.2. Emotional-Based AI Systems

Research has been done to develop emotional systems in various settings, such as emotions in music, art, and so on. The authors present some efforts below.

Marreiros et al. [20] designs a Ubiquitous Group Decision Support System (u-GDSS) that enables asynchronous and distributed computational services. One of the most interesting elements of this research is a multiagent-based simulator of emotional group decision-making. Zhou et al. [24] incorporates affective computing, emotion ontology within an emotion-aware service-oriented architecture. This framework allows us to publish emotion-sensitive services. Sharada & Ramanaiah [25] proposes an intelligent agent framework based on a neuro-fuzzy system to process the events. The emotion generation is based on a hopfield network.

Setiono et al. [26] proposes a game design with affective computing where the experience of the players is improved through the collection and understanding of the player's emotions. Han et al. [27] proposes a human-centric lifelong learning framework where the added value is affective computing. The results of their research prove that the incorporation of affective computing greatly improves the conventional alternatives. Kratzwald et al. [28] proposes a personalized learning transfer approach that uses sentiment analysis to achieve significant performance improvements.

In addition, Fuzzy Cognitive Maps have also been used as an interface between emotions, mood and behavior of human beings. Salmeron [29] builds emotional robots that operate in near real-time and improve their sensitivity. Salmeron & Lopez [30], Salmeron [31] presents a FCM-based proposal for generate synthetic emotions. This is the starting point of this research. FCMs have several valuable elements for the generation of synthetic emotions, such as flexible and adaptive reasoning and a high abstraction level [32,33]. Furthermore, this technique has been widely used to model and analyze complex dynamic systems [34–36]. As cognition tool, an FCM is easy to use and it can model knowledge and reasoning in an efficient way.

3. Fuzzy Grey Cognitive Maps
3.1. Fundamentals

Grey Systems Theory (GST) is a so interesting set of solving problem tools within environments with high uncertainty, under discrete small and incomplete data sets [37]. GST was created to analyze small data samples with poor information quality. GST has found successful applications in energy, transportation, military science, business, meteorology, medicine, agriculture, industry, and others.

Fuzzy Grey Cognitive Map is based on FCMs and GST, and it has become a very worthy theory for solving problems within domains with high uncertainty [38]. FGCMs offer an intuitive way to model and reason about concepts without loss of precision. An advantage of FGCMs is that non-technical decision-makers can understand all the problems in a given scenario using decision models represented as causal graphs. Furthermore, an FGCM allows locating the most critical factor that impacts the expected target or output concept.

The FGCM nodes are representing relevant concepts for the problem. The influence between nodes concepts are modeled by directed edges. An edge linking two nodes represents the grey causal impact of the causal concept on the effect concept. As FCMs, the FGCM models are represented by a (grey) adjacency matrix (A).

$$A = \begin{pmatrix} & c_1 & \cdots & c_n \\ c_1 & \otimes_{11} & \cdots & \otimes_{1n} \\ \vdots & \vdots & \ddots & \vdots \\ c_n & \otimes_{n1} & \cdots & \otimes_{nn} \end{pmatrix} \quad (1)$$

FGCMs can be considered as a special type of dynamic system that includes feedback, where the effect of the change in one node can impact other nodes, which successively can impact the concept that initiates the change. A FGCM models unstructured knowledge through causalities through grey concepts and grey relationships between them based on FCM [38–43].

Because FGCMs are hybrid methods that combine grey systems theory and neural networks, the state of each node (concept) is measured by its grey weight as follows

$$\otimes_{ij} = [\underline{\otimes}_{ij}, \overline{\otimes}_{ij}] \quad \underline{\otimes}_{ij} \quad \overline{\otimes}_{ij} \quad [\,1, +1] \quad [0, +1] \quad (2)$$

where i is the pre-synaptic (cause) node and j is the post-synaptic (effect) one. Note that if the FGCM is unipolar, then upper $\underline{\omega}$ and lower $\overline{\omega}$ weights belong to range $[0,+1]$. However, if the FGCM is bipolar, then upper and lower weights belong to range $[-1,+1]$.

FGCM dynamics begins with an initial grey vector state $c\ (0)$, which models a proposed initial imprecise stimuli. The initial grey vector state with n nodes is denoted as

$$\begin{aligned} c\ (0) &= (c_1(0), c_2(0), \ldots, c_n(0)) \\ &= ([\underline{c}_1(0), \overline{c}_1(0)], [\underline{c}_2(0), \overline{c}_2(0)], \ldots, [\underline{c}_n(0), \overline{c}_n(0)]) \end{aligned} \quad (3)$$

The updated nodes states are computed in an iterative inference process with an activation function (usually sigmoid or hyperbolic tangent function) [38,44,45], which maps monotonically the grey node value into a normalized range $[0,+1]$ or $[-1,+1]$, depending of the selected function. Note that grey arithmetic is detailed as [38]. Each single node would be updated as follows

$$c_j(t+1) = f\left(\sum_{i=1}^{n} \omega_{ij}\ c_i(t)\right) \quad (4)$$
$$[\underline{c}_j(t+1), \overline{c}_j(t+1)]$$

If the nodes has memory of the previous state the updating equation is as follows

$$c_j(t+1) = f\left(c_i(t) \sum_{i=1}^{n} \omega_{ij}\ c_i(t)\right) \quad (5)$$

where $\sum$ is the summation of grey numbers.

The most used activation function in FGMCs is unipolar sigmoid function when the nodes' value maps in the range $[0,1]$. If $f\ ( )$ is a sigmoid, then the i component of the grey vector state at $t+1$ iteration $(c\ (t+1))$ after the iterations would be as follows

$$c_i(t+1) = \left[\left(1+e^{-\lambda\ \underline{c}_i(t)}\right)^{-1}, \left(1+e^{-\lambda\ \overline{c}_i(t)}\right)^{-1}\right]. \quad (6)$$

Morever, the activation function $f\ ( )$ would be the hyperbolic tangent when the nodes' states map in the range [-1, +1]. It is computed as follows

$$c_i(t+1) = \left[\frac{e^{2\lambda\ \underline{c}_i(t)}-1}{e^{2\lambda\ \underline{c}_i(t)}+1}, \frac{e^{2\lambda\ \overline{c}_i(t)}-1}{e^{2\lambda\ \overline{c}_i(t)}+1}\right] \quad (7)$$

The nodes' states evolve along the FGCM dynamics and it could lead to three different scenarios.

- If the stability is reached, the FGCM inference process stop. It achieves a steady pattern of nodes' states, the so-called grey fixed-point attractor, or grey hidden pattern. This steady grey vector state shows the impact of the initial grey vector state on the final state of each FGCM grey node.
- In addition, the grey vector state could keep cycling between some fixed states. This situation is known as the limit grey cycle.
- A third possible state with a continuous activation function would be a grey chaotic attractor. It is when, instead of a steady-state, the FGCMs keep generating different grey vector states for each iteration.

FGCM includes greyness as an uncertainty measurement. Higher values of greyness mean that the results have a higher uncertainty degree. It is computed as follows

$$\phi(c_i) = \frac{\ell(c_i)}{\ell(\psi)} \quad (8)$$

where $\ell(c_i) = \overline{c}_i - \underline{c}_i$ is the absolute value of the length of grey node c_i state value, and $\ell(\psi)$ is the absolute value of the range in the information space, denoted by ψ. It is computed as follows

$$\ell(\psi) = \begin{cases} 1 & if \quad c_i, \omega_i \in [0,1] \quad c_i, \omega_i \in [-1,+1] \\ 2 & if \quad c_i, \omega_i \in [-1,+1] \end{cases} \quad (9)$$

3.2. FGCM Advantages over FCM

FGCMs have several advantages over conventional FCM [32,33,38,41,46,47]. A FGCM allows us to calculate the desired steady states managing the uncertainty and hesitation existing in the raw data (for instance, due to source noise) for the causal relationships between nodes, as well as within the states of the initial nodes.

Unlike FCMs, FGCM states have weights with grey numbers. In this way, FGCMs are able to model multi-meaning uncertainty in the relationships between concepts.

FGCM is an FCM generalization and it is considered closer to human decision-making than FCM is. It handles the inner hesitancy and uncertainty in complex systems by including greyness in edges and nodes. Indeed, the FGCMs' reasoning process output includes a degree of greyness expressed in grey values representing the certainty of the results.

FGCMs are also able to model more types of relationships than an FCM can. For example, FGCMs can run successfully models with edges where the intensity is just partially known or even is not known at all (e.g., $\omega_{ij} \in [-1,+1]$).

It is important to consider that, even in the case the dynamics of an FCM would finish with the same vector state as one FGCM after the whitenization, FGCMs still handle better the grey uncertainty and inner fuzziness of human emotions.

4. Proposal

Methodology

Figure 2 shows the flowchart of our methodological proposal. The starting points are the input data. It includes three kinds of input data. Firstly, the environment is a set of variables representing the influence of the environment over the affective state. Moreover, the mood and the temperament are input data because each individual has its own mood and temperament with the differences between them detailed before.

The effective engine is composed of FGCM-based models for building synthetic emotions. The reactions have influence over the mood. Afterwards, the higher state is selected and the arousal and the valence are computed. The affective state is computed using arousal and valence. If the system keeps running, the process is executed again. Note that the environment data is changing over time and it has an impact on the affective state.

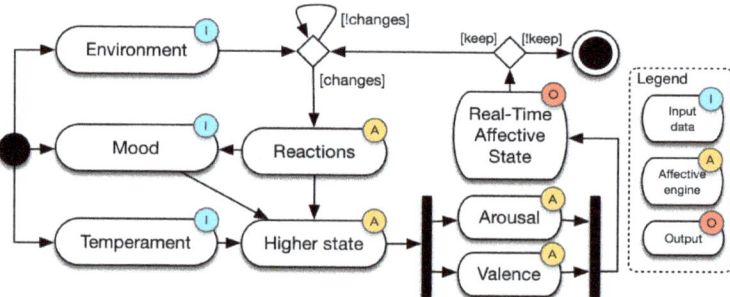

Figure 2. Architecture of the proposal.

5. Experiments and Discussion

With the intention of testing the proposal, this research analyzes two case studies of an artificial experiment. The objective is the simulation of the emotions of an autonomous system produced by the environmental conditions in a hospital facility.

It should be noted that the objective of the model is not to design a real-world emotional system, but only to test the FGCM approach for simulating synthetic emotions of people in the queue in a theoretical empathic building. For that reason, the authors have designed an FGCM-based emotional model shown in Figure 3. The concepts in this model are detailed in Table 1. Nodes c_1 and c_2 model arousal and valence respectively. They are the output concepts because those nodes are used to identified the emotions.

In each case of this experiment, the authors have designed a different initial vector state. In ths test case, the initial grey vector state $c_1(0)$ models the initial grey state values of the events at a given time of the process. As a result of the FGCM dynamics the final grey vector $c(t)$ models the achieved steady state. The steady grey vector $c(t)$ is the steady vector in the convergence region. The steady state of nodes c_1 and c_2, their greyness and the detected emotion are analysed.

Moreover, the authors analyze the FGCM dynamics in both cases with different settings. The setting is composed by the memory and slope. If the nodes do not have memory, then the updating equation is Equation (5). If the nodes have memory, then the updating equation is Equation (4). The activation function is the hyperbolic tangent because the emotional model needs negative values. The slope is the λ parameter of the Equation (7). According to literature [48], the slopes applied for both activation functions are 1, 3, and 5.

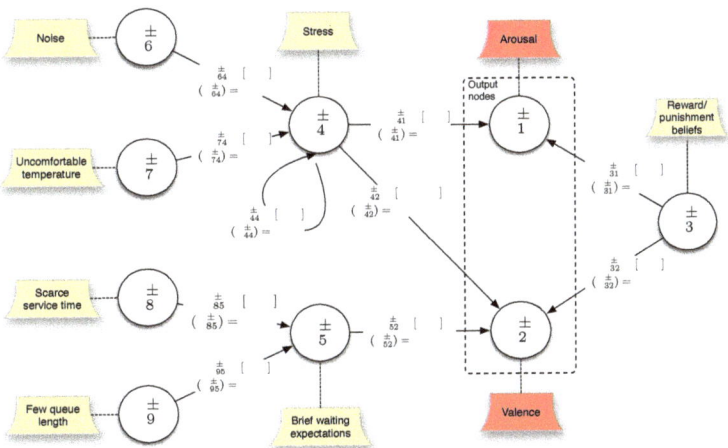

Figure 3. Fuzzy Cognitive Grey Map (FGCM)-based experimental model.

Table 1. FGCM nodes and description.

Node ($c_i^\pm$)	Label	Description
c_1	Arousal	State of being awake or reactive to stimuli
c_2	Valence	The intrinsic attractiveness (positive valence) or aversiveness (negative valence) of an emotion
c_3	Reward/Punishment	Reward is related with the queue's purpose
c_4	Stress	A person's response to a stressor such as noise or uncomfortable temperature
c_5	Waiting expectations	Waiting time
c_6	Noise	Environmental noise
c_7	Uncomfortable	Temperature higher or lower than comfortable
c_8	Scarce service time	Waiting time for each person
c_9	Few queue length	People in the queue

5.1. Experiment 1

For the first synthetic case study, the initial grey vector state is shown in Equation (10). Table 2 shows the results of this experiment with the different settings. Figure 4 show a graphical representation of the emotions achieved with each setting.

$$c_1(0) = ([0,0], [0,0], [.2,.2], [0,0], [0,0], [.2,.3], [.2,.1], [.1,.3], [.3,.4]) \quad (10)$$

Table 2. Results of experiment 1.

			Steady State			Greyness	
m	$f^\pm(\cdot)$	Slope	c1	c2	Emotion	c1	c2
F	tanh	1	[0.0, 1×10^{-6}]	[1×10^{-6}, 0.0]	neutral	6.3×10^{-7}	3.78×10^{-7}
F	tanh	3	[0.0, 1×10^{-5}]	[6×10^{-6}, 0.0]	neutral	5.03×10^{-6}	3.02×10^{-6}
F	tanh	5	[0.0, 0.1360]	[−0.0819, −0.0]	ligth nervous	6.8×10^{-2}	4.10×10^{-2}
T	tanh	1	[0.0380, 0.1766]	[0.1308, 0.4200]	ligth pleased	6.93×10^{-2}	1.45×10^{-1}
T	tanh	3	[0.3275, 0.9073]	[0.8188, 0.9958]	med-strong happy	2.90×10^{-1}	8.85×10^{-2}
T	tanh	5	[0.7331, 0.9990]	[0.9953, 0.9999]	strongly happy	1.33×10^{-1}	2.36×10^{-3}

Note that m means memory, F false and T true. Higher values of greyness are highlighted.

The achieved emotion with hyperbolic tangent as activation function is strongly related with the selected setting, especially the memory of the updating function. If the function has no memory (Equation (4)), then the emotion is almost neutral. However, if the function has memory (Equation (5)), then the emotion goes from pleased to happy as the slope increases.

The lower values of greyness for nodes c_1 and c_2 are achieved without memory (Equation (4)), and 1.0 as slope. The higher value of greyness for node c_1 is achieved with memory (Equation (5)), and 3.0 as slope. The higher value of greyness for node c_2 is achieved with memory (Equation (5)), and 1.0 as slope.

5.2. Experiment 2

For the second synthetic case study, the initial grey vector state is shown in Equation (11). Table 3 shows the results of this experiment with the different settings. Figure 5 show a graphical representation of the emotions achieved with each setting.

$$c_2(0) = ([[.0,.0],[.0,.0],[.0,.0],[.7,.6],[.2,.3],[.1,.0],[.0,.0],[.6,.7],[.4,.1]]) \quad (11)$$

The values of arousal (c_1) and valence (c_2) with hyperbolic tangent as activation function allow to compute peaceful and neutral as the achieved emotions. The achieved emotion is strongly related to the selected setting, especially the memory of the activation function. If the updating function has no memory (Equation (4)), then the emotion is mostly neutral. However, if the activation function has memory (Equation (5)), then the emotion is peaceful increasing intensity when the slope increases.

The lower values of greyness for nodes c_1 and c_2 are achieved without memory (Equation (4)), and 1.0 as slope. The higher value of greyness for node c_1 is achieved with memory (Equation (5)), and 1.0 as slope. The higher value of greyness for node c_2 is achieved with memory (Equation (5)), and 1.0 as slope.

Table 3. Results of experiment 2.

			Steady State			Greyness	
m	$f^{\pm}(\cdot)$	Slope	c1	c2	Emotion	c1	c2
F	tanh	1.0	$[1 \times 10^{-6}, 0.0]$	$[0.0, 1 \times 10^{-6}]$	neutral	6.61×10^{-7}	3.96×10^{-7}
F	tanh	3.0	$[1 \times 10^{-5}, 0.0]$	$[0.0, 6 \times 10^{-6}]$	neutral	5.21×10^{-6}	3.13×10^{-6}
F	tanh	5.0	$[-0.1360, 0.0]$	$[0.0, 0.0820]$	almost neutral	6.80×10^{-2}	4.10×10^{-2}
T	tanh	1.0	$[-0.4135, -0.1936]$	$[0.1794, 0.6163]$	medium peaceful	1.10×10^{-1}	2.18×10^{-1}
T	tanh	3.0	$[-0.9966, -0.9274]$	$[0.8990, 0.9999]$	strongly peaceful	3.46×10^{-2}	5.04×10^{-2}
T	tanh	5.0	$[-1.0, -0.9993]$	$[0.9978, 1.0]$	strongly peaceful	3.26×10^{-4}	1.09×10^{-3}

Note that m means memory, F false and T true. Higher values of greyness are highlighted.

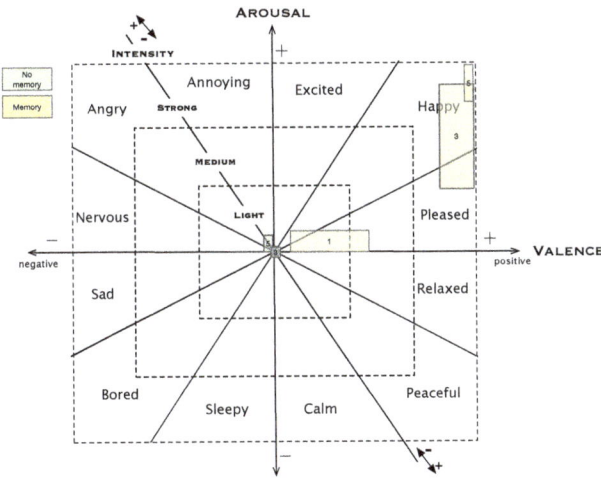

Figure 4. Experiment 1.

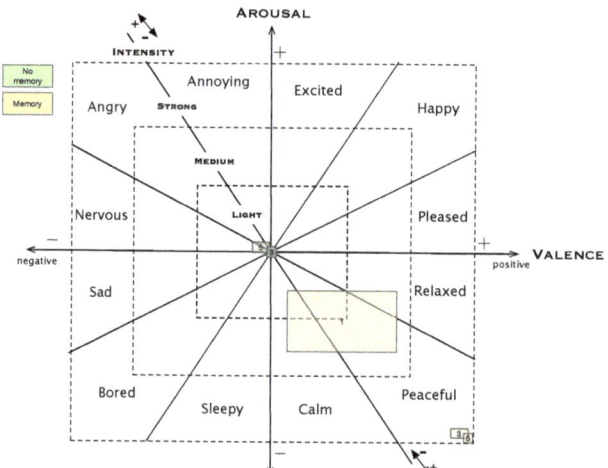

Figure 5. Experiment 2—Hyperbolic tangent.

6. Conclusions

This paper shows an FGCM-based system for synthetic emotions. FGCM is a grey graph for modeling causal reasoning within complex problems with high uncertainty. This research proves that it is possible to generate or simulate emotions obtained from sensors' raw data.

Note that this research is not an empirical one. An FGCM-based proposal based on sensors' raw data, concepts and output nodes is shown. Indeed, the aim is not to model a real-world system, but this research proposes an FGCM-based theoretical proposal so that ongoing research of real-world practitioners can apply to generate or simulate synthetic emotions within their own applications or systems.

The experiments' results prove that the outlet of this proposal is strongly related to the setting applied. According to the results, FGCMs with memory nodes are the best option for emotion modeling, and the lower slopes target emotions with less intensity. As a limitation, FGCMs are strongly related with their own setting and validation is not straightforward.

Author Contributions: conceptualization, J.L.S.; data curation, J.L.S.; formal analysis, J.L.S.; funding acquisition, A.R.-C.; investigation, J.L.S.; methodology, J.L.S.; project administration, A.R.-C.; validation, J.L.S. and A.R.-C.; writing—original draft, J.L.S.; writing—review and editing, J.L.S. All authors have read and agreed to the published version of the manuscript.

Funding: Ruiz-Celma was funded by the Government of Extremadura and the European Regional Development Fund, (Una manera de hacer Europa), through GR18137 and IB18008 support.

Institutional Review Board Statement: Not applicable.

Informed Consent Statement: Not applicable.

Data Availability Statement: Not applicable.

Acknowledgments: Salmeron would like to thank Tessella (Altran group, part of Capgemini) for their kind support.

Conflicts of Interest: The authors declare no conflict of interest.

References

1. Brun, Y.; Serugendo, G.D.M.; Gacek, C.; Giese, H.; Kienle, H.; Litoiu, M.; Muller, H.; Pezze, M.; Shaw, M. Engineering Self-Adaptive Systems through Feedback Loops, In *Software Engineering for Self-Adaptive Systems. Lecture Notes in Computer Science*, Cheng B.H.C., de Lemos R., Giese H., Inverardi P., Magee J., Eds.; Springer: Heidelberg/Berlin, Germany, 2009; pp. 48–70.
2. Precup, R.-E.; Preitl , S.; Petriu, E.; Bojan-Dragos, C.-A.; Szedlak-Stinean, A.-I.; Roman, R.-C.; Hedrea, E.-L. Model-Based Fuzzy Control Results for Networked Control Systems. *Rep. Mech. Eng.* **2020**, *1*, 10–25.
3. Ghosh, I.; Datta Chaudhuri, T. FEB-Stacking and FEB-DNN Models for Stock Trend Prediction: A Performance Analysis for Pre and Post Covid-19 Periods. *Decis. Mak. Appl. Manag. Eng.* **2021** *4*, 51–84.
4. Tziallas, G.; Theodoulidis, B. A controller synthesis algorithm for building self-adaptive software. *Inf. Softw. Technol.* **2004**, *46*, 719–727.
5. Khakpour, N.; Jalili, S.; Talcott, C.; Sirjani, M.; Mousavi, M.R. PobSAM: Policy-based Managing of Actors in Self-Adaptive Systems. *Electron. Notes Theor. Comput. Sci.* **2010**, *263*, 129–143
6. Lee-Johnson, C.P.; Carnegie, D.A. Mobile Robot Navigation Modulated by Artificial Emotions. *IEEE Trans. Syst. Man, Cybern. Part B Cybern.* **2010**, *40*, 469–480.
7. Shurong, N.; Jie, P.; Guangmei, X.; Guangping, Z.; Xuyan, T. Study on Artificial Emotion Model. In Proceedings of the ICNN&B '05. International Conference on Neural Networks and Brain, Beijing, China, 13–15 October 2005; Volume 3, pp. 1420–1424.
8. Hoerger, M.; Quirk, S.W. Affective forecasting and the Big Five. *Personal. Individ. Differ.* **2010**, *49*, 972–976
9. Tao, J.; Tan, T.; Picard, R.W. *Affective Computing and Intelligent Interaction*; Springer: Berlin, Germany, 2005.
10. Guojiang, W.; Xiaoxiao, W.; Kechang, F. Behaviour decision model of intelligent agent based on artificial emotion. In Proceedings of the 2nd International Conference on Advanced Computer Control (ICACC), Shenyang, China, 29–31 January 2010; pp. 185–189.
11. Albornoz, E.M.; Milone, D.H. & Rufiner, H.L. Spoken emotion recognition using hierarchical classifiers. *Comput. Speech Lang.* **2011**, *25*, 556–570.
12. Clavel, C.; Vasilescu, I.; Devillers, L.; Richard, G.; Ehrette, T. Fear-type emotion recognition for future audio-based surveillance systems. *Speech Commun.* **2008**, *50*, 487–503.
13. Devillers, L.; Vidrascu, L. Speaker Classification II: Selected Projects. *Lecture Notes in Computer Science*; Chapter: Real-Life Emotion Recognition in Speech; Springer: Berlin/Heidelberg, Germany, 2007; Volume 4441/2007, pp. 34–42.
14. Tacconi, D.; Mayora, O.; Lukowicz, P.; Arnrich, B.; Setz, C.; Trster, G.; Haring, C. Activity and emotion recognition to support early diagnosis of psychiatric diseases. In Proceedings of the 2nd International Conference on Pervasive Computing Technologies for Healthcare'08 Tampere, Tampere, Finland, 30 January– 1 February 2008; pp. 100–102.
15. Yildirim, S.; Narayanan, S.; Potamianos, A. Detecting emotional state of a child in a conversational computer game. *Comput. Speech Lang.* **2011**, *25*, 29–44.
16. Murray, I.R.; Arnott, J.L. Applying an analysis of acted vocal emotions to improve the simulation of synthetic speech. *Comput. Speech Lang.* **2008**, *22*, 107–129.
17. Schindler, K.; Van Gool, L.; de Gelder, B. Recognizing emotions expressed by body pose: A biologically inspired neural model. *Neural Netw.* **2008**, *21*, 1238–1246.
18. Vinhas, V.; Reis, L.P.; Oliveira, E. Dynamic multimedia content delivery based on real-time user emotions. Multichannel online biosignals towards adaptative GUI and content delivery. In Proceedings of the International Conference on Bio-inspired Systems and Signal Processing & Biosignals Porto, Portugal, 14–17 January 2009; pp. 299–304.
19. Ortony, A.; Clore, G.; Collins, A. *The Cognitive Structure of Emotions*; Cambridge University Press: Cambridge, UK, 1988.
20. Marreiros, G.; Santos, R.; Ramos, C.; Neves, J.; Novais, P.; Machado, J.; Bulas-Cruz, J. Ambient Intelligence in Emotion Based Ubiquitous Decision Making. In Proceedings of the Artificial Intelligence Techniques for Ambient Intelligence, IJCAI'07—Twentieth International Joint Conference on Artificial Intelligence, Hyderabad, India, 6–12 January, 2007.
21. Thayer, R.E. *The Biopsychology of Mood and Arousal*; Oxford University Press: New York, NY, USA, 1989.
22. Acampora, G.; Loia, V.; Vitiello, A. Distributing Emotional Services in Ambient Intelligence through Cognitive Agents. *Serv. Oriented Comput. Appl.* **2011**, *5*, 17–35.
23. Yang, Y.-H.; Lin, Y.-C.; Su, Y.-F.; Chen, H.H. Music emotion classification: A regression approach. In Proceedings of the IEEE International Conference Multimedia & Expo, Beijing, China, 2–5 July 2007; pp. 208–211.
24. Zhou, J.; Yu, C.; Riekki, J.; Karkkainen, E. AmE framework: A model for emotion-aware ambient intelligence. In Proceedings of the The Second International Conference on Affective Computing and Intelligent Interaction (ACII2007), Lisbon, Portugal, 12–14 September 2007.
25. Sharada, G.; Ramanaiah, O.B.V. An Artificial Intelligence Based Neuro-Fuzzy System Emotional Intelligence. *Int. J. Comput. Appl.* **2010**, *1*, 74–79.
26. Setiono, D.; Saputra, D.; Putra, K.; Moniaga, J.V.; Chowandaa, A. Enhancing Player Experience in Game With Affective Computing. *Procedia Comput. Sci.* **2021**, *179*, 781–788
27. Han, J.; Zhang, Z.; Pantic, M.; Schuller, B. Internet of emotional people: Towards continual affective computing cross cultures via audiovisual signals. *Future Gener. Comput. Syst.* **2021**, *114*, 294–306.
28. Kratzwald, B.; Ilić, S.; Kraus, M.; Feuerriegel, S.; Prendinger, H. Deep learning for affective computing: Text-based emotion recognition in decision support. *Decis. Support Syst.* **2018**, *115*, 24–35.
29. Salmeron, J.L. Augmented fuzzy cognitive maps for modelling LMS critical success factors. *Knowl. Based Syst.* **2009**, *22*, 275–278.

30. Salmeron, J.L.; Lopez, C. Forecasting Risk Impact on ERP Maintenance with Augmented Fuzzy Cognitive Maps. *IEEE Trans. Softw. Eng.* **2011**, *38*, 439–452.
31. Salmeron, J.L. Fuzzy cognitive maps for artificial emotions forecasting. *Appl. Soft Comput.* **2012**, *12*, 3704–3710.
32. Salmeron, J.L.; Rahimi, S.A.; Navalie, A.M.; Sadeghpour, A. Medical Diagnosis of Rheumatoid Arthritis using Data driven PSO-FCM. *Neurocomputing* **2017**, *232*, 104–112.
33. Salmeron, J.L.; Ruiz-Celma, A.; Mena, A. Learning FCMs with multi-local and balanced memetic algorithms for forecasting drying processes. *Neurocomputing* **2017**, *232*, 52–57.
34. Salmeron, J.L.; Vidal, R.; Mena, A. Ranking Fuzzy Cognitive Maps based scenarios with TOPSIS. *Expert Syst. Appl.* **2012**, *39*, 2443–2450.
35. Vanhoenshoven, F.; Napoles, G.; Froelich, W.; Salmeron, J.L.; Vanhoof, K.; Pseudoinverse Learning of Fuzzy Cognitive Maps for Multivariate Time Series Forecasting. *Appl. Soft Comput.* **2020**, *95*, 106461.
36. Salmeron, J.L.; Papageorgiou, E.I. A Fuzzy Grey Cognitive Maps-based Decision Support System for Radiotherapy Treatment Planning. *Knowl. Based Syst.* **2012**, *30*, 151–160.
37. Deng, J.L. Introduction to grey system theory. *J. Grey Syst.* **1989**, *1*, 1–24
38. Salmeron, J.L. Modelling grey uncertainty with Fuzzy Grey Cognitive Maps. *Expert Syst. Appl.* **2010**, *37*, 7581–7588.
39. Froelich, W.; Salmeron, J.L. Evolutionary Learning of Fuzzy Grey Cognitive Maps for the Forecasting of Multivariate, Interval-Valued Time Series. *Int. J. Approx. Reason.* **2014**, *55*, 1319–1335.
40. Rodriguez-Repiso, L.; Setchi, R.; Salmeron, J.L. Modelling IT Projects success with Fuzzy Cognitive Maps. *Expert Syst. Appl.* **2007**, *32*, 543–559.
41. Salmeron, J.L. An Autonomous FGCM-based System for Surveillance Assets Coordination. *J. Grey Syst.* **2016**, *28*, 27–35.
42. Salmeron, J.L.; Gutierrez, E. Fuzzy Grey Cognitive Maps in Reliability Engineering. *Appl. Soft Comput.* **2012**, *12*, 3818–3824.
43. Xirogiannis, G.; Glykas, M. Fuzzy cognitive maps in business analysis and performance-driven change. *IEEE Trans. Eng. Manag.* **2004**, *51*, 334–351.
44. Papageorgiou, E.I.; Salmeron, J.L. Learning Fuzzy Grey Cognitive Maps using Nonlinear Hebbian-based approach. *Int. J. Approx. Reason.* **2012**, *53*, 54–65.
45. Salmeron, J.L.; Papageorgiou, E.I. Fuzzy Grey Cognitive Maps and Nonlinear Hebbian Learning in process control. *Appl. Intell.* **2014**, *41*, 223–234.
46. Napoles. G.; Salmeron, J.L.; Vanhoof, K. Construction and Supervised Learning of Long-Term Grey Cognitive Networks. *IEEE Trans. Cybern.* **2021**, *51*, 686–695.
47. Salmeron, J.L.; Palos, P. Uncertainty propagation in Fuzzy Grey Cognitive Maps with Hebbian-like learning algorithms. *IEEE Trans. Cybern.* **2019**, *49*, 211–220.
48. Bueno, S.; Salmeron, J.L. Benchmarking main activation functions in fuzzy cognitive maps. *Expert Syst. Appl.* **2009**, *36* (3 Part 1), 5221–5229.

Article

Prediction of Important Factors for Bleeding in Liver Cirrhosis Disease Using Ensemble Data Mining Approach

Aleksandar Aleksić [1], Slobodan Nedeljković [2], Mihailo Jovanović [3], Miloš Ranđelović [4], Marko Vuković [5], Vladica Stojanović [6], Radovan Radovanović [7], Milan Ranđelović [8] and Dragan Ranđelović [1,*]

1. Faculty of Diplomacy and Security, University Union-Nikola Tesla Belgrade, 11000 Beograd, Serbia; aleksandar.aleksic@fdb.edu.rs
2. Ministry of Interior, Government of the Republic of Serbia, 11000 Beograd, Serbia; slobodan.nedeljkovic@mup.gov.rs
3. Office for Information Technologies and e-Government, Government of the Republic of Serbia, 11000 Beograd, Serbia; mihailo.jovanovic@gov.rs
4. Magna Seating D.O.O., 25250 Odžaci, Serbia; micii84@gmail.com
5. Public Utillity Company for Underground Exploatation of Coal Resavica, 11000 Beograd, Serbia; vukovic984@gmail.com
6. Department of Information Technology, University of Criminal Investigation and Police Studies, 11000 Beograd, Serbia; vladica.stojanovic@kpa.edu.rs
7. Department of Forensic Engineering, University of Criminal Investigation and Police Studies, 11000 Beograd, Serbia; radovan.radovanovic@kpa.edu.rs
8. Science Technology Park Niš, 18000 Niš, Serbia; milan.randjelovic@ntp.rs
* Correspondence: dragan.randjelovic@fdb.edu.rs

Received: 17 September 2020; Accepted: 13 October 2020; Published: 30 October 2020

Abstract: The main motivation to conduct the study presented in this paper was the fact that due to the development of improved solutions for prediction risk of bleeding and thus a faster and more accurate diagnosis of complications in cirrhotic patients, mortality of cirrhosis patients caused by bleeding of varices fell at the turn in the 21th century. Due to this fact, an additional research in this field is needed. The objective of this paper is to develop one prediction model that determines most important factors for bleeding in liver cirrhosis, which is useful for diagnosis and future treatment of patients. To achieve this goal, authors proposed one ensemble data mining methodology, as the most modern in the field of prediction, for integrating on one new way the two most commonly used techniques in prediction, classification with precede attribute number reduction and multiple logistic regression for calibration. Method was evaluated in the study, which analyzed the occurrence of variceal bleeding for 96 patients from the Clinical Center of Nis, Serbia, using 29 data from clinical to the color Doppler. Obtained results showed that proposed method with such big number and different types of data demonstrates better characteristics than individual technique integrated into it.

Keywords: ensemble techniques; data mining; classification and discrimination; linear regression; applied mathematics general; prediction theory; theory of mathematical modeling; medical applications

1. Introduction

Determination of relevant predictors in many fields of human life is important research challenge, including medicine. Research described in this paper is motivated from the fact that from one side, the liver disease causes about 3.5% of all deaths, which is a big number from approximately two million deaths per year worldwide, and that bleeding of varices is most common complication for successful treatment of liver cirrhosis [1]. On the other side, fact that the development of improved computer solutions for prediction of factors of bleeding, at the beginning of the 21th century, enables significantly more comprehensive, accurate, and fast diagnosis. Namely, the best way to determine esophageal varices is through gastrointestinal endoscopy. Since less than 50% of cirrhotic patients have varices and endoscopy is a nonconforming intervention, this way, a noninvasive methodology for predicting patients with the highest risk of bleeding and then applying endoscopy is the right choice [2]. In that way, good prediction indirectly reduces mortality of cirrhosis patients caused by bleeding of varices, so that further researches in this area impose itself as a serious challenge [3].

Basic idea of authors in research proposed in this paper was to apply concept of the classification algorithm, as one of a group of machine learning algorithms, so that a two-class classifier classifies the results into two classes, which is in each classification procedure completely defined with suitable 2 × 2 confusion matrix that content number of a true and false positive classification attempts and true and false negative classification attempts and could be applied in prediction of significant factors for bleeding in liver cirrhosis. Namely, concepts of diagnostic sensitivity and specificities are commonly used in the field of laboratory medicine [4]. Diagnostic test results are classified as positive or negative, where positive results imply the possibility of illness, whereas negative results indicate higher probability of absence of the illness. However, most of these tests are conducted by the instruments with high but not perfect accuracy, thus introducing certain errors in the diagnosis results and causing false positive and false negative results. Diagnosis sensitivity that is also known as true positive rate represents the possibility to detect ill patients actually, and it is defined as the number of true positive over the total number of ill patients, including the true positive and false negative patients. Hence, proper detection should discover patients with positive results within ill patients. On the other hand, specificity that is also known as a true negative rate represents possibility to detect healthy patients, and it is defined as the number of true negative patients over the total number of healthy patients, including the true negative and false positive ones. Thus, proper determination should also provide negative result for healthy patients. Assuming that determination provides only positive result, then the sensitivity will be 100%, but in that case, healthy patients would be falsely identified as ill [5]. In theory of statistic, experiments can be used to affirm hypotheses on differences and relationship between two or more groups of variables, and such experiments are called tests, or they can be used to determine influence of variables on dependent variable(s), such multifactor experiments are called valuations, [6] and such one is applied in the presented case study in this paper. Data mining approach, where belongs classification methodology, has been widely used in different fields of human life, such as economics [7], justice [8], medicine [9], etc. Data mining has also been applied for solving various problems, especially in diagnosis in medicine [10] and in the field of diagnosis of liver cirrhosis as in [11]. Bioinformatics and data mining have been the research hot topics in the computational science field [12–16]. Data mining is generally a two stage methodology that in the first stage involves the collection and management of a large amounts of data, which in second stage is used to determine patterns and relationships in collected data using machine learning algorithms. [17–20].

It is known that esophagus bleeding is not only the most frequent but also the most severe complication in cirrhotic patients that directly threatens patient's life [21–24]. Because of this fact, the main objective of this paper is to analyze as many factors as possible, which cause this bleeding, and specifically in this study, we have determined 29 factors, which belong to different types of data, from clinical and biochemical view, obtained via endoscopic and ultrasound data to the color Doppler data. In this way, we aimed to be as comprehensive as possible and determine and rank these factors as risk indicators of varices bleeding. Consequently, due to high mortality ratio caused by bleeding of varices, considering the bleeding risk assessment is crucial for proper therapy admission. The case study, we included 96 cirrhotic patients from the Clinical Center of Nis, Serbia. This mentioned study studied risks of initial varices in cirrhosis patients, as well as risks of early and late bleeding reoccurrence. As the main result of this study, authors proposed model which predicts the assessment of the significance of the individual parameters for variceal bleeding and survival probability of cirrhotic patients, which is in addition to the above adequate therapy very important and for determination of patient priority on the liver transplant waiting lists. Namely, in literature and practice connected with the problem of bleeding in liver cirrhosis, we can find research gap between request that for considering this problem, it is necessary to include more different types of parameters and, e.g., uncomfortable endoscopy, which, in turn, may be cost ineffective because less than 50% of a cirrhosis patients are with varices, from the medical standpoint from one side [25]. From the other mathematical side, we have the research gap between the need to include as many factors as possible in the consideration of bleeding problems in liver cirrhosis, which, in turn, cause the undesirable occurrence of noise in the data and, consequently, the need to reduce their number provided that the accuracy of the prediction is maintained [26]. Due to this fact, it is becoming more common request for using more noninvasive factors as possible, which is commonly solved using data mining technique. We can find more articles that deals with using different techniques of data mining for determination of risk indicators in different complications in disease liver cirrhosis [27–29] and risk for variceal bleeding as in [30,31]. Because two main methodologies of data mining approach are used in this paper, data mining classification technique with feature selection and logistic regression for prediction of variceal bleeding in cirrhotic patients, it is necessary to present the state of the art closely observed on the subject methodology, which solves the considered problem. This enabled authors to produce one new ensemble data mining model whose validity is proven by the results obtained in the case study. In literature, we find few papers that deals with machine learning approaches, which studied general complications in liver cirrhosis disease as, e.g., in [32,33], also on prediction of esophageal varices [34–38], and we found different forms of their integration but we did not find integration that we propose in this paper.

Authors as the subject of the paper set the answer to the research question, i.e., proof of the hypothesis, that it is possible to integrate classification method with attribute reduction also and regression into one ensemble method, which has better characteristics than each of them individually applied. To confirm the hypothesis and answer the research question, the authors used the results obtained with application of their novel proposed model in the case study described in previous paragraph of this section.

The remaining of this paper is organized as follows. After Section 1 Introduction, which after short explanation of motivation for authors to work on this paper, describes in four paragraphs the concept, objectives and existing research gap, contribution, and the organization of the paper and gives author's review of world literature which deal with bleeding problems in liver cirrhosis as well as with application of classification and logistic regression in prediction models, the other sections continues. Next, Section 2 Materials and Methods is part of paper that presents the background, which enables solving of the considered problem to be solved in this paper, introducing the methodology adopted in the proposed solution. In Section 3 Results are presented results obtained with proposed new methodology at concrete case study performed in the Clinical Center of Nis, Serbia. In Section 4 Discussion, authors discuss possibilities of theirs proposed approach and especially to clinical interpretation of the results, and in the end of this paper are conclusion remarks in Section 5 Conclusions.

2. Materials and Methods

2.1. Materials

2.1.1. Determination of Relevant Predictors of Bleeding Problems

The aim of this paper is to apply the integrated data mining methodology to the prediction on risk indicators of bleeding of varices using comprehensive analyze of different types of the clinical, biochemical, endoscopic, ultrasound, and color Doppler data [36]. As mentioned previously, the study included 96 cirrhotic patients. In order to conduct the case study more efficiently, two groups of patients were formed according to whether they previously had bleeding. The group of patients with episodes of bleeding of varices was divided into two subgroups, namely, patients with and without endoscopic sclerosis of esophagus varicosity. Clinical and biochemical parameters (Child–Pugh and MELD score) were analyzed along with endoscopic parameters (size, localization, and varicosity appearance) and ultrasound and color Doppler parameters. So big number of 29 considered factors in which 5 different type of parameters are used, because of the high mortality rate due to bleeding of varices, it is necessary to have precise risk assessment of bleeding for timely implementation of therapeutic interventions and also to assess precise prognosis and survival rate of patients with cirrhosis, which is important for appropriate therapy of patients and good patient prioritization on the waiting list for liver transplantation.

Benedeto-Stojanov et al. in [37] considered the bleeding problem in cirrhotic patients with the aim to evaluate the survival prognosis of patients with liver cirrhosis using the Model of End-stage Liver Disease (MELD) and Child–Pugh scores and to analyze the MELD score prognostic value in patients with both the liver cirrhosis and the bleeding of varices. Benedeto-Stojanov et al. studied in [38] the bleeding of varices as the most common life-threating complication of a cirrhotic patient with the aim to analyze the sources of gastroesophageal bleeding in cirrhotic patients and to identify the risk factors of bleeding from esophageal varices. Durand and Valla in [39] introduced a MELD score that was originally designed for assessing the prognosis of cirrhotic patients that underwent the transjugular intrahepatic portosystemic shunt (TIPS) and defined it as a continuous score relying on three objective variables. In the case of TIPS, MELD score has been proven as a robust marker of early mortality across a wide spectrum of causes of cirrhosis, but even though, 10–20% of patients have been still misclassified. In [40], authors described their developed Rockall risk scoring system for predicting the outcome of upper gastrointestinal (GI) bleeding, including bleeding of varices with the aim to investigate the mortality rate of first bleeding of varices and the predictability of each scoring system. Kleber and Sauerbruch studied in [41] the hemodynamic and endoscopic parameters as well as liver function and coagulation status and patient's history regarding the bleeding incidence. The following parameters were found to be correlated with an increased risk of bleeding: the first year after diagnosis of varices, positive history of bleeding of varices, presence of varices with large diameters, high blood pressure or a red color sign, concomitant gastric varices or development of a liver cell carcinoma. Authors concluded in [42] that using MELD score-based allocation, many current transplant recipients have shown advanced end-stage liver disease with an elevated international normalized ratio (INR).

The relationship between abnormalities in coagulation tests and the risk of bleeding has recently been investigated in patients with liver disease. In [32], we can notice that risk factors for mortality and rebleeding following acute variceal hemorrhage (AVH) were not well enough and completely established, and they tried to determine risk factors for emergence of mortality in 6-week and rebleeding within 5 days in cirrhotic patients and AVH.

2.1.2. Methods of Aggregation in Classification and Prediction Models

Boosting as an ensemble algorithm is one of the most important recent technique in classification methodology. Boosting sequentially applies classification algorithm to readjust the training data and then takes a weighted majority of the votes of a series of classifiers. Even being simple, this strategy improves performances of many classification algorithms significantly. For a two-class problem, boosting can be viewed as an approximation to additive modeling on the logistic scale using the maximum Bernoulli likelihood as a criterion [43]. Over the past few years, boosting technique has appeared as one of the most powerful methods for predictive analytics. Some implementations of powerful boosting algorithms [44] can be used for solving the regression and classification problems, using continuous and/or categorical predictors [45,46]. Finally, using predictive analytics with gradient boosting in clinical medicine is discussed in [47].

We can find a different kind of mentioned ensemble algorithm in prediction of most important factors using other methodologies as well as aggregation methods in decision-making problem, e.g., [48,49].

In computer science, e.g., a logistic model tree (LMT) represents a classification model which has an associated supervised training algorithm in which logistic regression and decision tree learning are combined [50].

2.2. Methods

2.2.1. Classification Method for Relevant Predictor Determination

Classification is frequently studied methodology in field of machine learning. Classification algorithm, as a predictive method, represents a supervised machine learning technique and implies the existence of a group of labeled instances for each class of objects and predicts the value of a (categorical) attribute (i.e., class) based on the values of other attributes, which are called predicting attributes [51]. The algorithm tries to discover relationships between the attributes in order to achieve accurate prediction of the outcome. The prediction result depends on the input and discovered relationships between the attributes. Some of the most common classification methods are classification and decision trees (e.g., ID3, C4.5, CART, SPRINT, THAID, and CHAID), Bayesian classifiers (e.g., Naive Bayes and Bayes Net), artificial neural networks (Single-Layer Perceptron, Multilayer Perceptron, Radial Base Function Network, and Support Vector Machine), k-nearest neighbor classifier (K-NN), regression-based methods (e.g., Linear Regression and Simple Logistic), and classifiers based on association rules (e.g., RIPPER, CN2, Holte's 1R, and C4.5) [52]). Selection of the most appropriate classification algorithm for a certain application is one of crucial points in data mining-based application and processes.

Consider a classifier that classifies the results into two classes, positive and negative. Then, the possible prediction results are as shown in Table 1.

Table 1. The confusion matrix of a two-class classifier.

		Predicted	
		Positive	Negative
True	Positive	TP	FN
	Negative	FP	TN

It should be noted that in Table 1, TP + FN + FP + TN = N where N is the total number of members in the considered set to be classified. The matrix presented in Table 1 is called a 2 × 2 confusion matrix. As presented in Table 1, there are four results, true positive (TP), false positive (FP), true negative (TN), and false negative (FN). It is important to notice that these numbers are counts, i.e., integers, not ratios, i.e., fractions. Based on the possible results that are presented in Table 1, for a two-class classifier, the accuracy, precision, recall, and F1 measure can be, respectively, calculated as:

$$\text{Accuracy} = (TP + TN)/N \tag{1}$$

$$\text{Precision} = TP/(TP + FP) \tag{2}$$

$$\text{Recall(Sensitivity)} = TP/(TP + FN) \tag{3}$$

$$\text{Specificity} = TN/(TN + FP). \tag{4}$$

Method based on the Receiver Operating Characteristic (ROC) curves are widely used in evaluation of prediction performance of a classifier. These represent on the OX axe, the rate of false positive cases and on the OY axe, the rate of true positive cases [53].

The ROCs of five classifiers denoted as A–E are displayed in Figure 1. A discrete classier output only a class label. Also, a discrete classifier produces an (*FP_Rate* and *TP_Rate*) pair, which corresponds to a single point in the ROC space, where *FP_Rate* represents false positive rate and *TP_Rate* represents true positive rate. A binary classifier is represented by a point on the graph (*FP_Rate* and *TP_Rate*), as follows [54]:

- Point (0,1) of the ROC plot represents perfect, ideal prediction, where the samples are classified correctly as positive or negative;
- Point (1,1) represents a classifier that classifies all cases as positive;
- Point (1,0) represents a classifier that classifies all samples incorrectly.

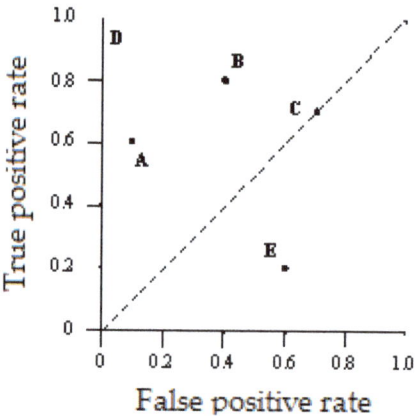

Figure 1. The Receiver Operating Characteristic (ROC) graph of five discrete classifiers.

Generally, in the ROC space, a point is classified more accurately when its true positive rate is higher and false positive rate is lower. In the ROC graph, classifiers appearing on the left-hand side of the ROC graph, which are near the *y*-axis, are considered as conservative. Namely, these classifiers make positive classifications only based on a strong evidence, so there can be only a few false positive errors, but there is also a low true positive rate as well. On the other hand, classifiers on the upper right-hand side of the ROC graph are considered as liberal. These classifiers make positive classifications based on weak evidence, so they classify almost all positives correctly, but they often have high false positive rate. For instance, in Figure 1, classifier A is more conservative than classifier B.

Decision trees or rule sets only make a decision on one of two classes a sample belong to in the case considered in this paper. When a discrete classifier is applied to a sample set, it yields to a single confusion matrix, which in turn corresponds to one ROC point. Thus, a discrete classifier produces only a single point in ROC space. On the other hand, the output of Naive Bayes classifier or neural networks is a probability or a score, i.e., a numeric value that represents the degree to which a particular instance is a member of a certain class [55].

Many classifiers scan yield to incorrect results. For instance, logistic regression provides approximately well-calibrated probabilities; in the Support Vector Machine (SVM) and similar methods, the outputs have to be converted into reasonable probabilities; regression analysis establishes a relationship between a dependent or outcome variable and a set of predictors. Namely, regression, as a data mining technique, belongs to supervised learning. Supervised learning partitions data into training and validation data sets, so regression model is constructed using only a part of the original data, that is, training data.

The classification performance of a classifier can be evaluated using:

- a user-defined data set,
- the *n*-fold cross validation division of the input data set,
- division of the input data set into the training and test sets.

The data are divided into two sets, training set and test set. The training set is used to train a selected classification algorithm, and test set is used to test the trained algorithm. If the classifier classifies most instances in the training set correctly, it is considered that it can classify correctly some other data as well. However, if many samples are incorrectly classified, it is considered that the trained model is unreliable. In addition to training and testing as a common approach to efficient use, model validation is most often used [56] to:

- select the best model from multiple candidates
- determine the optimal configuration of model parameters
- avoid over- or underfitting problems.

In summary, the classification model is defined by its true positive rate, false positive rate, precision, F1 measure, and confusion matrix, which represent basic parameters of precision evaluation of the implemented classifier.

2.2.2. Calibration Method

Calibration is applicable in the case a classifier output is the probability value. Calibration refers to the adjustment of the posterior probability output by a classification algorithm towards the true prior probability distribution of target classes. In many studies [57–59], machine learning and statistical models were calibrated to predict that for every given data row the probability that the outcome is 1. In classification, calibration is used to transform classifier scores into class membership probabilities [11,60]. The univariate calibration methods, such as logistic regression, exist for transforming classifier scores into class membership probabilities in the two-class case [61]. Logistic regression represents a statistical method for analyzing a dataset including one or more independent variables that determine an outcome, which is measured with a dichotomous variable, where there are only two possible outcomes, i.e., it contains only the data coded as 1, which is positive result (TRUE, success, pregnant, etc.), or 0, which is negative result (FALSE, failure, nonpregnant, etc.).

Logistic regression generates the coefficients, and the corresponding standard errors and significance levels, to predict a logit transformation of the probability of presence of a characteristic of interest, which can be expressed as:

$$\text{logit}(p) = b_0 + b_1 X_1 + b_2 X_2 + b_3 X_3 + \ldots + b_k X_k, \quad (5)$$

where p denotes the probability of presence of the characteristic of interest. The logit transformation is defined as the logged odds as follows:

$$\text{odds} = \frac{p}{1-p} = \frac{\text{probability of presence of characteristics}}{\text{probability of absence of characteristics}} \quad (6)$$

$$\text{logit}(p) = \ln\left(\frac{p}{1-p}\right). \quad (7)$$

Logistic regression selects parameters that increase the probability of observing sample values, instead of selecting parameters that minimize the sum of square errors (as in ordinary regression). The regression coefficients are coefficients $b_0, b_1, \ldots, b_k$ in the regression Equation (8). In the logistic regression, coefficients indicate the change (an increase when $b_i > 0$, or a decrease when $b_i < 0$) in the predicted logged odds of the characteristic of interest for a one-unit change in the independent variables. When the independent variables that are denoted as X_a and X_b in (8) are dichotomous variables (e.g., smoking and sex), then the influence of these variables on the dependent variable can be compared by matching their regression coefficients b_a and b_b. By applying the exponential function on the both sides of the regression Equations (7) and (5), considering Equation (6) as well, Equation (7) can be rewritten as the following equation:

$$\text{odds} = \frac{p}{1-p} = e^{b_0} \times e^{b_1 x_1} \times e^{b_2 x_2} \times e^{b_3 x_3} \times \ldots \times e^{b_k x_k}. \tag{8}$$

Thus, according to (8), when a variable X_i increases by one, while all other factors remain unchanged, then the odds will increase by a factor $e^b{}_i$, which is expressed as:

$$e^{b_t(1+x_t)} - e^{b_t x_t} = e^{b_t(1+x_t) - b_t x_t} = e^{b_t + b_t x_t - b_t x_t} = e^{b_t}. \tag{9}$$

The odds ratio (OR) of an independent variable X_i is notated as factor $e^b{}_i$, and it denotes a relative amount by which the odds of the outcome increase (OR greater than 1) or decrease (OR less than 1) when the value of the independent variable is increased by one.

2.2.3. Aggregation Method of Boosting using Classification and Calibration

Boosting as ensemble algorithm, which often uses more different supervised machine learning algorithms with minimum two from decision trees, classification and regression algorithm has become one of the most powerful and popular approaches in knowledge discovery and data mining field. It is commonly applied in science and technology when exploring large and complex data for discovering useful patterns is required, which allows different ways of modeling knowledge extraction from the large data sets [62].

In supervised learning, feature selection is most often viewed as a search problem in a space of feature subsets. In order to conduct our search, we must determine a starting point, a strategy for traversing trough the space of subsets, a function for evaluation, and a criterion to stop. This formulation allows that a variety of solutions can be developed, but usually two method types are considered, called filter methods and wrapper methods. Filter methods use an evaluation function that relies solely on data properties. Due to that fact, it is independent on any particular algorithm, and wrapper methods use inductive algorithm to estimate the value of a given subset. In our approach, there method types are combined: filter (information gain, gain ratio, and other four classifiers) and wrapper (search guided by the accuracy) [63].

As mentioned previously, the ROC analysis has been used in medicine, radiology, biometrics, and other areas for many decades, and recently, it has been increasingly used in machine learning and data mining research. In this study, the authors used the areas under the ROC curves to identify the classification accuracy of more classifiers, which is most important for proposed model to order the minimal number of attributes enough to give maximum value on the ROC curve [64].

In addition, most popular calibrating methods use isotonic regression to fit a piecewise-constant nondecreasing function. Isotonic regression is a useful nonparametric regression technique for fitting an increasing function to a given dataset. An its alternative is to use a parametric model and that most common model called univariate logistic regression. The model is defined as:

$$l = \log(p/(1-p)) = a + bf, \tag{10}$$

where f denotes a prediction score and p denotes the corresponding estimated probability for predicted binary response variable y. Equation (10) shows that the logistic regression model is essentially a linear model with intercept a and coefficient b, so it can be rewritten as:

$$p = \frac{1}{1 + e^{-(a+bf)}}. \tag{11}$$

Assume f_i is prediction score on the training set, and let $y_i \in "\{0, 1\}$ be the 2009 true label of the predicted variable. The parameters a and b are chosen to minimize the total sum $\sum_i l(p, y_i)$.

For example, in paper [35], which deals with prediction of risk of bleeding of varices using 25 attributes, we can find one aggregation of six classification's algorithms and six feature selection classifiers and that three from wrapper and three from filter group proposes model, which gives best solution than each of aggregated methods individually.

In this paper, authors propose model which:

- integrates classification (choosing the best of 5 selected)
- uses attribute reduction (choose from 5 proposed classifiers the one that reaches the maximum ROC value with the least number of attributes)
- than uses regression (which performs a fine calibration of the obtained results) as one boosting method, which has better characteristics and gives better results than any of those integrated into it, when they are individually applied. To confirm the hypothesis and answer the research question, the authors used the results provided by the case study described in Section 2.1 Material of this paper uses the procedure of obtaining significant bleeding predictors and setting great importance for further treatment and prevention of bleeding, which is summarized in Algorithm 1.

Algorithm 1: Procedure of obtaining significant predictors of bleeding in cirrhotic patients.

1. Determine an optimal classification algorithm with the highest value of ROC among enough number of minimum five algorithms, each from different class of classifiers, e.g., Naive Bayes, J48 Decision Trees, HyperPipes, Ada LogitBoost, and PART.
2. Perform attribute ranking according to the informativeness of the attribute that provides information on the presence of a certain attribute in a particular class. Using enough number of classifiers for attribute selection we proposed minimum of five classifiers, i.e., chi-square attribute evaluation, gain-ratio attribute evaluation, information-gain attribute evaluation, relief attribute evaluation, and symmetrical uncertainty attribute evaluation, to determine the feature subset methods and determine the set of attribute ranks $R = \{r_1, r_2, \ldots, r_n\}$, where n is the starting number of attributes.
3. Compute a subset $A' = \{a_1, a_2, \ldots, a_m\}$ of the starting set $A = \{a_1, a_2, \ldots, a_n\}$, m < = n of attributes as the most "useful" amongst. The ROC value is obtained by the optimal classification algorithm determined in Step 1.
4. Univariate logistic regression is used to calculate and the odds ratio for each attribute. Thus, a set of attributes with diverse distribution of attributes ranks is obtained $OR = \{or_1, or_2, \ldots, or_k\}$.
5. Over acquired subset of attributes $A' = \{a_1, a_2, \ldots, a_m\}$ in Step 3 with the set of attribute ranks $R = \{r_1, r_2, \ldots, r_n\}$ acquired in Step 2 performs the attribute rank calibration. Attribute calibration is performed on the basis of $OR = \{or_1, or_2, \ldots, or_k\}$ distribution of attribute influences acquired in Step 4.

The calibration process is given in Algorithm 2.

Algorithm 2: The pseudocode of the calibration process used most significant predictors of death income in cirrhotic patients part.

//Set the great importance for further treatment and prevention of bleeding for 15 predictive//variables
for $i = 1$ to $(n - 1)$ inclusive do:
/* if odds ratio value pair is out of order */
if OR[i] > OR [$i + 1$] **then**
/* swap attributes in subset A' and remember something changed */
swap (A[i], A[$i + 1$])
end if
end for

The ignored predictive variables are variables that have the accuracy less than 0.85%.

3. Results

The study from Benedeto-Stojanov and other coauthors in [36] involved 96 subjects, 76 (79.2%) male and 20 (20.8%) female participants. There were 55 patients without bleeding, of which 44 (80.0%)

were male and 11 (20.0%) were female. The group of 41 patients with bleeding included 32 (78.0%) male and 9 (22.0%) female participants. The average age of all patients was (56.99 ± 11.46) years. The youngest and oldest patients were 14 and 80 years old, respectively.

The data used in the study were obtained by the Clinical Center of Nis, Serbia. The original feature vector of patient data consisted of 29 features that were predictive variables. As the thirtieth variable, there was a two-case class variable result (yes/no), which was considered as a dependent variable. All predictive variables and dependent variable are shown in Table 2, where it can be seen that they were of numerical data type.

Table 2. List of features used in study.

Attribute Label and Name	Description
(A1) sex	Gender (male or female)
(A2) age	Age (year)
(A3) etiolog	Etiology
(A4) bilirub	Bilirubin (mg/dL)
(A5) album	Albumin (g/dL)
(A6) protrvr	Prothrombin time (s)
(A7) inr	International normalized ratio (s)
(A8) keratin	Creatinine (mg/dL)
(A9) ascites	Ascites
(A10) neurpor	Neurological dysfunction
(A11) pcsdr	Platelet count/spleen diameter ratio
(A12) uhranj	Body mass index
(A13) tromb	Thrombocytes (10^9/L)
(A14) veliki	Large esophageal varices
(A15) redcols	Red color signs
(A16) gastvar	Gastric varices
(A17) konggas	Congestive gastropathy
(A18) veljetre	Liver diameter (mm)
(A19) velslez	Spleen diameter (mm)
(A20) dijvport	Portal vein diameter (mm)
(A21) dzidavp	Portal vein wall thickness (mm)
(A22) dvldvms	Lienal + mesenteric superior vein diameter(mm)
(A23) kolcirk1	Collateral circulation
(A24) bpuvp	Flow speed in portal vein (m/s)
(A25) bpuvl	Flow speed in lienal vein (m/s)
(A26) konindvp	Congestion index in the portal vein (cm/s)
(A27) konindvl	Congestion index in the lienal vein (cm/s)
(A28) childps	Child–Pugh score
(A29) melds	MELD score
(A30) krvarenje	Bleeding (binominal response-dependent variable Yes, No)

In the case study, five classification algorithms were implemented, i.e., Naive Bayes, J48, Decision Trees, HyperPipes, Ada LogitBoost, and PART for designing prediction modes. Method of training set was applied in model for proposed classification algorithms where the authors chose the most famous from different groups of classifiers. This method was chosen and training set mode combined with test as well as 10-cross validation were not used because of a small number of instances in the case study.

The performance indicators of five classification algorithms are given in Table 3, where it can be seen that the LogitBoost classifier achieved the most accurate prediction results among all the models.

As presented in Table 3, the LogitBoost classifier achieved the F1 measure of 97.9%, accuracy of 98.0% (0.980), and the ROC of 0.999.

Table 3. Performance indicators obtained by the classification algorithms.

	Naive Bayes	J48	HyperPipes	LogitBoost	PART
Accuracy	0.900	0.918	0.688	0.980	0.959
Error	0.104	0.083	0.313	0.021	0.042
F1 measure	0.896	0.917	0.671	0.979	0.958
ROC	0.945	0.918	0.814	0.999	0.982

In Table 4, *CCI* denotes the number of correctly classified inputs, and *ICI* denotes the number of incorrectly classified inputs.

Table 4. Accuracy of the LogitBoost algorithm.

	CCI (%)	ICI (%)	TP_Rate	FP_Rate
LogitBoost	97.917	2.083	0.979	0.028

The LogitBoost classifier achieved a relatively good performance on classification tasks, due to the boosting algorithm [65]. Boosting process is based on the principle that finding many rough rules of thumb can be much easier than finding a single, highly accurate prediction rule. This classifier is a general method for accuracy improvement of learning algorithms. In the WEKA [66], LogitBoost classifier is implemented as class which performs additive logistic regression, which performed classification using a regression scheme as a base learner, and also can handle multiclass problems.

Feature selection is normally realized by searching the space of attribute subsets and evaluating each attribute. This is achieved by combining attribute subset evaluator with a search method. In this paper, five filter feature subset evaluation methods with a rank search or greedy search method were conducted to determine the best feature sets, and they are listed as follows:

(1) Chi-square attribute evaluation (CH),
(2) Gain-ratio attribute evaluation (GR),
(3) Information-gain attribute evaluation (IG),
(4) Relief attribute evaluation (RF) and
(5) Symmetrical uncertainty attribute evaluation (SU).

The feature ranks obtained by the above five methods on the training data are presented in Table 5.

Table 5. Results of the five ranking methods (bigger number mark highest rank).

	CH	GR	IG	RF	SU
(A15)	29	29	29	29	29
(A14)	28	28	28	28	16
(A17)	27	27	27	27	27
(A23)	26	25	26	26	9
(A25)	25	24	25	9	11
(A29)	24	26	24	15	1
(A24)	23	11	23	18	22
(A8)	22	22	22	17	25
(A9)	21	23	21	10	18
(A6)	20	20	20	13	26
(A7)	19	19	19	14	2
(A5)	18	18	18	22	21
(A11)	17	13	17	21	7
(A2)	16	16	16	11	28
(A3)	15	15	15	3	10
(A4)	14	14	14	8	23
(A10)	13	21	13	7	15
(A12)	12	17	12	23	19
(A22)	11	9	11	5	13
(A20)	10	7	10	2	8
(A21)	9	10	9	1	12
(A18)	8	6	8	4	4
(A19)	7	8	7	12	14
(A26)	6	2	6	16	3
(A13)	5	12	5	20	20
(A27)	4	5	4	6	5
(A28)	3	4	3	19	17
(A16)	2	3	2	24	6
(A1)	1	1	1	25	24

The ROC value shows relationship between sensitivity, which represents measure of the proportion of positives that are correctly identified TP, and specificity, which represents measure of the proportion of negative that are correctly identified, both in executed process of classification. The evaluation measures with variations of ROC values were generated from an open source data mining tool, WEKA, that offers a comprehensive set of state-of-the-art machine learning algorithms as well as set of autonomous feature selection and ranking methods. The generated evaluation measures are shown in Figure 2, where the x-axis represents the number of features, and the y-axis represents the ROC value of each feature subset generated by five filter classifiers. The maximum ROC value of all the algorithms and the corresponding cardinalities that are illustrated in Figure 2 are given numerically in Table 5. This is quite useful for finding an optimal size of the feature subsets with the highest ROC values. As given in Table 5, the highest ROC values were achieved by CH and IG classifiers. Although the CH and IG resulted in the ROC value of 0.999, the IG/CH could attain the maximum ROC value when the number of attributes reached the value of 15. Thus, it was concluded that IG has an optimal dimensionality in the dataset of patients.

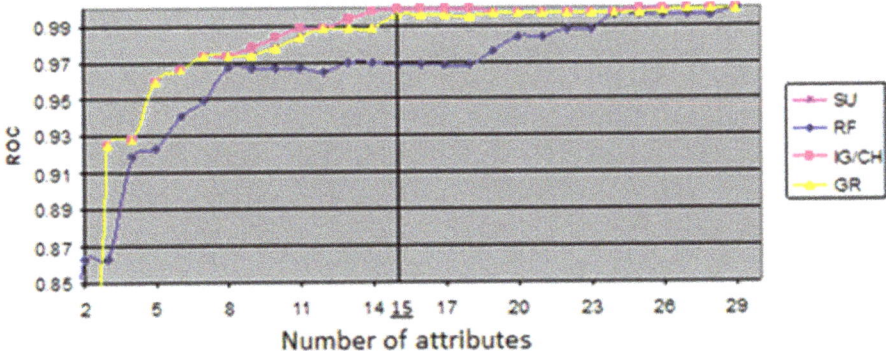

Figure 2. ROC value as a function of attribute number.

The top ranking features in Table 5 that were obtained by CH and IG classifiers were used for further predictive analysis as significant predictors of bleeding, and they were as follows: (A15)—Red color signs, (A14)—large esophageal varices, (A17)—congestive gastropathy, (A7)—international normalized ratio, (A23)—collateral circulation, (A24)—flow speed in portal vein, (A9)—ascites, (A8)—creatinine, (A6)—prothrombin time, (A29)—MELD score, (A2)—age, (A5)—albumin, (A11)—platelet count/spleen diameter ratio, (A3)—etiology, and (A25)—flow speed in lienal vein.

This study analyzes risks of initial bleeding of varices in cirrhotic patients, and the risks of early and late bleeding reoccurrence. The obtained results are important for further treatment and prevention of bleeding from esophageal varices, the most common and life-threatening complications of cirrhosis. Coauthors in this manuscript, Randjelovic and Bogdanovic, still used the univariate logistic regression analysis to demonstrate the most significant predictors of bleeding. Results of this analysis obtained using same input data are given in Table 6 [67].

Table 6. Odds ratio values for bleeding risk factors (univariate logistic regression).

Factor	P	OR	95% CI for OR	
			Lower Bound	Upper Bound
(A1)	0.816	1.125	0.417	3.033
(A2)	0.166	1.027	0.989	1.065
(A3)	0.606	0.629	0.108	3.662
(A4)	0.204	1.053	0.972	1.140
(A5)	0.962	1.013	0.602	1.703
(A6)	0.393	1.053	0.935	1.187
(A7)	0.421	1.640	0.491	5.470
(A8)	0.290	1.324	0.787	2.228
(A9)	0.631	1.417	0.342	5.865
(A10)	0.291	1.600	0.668	3.830
(A11)	0.020	0.998	0.997	0.999
(A12)	0.060	0.148	0.020	1.081
(A13)	0.023	0.992	0.985	0.999
(A14)	<0.001	24.589	7.368	82.060
(A15)	<0.001	194.997	35.893	1059.356

Table 6. Cont.

Factor	P	OR	95% CI for OR	
			Lower Bound	Upper Bound
(A16)	0.026	4.110	1.187	14.235
(A17)	<0.001	10.153	3.479	29.633
(A18)	0.078	0.986	0.970	1.002
(A19)	0.390	1.007	0.991	1.024
(A20)	0.405	0.936	0.800	1.094
(A21)	0.859	0.945	0.509	1.755
(A22)	0.600	0.960	0.826	1.117
(A23)	0.049	1.562	1.002	2.434
(A24)	0.958	1.441	0.030	11.321
(A25)	0.054	0.002	0.001	1.166
(A26)	0.676	0.294	0.001	91.338
(A27)	0.907	1.726	0.040	16.690
(A28)	0.574	1.048	0.890	1.233
(A29)	0.338	1.029	0.971	1.091

After conducting the experiment with the real medical data, important predictors of bleeding were determined by performing logistic regression analysis.

Univariate logistic regression analysis indicated the most significant predictors of bleeding in cirrhotic patients: the value of the Child–Pugh/Spleen Diameter ratio, platelet count, as well as the expression of large esophageal varices, red color signs, gastric varices, and congestive gastropathy collateral circulation. Approximate values were calculated relative risk (odds ratio—OR), and their 95% confidence intervals. The statistical significance was estimated by calculating the OR Wald (Wald) values.

The increase in the value of Child–Pugh/Spleen Diameter ratio for one unit resulted in the reduction in the risk of bleeding by 0.2% (from 0.1% to 0.3%, $p < 0.05$), while the increase in platelet count to 1×10^9/L yielded to the decrease in risk of bleeding by 0.8% (from 0.1% to 1.5%, $p < 0.05$). Expression of the following factors indicating an increased risk of bleeding: large esophageal varices 24.589 (7.368–82.060, $p < 0.001$), red color signs 194.997 (35.893–1059.356, $p < 0.001$), gastric varices 4.110 (1.187–14.235, $p < 0.05$), congestive gastropathy 10.153 (3.479–29.633, $p < 0.001$), and collateral circulation 1.562 (1.002–2.434, $p < 0.05$).

Following performed univariate logistic regression analysis, it is enabled that previously acquired set of 15 attributes with attribute rank given in columns one (CH) and three (IG) of Table 5 can be calibrated using results for OR given in column three (OR) in Table 6. The calibration process is showed in Table 7. It was carried out so that the mentioned set of 15 attributes from Table 5, which is given in the first row of Table 7 using extracting those of the 15 attributes for which OR > 1 in Table 6 is given in the second row of Table 7 and using extracting those of the 15 attributes for which OR < 1 in Table 6 is given in the third row of Table 7.

According to the results in Table 6, the independent (predictive) variables were A1–A29 attributed to number p smaller than 0.05, which significantly influenced on dependent, binary variable A30—bleeding.

According to the results in Table 7, we have 15 significant predictors given in first row. On the one hand, in second row, we have 12 predictors from this 15 with OR greater than one and characteristic when the predictive variable, bleeding, increased, and the risk that binary variable would acquire value Yes also increased.

Table 7. Top ranking feature subsets.

Ranking Subset	Attribute
Start top ranking attribute numbers based on ROC values in the descending order—Table 5	A15, A14, A17, A23, A25, A29, A24, A8, A9, A6, A7, A5, A11, A2, A3.
Top ranking attributes after calibration by OR values greater than one—Table 6	A15, A14, A17, A7, A23, A24, A9, A8, A6, A29, A2, A5.
Top ranking attributes after calibration by OR values smaller than one—Table 6	A11, A3, A25.

On the other hand, in third row we have 3 predictors from this 15 with OR smaller than one and characteristic when the predictive variable increased, and the risk that binary variable would acquire value Yes decreased.

4. Discussion

In the machine learning and statistics, dimensionality reduction is the process of reducing the number of random variables under a certain consideration and can be divided into feature selection and attribute importance determination.

Feature selection approaches [68–70] try to find a subset of the original variables. In this work, two strategies, namely, filter (Chi-square, information gain, gain ratio, relief and symmetrical uncertainty) and wrapper (search guided by the accuracy) approaches are combined. The performance of classification algorithm is commonly examined by evaluating the classification accuracy.

In this study, the ROC curves are used to evaluate the classification accuracy. By analyzing the experimental results presented in Table 3, it can be observed that the LogitBoost classification technique achieved better result than the other techniques using training mode of valuation applied classification algorithms.

The results of the comparative application of different classifiers conducted in described case study on feature subsets generated by the five different feature selection procedures are shown in Table 5. The LogitBoost classification algorithm is trained using decision stumps (one node decision trees) as weak learners. The IG attribute evaluation can be used to filter features, thus reducing the dimensionality of the feature space [71].

The experimental results presented on Table 8 show that IG feature selection significantly improves the all observed performance of the LogitBoost classification technique in spite of the fact that decision tree has inherited ability to focus on relevant features while ignoring the irrelevant ones (refer to Section 3).

Table 8. Performance of LogitBoost classification before and after information-gain attribute evaluation/Chi-square attribute evaluation (IG/CH) feature selection.

	LogitBoost before IG/CH Feature Selection	LogitBoost after IG/CH Feature Selection
Accuracy	0.980	0.990
Error	0.021	0.014
F1 measure	0.979	0.990
ROC	0.999	0.999

The authors performed 10-cross validation of the proposed model using Weka software and it confirmed the validity of the proposed model defined by the procedures given in the work with Algorithm 1 and Algorithm 2 as it is given in Table 9.

Table 9. Performance of LogitBoost before/after IG/CH feature selection using 10-cross validation.

	LogitBoost before IG/CH Feature Selection	LogitBoost after IG/CH Feature Selection
Accuracy	0.896	0.896
Error	0.104	0.104
F1 measure	0.896	0.896
ROC	0.930	0.948

As we mentioned in Section 3 Results, results of univariate regression on same data set [67] are used for fine calibration in proposed model. In that paper was considered comparison of use of classic and gradual regression in prediction of risk of variceal bleeding in cirrhotic patients.

Table 10 shows results obtained using multivariate gradual regression and recognizes only two factors as significant for risk of variceal bleeding, which are in comparison with results of proposed model evidently a worse result in terms of requested prediction.

Table 10. Odds ratio values for bleeding risk factors (multivariate logistic regression).

Factor	P	OR	95% CI for OR	
			Lower Bound	Upper Bound
Red color signs	<0.001	116.578	19.744	688.326
Congestive gastropathy	0.037	6.116	1.113	33.611
Constant	<0.001	0.010		

The regression calibration is a simple way to improve estimation accuracy of the errors-in-variables model [72].

It is shown that when variables are small, regression calibration using response variables outperforms the conventional regression calibration.

Expert clinical interpretation of obtained results for risk of bleeding prediction in cirrhotic patients could be given using decision tree diagram with feature subset of 15 attributes, which is practically equal to set of 29 attributes in the case without feature selection but more precise and accurate.

The run information part contains general information about the used scheme, the number of instances, 96 patients, in the case of 15 attributes is shown in Figure 3, i.e., the case of 29 attributes is shown in Figure 4, and in both cases as well as the attributes names.

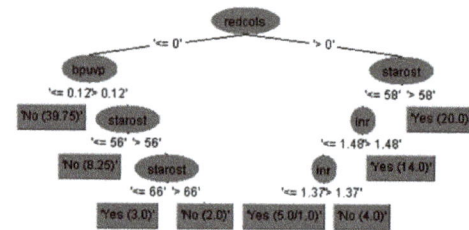

Figure 3. The decision tree with feature subsets (using 15 attributes).

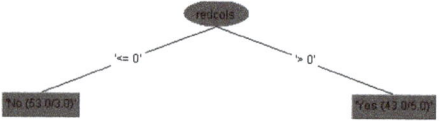

Figure 4. The decision tree without feature subsets (using 29 attributes).

The output for predicted variable represented by the decision tree given in Figure 3 can be interpreted using the If-Then 14 rules in Equation (12), as follows:

$$\text{If } (A15 =< 0.0) \text{ and } (A24 =< 0.12) \text{ then } A30 = No\ (39, 75/96). \tag{12}$$

Authors contribution is demonstrated in obtained result with application of proposed new ensemble boosting model of data mining, which integrates classification algorithm with attribute reduction and regression method for calibration and which shows that proposed model has a better characteristic than each of individually applied model and authors could not find in existing literature.

The authors confirmed originality of the proposed ensemble model by reviewing the state of the art, generally observed, end especially in the liver disease prediction, which are given in the introduction of the paper and could be confirmed by observation updated state of the art in both disciplines:

- in the different machine learning methodologies [73–75] and
- in the use of differently constructed ensemble methodologies [76,77].

Advantage of proposed model is, in fact, that it is evaluated on the case study including big number of different types of considered factors. Finally, one advantage of the proposed model is in the fact that it could be applied worldwide where it will generate prediction that is suitable according the specificity of each locality individual so that the paper is suitable for broad international interest and applications.

In such a way, authors confirmed the hypothesis and answered the research question set in introduction of this paper and thus contributed to the creation of a tool that can successfully and practically serve to solve their perceived research gap.

This described study has several limitations that must be addressed:

First, we collected data only from one medical center (as it is given in [78] as Supplementary Material) that reflects its particularities; the sample would be more representative if it is from many different localities, so that results can be generalized. Second, we evaluated small size of only 96 patient's information, although most of the variables were statistically significant. Third, we have not included all possible factors that could cause bleeding. Finally, we must notice that noninvasive markers may be useful only as a first step to possibly identify varices for cirrhosis patients and in this way to reduce the number of endoscopies.

In further work and research authors plan to test proposed model on the data set obtained in last 10 years in Clinical Center of Nis, Serbia. Authors also intend to include in further research at least two other clinical centers in Serbia or in the Western Balkans that are topologically distant and located in different locations with different features (hilly and lowland coastal locality) where the population has other habits and characteristics and, in this way, to obtain bigger size of cirrhotic patients and more representative sample for proposed model evaluation. Authors plan also to deal with determining more precise type and number in each type of classification algorithms and type and number of classifiers for feature selection used in proposed model. Finally, proposed model can be suggested for prediction and monitoring of risk of bleeding in cirrhotic patients, e.g., by implementing as a software tool.

5. Conclusions

Analysis of significance of factors that are influencing an event is a very complex task. Factors can be independent or dependent, quantitative or qualitative, i.e., deterministic or probabilistic nature, and there can be a complex relationship between them. Due to the importance of determination of risk factors for bleeding problems in cirrhotic patients and the fact that early prediction of varices bleeding in cirrhotic patients in last 20 years help this complication to be reduced, it is clear that it is necessary to develop an accurate algorithm for selection of the most significant factors of the mentioned problem.

Among all techniques of statistics, operation research, and data mining techniques, in this work, statistical univariate regression and data mining technique of classification are aggregated to obtain one boosting method, which has better characteristics than each of them individually. Data mining is used to find a subset of the original set of variables. Also, two strategies, filter (information gain and other) and wrapper (search guided by the accuracy) approaches, are combined. Regression calibration is utilized to improve estimation performance of the errors in variables model. Application of the bleeding risk factors-based univariate regression presented in this paper can help decision-making and higher risk identification of bleeding in cirrhotic patients.

The proposed method uses advantages of data mining decision tree method to make good beginning classification of considered predictors and then univariate regression is utilized for fine calibration of obtained results, resulting in developing a high-accuracy risk prediction model.

It is evident that the proposed ensemble model can be useful and extensible to other hospitals in the world treating this illness, the liver cirrhosis and its consequences as the bleeding of varices studied in this case.

Supplementary Materials: The following are available online at http://www.mdpi.com/2227-7390/8/11/1887/s1, Table S1: The data in study described in (Benedeto-Stojanov, 2010) 29 attributes—involved 96 subjects by Clinical Center of Nis, Serbia.

Author Contributions: Conceptualization: A.A.; Project administration: S.N.; Validation: M.J.; Writing—original draft: M.V.; Writing—review & editing: M.R. (Miloš Ranđelović); Formal analysis: M.R. (Milan Ranđelović); Software: V.S.; Investigation: R.R.; Supervision, Methodology: D.R. All authors have read and agreed to the published version of the manuscript.

Funding: This research received no external funding.

Conflicts of Interest: The authors declare no conflict of interest.

Abbreviations

MELD	Model of End-Stage Liver Disease
TIPS	Transjugular Intrahepatic Portosystemic Shunt
GI	Gastrointestinal
INR	International normalized ratio
AVH	Acute variceal hemorrhage
LMT	Logistic model tree
K-NN	K-nearest neighbor
TP	True positive
TN	True negative
FP	False positive
FN	False negative
ROC	Receiver Operating Characteristic
SVM	Support Vector Machine
P	Probability
OR	Odds ratio
CCI	Correctly classified inputs
ICI	Incorrectly classified inputs
CI	Confidence interval
CH	Chi-square
GR	Gain ratio
IG	Information gain
RF	Relief attribute evaluation
SU	Symmetrical uncertainty

References

1. Liu, Y.; Meric, G.; Havulinna, A.S.; Teo, M.S.; Ruuskanen, M.; Sanders, J.; Zhu, Q.; Tripathi, A.; Verspoor, K.; Cheng, S.; et al. Early prediction of liver disease using conventional risk factors and gut microbiome-augmented gradient boosting. *medRxiv* **2020**. [CrossRef]

2. Rajoriya, N.; Tripathi, D. Historical overview and review of current day treatment in the management of acute variceal haemorrhage. *World J. Gastroenterol.* **2014**, *20*, 6481–6494. [CrossRef]
3. Barbu, L.; Mărgăritescu, N.D.; Şurlin, M. Diagnosis and Treatment Algorithms of Acute Variceal Bleeding. *Curr. Health Sci. J.* **2017**, *43*, 191–200. [PubMed]
4. Matheny, M.; Thadeney Israni, S.; Ahmed, M.; Whicher, D. (Eds.) *Artificial Inelligence in Health Care: The Hope, the Hype, the Promise, the Peril*; National Academy of Medicine, NAM Special Publication: Washington, DC, USA, 2019.
5. Zhu, W.; Zeng, N.; Wang, N. Sensitivity, Specificity, Accuracy, Associated Confidence Interval and ROC Analysis with Practical SAS Implementations. In Proceedings of the NESUG 2010 Conference, Baltimore, MD, USA, 14–17 November 2010. Available online: www.lexjansen.com/cgi-bin/xsl_transform.php?x=nesug2010#NESUG2010-hl006 (accessed on 1 August 2020).
6. Kempthorne, O. *The Design and Analysis of Experiments*; John Wiley&Sons Inc: New York, NY, USA, 1952.
7. Koop, G. *Analysis of Economic Data*; Wiley: Chichester, UK, 2000.
8. Oatley, G.; Ewart, B. Data mining and crime analysis. *Wiley Interdiscip. Rev. Data Min. Knowl. Discov.* **2011**, *1*, 147–153. [CrossRef]
9. Elrazek, A.E.A.; Elbana, A. Validation of Data Mining Advanced Technology in Clinical Medicine. *Appl. Math. Inf. Sci.* **2016**, *10*, 1637–1640. [CrossRef]
10. Chimieski, B.F.; Fagundes, R.D.R. Asociation and Clasifcation Data Mining Algorithms Comparison over Medical Datasets. *J. Health Inform.* **2013**, *5*, 44–51.
11. D'Amico, G.; Garcia-Tsao, G.; Pagliaro, L. Natural history and prognostic indicators of survival in cirrhosis: A systematic review of 118 studies. *J. Hepatol.* **2006**, *44*, 217–231. [CrossRef] [PubMed]
12. Kumar, R.P.; Rao, M.; Kaladhar, D.; Raghavendra, P.K.; Malleswara, R.; Dsvgk, K. Data Categorization and Noise Analysis in Mobile Communication Using Machine Learning Algorithms. *Wirel. Sens. Netw.* **2012**, *4*, 113–116. [CrossRef]
13. Lavrač, N. Selected techniques for data mining in medicine. *Artif. Intell. Med.* **1999**, *16*, 3–23. [CrossRef]
14. Cios, K.J.; Moore, G.W. Uniqueness of medical data mining. *Artif. Intell. Med.* **2002**, *26*, 1–24. [CrossRef]
15. Richards, G.; Rayward-Smith, V.J.; Sönksen, P.; Carey, S.; Weng, C. Data mining for indicators of early mortality in a database of clinical records. *Artif. Intell. Med.* **2001**, *22*, 215–231. [CrossRef]
16. Warner, J.L.; Zhang, P.; Liu, J.; Alterovitz, G. Classification of hospital acquired complications using temporal clinical information from a large electronic health record. *J. Biomed. Inform.* **2016**, *59*, 209–217. [CrossRef]
17. Hall, M.; Frank, E.; Holmes, G.; Pfahringer, B.; Reutemann, P.; Witten, I.H. The WEKA data mining software. *ACM SIGKDD Explor. Newsl.* **2009**, *11*, 10–18. [CrossRef]
18. Berman, J.J. Confidentiality issues for medical data miners. *Artif. Intell. Med.* **2002**, *26*, 25–36. [CrossRef]
19. Chen, W.; Cockrell, C.H.; Ward, K.; Najarian, K. Predictability of intracranial pressure level in traumatic brain injury: Features extraction, statistical analysis and machine learning-based evaluation. *Int. J. Data Min. Bioinform.* **2013**, *8*, 480–494. [CrossRef]
20. Bardsiri, M.K.; Eftekhari, M. Comparing ensemble learning methods based on decision tree classifiers for protein fold recognition. *Int. J. Data Min. Bioinform.* **2014**, *9*, 89–105. [CrossRef]
21. Kovačić, Z.J. *Multivarijaciona Analiza*; Ekonomski Fakultet: Beograd, Srbija, 1994.
22. Xu, X.-D.; Dai, J.-J.; Qian, J.-Q.; Pin, X.; Wang, W.-J. New index to predict esophageal variceal bleeding in cirrhotic patients. *World J. Gastroenterol.* **2014**, *20*, 6989–6994. [CrossRef]
23. Kumar, M.K.; Sreedevi, M.; Reddy, Y.C.A.P. Survey on machine learning algorithms for liver disease diagnosis and prediction. *Int. J. Eng. Technol.* **2018**, *7*, 99–102. [CrossRef]
24. Jain, D.; Singh, V. Feature selection and classification systems for chronic disease prediction: A review. *Egypt. Inform. J.* **2018**, *19*, 179–189. [CrossRef]
25. Provost, F.; Fawcett, T. Analysis and visualization of classifier performance: Comparison under imprecise class and cost distributions. In Proceedings of the 3rd International Conference on Knowledge Discovery and Data Mining, Newport Beach, CA, USA, 14–17 August 1997; pp. 14–17.
26. Joloudari, J.H.; Saadatfar, H.; Dehzangi, A.; Shamshirband, S. Computer-aided decision-making for predicting liver disease using PSO-based optimized SVM with feature selection. *Inform. Med. Unlocked* **2019**, *17*, 100255. [CrossRef]
27. Goldis, A.; Lupușoru, R.; Goldis, R.; Rațiu, I. Prognostic Factors in Liver Cirrhosis Patients with Upper Gastrointestinal Bleeding. *Biol. Med.* **2017**, *10*, 1–6. [CrossRef]

28. Al Ghamdi, M.H.; Fallatah, H.I.; Akbar, H.O. Transient Elastography (Fibroscan) Compared to Diagnostic Endoscopy in the Diagnosis of Varices in Patients with Cirrhosis. *Sci. J. Clin. Med.* **2016**, *5*, 55–59. [CrossRef]
29. Wu, C.-C.; Yeh, W.-C.; Hsu, W.-D.; Islam, M.; Nguyen, P.A.; Poly, T.N.; Wang, Y.-C.; Yang, H.-C.; Li, Y.-C. Prediction of fatty liver disease using machine learning algorithms. *Comput. Methods Programs Biomed.* **2019**, *170*, 23–29. [CrossRef] [PubMed]
30. Abd Elrazek, E.M.A.; Hamdy, A.M. Prediction analysis of esophageal variceal degrees using data mining: Is validated in clinical medicine? *Global. J. Comp. Sci. Technol.* **2013**, *13*, 1–5.
31. Augustin, S.; Muntaner, L.; Altamirano, J.T.; González, A.; Saperas, E.; Dot, J.; Abu–Suboh, M.; Armengol, J.R.; Malagelada, J.R.; Esteban, R.; et al. Predicting early mortality after acute variceal hemorrhage based on classification and regression tree analysis. *Liver Pancreas Biliary Tract* **2009**, *7*, 1347–1354. [CrossRef]
32. Breiman, L.; Friedman, J.H.; Olshen, R.A.; Stone, C.J. *Classification and Regression Trees*; Wadsworth & Brooks/Cole Advanced Books & Software: Monterey, CA, USA, 1984.
33. Abu-Hanna, A.; De Keizer, N. Integrating classification trees with local logistic regression in Intensive Care prognosis. *Artif. Intell. Med.* **2003**, *29*, 5–23. [CrossRef]
34. Abdel-Aty, M.; Fouad, M.; Sallam, M.M.; Elgohary, E.A.; Ismael, A.; Nawara, A.; Hawary, B.; Tag-Adeen, M.; Khaled, S. Incidence of HCV induced—Esophageal varices in Egypt. *Medicine* **2017**, *96*, e5647. [CrossRef]
35. El-Salam, S.M.A.; Ezz, M.M.; Hashem, S.; Elakel, W.; Salama, R.; Elmakhzangy, H.; Elhefnawi, M. Performance of machine learning approaches on prediction of esophageal varices for Egyptian chronic hepatitis C patients. *Inform. Med. Unlocked* **2019**, *17*, 100267. [CrossRef]
36. Benedeto-Stojanov, D. *Indikatori Rizika Varikoznog Krvarenja u Bolesnika sa Cirozom Jetre*; Medicinski Fakultet: Niš, Srbija, 2010.
37. Benedeto-Stojanov, D.; Nagorni, A.; Bjelaković, G.; Stojanov, D.; Mladenović, B.; Djenić, N. The model for the end-stage liver disease and Child-Pugh score in predicting prognosis in cirrhotic patients and esophageal bleeding of varices. *Vojnosanit. Pregl.* **2009**, *66*, 724–728. [CrossRef]
38. Benedeto-Stojanov, D.; Nagorni, A.; Bjelaković, G.; Mladenović, B.; Stojanov, D.; Djenić, N. Risk and causes of gastroesophageal bleeding in cirrhotic patients. *Vojnosanit. Pregl.* **2007**, *64*, 585–589. [CrossRef]
39. Durand, F.; Valla, D. Assessment of Prognosis of Cirrhosis. *Semin. Liver Dis.* **2008**, *28*, 110–122. [CrossRef] [PubMed]
40. Lee, J.Y.; Lee, J.H.; Kim, S.J.; Choi, D.R.; Kim, K.H.; Kim, Y.B.; Kim, H.Y.; Yoo, J.Y. Comparison of predictive factors related to the mortality and rebleeding caused by bleeding of varices: Child-Pugh score, MELD score, and Rockall score. *Taehan Kan Hakhoe Chi* **2002**, *8*, 458–464. [PubMed]
41. Kleber, G.; Sauerbruch, T. Risk indicators of bleeding of varices. Y. *Gastroenterology* **1988**, *26*, 19–23.
42. Esmat Gamil, M.; Pirenne, J.; Van Malenstein, H.; Verhaegen, M.; Desschans, B.; Monbaliu, D.; Aerts, R.; Laleman, W.; Cassiman, D.; Verslype, C.; et al. Risk factors for bleeding and clinical implications in patients undergoing liver transplantation. *Transplant Proc.* **2012**, *44*, 2857–2860. [CrossRef] [PubMed]
43. Aggarwal, C. *Machine Learning for Text*; Springer Nature: Lawrence Livermore National Labaratory: Livermore, CA, USA, 2018; ISBN 978-3-319-73530-6.
44. Friedman, J.H. *Data Mining and Statistics: What's the Connection?* Technical Report; Department of Statistics: Stanford University: Stanford, CA, USA, 1997.
45. Friedman, J.H.; Hastie, T.; Tibshirani, R. *Additive Logistic Regression: A Statistical View of Boosting*; Technica Report; Department of Statistics, Stanford University: Stanford, CA, USA, 1998.
46. Hastie, T.; Tibshirani, R.; Friedman, J. *The Elements of Statistical Learning, Data Mining, Inference, and Prediction*; Springer Series in Statistics; Springer: Berlin, Germany, 2008.
47. Zhang, Z.; Zhao, Y.; Canes, A.; Steinberg, D.; Lyashevska, O. Predictive analytics with gradient boosting in clinical medicine. *Ann. Transl. Med.* **2019**, *7*, 152. [CrossRef]
48. Žižović, M.; Pamučar, D. New model for determining criteria weights: Level Based Weight Assessment (LBWA) model. *Decis. Mak. Appl. Manag. Eng.* **2019**, *2*, 126–137. [CrossRef]
49. Roy, J.; Pamučar, D.; Adhikary, K.; Kar, K. A rough strength relational DEMATEL model for analysing the key success factors of hospital service quality. *Decis. Making: Appl. Manag. Eng.* **2018**, *1*, 121–142. [CrossRef]
50. Niculescu-Mizil, A.; Caruana, R. Obtaining calibrated probabilities from boosting. In Proceedings of the 21st Conference on Uncertainty in Artificial Intelligence (UAI'05), Edinburgh, Scotland, 26–29 July 2005; pp. 413–420.

51. Tan, P.N.; Steinbach, M.; Kumar, V. Classification: Basic Concepts, Decision Trees, and Model Evaluation. In *Introduction to Data Mining*; Addison-Wesley: Boston, MA, USA, 2005; ISBN 0321321367.
52. Romero, C.; Ventura, S.; Espejo, P.; Hervas, C. Data mining algorithms to classify students. In Proceedings of the 1st IC on Educational Data Mining (EDM08), Montreal, QC, Canada, 20–21 June 2008; pp. 20–21.
53. Fawcett, T. *ROC Graphs: Notes and Practical Considerations for Data Mining Researchers*; Technical Report HPLaboratories: Palo Alto, CA, USA, 2003.
54. Vuk, M.; Curk, T. ROC curve, lift chart and calibration plot. *Metodoloski Zv.* **2006**, *3*, 89–108.
55. Dimić, G.; Prokin, D.; Kuk, K.; Micalović, M. Primena Decision Trees i Naive Bayes klasifikatora na skup podataka izdvojen iz Moodle kursa. In Proceedings of the Conference INFOTEH, Jahorina, Bosnia and Herzegovina, 21–23 March 2012; Volume 11, pp. 877–882.
56. Xu, Y.; Goodacre, R. Splitting Training and Validation Set: A Comparative Study of Cross-Validation, Bootstrap and Systematic Sampling for Estimating the Generalization Performance of Supervised Learning. *J. Anal. Test.* **2018**, *2*. [CrossRef]
57. Bella, A.; Ferri, C.; Hernández-Orallo, J.; Ramírez-Quintana, M.J. Calibration of machine learning models. In *Handbook of Research on Machine Learning Applications*; IGI Global: Hershey, PA, USA, 2009.
58. Sousa, J.B.; Esquvel, M.L.; Gaspar, R.M. Machine learning Vasicek model calibration with gaussian processes. *Commun. Stat. Simul. Comput.* **2012**, *41*, 776–786. [CrossRef]
59. Zadrozny, B.; Elkan, C. Obtaining calibrated probability estimates from decision trees and naive bayesian classifiers. In *Proceedings of the Eighteenth International Conference on Machine Learning, Williamstown, MA, USA, 28 June–1 July 2001*; Morgan Kaufmann Publishers, Inc.: San Francisco, CA, USA; pp. 609–616.
60. Agarwal, N. Calibration of Models. 2019. Available online: https://www.changhsinlee.com/python-calibration-plot/ (accessed on 1 August 2020).
61. Friedman, J.; Hastie, T.; Tibshirani, R. Additive Logistic Regression: A Statistical View of Boosting. *Ann. Stat.* **2000**, *28*, 337–407. [CrossRef]
62. Blagus, R.; Lusa, L. Bosting for high-dimensional two-class prediction. *BMC Bioinform.* **2015**, *16*, 300. [CrossRef] [PubMed]
63. Srimani, P.K.; Koti, M.S. Medical Diagnosis Using Ensemble Classifiers-A Novel Machine Learning Approach. *J. Adv. Comput.* **2013**, *1*, 9–27. [CrossRef]
64. Bettinger, R. Cost Sensitive Classifier Selection Using the ROC Convex Hull Method. 2003. Available online: https://www.reserachgate.net/publication/228969570 (accessed on 1 August 2020).
65. Kotsiantis, S.B.; Pintelas, P.E. Logitboost of Simple Bayesian Classifier. *Informatica* **2005**, *29*, 53–59.
66. WEKA Software. The University of Waikato: Hillcrest, New Zealand, 2009. Available online: http://www.cs.waikato.ac.nz/ml/weka (accessed on 1 August 2020).
67. Randjelovic, D.; Bogdanovic, D. Health Risk Factors Assessment using Gradual and Classic Logistics Regression Analysis. In Proceedings of the 1st WSEAS International Conference on Advances in Environment, Biotechnology and Biomedicine, Tomas Bata University, Zlin, Czech Republic, 20–22 September 2012; pp. 378–385.
68. Fodor, I.K. *A Survey of Dimension Reduction Techniques*; Technical Report UCRL-ID-148494; Lawrence Livermore National Lab.: Livermore, CA, USA, 2002.
69. Bachu, V.; Anuradha, J. A Review of Feature Selection and Its Methods. *Cybern. Inf. Technol.* **2019**, *19*, 3. [CrossRef]
70. Guyon, I.; Elisseeff, A. An introduction to variable and feature selection. *J. Mach. Learn. Res.* **2003**, *3*, 1157–1182.
71. Zeeshan, A.R.; Awais, M.M.; Shamail, S. Impact of Using Information Gain in Software Defect Prediction Models. In *Lecture Notes in Computer Science: Intelligent Computing Theory*; Springer: Berlin/Heidelberg, Germany, 2014; Volume 8588, pp. 637–648.
72. Huang, S.Y.H. Regression calibration using response variables in linear models. *Stat. Sin.* **2005**, *15*, 685–696.
73. Baitharu, T.R.; Pani, S.K. Analysis of Data Mining Techniques for Healthcare Decision Support System Using Liver Disorder Dataset. *Procedia Comput. Sci.* **2016**, *85*, 862–870. [CrossRef]
74. Marozas, M.; Zykus, R.; Sakalauskas, A.; Kupcinskas, L.; Lukoševičius, A. Noninvasive Evaluation of Portal Hypertension Using a Supervised Learning Technique. *J. Health Eng.* **2017**, *2017*, 1–10. [CrossRef]

75. Shung, D.L.; Au, B.; Taylor, R.A.; Tay, J.K.; Laursen, S.B.; Stanley, A.J.; Dalton, H.R.; Ngu, J.; Schultz, M.; Laine, L. Validation of a Machine Learning Model That Outperforms Clinical Risk Scoring Systems for Upper Gastrointestinal Bleeding. *Gastroenterology* **2020**, *158*, 160–167. [CrossRef] [PubMed]
76. Latha, C.B.C.; Jeeva, S.C. Improving the accuracy of prediction of heart disease risk based onensemble classification techniques. *Inform. Med. Unlocked* **2019**, *16*, 100203. [CrossRef]
77. Nahar, N.; Ara, F.; Neloy, M.; Istiek, A.; Barua, V.; Hossain, M.S.; Andersson, K. A Comparative Analysis of the Ensemble Method for Liver Disease Prediction. In Proceedings of the ICIET 2019 Conference, Dhaka, Bangladesh, 23–24 December 2019.
78. Available online: http://www.diplomatija.com/wp-content/uploads/2020/02/The-data-in-study-described-in-Benedeto-Stojanov2010-29-attributes-involved-96-subjects-by-Clinical-center-of-Nis-Serbia.xlsx (accessed on 1 August 2020).

Publisher's Note: MDPI stays neutral with regard to jurisdictional claims in published maps and institutional affiliations.

© 2020 by the authors. Licensee MDPI, Basel, Switzerland. This article is an open access article distributed under the terms and conditions of the Creative Commons Attribution (CC BY) license (http://creativecommons.org/licenses/by/4.0/).

Article

Development of a Novel Integrated CCSD-ITARA-MARCOS Decision-Making Approach for Stackers Selection in a Logistics System

Alptekin Ulutaş [1], Darjan Karabasevic [2,*], Gabrijela Popovic [2], Dragisa Stanujkic [3], Phong Thanh Nguyen [4] and Çağatay Karaköy [1]

1. Department of International Trade and Logistics, Faculty of Economics and Administrative Sciences, Sivas Cumhuriyet University, Sivas 58140, Turkey; aulutas@cumhuriyet.edu.tr (A.U.); ckarakoy@cumhuriyet.edu.tr (Ç.K.)
2. Faculty of Applied Management, Economics and Finance, University Business Academy in Novi Sad, Belgrade, Serbia, Jevrejska 24, 11000 Belgrade, Serbia; gabrijela.popovic@mef.edu.rs
3. Technical Faculty in Bor, University of Belgrade, Vojske Jugoslavije 12, 19210 Bor, Serbia; dstanujkic@tfbor.bg.ac.rs
4. Department of Project Management, Ho Chi Minh City Open University, Ho Chi Minh City 7000000, Vietnam; phong.nt@ou.edu.vn
* Correspondence: darjan.karabasevic@mef.edu.rs or darjankarabasevic@gmail.com

Received: 8 September 2020; Accepted: 28 September 2020; Published: 1 October 2020

Abstract: The main goal of this paper is to propose a Multiple-Criteria Decision-Making (MCDM) approach that will facilitate decision-making in the field of logistics—i.e., in the selection of the optimal equipment for performing a logistics activity. For defining the objective weights of the criteria, the correlation coefficient and the standard deviation (CCSD method) are applied. Furthermore, for determining the semi-objective weights of the considered criteria, the indifference threshold-based attribute ratio analysis method (ITARA) is used. In this way, by combining these two methods, the weights of the criteria are determined with a higher degree of reliability. For the final ranking of the alternatives, the measurement of alternatives and ranking according to the compromise solution method (MARCOS) is utilized. For demonstrating the applicability of the proposed approach, an illustrative case study pointing to the selection of the best manual stacker for a small warehouse is performed. The final results are compared with the ones obtained using the other proved MCDM methods that confirmed the reliability and stability of the proposed approach. The proposed integrated approach shows itself as a suitable technique for applying in the process of logistics equipment selection, because it defines the most influential criteria and the optimal choice with regard to all of them in a relatively easy and comprehensive way. Additionally, conceiving the determination of the criteria with the combination of objective and semi-objective methods enables defining the objective weights concerning the attitudes of the involved decision-makers, which finally leads to more reliable results.

Keywords: MCDM; the CCSD method; the ITARA method; the MARCOS method; stackers; logistics

1. Introduction

Logistics has long been considered a key factor in economic development, spatial integration, and market integration in the developed world [1]. During the 1960s, logistics as a concept of the integration of the process of the distribution of goods gained its place in the theory and practice of business management. Within the logistics sector, there are three basic approaches: physical distribution management, materials management, and business logistics. The important issue that logistics is faced with is certainly the question of the selection of adequate equipment for dealing with material resources.

The efficiency of the performance of logistics activities strongly depends on the use of optimal equipment in the warehouse or for the transportation of the goods. Bad choices could lead to the damage or contamination of goods, delays in delivery, and an increase in costs [2]. Furthermore, the selection of equipment directly influences the performance of the company, so this kind of decision could be considered as strategic and of great importance [3]. In the case of manufacturing equipment selection, the selection of the equipment needed for performing logistics activities requires defining the crucial features of the equipment, comparing them with the equipment offered on the market, and selecting the most suitable one [4]. The costs are considered as the most influential criterion in equipment selection, but they could not be treated as the only one.

Decisions regarding equipment purchasing affect various criteria that are often mutually opposing. Besides this, making a decision based on only one or a few criteria as well as making a decision based on previous experience and intuition will not lead to a reasonable decision. The use of techniques based on mathematics and statistics increases the reliability of the decision and contributes to the assurance of the selection that is made. The utilization of the Multiple-Criteria Decision-Making (MCDM) method could be a suitable means for the facilitation of a decision process regarding logistics equipment selection.

Recently, the field of Multi-Criteria Decision-Making (MCDM) has been rapidly evolving, thanks to the large number of scientific publications dealing with the adoption of individual decisions based on employed techniques and methods that belong to the specified domain [5]. MCDM is quite a suitable tool for solving complex decision-making problems because of its ability to evaluate different alternatives using a specific set of criteria [6].

The main aim of this paper is to develop a novel integrated MCDM-based approach for equipment selection in a logistics system. The correlation coefficients (CC) and standard deviations (SD)—i.e., the CCSD method [7]—will be applied for determining the objective weights of the criteria. Besides that, the indifference threshold-based attribute ratio analysis method (ITARA) [8], as a semi-objective method, will be also applied for determining the weights of the criteria. Therefore, the weights of the criteria will be determined by applying a combined CCSD-ITARA approach in order to make an objective determination of criteria significance where the subjectivity—i.e., perspective of the decision-makers—is included to a moderate degree. When it comes to the ranking of the alternatives, the measurement of alternatives and ranking according to the compromise solution method (MARCOS) [9] will be applied. The applicability of the proposed approach will be demonstrated through the illustrative case study, pointing to the selection of a suitable type of stacker for purchasing. The proposed approach enables the facilitation of the selection process regarding the purchasing of logistics equipment, which is a manual stacker in the considered case. Thus, the practitioners could observe all the involved criteria and, based on them, select the most appropriate alternative. Scientifically, the proposed combination of methods is completely new, and its possibilities have not been fully tested yet. In this case, it is used for the facilitation of decision and selection processes in the logistics field, but its potential could be further explored in other areas as well.

The rest of the paper is organized as follows: In Section 1, introductory considerations are given. A literature review is presented in Section 2. Section 3 demonstrates the methodology. An illustrative case study is described in Section 4. Finally, at the end of the manuscript the conclusions are given.

2. Literature Review

Decision-making is a process as old as humanity itself. Every day, each of us usually makes a large number of decisions. However, one of the problems that arise is to choose from the multitude of possible solutions the solution by which we will achieve the desired goal to the greatest degree, taking into account the objective limitations, which, to a greater or lesser extent, limit our freedom of judgment [10–12]. As could be inferred, the decision process involves the synergy of action of the human factor, mathematical methods, and IT tools [13]. In each study on the issue of decision-making, attention is focused on three general concepts—namely, the decision-making process, the decision-maker, and the decision itself—with the constant attempt to find a suitable way to make an appropriate decision. Intending to facilitate the decision process, scholars have proposed various methods that belong to the MCDM field.

MCDM has been developed as an integral part of operational research in order to create mathematical tools aimed at supporting the subjective evaluation of criteria by decision-makers [14,15]. MCDM is created in such a way that facilitates the selection of the most desirable alternative, the classification of the alternatives into a smaller number of categories, and the ranking of these alternatives following subjective requirements [16,17]. As already mentioned, there are a whole range of various MCDM techniques that have been applied to solving different types of complex problems. Each of the developed MCDM methods has its advantages, disadvantages, and limitations. Additionally, according to the problem that is being solved, it is necessary to consider an adequate technique [18–20].

Thus, MCDM considers situations in which the decision-maker must choose one of the alternatives from a set of available alternatives, which are judged based on several often-conflicting criteria [17,20]. The remarkably extensive development of the field of decision-making theory over the past few decades certainly has contributed to the presence of a multitude of MCDM methods. Perhaps the best-known and most widely applied MCDM methods are: simple additive weighting (SAW) [21]; the analytic hierarchy process (AHP) [22]; the analytic network process (ANP) [23]; elimination et choix traduisant la realité (ELECTRE) [24]; the preference ranking organization method for enrichment evaluation (PROMETHEE) [25]; the technique for order performance by similarity to ideal solution (TOPSIS) [26]; Višekriterijumska optimizacija i kompromisno rešenje (VIKOR) [27]; the complex proportional assessment of alternatives (COPRAS) [28]; and so forth.

In order to cope with a wider spectrum of problems, there is a new generation of newly developed MCDM methods and MCDM-based approaches, such as a new additive ratio assessment method (ARAS) [29]; multi-objective optimization on the basis of the ratio analysis method (MOORA) [30]; multi-objective optimization by ratio analysis plus full multiplicative form (MULTIMOORA) [31]; the step-wise weight assessment ratio analysis method (SWARA) [32]; the pivot pair-wise relative criteria importance assessment method (PIPRECIA) [33]; the multi-attributive ideal-real comparative analysis method (MAIRCA) [34]; the full consistency method (FUCOM) [35]; the evaluation based on distance from the average solution method (EDAS) [36]; a combined compromise solution method (CoCoSo) [37]; and so on. It is important to note that some of the aforementioned methods are used for weight determination and some of them for the ranking of alternatives.

Until now, MCDM methods have been used in the logistics field to contribute to and simplify the decision process regarding the various issues. A very popular theme that occupied scientific attention is certainly the question of reverse logistics [38–40]. Thence, the authors examined the problem of the selection of the logistics center or warehouse location [41,42]. The issue of humanitarian logistics is resolved by applying different MCDM techniques too [43,44]. The selection of the partners suitable for performing the logistics activities has been also performed by applying MCDM methods [45,46].

The topic connected to the equipment selection pointed to material handling is also present in the works of various authors. For example, Mathew and Sahu [47] used four methods for resolving the problem of equipment selection, and they are: CODAS, EDAS, MOORA, and WASPAS. The authors also based the selection of the equipment on the fuzzy axiomatic design principles [48]. Suitable equipment is selected in the fuzzy environment too [49]. Saputro and Rouyendegh [50] used the TOPSIS and MOMILP methods to find the best solution regarding the equipment for the warehouse. As can be concluded, there is enough space for observing the issue of the selection of the appropriate equipment for a logistics center. With that aim, in this paper an integrated approach based on the CCSD, ITARA, and MARCOS methods is proposed. The main reason for involving the CCSD and ITARA methods in the procedure of determining the criteria weights relies on the fact that they enable the definition of the criteria weights in an objective way but with incorporating a hint of the subjectivity of the decision-maker. In some cases, it is necessary to incorporate the requirements of the decision-maker to some suitable extent because the decision-maker knows what his/her possibilities and requests are. The MARCOS method, which is utilized for the final ranking of the considered alternatives, is a relatively recently proposed method whose possibilities have not been completely examined until now. The mentioned method enables the selection of a compromise solution that is optimal for the present conditions and fulfills all the given criteria to a satisfying degree.

3. Methodology

In this study, an integrated model including the CCSD, ITARA, and MARCOS methods is applied to determine the best stacker (Figure 1).

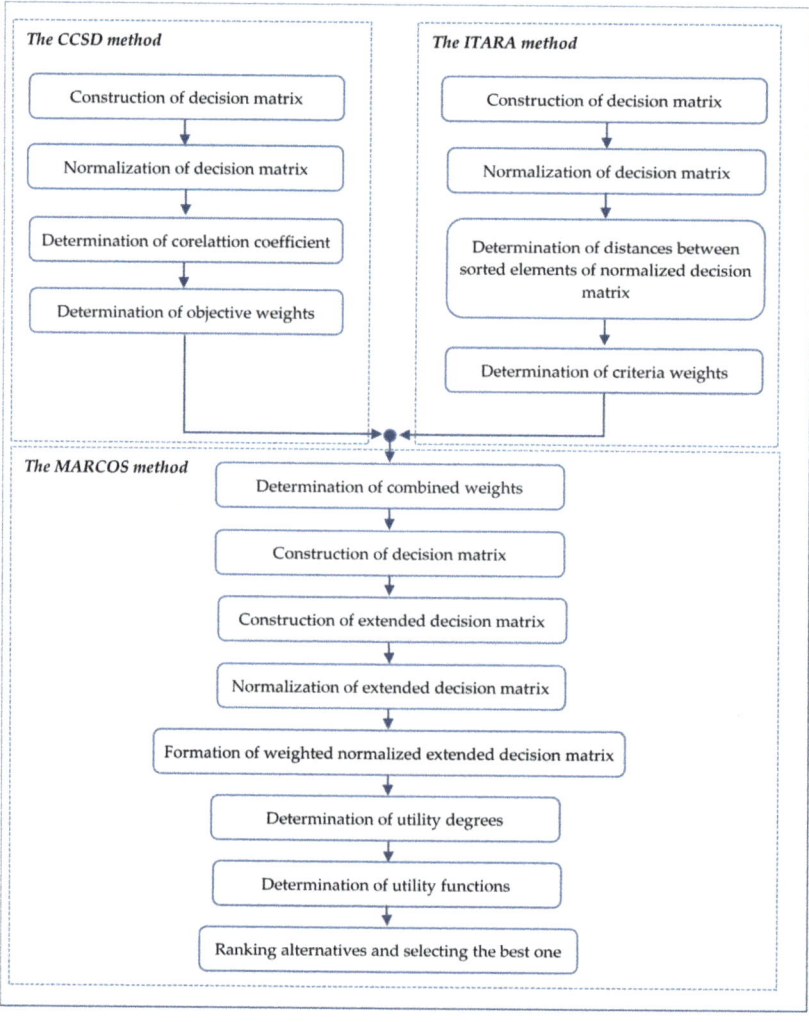

Figure 1. The computational procedure of the integrated CCSD-ITARA-MARCOS approach.

The CCSD and ITARA methods are used to determine weights of the criteria, whereas the MARCOS method is used to rank the alternatives—i.e., in our case, stackers—and to select the best one.

3.1. The CCSD Method

The CCSD method was developed by Wang and Luo [7]. The CCSD method is an objective weighting method. However, so far the CCSD method has been used for solving a variety of problems, such as problems in the supply chain [51,52], technological forecasting [53], financial performance evaluation [54], environmental issues [55], and so forth.

The steps of this method are as follows [7,53]:

Step 1: A decision matrix (G) is constructed. This matrix includes m alternatives, $B_1, \ldots, B_m$ based on the n criteria, $T_1, \ldots, T_n$.

$$G = [g_{ij}]_{m \times n}. \tag{1}$$

In Equation (1), g_{ij} denotes the performance of the ith alternative on the jth criterion.

Step 2: This matrix is normalized using Equation (2) (for beneficial criteria) and Equation (3) (for cost criteria).

$$h_{ij} = \frac{g_{ij} - \min(g_{ij})}{\max(g_{ij}) - \min(g_{ij})}, \tag{2}$$

$$h_{ij} = \frac{\max(g_{ij}) - g_{ij}}{\max(g_{ij}) - \min(g_{ij})}. \tag{3}$$

Step 3: The criterion T_j is removed to take into account its impact on decision-making. With criterion T_j, the performance value is computed using Equation (4) [56].

$$d_{ij} = \sum_{k=1,\ k \neq j}^{n} h_{ik} w_k. \tag{4}$$

In Equation (4), w_k denotes the weight of kth criterion calculated using some method for the subjective criteria weights determination, such as the AHP, SWARA, or PIPRECIA methods.

Step 4: The correlation coefficient (R_j) between T_j criterion's value and d_{ij} is computed using Equation (5).

$$R_j = \frac{\sum_{i=1}^{m}(h_{ij} - \overline{h}_j)(d_{ij} - \overline{d}_j)}{\sqrt{\sum_{i=1}^{m}(h_{ij} - \overline{h}_j)^2 \sum_{i=1}^{m}(d_{ij} - \overline{d}_j)^2}}, \tag{5}$$

where:

$$\overline{h}_j = \frac{\sum_{i=1}^{m} h_{ij}}{m}, \tag{6}$$

$$\overline{d}_j = \frac{\sum_{i=1}^{m} d_{ij}}{m}. \tag{7}$$

Step 5: In order to determine the objective weights (w_{jC}) of criteria, a non-linear optimization model is written as:

$$\text{Minimize } J = \sum_{j=1}^{n} \left(w_{jC} - \frac{\sigma_j \sqrt{1-R_j}}{\sum_{k=1}^{n} \sigma_k \sqrt{1-R_k}} \right)^2, \tag{8}$$

$$\text{s.t. } \sum_{j=1}^{n} w_{jC} = 1.$$

In Equation (8), σ_j denotes T_j criterion's standard deviation, and it can be calculated using Equation (9).

$$\sigma_j = \sqrt{\frac{1}{m} \sum_{i=1}^{m} (h_{ij} - \overline{h}_j)^2}. \tag{9}$$

The non-linear model indicated in Equation (8) is solved using MS Excel Solver (Microsoft corp., Redmond, WA, USA), Lingo 16 (Lindo Systems, Chicago, IL, USA), and MATLAB (The MathWorks, Inc., Natick, MA, USA).

3.2. The ITARA Method

The ITARA method was recently developed by Hatefi [8] and is a semi-objective method for determining the weights of criteria. The steps of the ITARA method are as follows [8]:

Step 1: A decision matrix (G) is constructed. This matrix was indicated in Equation (1).

Step 2: Normalized values and NIT_j (Normalized Indifference Threshold) are obtained using Equations (10) and (11), respectively.

$$e_{ij} = \frac{g_{ij}}{\sum_{i=1}^{m} g_{ij}}, \qquad (10)$$

$$NIT_j = \frac{IT_j}{\sum_{i=1}^{m} g_{ij}}. \qquad (11)$$

In Equation (11), IT_j denotes the Indifference Threshold of the jth criterion.

Step 3: Normalized values are sorted in ascending order, then they are named ρ_{ij} in such a way that $\rho_{ij} \le \rho_{i+1,j}$.

Step 4: The distance (γ_{ij}) between $\rho_{i+1,j}$ and ρ_{ij} is computed as follows.

$$\gamma_{ij} = \rho_{i+1,j} - \rho_{ij}. \qquad (12)$$

Step 5: The difference (ε_{ij}) between γ_{ij} and NIT_j is calculated as follows.

$$\varepsilon_{ij} = \begin{cases} \gamma_{ij} - NIT_j & for\ \gamma_{ij} > NIT_j, \\ 0 & for\ \gamma_{ij} \le NIT_j, \end{cases} \forall_i \in M, \forall_j \in N. \qquad (13)$$

Step 6: The weights of the criteria (w_{jI}) are computed as follows.

$$w_{jI} = \frac{v_j}{\sum_{j=1}^{n} v_j}, \qquad (14)$$

where:

$$v_j = \left(\sum_{i=1}^{m-1} \varepsilon_{ij}^p \right)^{1/p}. \qquad (15)$$

These weights are combined using Equation (16) [57].

$$w_{jCO} = \frac{w_{jC} w_{jI}}{\sum_{j=1}^{n} w_{jC} w_{jI}}. \qquad (16)$$

3.3. The MARCOS Method

The MARCOS method is developed by Stević et al. [9]. Although the method is new, so far it has been applied for solving different decision-making problems, such as the assessment of project management software [58], supplier selection [59], the evaluation of human resources [60], road traffic analysis [61], and so on.

In our study, the MARCOS method is used to rank stackers and to determine the best one. The steps of this method are as follows [9]:

Step 1: The decision matrix is constructed. This matrix was indicated in Equation (1).

Step 2: An extended decision matrix (U) is formed.

$$U = \begin{array}{c} \\ AAI \\ B_1 \\ B_2 \\ \ldots \\ B_m \\ AI \end{array} \begin{array}{c} T_1 \quad T_2 \quad \ldots \quad T_n \\ \left[\begin{array}{cccc} g_{aa1} & g_{aa2} & \cdots & g_{aan} \\ g_{11} & g_{12} & \cdots & g_{1n} \\ g_{21} & g_{22} & \cdots & g_{2n} \\ \ldots & \ldots & \ldots & \ldots \\ g_{m1} & g_{m2} & \cdots & g_{mn} \\ g_{ai1} & g_{ai2} & \cdots & g_{ain} \end{array} \right] \end{array}. \quad (17)$$

While the ideal solution (AI) is the best alternative, the anti-ideal solution (AAI) is the worst alternative. These values are computed as follows.

$$AI = \max(g_{ij}) \text{ if } j \in BN \text{ and } AI = \min(g_{ij}) \text{ if } j \in CS, \quad (18)$$

$$AAI = \min(g_{ij}) \text{ if } j \in BN \text{ and } AAI = \max(g_{ij}) \text{ if } j \in CS. \quad (19)$$

In Equations (18) and (19), BN denotes the beneficial criteria and CS presents the cost criteria.

Step 3: The extended decision matrix is normalized using Equations (20) and (21).

$$y_{ij} = \frac{g_{aij}}{g_{ij}} \text{ if } j \in CS, \quad (20)$$

$$y_{ij} = \frac{g_{ij}}{g_{aij}} \text{ if } j \in BN. \quad (21)$$

In Equations (20) and (21), y_{ij} is an element of the normalized matrix ($Y = [y_{ij}]_{m \times n}$).

Step 4: The normalized values are multiplied by the weights (w_{jCO}) of criteria by using Equation (22) to identify the weighted matrix ($C = [c_{ij}]_{m \times n}$).

$$c_{ij} = y_{ij} \times w_{jCO}. \quad (22)$$

Step 5: The utility degrees (Z_i) of the alternatives are computed concerning the anti-ideal and ideal solution, respectively.

$$Z_i^- = \frac{S_i}{S_{aai}}, \quad (23)$$

$$Z_i^+ = \frac{S_i}{S_{ai}}, \quad (24)$$

where:

$$S_i = \sum_{i=1}^{n} c_{ij}. \quad (25)$$

Step 6: The utility functions ($f(Z_i)$) of the alternatives are determined using Equation (26).

$$f(Z_i) = \frac{Z_i^+ + Z_i^-}{1 + \frac{1-f(Z_i^+)}{f(Z_i^+)} + \frac{1-f(Z_i^-)}{f(Z_i^-)}}, \quad (26)$$

where:

$$f(Z_i^-) = \frac{Z_i^+}{Z_i^+ + Z_i^-}, \quad (27)$$

$$f(Z_i^+) = \frac{Z_i^-}{Z_i^+ + Z_i^-}. \quad (28)$$

In Equation (27), $f(Z_i^-)$ denotes the utility function concerning the anti-ideal solution. In Equation (28), $f(Z_i^+)$ presents the utility function concerning the ideal solution.

Step 7: The alternatives are ranked with respect to the final utility function. The alternative with the highest final utility function is determined as the best one.

4. An Illustrative Case Study

In this study, the best manual stacker will be selected for small warehouses. For this, two logistics experts were asked to identify suitable alternatives for small warehouses and evaluation criteria. The logistics experts identified eight alternatives and five criteria, which are the Price of Stacker (PS) (USD), Capacity (CPC) (kg), Lift Height (LH) (mm), Warranty Period (WRP) (Month), and Fork Length (FL) (mm). All the data are obtained from websites selling stackers. Table 1 indicates the decision matrix.

Table 1. Decision matrix.

Stackers \ Criteria	PS	CPC	LH	WRP	FL
Stc1	660	1000	1600	18	1200
Stc2	800	1000	1600	24	900
Stc3	980	1000	2500	24	900
Stc4	920	1500	1600	24	900
Stc5	1380	1500	1500	24	1150
Stc6	1230	1000	1600	24	1150
Stc7	680	1500	1600	18	1100
Stc8	960	2000	1600	12	1150

First of all, the CCSD method is applied to the above matrix to determine the objective weights of the criteria. The results of the CCSD are indicated in Table 2.

Table 2. The results of the CCSD.

Weights \ Criteria	PS	CPC	LH	WRP	FL
w_{jC}	0.1833	0.1942	0.1707	0.2114	0.2404

Then, the value of IT_j for each criterion is determined by the experts. These values are indicated in Table 3.

Table 3. The value of IT_j.

Criteria	PS	CPC	LH	WRP	FL
IT_j	120	100	100	4	100

The steps of the ITARA method are applied to the decision matrix to achieve the weights of the criteria. The results of the ITARA method, the results of the CCSD, and the combined weights of criteria are indicated in Table 4.

Table 4. The results of the ITARA, CCSD, and combined weights.

Weights \ Criteria	PS	CPC	LH	WRP	FL
w_{jC}	0.1833	0.1942	0.1707	0.2114	0.2404
w_{jI}	0.1097	0.3393	0.3698	0.1063	0.0748
w_{jCO}	0.1061	0.3476	0.3330	0.1185	0.0949

The combined weights are transferred to the MARCOS method. Then, the extended decision matrix is formed using step 2 of the MARCOS method. Table 5 indicates the extended decision matrix.

Table 5. The extended decision matrix.

Stackers / Criteria	PS	CPC	LH	WRP	FL
AAI	1380	1000	1500	12	900
Stc1	660	1000	1600	18	1200
Stc2	800	1000	1600	24	900
Stc3	980	1000	2500	24	900
Stc4	920	1500	1600	24	900
Stc5	1380	1500	1500	24	1150
Stc6	1230	1000	1600	24	1150
Stc7	680	1500	1600	18	1100
Stc8	960	2000	1600	12	1150
AI	660	2000	2500	24	1200

Then, the extended decision matrix is normalized using Equations (20) and (21). Table 6 presents the normalized matrix.

Table 6. The normalized matrix.

Stackers / Criteria	PS	CPC	LH	WRP	FL
AAI	0.4783	0.5000	0.6000	0.5000	0.7500
Stc1	1.0000	0.5000	0.6400	0.7500	1.0000
Stc2	0.8250	0.5000	0.6400	1.0000	0.7500
Stc3	0.6735	0.5000	1.0000	1.0000	0.7500
Stc4	0.7174	0.7500	0.6400	1.0000	0.7500
Stc5	0.4783	0.7500	0.6000	1.0000	0.9583
Stc6	0.5366	0.5000	0.6400	1.0000	0.9583
Stc7	0.9706	0.7500	0.6400	0.7500	0.9167
Stc8	0.6875	1.0000	0.6400	0.5000	0.9583
AI	1.0000	1.0000	1.0000	1.0000	1.0000

Then, the normalized values are multiplied by weights (w_{jCO}) of the criteria using Equation (22) to determine the weighted matrix. Table 7 indicates the weighted matrix.

Table 7. The weighted matrix.

Stackers / Criteria	PS	CPC	LH	WRP	FL
AAI	0.0507	0.1738	0.1998	0.0593	0.0712
Stc1	0.1061	0.1738	0.2131	0.0889	0.0949
Stc2	0.0875	0.1738	0.2131	0.1185	0.0712
Stc3	0.0715	0.1738	0.3330	0.1185	0.0712
Stc4	0.0761	0.2607	0.2131	0.1185	0.0712
Stc5	0.0507	0.2607	0.1998	0.1185	0.0909
Stc6	0.0569	0.1738	0.2131	0.1185	0.0909
Stc7	0.1030	0.2607	0.2131	0.0889	0.0870
Stc8	0.0729	0.3476	0.2131	0.0593	0.0909
AI	0.1061	0.3476	0.3330	0.1185	0.0949

Using Equations (23)–(28), the results of the MARCOS method are obtained. The results of the MARCOS method and the rankings of stackers are indicated in Table 8.

Table 8. The results of the MARCOS method.

Results \ Stackers	Z_i^-	Z_i^+	$f(Z_i^-)$	$f(Z_i^+)$	$f(Z_i)$	Rankings
Stc1	1.2199	0.6767	0.3568	0.6432	0.5649	6
Stc2	1.1970	0.6640	0.3568	0.6432	0.5543	7
Stc3	1.3843	0.7679	0.3568	0.6432	0.6410	2
Stc4	1.3331	0.7395	0.3568	0.6432	0.6173	4
Stc5	1.2988	0.7205	0.3568	0.6432	0.6014	5
Stc6	1.1774	0.6531	0.3568	0.6432	0.5452	8
Stc7	1.3567	0.7526	0.3568	0.6432	0.6283	3
Stc8	1.4128	0.7837	0.3568	0.6432	0.6542	1

According to the results of the MARCOS method, the rankings of the stackers are as follows: Stc8, Stc3, Stc7, Stc4, Stc5, Stc1, Stc2, and Stc6. As can be seen from the input data presented in Table 1, the parameters connected to the Stc8 are always medium to high, which finally emphasizes this choice as a compromise and optimal.

In order to confirm the stability and reliability of the proposed model, the gained results are compared with the results obtained using the following MCDM methods: the weighted aggregated sum product assessment (WASPAS) method [62], additive ratio assessment (ARAS) [29], and grey relational analysis (GRA) [63]. The comparison of the gained ranking orders of the alternatives is shown in Figure 2.

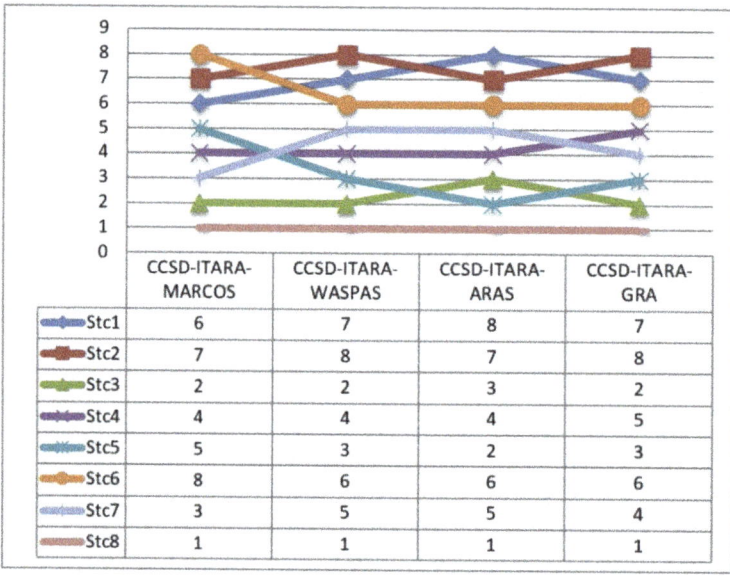

Figure 2. Testing the stability of the proposed approach.

5. Discussion and Conclusions

The selection of equipment for dealing with materials during the logistics process is a very important task for decision-makers because this choice has a significant impact on the future operation of a logistics center. This kind of decision could be treated as strategic because the selected type of equipment could contribute to decreasing costs, shortening the time needed for performing an activity, and providing a higher security for goods and products. All of the points mentioned lead to the conclusion that these decisions require an analytical approach that involves all the criteria that are important for performing the evaluation process. For that matter, the MCDM methods could be a suitable and useful tool that facilitates the decision process and enables the making of a proper decision for the given conditions. For the facilitation of a decision-making process regarding equipment selection in the logistics field, in this paper we proposed the application of a novel integrated CCSD-ITARA-MARCOS MCDM model. The usefulness of this integrated model is demonstrated through the illustrative case study and pointed to the selection of the appropriate manual stacker. Additionally, two domain experts were involved in the evaluation process in regard to identifying suitable alternatives—i.e., manual stackers for small warehouses—according to the given set of evaluation criteria.

In the conducted case study, the weights of the evaluation criteria were determined by applying and combining the CCSD method and the ITARA method. When it comes to the process of determining weights, both the methods are convenient and easy to apply. The main difference between these methods is their orientation. The CCSD method is objective, whereas the ITARA method is semi-objective. Additionally, the CCSD method does not need a specific normalization method and can include more data on criteria weights [7], whereas the ITARA method belongs to a group of methods that are based on measuring data dispersion. The reason for employing objective and semi-objective methods when it comes to the determination of weights of criteria is that subjective methods often led to a decrease in the accuracy of evaluation with the increase in the number of criteria [8]. The main advantage of this combination relies on the fact that the standpoint of the decision-maker is appreciated to a certain degree. Namely, every decision-maker has a particular attitude regarding the criteria, meaning that for someone something is more important than to for another. If the significance of criteria is determined only on an objective basis then the individual dimension is lost. In this case, combining the objective and semi-objective methods for obtaining the criteria significance reflects the intention of the preservation of the objectiveness of evaluation together with acknowledging the preferences of decision-makers without disturbing the reliability of criteria significance determination.

The final ranking order is obtained by utilizing the newly developed MARCOS method. The MARCOS method primarily is based on testing the reference values of alternatives related to ideal values [9]. Thus, the given method emphasizes the alternative that represents some kind of compromise solution regarding the given requirements. The final evaluation and ranking order are strongly influenced by determining the criteria significance. In the present case, as was previously stated, the significance of the criteria is determined very thoughtfully and carefully, and all because of gaining the most reliable results. It is undeniable that the MARCOS method is easy to use and that it facilitates the decision process, but in combination with the CCSD and ITARA applied for determining the importance of the considered criteria, the reliability of the performed evaluation and the gained ranking order increased.

Following the results of the applied integrated model, the stacker designated as Stc8 is the best in terms of the evaluated criteria. With the aim of testing the proposed approach based on the mentioned MCDM methods, the obtained results are compared with the results determined using the WASPAS, ARAS, and GRA methods. In the computing procedures of all three methods, the same weights of the criteria are involved, which were obtained by applying the CCSD-ITARA. In all observations, the stacker Stc8 is in first place and represents the best choice for the given conditions. Besides this, the stacker Stc3 is in the second place, except in the case when is applied in ARAS, when it is in 3rd place. Thus, in this way the reliability and stability of the proposed approach are completely confirmed.

The proposed integrated CCSD-ITARA-MARCOS model proved to be extremely successful when it comes to solving problems in a logistics system—i.e., a stacker selection problem. The use of the CCSD-ITARA-MARCOS model is very beneficial because it is very comprehensive and empowers us to make confident judgments. However, the applicability of the proposed model should not be limited only to the logistics field. Its potential and possibilities should be examined in other fields, such as information technologies, strategy selection, personnel selection, etc. In that way, all the aspects of the proposed model will be observed and the potential shortages could be resolved.

The key advantage of the introduced integrated model is its simplicity, ease of use, and objectivity that appreciates the standpoint of decision-makers to an acceptable degree. However, the main limitation of the proposed model is that it deals with crisp numbers. The decision-making environment is characterized by uncertainty and vagueness, so it is very difficult to correctly express the evaluation criteria through crisp numbers. In other words, the reliability of the performed evaluation decreases because unexpected changes could cause a situation where, for example, the first ranked alternative is not acceptable because the conditions have changed. In order to better incorporate uncertainty into the evaluation process, an extension with fuzzy, grey, and neutrosophic numbers is proposed. In this way, the proposed model would be improved and the possibility of making impropriate decisions would be reduced. Furthermore, by involving a greater number of decision-makers, the subjective dimension could be incorporated to a greater extent and interesting results would be obtained.

Besides the mentioned shortages, the CCSD-ITARA-MARCOS model proved its applicability and ability to help in the process of decision-making. Overall, the proposed hybrid model is flexible, adaptable, and effective, and it can help decision-makers solve problems in other areas as well. Additionally, the model is quite simple and can be easily modified depending on the problem one wants to solve.

Author Contributions: Conceptualization, A.U., D.K., and G.P.; methodology, A.U., D.K., D.S., and Ç.K.; validation, P.T.N.; data curation, G.P.; writing—original draft preparation, D.S. and Ç.K.; writing—review and editing, A.U., and P.T.N.; supervision, D.K. All authors have read and agreed to the published version of the manuscript.

Funding: This research received no external funding.

Conflicts of Interest: The authors declare no conflict of interest.

References

1. Tadić, S.; Zečević, S.; Petrović-Vujačić, J. Global trends and logistics development. *Ekon. Vidici* **2013**, *18*, 519–532.
2. Mohsen; Hassan, M.D. A framework for selection of material handling equipment in manufacturing and logistics facilities. *J. Manuf. Technol. Manag.* **2010**, *21*, 246–268. [CrossRef]
3. Tuzkaya, G.; Gülsün, B.; Kahraman, C.; Özgen, D. An integrated fuzzy multi-criteria decision making methodology for material handling equipment selection problem and an application. *Expert Syst. Appl.* **2010**, *37*, 2853–2863. [CrossRef]
4. Tabucanon, M.T.; Batanov, D.N.; Verma, D.K. Decision support system for multicriteria machine selection for flexible manufacturing systems. *Comput. Ind.* **1994**, *25*, 131–143. [CrossRef]
5. Zavadskas, E.K.; Turskis, Z.; Stević, Ž.; Mardani, A. Modelling procedure for the selection of steel pipes supplier by applying fuzzy AHP method. *Oper. Res. Eng. Sci. Theory Appl.* **2020**, 39–53. [CrossRef]
6. Đalić, I.; Stević, Ž.; Karamasa, C.; Puška, A. A novel integrated fuzzy PIPRECIA–interval rough SAW model: Green supplier selection. *Decis. Mak. Appl. Manag. Eng.* **2020**, *3*, 126–145. [CrossRef]
7. Wang, Y.M.; Luo, Y. Integration of correlations with standard deviations for determining attribute weights in multiple attribute decision making. *Math. Comput. Model.* **2010**, *51*, 1–12. [CrossRef]
8. Hatefi, M.A. Indifference threshold-based attribute ratio analysis: A method for assigning the weights to the attributes in multiple attribute decision making. *Appl. Soft Comput.* **2019**, *74*, 643–651. [CrossRef]
9. Stević, Ž.; Pamučar, D.; Puška, A.; Chatterjee, P. Sustainable supplier selection in healthcare industries using a new MCDM method: Measurement of alternatives and ranking according to COmpromise solution (MARCOS). *Comput. Ind. Eng.* **2020**, *140*, 106231. [CrossRef]
10. Popovic, G.; Stanujkic, D.; Brzakovic, M.; Karabasevic, D. A multiple-criteria decision-making model for the selection of a hotel location. *Land Use Policy* **2019**, *84*, 49–58. [CrossRef]
11. Karabašević, D.; Zavadskas, E.K.; Stanujkic, D.; Popovic, G.; Brzakovic, M. An Approach to Personnel Selection in the IT Industry Based on the EDAS Method. *Transform. Bus. Econ.* **2018**, *17*, 54–65.
12. Stanujkic, D.; Karabasevic, D.; Zavadskas, E.K. A New Approach for Selecting Alternatives Based on the Adapted Weighted Sum and the SWARA Methods: A Case of Personnel Selection. *Econ. Comput. Econ. Cybern. Stud. Res.* **2017**, *51*, 39–56.

13. Hansson, S.O.; Hadorn, G.H. Argument-based decision support for risk analysis. *J. Risk Res.* **2018**, *21*, 1449–1464. [CrossRef]
14. Zavadskas, E.K.; Turskis, Z.; Kildienė, S. State of art surveys of overviews on MCDM/MADM methods. *Technol. Econ. Dev. Econ.* **2014**, *20*, 165–179. [CrossRef]
15. Stanujkic, D.; Zavadskas, E.K.; Liu, S.; Karabasevic, D.; Popovic, G. Improved OCRA method based on the use of interval grey numbers. *J. Grey Syst.* **2017**, *29*, 49–60.
16. Mardani, A.; Jusoh, A.; Nor, K.; Khalifah, Z.; Zakwan, N.; Valipour, A. Multiple criteria decision-making techniques and their applications–a review of the literature from 2000 to 2014. *Econ. Res. Ekon. Istraživanja* **2015**, *28*, 516–571. [CrossRef]
17. Popovic, G.; Stanujkic, D.; Karabasevic, D. A framework for the evaluation of hotel property development projects. *Int. J. Strat. Prop. Manag.* **2019**, *23*, 96–107. [CrossRef]
18. Bakir, M.; Akan, Ş.; Kiraci, K.; Karabasevic, D.; Stanujkic, D.; Popovic, G. Multiple-Criteria Approach of the Operational Performance Evaluation in the Airline Industry: Evidence from the Emerging Markets. *Rom. J. Econ. Forecast.* **2020**, *23*, 149.
19. Stanujkic, D.; Karabasevic, D.; Zavadskas, E.K.; Smarandache, F.; Brauers, W.K. A bipolar fuzzy extension of the MULTIMOORA method. *Informatica* **2019**, *30*, 135–152. [CrossRef]
20. Karabasevic, D.; Maksimovic, M.; Stanujkic, D.; Brzakovic, P.; Brzakovic, M. The evaluation of websites in the textile industry by applying ISO/IEC 9126-4 standard and the EDAS method. *Ind. Text.* **2018**, *69*, 489–494.
21. Churchman, C.W.; Ackoff, R.L. An approximate measure of value. *J. Oper. Res. Soc. Am.* **1954**, *2*, 172–187. [CrossRef]
22. Saaty, T.L. *The Analytic Hierarchy Process*; McGraw-Hill: New York, NY, USA, 1980.
23. Saaty, T.L. *Decision Making with Dependence and Feedback: Analytic Networkprocess*; RWS Publications: Pittsburgh, PA, USA, 1996.
24. Roy, B. *Multicriteria for Decision Aiding*; Kluwer: London, UK, 1996.
25. Brans, J.P.; Vincke, P. A preference ranking organization method: The PROMETHEE method for MCDM. *Manag. Sci.* **1985**, *31*, 647–656. [CrossRef]
26. Yoon, K.P.; Hwang, C.L. *Multiple Attribute Decision Making: An Introduction*; Sage Publications: Thousand Oaks, CA, USA, 1995; Volume 104.
27. Opricovic, S. *Multicriteria Optimization of Civil Engineering Systems*; Faculty of Civil Engineering: Belgrade, Serbia, 1998. (In Serbian)
28. Zavadskas, E.K.; Kaklauskas, A.; Sarka, V. The new method of multi-criteria complex proportional assessment of projects. *Techological Econ. Dev. Econ.* **1994**, *1*, 131–139.
29. Zavadskas, E.K.; Turskis, Z. A new additive ratio assessment (ARAS) method in multicriteria decision-making. *Technol. Econ. Dev. Econ.* **2010**, *16*, 159–172. [CrossRef]
30. Brauers, W.K.; Zavadskas, E.K. The MOORA method and its application to privatization in a transition economy. *Control Cybern.* **2006**, *35*, 445–469.
31. Brauers, W.K.M.; Zavadskas, E.K. Project management by MULTIMOORA as an instrument for transition economies. *Technol. Econ. Dev. Econ.* **2010**, *16*, 5–24. [CrossRef]
32. Keršuliene, V.; Zavadskas, E.K.; Turskis, Z. Selection of rational dispute resolution method by applying new step-wise weight assessment ratio analysis (SWARA). *J. Bus. Econ. Manag.* **2010**, *11*, 243–258. [CrossRef]
33. Stanujkic, D.; Zavadskas, E.K.; Karabasevic, D.; Smarandache, F.; Turskis, Z. The use of Pivot Pair-wise Relative Criteria Importance Assessment method for determining weights of criteria. *Rom. J. Econ. Forecast.* **2017**, *20*, 116–133.
34. Gigović, L.; Pamučar, D.; Bajić, Z.; Milićević, M. The combination of expert judgment and GIS-MAIRCA analysis for the selection of sites for ammunition depots. *Sustainability* **2016**, *8*, 372. [CrossRef]
35. Pamučar, D.; Stević, Ž.; Sremac, S. A new model for determining weight coefficients of criteria in mcdm models: Full consistency method (FUCOM). *Symmetry* **2018**, *10*, 393. [CrossRef]
36. Keshavarz Ghorabaee, M.; Zavadskas, E.K.; Olfat, L.; Turskis, Z. Multi-criteria inventory classification using a new method of evaluation based on distance from average solution (EDAS). *Informatica* **2015**, *26*, 435–451. [CrossRef]
37. Yazdani, M.; Zarate, P.; Zavadskas, E.K.; Turskis, Z. A Combined Compromise Solution (CoCoSo) method for multi-criteria decision-making problems. *Manag. Decis.* **2019**, *57*, 2501–2519. [CrossRef]

38. Wadhwa, S.; Madaan, J.; Chan, F.T.S. Flexible decision modeling of reverse logistics system: A value adding MCDM approach for alternative selection. *Robot. Comput. Integr. Manuf.* **2009**, *25*, 460–469. [CrossRef]
39. Prakash, C.; Barua, M.K. A combined MCDM approach for evaluation and selection of third-party reverse logistics partner for Indian electronics industry. *Sustain. Prod. Consum.* **2016**, *7*, 66–78. [CrossRef]
40. Wang, H.; Jiang, Z.; Zhang, H.; Wang, Y.; Yang, Y.; Li, Y. An integrated MCDM approach considering demands-matching for reverse logistics. *J. Clean. Prod.* **2019**, *208*, 199–210. [CrossRef]
41. Żak, J.; Węgliński, S. The selection of the logistics center location based on MCDM/A methodology. *Transp. Res. Procedia* **2014**, *3*, 555–564. [CrossRef]
42. Mihajlović, J.; Rajković, P.; Petrović, G.; Ćirić, D. The selection of the logistics distribution center location based on MCDM methodology in southern and eastern region in Serbia. *Oper. Res. Eng. Sci. Theory Appl.* **2019**, *2*, 72–85. [CrossRef]
43. Celik, E.; Gumus, A.T.; Alegoz, M. A trapezoidal type-2 fuzzy MCDM method to identify and evaluate critical success factors for humanitarian relief logistics management. *J. Intell. Fuzzy Syst.* **2014**, *27*, 2847–2855. [CrossRef]
44. Budak, A.; Kaya, İ.; Karaşan, A.; Erdoğan, M. Real-time location systems selection by using a fuzzy MCDM approach: An application in humanitarian relief logistics. *Appl. Soft Comput.* **2020**, *92*. [CrossRef]
45. Aguezzoul, A. Third-party logistics selection problem: A literature review on criteria and methods. *Omega* **2014**, *49*, 69–78. [CrossRef]
46. Jamshidi, A.; Jamshidi, F.; Ait-Kadi, D.; Ramudhin, A. A review of priority criteria and decision-making methods applied in selection of sustainable city logistics initiatives and collaboration partners. *Int. J. Prod. Res.* **2019**, *57*, 5175–5193. [CrossRef]
47. Mathew, M.; Sahu, S. Comparison of new multi-criteria decision making methods for material handling equipment selection. *Manag. Sci. Lett.* **2018**, *8*, 139–150. [CrossRef]
48. Khandekar, A.V.; Chakraborty, S. Selection of material handling equipment using fuzzy axiomatic design principles. *Informatica* **2015**, *26*, 259–282. [CrossRef]
49. Hadi-Vencheh, A.; Mohamadghasemi, A. A new hybrid fuzzy multi-criteria decision making model for solving the material handling equipment selection problem. *Int. J. Comput. Integr. Manuf.* **2015**, *28*, 534–550. [CrossRef]
50. Eko Saputro, T.; Daneshvar Rouyendegh, B. A hybrid approach for selecting material handling equipment in a warehouse. *Int. J. Manag. Sci. Eng. Manag.* **2016**, *11*, 34–48. [CrossRef]
51. Singh, R.K.; Benyoucef, L. A consensus based group decision making methodology for strategic selection problems of supply chain coordination. *Eng. Appl. Artif. Intell.* **2013**, *26*, 122–134. [CrossRef]
52. Hanane, A.; Brahim, O.; Bouchra, F. CCSD and TOPSIS methodology for selecting supplier in a paper company. In Proceedings of the 2016 4th IEEE International Colloquium on Information Science and Technology (CiSt), Tangier, Morocco, 24–26 October 2016; pp. 275–280.
53. Dahooie, J.H.; Zavadskas, E.K.; Firoozfar, H.R.; Vanaki, A.S.; Mohammadi, N.; Brauers, W.K.M. An improved fuzzy MULTIMOORA approach for multi-criteria decision making based on objective weighting method (CCSD) and its application to technological forecasting method selection. *Eng. Appl. Artif. Intell.* **2019**, *79*, 114–128. [CrossRef]
54. Heidary Dahooie, J.; Zavadskas, E.K.; Vanaki, A.S.; Firoozfar, H.R.; Lari, M.; Turskis, Z. A new evaluation model for corporate financial performance using integrated CCSD and FCM-ARAS approach. *Econ. Res. Ekon. Istraživanja* **2019**, *32*, 1088–1113. [CrossRef]
55. Kim, I.; Park, K.; Lee, K.; Park, M.; Lim, H.; Shin, H.; Kim, S.D. Application of various cytotoxic endpoints for the toxicity prioritization of fine dust (PM2.5) sources using a multi-criteria decision-making approach. *Environ. Geochem. Health* **2019**, *42*, 1775–1788. [CrossRef]
56. Hwang, C.L.; Yoon, K. Methods for multiple attribute decision making. In *Multiple Attribute Decision Making*; Springer: Berlin/Heidelberg, Germany, 1981; pp. 58–191.
57. Zavadskas, E.K.; Podvezko, V. Integrated determination of objective criteria weights in MCDM. *Int. J. Inf. Technol. Decis. Mak.* **2016**, *15*, 267–283. [CrossRef]
58. Puška, A.; Stojanović, I.; Maksimović, A.; Osmanović, N. Evaluation software of project management used measurement of alternatives and ranking according to compromise solution (MARCOS) method. *Oper. Res. Eng. Sci. Theory Appl.* **2020**, *3*, 89–102.

59. Badi, I.; Pamucar, D. Supplier selection for steelmaking company by using combined Grey-MARCOS methods. *Decis. Mak. Appl. Manag. Eng.* **2020**, *3*, 37–48. [CrossRef]
60. Stević, Ž.; Brković, N. A Novel Integrated FUCOM-MARCOS Model for Evaluation of Human Resources in a Transport Company. *Logistics* **2020**, *4*, 4. [CrossRef]
61. Stanković, M.; Stević, Ž.; Das, D.K.; Subotić, M.; Pamučar, D. A new fuzzy MARCOS method for road traffic risk analysis. *Mathematics* **2020**, *8*, 457. [CrossRef]
62. Zavadskas, E.K.; Turskis, Z.; Antucheviciene, J.; Zakarevicius, A. Optimization of weighted aggregated sum product assessment. *Elektronika Ir Elektrotechnika* **2012**, *122*, 3–6. [CrossRef]
63. Deng, J. Control problems of grey systems. *Syst. Control Lett.* **1982**, *1*, 288–294.

© 2020 by the authors. Licensee MDPI, Basel, Switzerland. This article is an open access article distributed under the terms and conditions of the Creative Commons Attribution (CC BY) license (http://creativecommons.org/licenses/by/4.0/).

Article

Application of Improved Best Worst Method (BWM) in Real-World Problems

Dragan Pamučar [1],*, Fatih Ecer [2], Goran Cirovic [3] and Melfi A. Arlasheedi [4]

1. Department of Logistics, Military Academy, University of Defence in Belgrade, Military Academy, Pavla Jurisica Sturma 33, 11000 Belgrade, Serbia
2. Department of Business Administrative, Faculty of Economics and Administrative Sciences, Afyon Kocatepe University, ANS Campus, 03030 Afyonkarahisar, Turkey; fatihecer@gmail.com
3. Faculty of Technical Sciences, University of Novi Sad, Trg Dositeja Obradovica 6, 2100 Novi Sad, Serbia; cirovic@sezampro.rs
4. Department of Quantitative Methods, School of Business, King Faisal University, 31982 Al-Ahsa, Saudi Arabia; malrasheedy@kfu.edu.sa
* Correspondence: dragan.pamucar@va.mod.gov.rs

Received: 12 July 2020; Accepted: 7 August 2020; Published: 11 August 2020

Abstract: The Best Worst Method (BWM) represents a powerful tool for multi-criteria decision-making and defining criteria weight coefficients. However, while solving real-world problems, there are specific multi-criteria problems where several criteria exert the same influence on decision-making. In such situations, the traditional postulates of the BWM imply the defining of one best criterion and one worst criterion from within a set of observed criteria. In this paper, an improvement of the traditional BWM that eliminates this problem is presented. The improved BWM (BWM-I) offers the possibility for decision-makers to express their preferences even in cases where there is more than one best and worst criterion. The development enables the following: (1) the BWM-I enables us to express experts' preferences irrespective of the number of the best/worst criteria in a set of evaluation criteria; (2) the application of the BWM-I reduces the possibility of making a mistake while comparing pairs of criteria, which increases the reliability of the results; and (3) the BWM-I is characterized by its flexibility, which is expressed through the possibility of the realistic processing of experts' preferences irrespective of the number of the criteria that have the same significance and the possibility of the transformation of the BWM-I into the traditional BWM (should there be a unique best/worst criterion). To present the applicability of the BWM-I, it was applied to defining the weight coefficients of the criteria in the field of renewable energy and their ranking.

Keywords: BWM; BWM-I; criteria weights; multi-criteria; renewable energy

1. Introduction

In everyday life, we meet and analyze problems to find an optimal solution, i.e., the task of optimization. We meet them almost everywhere—in technical and economic systems, in the family, and elsewhere. The decision-making process and the choice of "the best" alternative is most frequently based on the analysis of more than one criterion and a series of limitations. When speaking about decision-making with the application of several criteria, decision-making may be referred to as multi-criteria decision-making (MCDM) [1,2]. The essence of the problem of MCDM is reduced to the ranking of an alternative from within the considered set by applying specific mathematical tools and/or logical preferences. Finally, a decision is made on the choice of the best alternative, taking into consideration different evaluation criteria. MCDM is an integral part of the contemporary science of decision-making and the science of management and systems engineering, which has broadly been applied in many fields, such as engineering, economics, medicine, logistics, the military field, and management [3,4].

While solving MCDM problems, the inevitable phase implies the determination of criteria weight coefficients. Studying the available literature enables us to note that there is no unique division of the methods for determining criteria weights and that, for the most part, their division has been made per the authors' understanding of and needs for solving a real-world problem. According to [5], one of the classification methods for determining criteria weights is implying their division into objective and subjective models. Objective models imply the calculation of criteria weight coefficients based on the criteria value in the initial decision-making matrix. The most well-known objective models include the Entropy Method [6], the CRITIC method (CRiteria Importance Through Intercriteria Correlation) [7], and the FANMA method, which is named after the authors of the method [8].

On the other hand, subjective models imply the application of the methodology, implying the direct participation of decision-makers who express their preferences according to the significance of criteria. Subjective models differ from each other in the number of participants and the techniques applied, as well as how the criteria final weights are formed. A big group of subjective models consists of the models based on pairwise comparisons. Thurstone [9] was the first to introduce the pairwise comparison method, which represents a structured manner of defining the decision-making matrix. Pairwise comparisons are used to show the relative significances of m actions in situations when it is impossible or senseless to assign rates to actions in relation to criteria. One of the most frequently used methods based on pairwise comparisons is the Analytic Hierarchy Process (AHP) method [10].

Motivation for the Modification of the Traditional Best Worst Method

In the last few years, the Best Worst Method (BWM) has significantly ranked in the field of MCDM as a model providing reliable and relevant results for optimal decision-making. Rezaei [11] developed the BWM to overcome some shortcomings of the AHP, which first of all pertain to a large number of comparisons in criteria pairs. By applying the BWM, optimal values of weight coefficients are obtained with only *2n-3* comparisons in criteria pairs. A small number of comparisons in pairs remove inconsistencies during the comparison of criteria. That exerts a further influence on obtaining more reliable results (in relation to the AHP), since transitivity relations are less undermined, which further influences a greater consistency of the results. Differently from the AHP, in the BWM, only reference comparisons implying the defining of the advantages of the best criterion over all other criteria and the advantage of such other criteria over the worst criterion are realized. This procedure is much simpler and more accurate, and it eliminates redundant (secondary) comparisons.

The BWM implies that one best criterion and one worst criterion representing reference points for pairwise comparisons with other criteria are defined in every MCDM problem from within a set of evaluation criteria. However, in numerous real-world problems, there are situations in which there is no unique best and/or worst criterion/criteria, but there are two or more best and/or worst criteria. Such situations are impossible to solve by the traditional BWM [11], but a consensus of the decision-maker on the defining of the unique best and/or worst criterion/criteria is required instead. We are going to illustrate this problem with the following example. The decision-maker observes a set of four criteria put in order according to significance C1 = C2 > C3 > C4, for which weight coefficients need to be defined. The traditional BWM implies that the decision-maker should adapt (modify) his/her preferences to the BWM's algorithm, which implies the defining of the unique best criterion, about which the comparison of the three remaining criteria will be made. In that manner, objectivity in the decision-making process is undermined. If, based on a consensus, we were to define that criterion C1 is the best criterion, then, since the difference between C1 and C2 is minimal, we would take the smallest value from the 9-degree scale, namely $a_{12} = 2$. This means that the weight coefficients of the criteria C1 and C2 should be in a 2:1 ratio, which does not represent the decision-maker's real preference. Solving this problem by applying the traditional BWM, the weight coefficients that are in an approximate ratio $w_1 \approx 2 \cdot w_2$ are obtained. In this paper, the authors have developed an improved BWM (BWM-I), which enables us to solve a problem such as this or similar problems. The BWM-I enables us to realistically perceive the decision-maker's preferences irrespective of the number of best/worst criteria in a problem. Besides, in the case of a larger number of best/worst criteria, the number of criteria pairwise comparisons is reduced (decreases) in the BWM-I from *2n-3* to *2n-5*. In that way, the model's algorithm is simplified, and the reliability of results is increased. In the case when there is a unique best/worst criterion, the BWM-I transforms into the traditional BWM with *2n-3* comparisons. This flexibility recommends the application of the BWM-I in complex studies in which criteria and experts' preferences differ depending on experts' preferences.

2. Applications of BWM: A Literature Review

In order to calculate weights of evaluation criteria in an MCDM problem, some MCDM methods can be utilized, such as stepwise weight assessment ratio analysis (SWARA) [12], the analytic hierarchy process (AHP) [13–15], the analytic network process (ANP), the full consistency method (FUCOM) [16,17], criteria importance through intercriteria correlation (CRITIC) [18], Entropy [19], level-based weight assessment (LBWA) [20], and so on. As one of the latest weighting methods, BWM is based on pairwise comparisons to extract criteria weights. By only conducting *2n-3* comparisons, as mentioned before, the BWM overcomes the inconsistency problem encountered during pairwise comparisons.

During the past five years, the BWM has already been utilized in numerous real-world problems, such as energy, supply chain management, transportation, manufacturing, education, investment, performance evaluation, airline industry, communication, healthcare, banking, technology, and tourism. Moreover, there are numerous studies in which only the BWM method is used (singleton integration), as well as the papers employing this method together with other methods (multiple integrations).

Van de Kaa et al. [21] used the BWM to compare three communication factors and [22] applied the method to the evaluation of technical and performance criteria in supply chain management. Similarly, [23–25] studied the BWM to determine sustainable criteria weights in sustainable supply chain management. Both [26,27] applied the BWM to the selection of the mobile phone. In another study, the BWM was employed to evaluate cars [28]. Ghaffari [29] employed the method to evaluate the key success factors in the development of technological innovation. In addition, [30] applied the BWM in the development of a strategy for overcoming barriers to energy efficiency in buildings. This method is used by [31] to assess the factors influencing information-sharing arrangements. Furthermore, [24] employed the BWM to evaluate the research and development (R&D) performance of firms. Yadollahi et al. [32] applied the BWM in order to prioritize the factors of the service experience in the banking industry. Finally, [33] applied the method to the selection of the bioethanol facility location.

As mentioned above, the BWM has been combined with other robust techniques in order to obtain better results. For instance, fuzzy information and interval values were utilized to integrate with the method. To represent uncertainty in the BWM, [34,35] used fuzzy sets in manufacturing and performance evaluation, respectively. While [36] applied triangular fuzzy sets in performance evaluation, similarly, [37,38] employed the method with the variants of the Technique for Order of Preference by Similarity to Ideal Solution (TOPSIS) method in the supply chain management, the energy sector, and investment, respectively. Furthermore, researchers have integrated the Multicriteria Optimization and Compromise Solution (VIKOR) method with the BWM. For instance, [39–41] applied the BWM–VIKOR integration to supplier selection and the green performance of airports, respectively. In another study, [42] proposed a BWM-interval type-2 fuzzy TOPSIS framework for the selection of the most proper green supplier. In order to select a location for wind plants, [43] used the BWM and the MultiAtributive Ideal-Real Comparative Analysis (MAIRCA) integration. Moreover, [44] studied a rough BWM and Simple Aditive Weighting (SAW) approach to wagon selection. In order to assess firms' performance in product development, [45] applied the fuzzy BWM and the fuzzy Analytic Network Process (ANP) methodologies. Another study suggested the fuzzy BWM and the fuzzy COPRAS methodologies for the analysis of the key factors of sustainable architecture [46]. In order to assess and rank foreign companies, [47] proposed the BWM, ELimination Et Choice Translating REality (ELECTRE) III, and Preference Ranking Organization METHod for Enrichment of Evaluations (PROMETHEE) II multi-criteria models. Another study by [48] introduced the interval rough BWM-based Weighted Aggregated Sum Product ASsessment (WASPAS) and Multi-Attributive Border Approximation area Comparison (MABAC) models for the evaluation of third-party logistics providers. An integrated model including the BWM, TOPSIS, Gray Relational Analysis (GRA), and Weighted Sum Approach (WSA) was proposed for turning operations [49]. For web service selection, [50] employed the BWM, VIKOR, SAW, TOPSIS, and COmplex PRoportional ASsessment (COPRAS). Finally, [51] proposed the BWM-based MAIRCA multi-criteria methodology for neighborhood selection.

What is common to all these studies is that they apply the traditional algorithm of the BWM, which implies that one best criterion and one worst criterion are defined through a consensus. In the literature, there are numerous examples of studies implying the defining of criteria weight coefficients irrespective of whether there are one best or worst criterion, or several best or worst criteria [52–55]. In such studies, the algorithm of the traditional BWM would not be able to provide objective results, since it requires the adaptation of experts' preferences to one best/worst criterion. For that reason, the BWM-I that eliminates this problem and enables us to define criteria weights through a realistic perception of experts' preferences has been developed in this paper. The algorithm of the BWM-I is presented in the following section.

3. Improved Best Worst Method (BWM-I)

The BWM-I provides decision-makers with the possibility of choosing as many best/worst criteria as there are in the real decision-making problem. The determination of evaluation criteria weight coefficients by the application of the BWM-I implies the following steps:

Step 1. Defining a set of evaluation criteria $C = \{c_1, c_2, \ldots c_n\}$, where n represents the total number of the criteria.

Step 2. Determining the best and the worst criteria, i.e., as many best and worst criteria as there are in the decision-making model. Simultaneously, m_b and m_w denote the number of the best and the worst criteria in the model, respectively.

Step 3. Determining the advantages of the best criterion/criteria from within the set C over the other criteria. A 9-degree numeric scale is used to determine the advantage(s). If the criteria C_1 and C_2 are marked as the best criterion, then an improved best-to-others vector (M-BO) is obtained by the application of expression (1), namely:

$$A_B = (m_b a_{BB}, a_{B(m_b+1)}, a_{B(m_b+2)}, \ldots, a_{Bn}) \qquad (1)$$

where a_{Bn} represents the advantage of the best criterion B over the criterion j, and m_b represents the number of the best criteria in the model, whereas $a_{BB} = 1$. It is clear that for $m_b = 1$, expression (1) transforms into a classical best-to-others (BO) vector, as in the traditional BWM.

Step 4. Determining the advantages of all the criteria from within the set C over the worst criterion/criteria. In order to determine the advantage(s), as in Step 3, a 9-degree numeric scale is used. If we mark the criterion C_{n-1} and the criterion C_n, i.e., $m_w = 2$, as the worst criterion, then a modified others-to-worst vector (M-OW) is obtained by the application of expression (2), as follows:

$$A_W = (a_{1W}, a_{2W}, \ldots, a_{(n-3)W}, a_{(n-2)W}, m_w a_{nW}) \qquad (2)$$

where a_{jW} represents the advantage of the criterion j over the worst criterion W, m_w represents the number of the worst criteria in the model, whereas $a_{WW} = 1$. For $m_w = 1$, expression (2) transforms into a classical OW vector, as in the traditional BWM.

Step 5. Calculating the optimal values of the weight coefficients of the criteria from within the set C, $(w_1^*, w_2^*, \ldots, w_n^*)$. Since the BWM algorithm defining weight coefficients in the case when there is one or more than one best and/or worst criterion/criteria (i.e., $m_b \geq 1$ and $m_w \geq 1$) is considered here, the postulates for solving the optimization model must be defined.

The optimal values of weight coefficients are obtained once the condition stipulating that for each pair w_B/w_j and w_j/w_W, it is applicable that $w_B/w_j = a_{Bj}$ and $w_j/w_W = a_{jW}$ is met. Since we are considering the case where $m_b \geq 1$ and/or $m_w \geq 1$, it is necessary that the mentioned conditions should be revised, so there is the condition that $w_B/w_j = m_b a_{Bj}$ and $w_j/w_W = m_w a_{jW}$, where the weight coefficients w_B and w_W represent the weights of the unique best and the unique worst criteria. The unique best and worst criteria (C_B and C_W) represent all the criteria that are marked as the best and the worst criteria in the set $C = \{c_1, c_2, \ldots c_n\}$. In addition, since $w_B/w_W = m_b a_{BW}/m_w$, we obtain $\frac{w_B}{w_W} \frac{m_W}{m_b} = a_{BW}$. It arises from the aforementioned factors that the weight coefficient of the unique best criterion (w_B) represents the sum of all the weight coefficients of the criteria that are marked as the best criteria in the set $C = \{c_1, c_2, \ldots c_n\}$, i.e.,

$$w_B = \sum_{l=1}^{b} w_l \tag{3}$$

where w_l represents the weight coefficients of all the criteria in the set $C = \{c_1, c_2, \ldots c_n\}$ that are marked as the best criteria, whereas b represents the total number of the best criteria from the set C.

The unique worst criterion is defined similarly. The weight coefficient of the unique worst criterion (w_W) represents the sum of all weight coefficients of the criteria that are marked as the worst criteria in the set $C = \{c_1, c_2, \ldots c_n\}$, i.e.,

$$w_W = \sum_{k=1}^{v} w_k \tag{4}$$

where w_k represents the weight coefficients of all the criteria that are marked as the worst criteria in the set $C = \{c_1, c_2, \ldots c_n\}$, and v represents the total number of the worst criteria from within the set C. Since the optimal values of weight coefficients should meet the condition stipulating that the maximum absolute values of the differences should be $\left|\frac{w_B}{m_b \cdot w_j} - a_{Bj}\right|$ and $\left|\frac{w_j}{m_w \cdot w_W} - a_{jW}\right|$, all such absolute values must be minimized for each j, i.e.,

$$\min\max_j \left\{ \left|\frac{w_B}{m_b \cdot w_j} - a_{Bj}\right|, \left|\frac{w_j}{m_w \cdot w_W} - a_{jW}\right| \right\}$$
s.t.
$$w_B + w_W + \sum_{j=1}^{n-(m_b+m_w)} w_j = 1 \tag{5}$$
$$w_B, w_W, w_j \geq 0 \, \forall j$$

The model presented in (5) is equivalent to the following model.

$$\min \xi$$
s.t.
$$\left|\frac{w_B}{m_b \cdot w_j} - a_{Bj}\right| \leq \xi, \forall w_j \neq w_W$$
$$\left|\frac{w_j}{m_w \cdot w_W} - a_{jW}\right| \leq \xi,\, \forall w_j \neq w_B \tag{6}$$
$$\left|\frac{w_B}{w_W} \frac{m_W}{m_b} - a_{BW}\right| \leq \xi,$$
$$w_B + w_W + \sum_{j=1}^{n-(m_b+m_w)} w_j = 1$$
$$w_B, w_W, w_j \geq 0 \, \forall j$$

Should $m_b > 1$ and/or $m_w > 1$, then the total number of the criteria in the model is reduced (decreases) by the introduction of the unique best and the unique worst criteria. Then, we obtain a smaller number of comparisons, i.e., the total number of comparisons in the model is reduced from $2n - 3$ (in the traditional BWM) to $2n - 5$ (in the BWM-I). It is clear that, should $m_b = m_w = 1$, the models (5) and (6) transform into the classical optimization BWM model [11].

Example 1. *If a set of eight criteria $C_1, C_2, \ldots, C_8$ is observed, in which there are two best and two worst criteria; if we know that the criteria $C_1 = C_2$ are marked as the best, then the unique best criterion (C_B) that represents both criteria in model (6) is introduced. If the criteria $C_7 = C_8$ are marked as the worst, then the unique worst criterion (C_W) represents the criteria C_7 and C_8 and in model (6). Then, the total number of the criteria in the model is reduced to six, since $C_1 = C_2 = C_B$ and $C_7 = C_8 = C_W$. Thus, the total number of comparisons in pairs of criteria is reduced from 15 to 13.*

Should $m_b > 1$ and/or $m_w > 1$, then, based on conditions (3) and (4), it follows that by solving model (6), the values of the weight coefficients of the best criterion and the worst criterion increased by the number of the best and the worst criteria are obtained. Therefore, after solving model (6), the obtained values of the weights w_B and w_W need to be divided by m_b and m_w in order to obtain the final values of the weight coefficients of the best and the worst criteria. For example, if $m_b = m_w = 2$, the final values of the best and the worst (w_B^* and w_W^*) criteria obtained are $w_{B1}^* = w_{B2}^* = w_B/m_b = w_B/2$ and $w_{W1}^* = w_{W2}^* = w_W/m_w = w_W/2$. The values of the weights of the remaining criteria remain unchanged, and they are taken from the solution to model (6).

In order to more easily understand the algorithm of the BWM-I, the following part is dedicated to solving a simple example including five criteria taken from a study by [28]; then, a complex model implying the defining of the weight coefficients of a total of the 28 criteria grouped into six clusters is considered in the case study (Section 3).

Example 2. *While buying a car, the buyer applies five criteria for the evaluation of the alternative (the car): Quality (C1), Price (C2), Comfort (C3), Safety (C4), and Style (C5). The buyer has the evaluated criteria per the algorithm of the traditional BWM, as shown in Table 1.*

Table 1. The best-to-others and others-to-worst pairwise comparison vectors.

Best-to-Others Vector		Others-to-Worst Vector	
Best: $C2$ and $C4$	Evaluation	Worst: $C5$	Evaluation
C1	2	C1	4
C2	1	C2	9
C3	4	C3	2
C4	1	C4	9
C5	9	C5	1

Based on the data accounted for in Table 1, it is possible to conclude that the buyer considers the criteria Price (C2) and Safety (C4) as the most significant, whereas the criterion Style (C5) is rated as the least significant. The problem that appears here cannot be solved through the application of the traditional BWM, which requires the defining of the unique best and worst criteria. If we were to insist on the defining of the unique best criterion (as is required by the traditional BWM), then we would have to revise the BO vector to define a single best criterion. However, by doing so, we would exert an influence on the buyer's preferences, i.e., the buyer would not express his real preferences. Those revised preferences would further exert an influence on a non-objective choice of alternatives, which should be avoided. If the expert (in this case, the buyer) requires a high degree of rationality during the evaluation of the criteria, the multi-criteria decision-making methods also need to be used as support to such rational decision-making in order to meet that very same condition. Therefore, since it was impossible to apply the traditional BWM, the BWM-I was applied.

Based on the data from Table 1, we conclude that the number of the best criteria is $m_b = 2$, whereas the number of the worst criteria is $m_w = 1$. Based on that and expression (4), it is possible to define the model for the calculation of the optimal values of the weight coefficients of the BWM-I as follows:

$$\min \xi$$
s.t.
$$\left|\frac{w_B}{2 \cdot w_1} - 2\right| \leq \xi, \left|\frac{w_B}{2 \cdot w_3} - 4\right| \leq \xi, \left|\frac{w_B}{2 \cdot w_W} - 9\right| \leq \xi,$$
$$\left|\frac{w_1}{w_W} - 4\right| \leq \xi, \left|\frac{w_3}{w_W} - 2\right| \leq \xi, \qquad (7)$$
$$w_B + w_w + w_1 + w_3 = 1$$
$$w_B, w_W, w_1, w_3 \geq 0$$

By solving the presented model, the values of the weights $w_B = 0.7088$, $w_W = 0.0400$, $w_1^* = 0.1656$, and $w_3^* = 0.0856$, as well as $\xi = 0.140$, are obtained. Based on condition (3), we obtain $w_{B1}^* = w_2^* = 0.7088/2 = 0.3544$, i.e., $w_{B2}^* = w_4^* = 0.7088/2 = 0.3544$. Since $m_b = 1$, $w_W = w_5^* = 0.0400$ is obtained. So, the optimal values of the weight coefficients $w_j = (0.1656, 0.3544, 0.0856, 0.3544, 0.0400)^T$ are obtained characterized by a high consistency ratio:

$$CR = \frac{\xi}{CI} = \frac{0.140}{5.23} = 0.026.$$

Had the model of the traditional BWM [27] been applied to the presented example, optimization model (8) would have been obtained.

$$\min \xi$$
s.t.
$$\left|\frac{w_2}{w_1} - 2\right| \leq \xi, \left|\frac{w_2}{w_3} - 4\right| \leq \xi, \left|\frac{w_2}{w_4} - 1\right| \leq \xi, \left|\frac{w_2}{w_5} - 9\right| \leq \xi,$$
$$\left|\frac{w_1}{w_5} - 4\right| \leq \xi, \left|\frac{w_3}{w_5} - 2\right| \leq \xi, \left|\frac{w_4}{w_5} - 9\right| \leq \xi, \qquad (8)$$
$$w_1 + w_2 + w_3 + w_4 + w_5 = 1$$
$$w_1, w_2, w_3, w_4, w_5 \geq 0$$

By solving model (8), the following vectors of the weight coefficients $w_j = (0.1638, 0.3505, 0.0847, 0.3616, 0.0396)^T$ and $\xi = 0.1401$ are obtained. Based on the results obtained, we perceive that even though there is the defined condition that both best criteria (C2 and C4) are of the same significance, the values of the weight coefficients are different ($w_2 \neq w_4$), i.e., $w_2 = 0.3505$ and $w_4 = 0.3616$. The different values of the weight coefficients of the criteria C2 and C4 are a consequence of undermining the condition of the transitivity of relations between criteria. This is confirmed by the value of the consistency ratio (CR), which is $CR = 0.026$, just as in model (7).

The shown example has demonstrated that the traditional BWM model can be applied to the determination of the weights of a larger number of the best/worst criteria, but only in the case when the consistency ratio is ideal, i.e., when $CR = 0.00$. However, we may realistically expect that more than one best/worst criterion and the value $CR > 0$ will appear in solving real-world problems, especially those with a greater number of criteria. In such cases, the BWM-I is inevitably applied. Given the fact that the BWM-I is capable of transforming itself into the traditional BWM (in the case when $m_b = m_w = 1$), its application is also logical for a future objective perception of and solving real-world multi-criteria problems.

4. Case Study: The Application of BWM-I

In this chapter, the application of the BWM-I in solving a renewable energy source evaluation problem implying the existence of a larger number of the best/worst criteria within the framework of the dimensions/criteria is presented. The most common criteria for a renewable energy source evaluation involve technical, environmental, social, risk, political, and economic aspects. Thus, we introduce a six-dimensional model in order to define the weights of the drivers for renewable energy sources, as shown in Figure 1, in which several criteria are considered for each dimension. The six dimensions are technical (C1), economic (C2), social (C3), environmental (C4), risk (C5), and political (C6); each dimension comprises three to six criteria. Moreover, the criteria for the evaluation of renewable energy sources were achieved by reviewing the existing literature [56–64]. Consequently, the evaluation comprised of six dimensions and 28 criteria. The criteria and their descriptions are listed in Table 2.

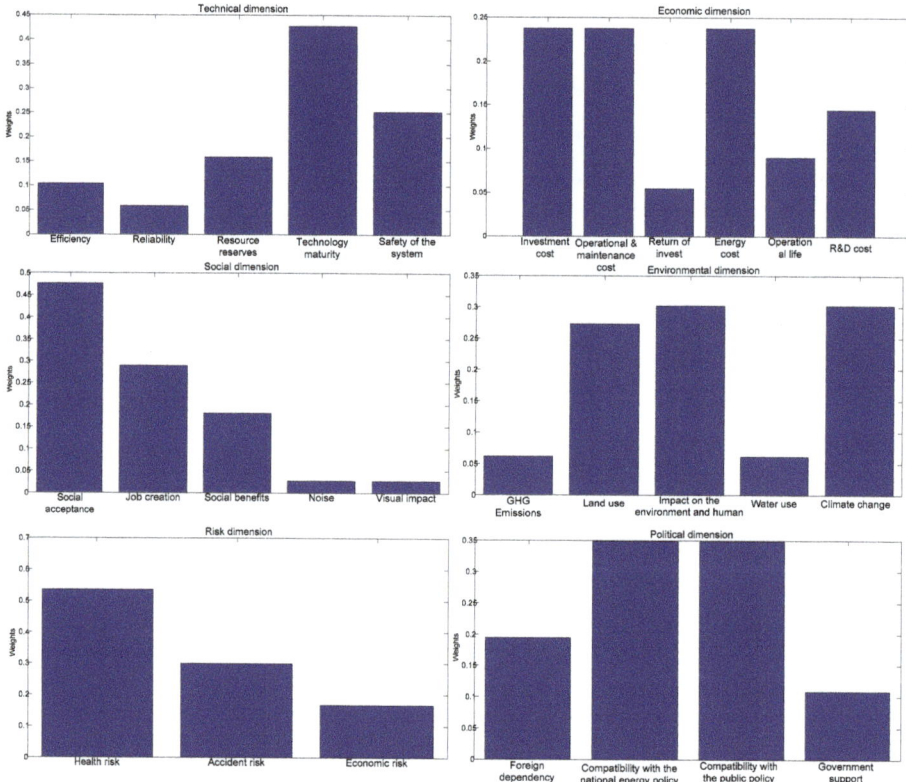

Figure 1. The local weights of the criteria according to the considered dimensions.

Table 2. The criteria and sub-criteria used in this paper.

Main Criteria	Sub-Criteria	Code	Definition	References
Technical (C1)	Efficiency	C11	How technology is widespread at the regional, national, and international levels.	[57–59]
	Reliability	C12	An energy system's ability to perform the required functions	[56,58,60]
	Resource reserves	C13	The availability of the energy source to generate energy	[58]
	Technology maturity	C14	The penetration of a specific technology in the energy mix at the regional, national, and international levels.	[58,60]
	Safety of the system	C15	The security of the workers and the local community	[56]

Table 2. Cont.

Main Criteria	Sub-Criteria	Code	Definition	References
Economic (C2)	Investment cost	C21	All costs of products and services, except for the costs of labor or the cost of equipment maintenance	[56,58–60]
	Operation and maintenance cost	C22	Operating the energy system adequately, as well as the costs related to the maintenance of the energy system	[56,58]
	Return of investment	C23	The time required to recover the investment	[56,58]
	Energy cost	C24	The cost of the energy-generating system	[60,63]
	Operational life	C25	The period during which the power plant can operate before being decommissioned	[56]
	R&D cost	C26	The expenses incurred for the R&D of technological innovations	[65]
Social (C3)	Social acceptance	C31	The opinions of residents, local authorities, and other stakeholders on an energy project	[56–58]
	Job creation	C32	Jobs created per unit of the energy produced	[57,58,61]
	Social benefits	C33	The contribution of an energy system to the improvement and advancement of local society	[56,58]
	Noise	C34	The noise generated during the lifecycle under consideration	[62]
	Visual impact	C35	The aesthetics of the installations of the energy system	[62]
Environmental (C4)	Greenhouse Gas (GHG) Emissions	C41	Lifecycle GHG emissions (in the equivalent emission of CO_2) from technology	[58,61,63]
	Land use	C42	The area used per unit of the energy produced	[58–61]
	Impact on the environment and humans	C43	The detriment level of the energy facility to humans and nature	[58–60,64]
	Water use	C44	Water consumed per unit of the energy produced	[60,61]
	Climate change	C45	The global warming potential	[57]
Risk (C5)	Health risk	C51	Emissions harmful to human health	[66]
	Accident risk	C52	Accidents of any type during the lifecycle considered	[57,59,62,66]
	Economic risk	C53	The risk financial stakeholders should bear for business in new plants	[60]
Political (C6)	Foreign dependency	C61	The dependency of countries on international legislations	[57,58]
	Compatibility with the national energy policy	C62	The national energy policy related to renewable energy sources	[58]
	Compatibility with the public policy	C63	Voluntary agreements and general codes of conduct in line with national priorities	[64]
	Government support	C64	Approving and adapting to renewable energy sources.	[64]

After defining the set of the evaluation criteria, the following steps of the BWM-I (Steps 3 and 4) imply the formation of the M-BO and M-OW vectors of the dimensions/sub-criteria, as shown in Table 3.

Table 3. The best-to-others (M-BO) and modified others-to-worst (M-OW) vectors of the dimensions/sub-criteria.

Dimensions			
Best: $C4$	Preference	Worst: $C5$ and $C6$	Preference
$C1$	3	$C1$	3
$C2$	2	$C2$	4
$C3$	4	$C3$	2
$C4$	1	$C4$	5
$C5$	5	$C5$	1
$C6$	5	$C6$	1
Technical sub-criteria			
Best: $C14$	Preference	Worst: $C12$	Preference
$C11$	4	$C11$	2
$C12$	7	$C12$	1
$C13$	3	$C13$	3
$C14$	1	$C14$	7
$C15$	2	$C15$	4
Economic sub-criteria			
Best: $C21$, $C22$ and $C24$	Preference	Worst: $C23$	Preference
$C21$	1	$C21$	4
$C22$	1	$C22$	4
$C23$	4	$C23$	1
$C24$	1	$C24$	4
$C25$	3	$C25$	2
$C26$	2	$C26$	3
Social sub-criteria			
Best: $C31$	Preference	Worst: $C34$ and $C35$	Preference
$C31$	1	$C31$	4
$C32$	2	$C32$	3
$C33$	3	$C33$	2
$C34$	4	$C34$	1
$C35$	4	$C35$	1
Environmental sub-criteria			
Best: $C43$ and $C45$	Preference	Worst: $C41$ and $C44$	Preference
$C41$	4	$C41$	1
$C42$	2	$C42$	2
$C43$	1	$C43$	4
$C44$	4	$C44$	1
$C45$	1	$C45$	4
Risk sub-criteria			
Best: $C51$	Preference	Worst: $C53$	Preference
$C51$	1	$C51$	3
$C52$	2	$C52$	2
$C53$	3	$C53$	1
Political sub-criteria			
Best: $C62$ and $C63$	Preference	Worst: $C64$	Preference
$C61$	2	$C61$	2
$C62$	1	$C62$	3
$C63$	1	$C63$	3
$C64$	3	$C64$	1

Table 3 enables us to note that in some M-BO and M-OW vectors, there are several best and worst criteria. So, based on the M-BO and M-OW dimensions, we notice the existence of one best criterion (Environmental—C4), whereas there are two worst criteria (Risk—C5 and Political—C6). In the Economic Sub-Criteria group, there are three best criteria (Investment cost—C21, Operation and maintenance cost—C22, and Energy cost—C24) and one worst criterion (Return of investment—C23). In the Social Sub-Criteria group, there is one best criterion (Social acceptance—C31) and two worst criteria (Noise—C34 and Visual impact—C35). The Environmental Sub-Criteria group is characteristic, since it contains two best criteria (Impact on the environment and humans—C43 and Climate change—C45) and two worst criteria (GHG Emissions—C41 and Water use—C44). In the Political Sub-Criteria group, there are two best criteria (Compatibility with the national energy policy—C62 and Compatibility with the public policy—C63) and one worst criterion (Government support—C64). In the remaining sub-criteria groups (the Technical Sub-Criteria and the Risk Sub-Criteria), there are the unique best and worst criteria, for which reason the traditional postulate of the BWM is used to define the weight coefficients of these sub-criteria groups.

Based on the M-BO and M-OW vectors (Table 3), the optimization models for the calculation of the weight coefficients of the dimensions/sub-criteria were defined. A total of seven BWM-I models were defined, some of which are shown in the next part.

Model 1 (Dimensions)

min ξ

s.t.

$$\begin{cases} \left|\frac{w_4}{w_1} - 3\right| \le \xi; \left|\frac{w_4}{w_2} - 2\right| \le \xi; \left|\frac{w_4}{w_3} - 4\right| \le \xi; \left|\frac{w_4}{2\cdot w_w} - 5\right| \le \xi; \\ \left|\frac{w_1}{2\cdot w_w} - 3\right| \le \xi; \left|\frac{w_2}{2\cdot w_w} - 4\right| \le \xi; \left|\frac{w_3}{2\cdot w_w} - 2\right| \le \xi; \\ w_1 + w_2 + w_3 + w_4 + w_w = 1 \\ w_j \ge 0, \forall j = 1, 2, \ldots, 5 \end{cases}$$

Model 2 (Technical sub – criteria)

min ξ

s.t.

$$\begin{cases} \left|\frac{w_{14}}{w_{11}} - 4\right| \le \xi; \left|\frac{w_{14}}{w_{12}} - 7\right| \le \xi; \left|\frac{w_{14}}{w_{13}} - 3\right| \le \xi; \left|\frac{w_{14}}{w_{15}} - 2\right| \le \xi; \\ \left|\frac{w_{11}}{w_{12}} - 2\right| \le \xi; \left|\frac{w_{13}}{w_{12}} - 3\right| \le \xi; \left|\frac{w_{14}}{w_{12}} - 7\right| \le \xi; \left|\frac{w_{15}}{w_{12}} - 2\right| \le \xi; \\ \sum_{j=1}^{3} w_j = 1 \\ w_j \ge 0, \forall j = 1, 2, 3 \end{cases}$$

...

Model 6 (Risk sub – criteria)

min ξ

s.t.

$$\begin{cases} \left|\frac{w_{51}}{w_{52}} - 2\right| \le \xi; \left|\frac{w_{51}}{w_{53}} - 3\right| \le \xi; \left|\frac{w_{51}}{w_{53}} - 3\right| \le \xi; \left|\frac{w_{52}}{w_{53}} - 2\right| \le \xi; \\ \sum_{j=1}^{3} w_j = 1; w_j \ge 0, \forall j = 1, 2, 3 \end{cases}$$

Model 7 (Political sub – criteria)

min ξ

s.t.

$$\begin{cases} \left|\frac{w_B}{2\cdot w_{61}} - 2\right| \le \xi; \left|\frac{w_B}{2\cdot w_{64}} - 3\right| \le \xi; \left|\frac{w_{61}}{w_{64}} - 2\right| \le \xi; \\ w_{61} + w_B + w_{64} = 1; w_j \ge 0, \forall j = 1, 2, 3 \end{cases}$$

By solving the presented models, the optimal values of the weight coefficients of the dimensions/sub-criteria are obtained, as shown in Table 4.

Table 4. The optimal values of the weight coefficients of the dimensions/sub-criteria.

Dimensions/Sub-Criteria	Code	Local Weights	Global Weights	Rank
Technical	C1	0.1674	-	3
Efficiency	C11	0.1037	0.0174	17
Reliability	C12	0.0586	0.0098	19
Resource reserves	C13	0.1584	0.0265	12
Technology maturity	C14	0.4278	0.0716	4
Safety of the system	C15	0.2514	0.0421	9
Economic	C2	0.2823	-	2
Investment cost	C21	0.2372	0.0670	5
Operation and maintenance cost	C22	0.2372	0.0670	5
Return of investment	C23	0.0545	0.0154	18
Energy cost	C24	0.2372	0.0670	5
Operational life	C25	0.0897	0.0253	13
R&D cost	C26	0.1441	0.0407	10

Table 4. Cont.

Dimensions/Sub-Criteria	Code	Local Weights	Global Weights	Rank
Social	C3	0.1178	-	4
Social acceptance	C31	0.4761	0.0561	8
Job creation	C32	0.2893	0.0341	11
Social benefits	C33	0.1799	0.0212	16
Noise	C34	0.0273	0.0032	25
Visual impact	C35	0.0273	0.0032	25
Environmental	C4	0.3972	-	1
GHG Emissions	C41	0.0617	0.0245	14
Land use	C42	0.2729	0.1084	3
Impact on the environment and humans	C43	0.3019	0.1199	1
Water use	C44	0.0617	0.0245	14
Climate change	C45	0.3019	0.1199	1
Risk	C5	0.0176	-	5
Health risk	C51	0.5348	0.0094	20
Accident risk	C52	0.2985	0.0053	23
Economic risk	C53	0.1667	0.0029	27
Political	C6	0.0176	-	5
Foreign dependency	C61	0.1945	0.0034	24
Compatibility with the national energy policy	C62	0.3484	0.0061	21
Compatibility with the public policy	C63	0.3484	0.0061	21
Government support	C64	0.1086	0.0019	28

In Table 4, the global and local values of the weight coefficients of the criteria are presented. The global weights of the criteria were obtained by multiplying the weight coefficient of the dimension with the weight coefficients of the sub-criterion. By solving model (6), the values of ξ^*, which are $\xi^*_{C1-C6} = 0.6277$, $\xi^*_{C11-C15} = 0.2984$, $\xi^*_{C21-C26} = 0.3542$, $\xi^*_{C31-C35} = 0.3542$, $\xi^*_{C41-C45} = 0.8939$, $\xi^*_{C51-C53} = 0.2087$, and $\xi^*_{C61-C64} = 0.2087$ were obtained. The values of ξ^* are used to determine the consistency ratio, as shown in Table 5.

Table 5. The consistency index and the consistency ratio of our modified Best Worst Method (BWM-I).

Criterion Level	C1–C6	C11–C15	C21–C26	C31–C35	C41–C45	C51–C53	C61–C64
a_{BW}	5	7	4	4	4	3	3
CI ($\max\xi$)	2.30	3.73	1.63	1.63	1.63	1.00	1.00
CR	0.27	0.08	0.22	0.22	0.55	0.21	0.21

The analysis of the results of the BWM-I from Table 5 allows us to conclude that the values of the consistency ratio are satisfactory [27].

According to the findings shown in Table 4, the environmental dimension is determined to be the most crucial dimension, with the significance of 0.3972, only to be followed by the economic and technical dimensions, with the comparative weights of 0.2823 and 0.1674, respectively. According to Figure 1, in the pairwise comparison of the evaluation criteria, both "Impact on the environment and humans" and "Climate change" ranked as the priority factor from the environmental aspect, only to be followed by "Land use". Furthermore, the three criteria (Investment cost, Operation and maintenance cost, and Energy cost) ranked the first in the ranking related to the economic dimension. "Technology maturity" and "social acceptance" were the most important criteria in terms of technological and social dimensions, respectively. Overall, according to the global weights, the most important criteria were "Climate change" (0.1199), "Impact on the environment and humans" (0.1199), "Land use" (0.1084), and "Technology maturity" (0.0716), indicating that the Climate change, Impact on the environment and humans, Land use, and Technology maturity criteria represent the four most crucial evaluation criteria for the determination of a suitable renewable energy source.

In order to show the sensitivity analysis of the BWM-I model, in the next section, we simulated the changes in the input parameters of the BO and OW vectors. In each group of criteria, another best or worst criterion was added, while the values of the remaining criteria in BO and OW vectors remained unchanged.

In the Dimensions group, two best criteria were selected (C4 and C2), while the remaining values of the criteria remained unchanged. In the Technical Sub-Criteria group, two criteria—C12 and C11—were selected as the worst criteria. In the Economic Sub-Criteria group, in addition to the three best criteria, the two worst criteria were selected (C23 and C25). In the Social Sub-Criteria group, two best criteria, C31 and C32, were added to the input BO and OW vectors. In the Risk Sub-Criteria group, in addition to the best criterion C51 and criterion C52, it was selected as the best criterion. In the Political Sub-Criteria group, in addition to C64, criterion C61 was also chosen as the worst criterion. After the implementation of these changes, the results shown in Figure 2 were obtained.

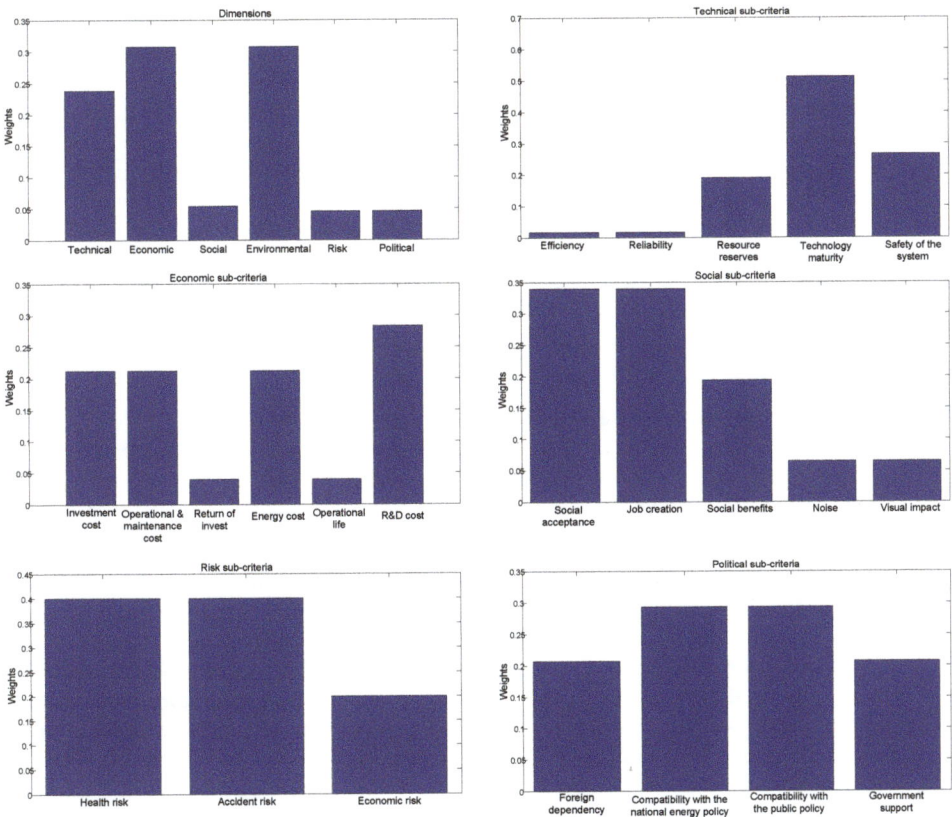

Figure 2. Results of modified M-BO and M-OW vectors of the dimensions/sub-criteria.

By analyzing the results from Figure 2, we notice that the model is sensitive to changes in the number of best and worst criteria in the input data. Despite the changes in the input data, the degree of consistency of the considered models remained within acceptable limits. The authors believe that the presented analysis shows the stability and robustness of the modified BWM methodology.

5. Managerial Implications

Integrating some methods into decision-making methodologies will make a significant contribution to the particular body of knowledge. Furthermore, it is valuable that the existing methods are made more efficient by completing their deficiencies. In decision theory, MCDM methods are utilized to solve many real-world problems. Improvement and development of the functionless side of an existing approach is always appreciated to continuously improve this branch of operations research, because businesses, politicians, researchers, and industries need such arrangements to make more reliable decisions.

The aim of this paper is pertinent to the fact that the BWM method, which is one of the new approaches in the field of MCDM, is ineffective if there is more than one best/worst criterion. Thus, this work suggests a novel strategy to solve an MCDM problem via some specific modifications to the main structure of the traditional BWM method. As a result, decision-makers will be able to easily cope with the problem of more than one best/worst criteria often encountered in real-world problems. Furthermore, by making fewer pairwise comparisons (only $2n-5$), they will not only have to deal with the problem of inconsistency but also save time. Therefore, it is as well believed that the present article will give a different point of view for future works.

The presented methodology eliminates deviations in expert preferences that occur as a consequence of adapting to the traditional BWM algorithm. The previous analysis showed apparent advantages, so it is expected that the proposed methodology will be accepted by the management when solving real-world problems. Most decision-makers readily accept tools that are logical and easy to understand. The BWM-I methodology can be included in the category of easy-to-understand decision-making tools. In particular, it is expected to be accepted and used by decision-makers who know the algorithm of the traditional BWM, as well as its advantages and disadvantages. In addition, the use of the BWM-I methodology as part of the set of tools that make up the decision support system will make it more acceptable to management structures. This tool will be acceptable for managers who require a more realistic view of the mutual relations between the criteria, as well as a realistic and rational view of expert preferences.

A few insights are extracted to increase the applicability of the proposed BWM-I methodology in real cases. Thereby, the implications are as follows:

- By preferring the BWM-I model, authorities can make more accurate decisions.
- Since the weight of each criterion is found according to the opinions of decision-makers, firms can improve their evaluation process through the BWM-I approach.
- Firms can create a better competitive advantage over their business competitors by determining the best alternatives with the BWM-I model.

Knowing that the decision-making process is accompanied by greater or lesser uncertainties caused by a dynamic environment, such a system eliminates further adjustment and deviation of expert preferences. As a result of this feature, the demonstrated methodology can help companies establish a rational, systematic approach to evaluating the internal and external factors that affect their business. The flexibility of the methodology in terms of reducing the number of pairwise comparisons is also valuable. It is expected that the flexibility of the BWM-I methodology will enable its application in complex studies in which criteria and expert preferences differ and in which no consensus is required in expert preferences.

6. Conclusions

The BWM method represents a very powerful tool for multi-criteria decision-making and defining criteria weight coefficients. Generally viewed, while solving real-world problems, there are specific multi-criteria problems in which there are several criteria with the same influence on decision-making. The traditional postulate of the BWM implies that while defining priority vectors (BO and OW), one best criterion and one worst criterion should be chosen from within a set of the observed criteria.

Then, the criteria are compared in pairs by defining the best-to-others (BO) and others-to-worst (OW) vectors. While defining the BO and OW vectors, the decision-maker may assign the same criteria preferences while comparing the BO and OW, which means that there may be several criteria with the same significance. However, the traditional BWM does not permit the defining of several best/worst criteria that will have the same significance, although it is frequently the case in real-world problems. As a result of that, by applying the traditional BWM, decision-makers are required to define one best/worst criterion should they believe that there are two or more best/worst criteria. In that way, the decision-maker's preferences are distorted to a certain extent, and no objective results are obtained. Should the small flexibility of the 9-degree scale be added to that as well, then the obtained values of criteria weights may significantly deviate from the preferences expressed by the decision-maker.

In this paper, the improvement of the traditional BWM is presented. The improved BWM (BWM-I) eliminates the shortcomings of the traditional BWM. It offers a possibility for decision-makers to express their preferences even in the cases when there is more than one best and worst criterion. The BWM-I was successfully tested on two examples in this paper. In the first example in Section 3, a case in which there are two best criteria is presented. The algorithm of the traditional BWM and the BWM-I was also applied to the same example. It was shown that the BWM-I has greater flexibility in expressing experts' preferences in relation to the traditional BWM. In the second example (Section 4), the BWM-I was applied to the defining of the weight coefficients of the criteria in the field of renewable energy and their ranking. In the presented example, all of the 28 criteria grouped into the six dimensions were subjected to evaluation. Through a combination of the seven models of the BWM-I, the advantages of the developed model and the possibilities of the objective processing of experts' preferences are demonstrated.

In comparison with the traditional BWM, the proposed BWM-I has several advantages according to the following:

(1) Due to non-determinedness and imprecision in data, it is realistic that more than one best and/or worst criterion/criteria with the same significance may appear in experts' preferences. The BWM-I enables a realistic expression of experts' preferences irrespective of the number of the best/worst criteria in a set of evaluation criteria.

(2) In case more than one best and worst criterion appear ($m_b > 1$ and $m_w > 1$) in the decision-making process, the application of the BWM-I reduces the number of comparisons from $2n-3$ (in the traditional BWM) to $2n-5$ (in the BWM-I). In that manner, the possibility of making a mistake while conducting a pairwise comparison of the criteria is also reduced, which further exerts an influence on the greater reliability of results.

(3) The flexibility of the BWM-I is expressed in two ways: (1) the possibilities of the realistic processing of experts' preferences irrespective of the number of the criteria with the same significance (even in the case of the best/worst criteria), and (2) in the case of $m_b = m_w = 1$, the BWM-I transforms into the traditional BWM. This flexibility opens the possibility of applying the BWM-I in complex studies, in which criteria and experts' preferences differ within the framework of the cluster(s)/group of criteria.

Future Research

The proposed BWM-I represents a tool that is capable of being successfully integrated with other MCDM techniques. The development of the hybrid multi-criteria models for group decision-making that would be based on the integration of the BWM-I into other MCDM tools represents one of the future directions of its application. The second logical step for the future improvement of the BWM-I is its application in an uncertain environment, such as fuzzy, rough, grey, neutrosophic, and so on [67,68]. In the last few years, numerous linguistic approaches, such as the expansions of linguistic variables in a neutrosophic environment and the unbalanced linguistic approach, have been developed. The mentioned approaches have attracted considerable attention to the decision-making field through the possibility of applying linguistic variables in the decision-making process. Connecting these linguistic approaches with the BWM-I and research into the possibility of the linguistic modeling of preferences are interesting and promising topics in future research.

Author Contributions: Conceptualization, methodology, validation, D.P. and F.E.; writing—original draft preparation, review and editing, D.P., F.E., G.C. and M.A.A. All authors have read and agreed to the published version of the manuscript.

Funding: This research received no external funding.

Conflicts of Interest: The authors declare no conflict of interest.

References

1. Stankovic, M.; Gladovic, P.; Popovic, V. Determining the importance of the criteria of traffic accessibility using fuzzy AHP and rough AHP method. *Decis. Mak. Appl. Manag. Eng.* **2019**, *2*, 86–104. [CrossRef]
2. Petrovic, G.; Mihajlovic, J.; Cojbasic, Z.; Madic, M.; Marinkovic, D. Comparison of three fuzzy MCDM methods for solving the supplier selection problem. *Facta Univ. Ser. Mech. Eng.* **2019**, *17*, 455–469. [CrossRef]
3. Hassanpour, M. Evaluation of Iranian Wood and Cellulose Industries. *Decis. Mak. Appl. Manag. Eng.* **2019**, *2*, 13–34. [CrossRef]
4. Diyaley, S.; Chakraborty, S. Optimization of multi-pass face milling parameters using metaheuristic algorithms. *Facta Univ. Ser. Mech. Eng.* **2019**, *17*, 365–383. [CrossRef]
5. Tzeng, G.-H.; Chen, T.-Y.; Wang, J.C. A weight-assessing method with habitual domains. *Eur. J. Oper. Res.* **1998**, *110*, 342–367. [CrossRef]
6. Shannon, C.E.; Weaver, W. *The Mathematical Theory of Communication*; The University of Illinois Press: Urbana, IL, USA, 1947.
7. Diakoulaki, D.; Mavrotas, G.; Papayannakis, L. Determining objective weights in multiple criteria problems: The CRITIC method. *Comput. Oper. Res.* **1995**, *22*, 763–770. [CrossRef]
8. Srdjevic, B.; Medeiros, Y.D.P.; Faria, A.S.; Schaer, M. Objektivno vrednovanje kriterijuma performanse sistema akumulacija. *Vodoprivreda* **2003**, *35*, 163–176. (In Serbian)
9. Thurstone, L.L. A law of comparative judgment. *Psychol. Rev.* **1927**, *34*, 273. [CrossRef]
10. Saaty, T.L. *Analytic Hierarchy Process*; McGraw-Hill: New York, NY, USA, 1980.
11. Rezaei, J. Best-worst multi-criteria decision-making method. *Omega* **2015**, *53*, 49–57. [CrossRef]
12. Hashemkhani Zolfani, S.; Yazdani, M.; Zavadskas, E.K. An extended stepwise weight assessment ratio analysis (SWARA) method for improving criteria prioritization process. *Soft Comput.* **2018**, *22*, 7399–7405. [CrossRef]
13. Ecer, F. An integrated Fuzzy AHP and ARAS model to evaluate mobile banking services. *Technol. Econ. Dev. Econ.* **2018**, *24*, 670–695. [CrossRef]
14. Ecer, F. Multi-criteria decision making for green supplier selection using interval type-2 fuzzy AHP: A case study of a home appliance manufacturer. *Oper. Res.* **2020**, 1–35. [CrossRef]
15. Badi, I.; Abdulshahed, A. Ranking the Libyan airlines by using full consistency method (FUCOM) and analytical hierarchy process (AHP). *Oper. Res. Eng. Sci. Theory Appl.* **2019**, *2*, 1–14. [CrossRef]
16. Pamučar, D.; Lukovac, V.; Božanić, D.; Komazec, N. Multi-criteria FUCOM-MAIRCA model for the evaluation of level crossings: Case study in the Republic of Serbia. *Oper. Res. Eng. Sci. Theory Appl.* **2018**, *1*, 108–129. [CrossRef]
17. Durmic, E.; Stevic, Z.; Chatterjee, P.; Vasiljevic, M.; Tomasevic, M. Sustainable supplier selection using combined FUCOM—Rough SAW model. *Rep. Mech. Eng.* **2020**, *1*, 34–43. [CrossRef]
18. Rostamzadeh, R.; Ghorabaee, M.K.; Govindan, K.; Esmaeili, A.; Nobar, H.B.K. Evaluation of sustainable supply chain risk management using an integrated fuzzy TOPSIS-CRITIC approach. *J. Clean. Prod.* **2018**, *175*, 651–669. [CrossRef]
19. Ecer, F. A Multi-criteria Approach Towards Assessing Corporate Sustainability Performances of Privately-owned Banks: Entropy-ARAS Integrated Model. *Eskişehir Osman. Univ. J. Econ. Adm. Sci.* **2019**, *14*, 365–390.
20. Zizovic, M.; Pamucar, D. New model for determining criteria weights: Level Based Weight Assessment (LBWA) model. *Decis. Mak. Appl. Manag. Eng.* **2019**, *2*, 1–12. [CrossRef]

21. Van de Kaa, G.; Fens, T.; Rezaei, J.; Kaynak, D.; Hatun, Z.; Tsilimeni-Archangelidi, A. Realizing smart meter connectivity: Analyzing the competing technologies Power line communication, mobile telephony, and radio frequency using the best worst method. *Renew. Sustain. Energy Rev.* **2019**, *103*, 320–327. [CrossRef]
22. Setyono, R.P.; Sarno, R. Vendor Track Record Selection Using Best Worst Method. In Proceedings of the 2018 International Seminar on Application for Technology of Information and Communication, Semarang, Indonesia, 7 October 2018; pp. 41–48.
23. Ahmadi, H.; Ku Kusi-Sarpong, S.; Rezaei, J. Assessing the social sustainability of supply chains using Best Worst Method. *Recourses Conserv. Recycl.* **2017**, *126*, 99–106. [CrossRef]
24. Salimi, N.; Rezaei, J. Evaluating firms' R&D performance using best worst method. *Eval. Program Plan.* **2018**, *66*, 147–155.
25. Beemsterboer, D.J.C.; Hendrix, E.M.T.; Claassen, G.D.H. On solving the Best-Worst Method in multi-criteria decision-making. *IFAC-PapersOnLine* **2018**, *51*, 1660–1665. [CrossRef]
26. Rezaei, J.; Wang, J.; Tavasszy, L. Linking supplier development to supplier segmentation using Best Worst Method. *Expert Syst. Appl.* **2015**, *42*, 9152–9164. [CrossRef]
27. Rezaei, J. Best-worst multi-criteria decision-making method: Some properties and a linear model. *Omega* **2016**, *64*, 126–130. [CrossRef]
28. Ghaffari, S.; Arab, A.; Nafari, J.; Manteghi, M. Investigation and evaluation of key success factors in technological innovation development based on BWM. *Decis. Sci. Lett.* **2017**, *6*, 295–306. [CrossRef]
29. Gupta, P.; Anand, S.; Gupta, H. Developing a roadmap to overcome barriers to energy efficiency in buildings using best worst method. *Sustain. Cities Soc.* **2017**, *31*, 244–259. [CrossRef]
30. Praditya, D.; Janssen, M. Assessment of factors influencing information sharing arrangements using the best-worst method. In Proceedings of the Conference on e-Business, e-Services and e-Society, Dlehi, India, 21 November 2017; Springer: Cham, Switzerland; pp. 94–106.
31. Yadollahi, S.; Kazemi, A.; Ranjbarian, B. Identifying and prioritizing the factors of service experience in banks: A Best-Worst method. *Decis. Sci. Lett.* **2018**, *7*, 455–464. [CrossRef]
32. Kheybari, S.; Kazemi, M.; Rezaei, J. Bioethanol facility location selection using best-worst method. *Appl. Energy* **2019**, *242*, 612–623. [CrossRef]
33. Raj, A.; Srivastava, S.K. Sustainability performance assessment of an aircraft manufacturing firm. *Benchmark. Int. J.* **2018**, *25*, 1500–1527. [CrossRef]
34. Torbati, A.R.; Sayadi, M.K. A New Approach to Investigate the Performance of Insurance Branches in Iran Using Best-Worst Method and Fuzzy Inference System. *J. Soft Comput. Decis. Support Syst.* **2018**, *5*, 13–18.
35. Khanmohammadi, E.; Zandieh, M.; Tayebi, T. Drawing a Strategy Canvas Using the Fuzzy Best–Worst Method. *Glob. J. Flex. Syst. Manag.* **2019**, *20*, 57–75. [CrossRef]
36. Gupta, H.; Barua, M.K. A framework to overcome barriers to green innovation in SMEs using BWM and Fuzzy TOPSIS. *Sci. Total Environ.* **2018**, *633*, 122–139. [CrossRef] [PubMed]
37. You, P.; Guo, S.; Zhao, H.; Zhao, H. Operation performance evaluation of power grid enterprise using a hybrid BWM-TOPSIS method. *Sustainability* **2017**, *9*, 2329. [CrossRef]
38. Askarifar, K.; Motaffef, Z.; Aazaami, S. An investment development framework in Iran's seashores using TOPSIS and best-worst multi-criteria decision making methods. *Decis. Sci. Lett.* **2018**, *7*, 55–64. [CrossRef]
39. Garg, C.P.; Sharma, A. Sustainable outsourcing partner selection and evaluation using an integrated BWM–VIKOR framework. *Environ. Dev. Sustain.* **2018**, 1–29. [CrossRef]
40. Cheraghalipour, A.; Paydar, M.M.; Hajiaghaei-Keshteli, M. Applying a hybrid BWM-VIKOR approach to supplier selection: A case study in the Iranian agricultural implements industry. *Int. J. Appl. Decis. Sci.* **2018**, *11*, 274–301. [CrossRef]
41. Kumar, A.; Aswin, A.; Gupta, H. Evaluating green performance of the airports using hybrid BWM and VIKOR methodology. *Tour. Manag.* **2020**, *76*, 103941. [CrossRef]
42. Yucesan, M.; Mete, S.; Serin, F.; Celik, E.; Gul, M. An integrated best-worst and interval type-2 fuzzy TOPSIS methodology for green supplier selection. *Mathematics* **2019**, *7*, 182. [CrossRef]
43. Pamučar, D.; Gigović, L.; Bajić, Z.; Janošević, M. Location selection for wind farms using GIS multi-criteria hybrid model: An approach based on fuzzy and rough numbers. *Sustainability* **2017**, *9*, 1315. [CrossRef]
44. Stević, Ž.; Pamučar, D.; Kazimieras Zavadskas, E.; Ćirović, G.; Prentkovskis, O. The selection of wagons for the internal transport of a logistics company: A novel approach based on rough BWM and rough SAW methods. *Symmetry* **2017**, *9*, 264. [CrossRef]

45. Alimohammadlou, M.; Bonyani, A. Fuzzy BWANP multi-criteria decision-making method. *Decis. Sci. Lett.* **2019**, *8*, 85–94. [CrossRef]
46. Amoozad Mahdiraji, H.; Arzaghi, S.; Stauskis, G.; Zavadskas, E. A hybrid fuzzy BWM-COPRAS method for analyzing key factors of sustainable architecture. *Sustainability* **2018**, *10*, 1626. [CrossRef]
47. Bonyani, A.; Alimohammadlou, M. Identifying and prioritizing foreign companies interested in participating in post-sanctions Iranian energy sector. *Energy Strategy Rev.* **2018**, *21*, 180–190. [CrossRef]
48. Pamučar, D.; Chatterjee, K.; Zavadskas, E.K. Assessment of third-party logistics provider using multi-criteria decision-making approach based on interval rough numbers. *Comput. Ind. Eng.* **2019**, *127*, 383–407. [CrossRef]
49. Sofuoglu, M.A.; Orak, S. A novel hybrid multi criteria decision making model: Application to turning operations. *Int. J. Intell. Syst. Appl. Eng.* **2017**, *5*, 124–131. [CrossRef]
50. Serrai, W.; Abdelli, A.; Mokdad, L.; Hammal, Y. Towards an efficient and a more accurate web service selection using MCDM methods. *J. Comput. Sci.* **2017**, *22*, 253–267. [CrossRef]
51. Hashemkhani Zolfani, S.; Pamucar, D.; Ecer, F.; Raslanas, S. Neighborhood Selection for a Newcomer via a Novel BWM-Based Revised MAIRCA Integrated Model; a Case from the Coquimbo-La Serena Conurbation, Chile. *Int. J. Strateg. Prop. Manag.* **2020**, *24*, 102–118. [CrossRef]
52. Ergu, D.; Kou, G.; Peng, Y.; Shi, Y. A simple method to improve the consistency ratio of the pair-wise comparison matrix in ANP. *Eur. J. Oper. Res.* **2013**, *213*, 246–259. [CrossRef]
53. Anane, M.; Kallali, H.; Jellali, S.; Ouessar, M. Ranking suitable sites for Soil Aquifer Treatment in Jerba Island (Tunisia) using remote sensing, GIS and AHP-multicriteria decision analysis. *Int. J. Water* **2008**, *4*, 121–135. [CrossRef]
54. Ishizaka, A. Comparison of Fuzzy logic, AHP, FAHP and Hybrid Fuzzy AHP for new supplier selection and its performance analysis. *Int. J. Integr. Supply Manag.* **2014**, *9*, 1–22. [CrossRef]
55. Pamucar, D.; Bozanic, D.; Lukovac, V.; Komazec, N. Normalized weighted geometric Bonferroni mean operator of interval rough numbers—Application in interval rough DEMATEL-COPRAS. *Facta Univ. Ser. Mech. Eng.* **2018**, *16*, 171–191. [CrossRef]
56. Haddad, B.; Liazid, A.; Ferreira, P. A multi-criteria approach to rank renewables for the Algerian electricity system. *Renew. Energy* **2017**, *107*, 462–472. [CrossRef]
57. Yilan, G.; Kadirgan, M.N.; Çiftçioğlu, G.A. Analysis of electricity generation options for sustainable energy decision making: The case of Turkey. *Renew. Energy* **2020**, *146*, 519–529. [CrossRef]
58. Büyüközkan, G.; Güleryüz, S. Evaluation of Renewable Energy Resources in Turkey using an integrated MCDM approach with linguistic interval fuzzy preference relations. *Energy* **2017**, *123*, 149–163. [CrossRef]
59. Çelikbilek, Y.; Tüysüz, F. An integrated grey based multi-criteria decision making approach for the evaluation of renewable energy sources. *Energy* **2016**, *115*, 1246–1258. [CrossRef]
60. Cavallaro, F.; Zavadskas, E.K.; Streimikiene, D.; Mardani, A. Assessment of concentrated solar power (CSP) technologies based on a modified intuitionistic fuzzy TOPSIS and trigonometric entropy weights. *Technol. Forecast. Soc. Chang.* **2019**, *140*, 258–270. [CrossRef]
61. Malkawi, S.; Azizi, D. A multi-criteria optimization analysis for Jordan's energy mix. *Energy* **2017**, *127*, 680–696. [CrossRef]
62. Cartelle Barros, J.; Coira, M.L.; De la Cruz López, M.P.; del Caño Gochi, A. Assessing the global sustainability of different electricity generation systems. *Energy* **2015**, *89*, 473–489. [CrossRef]
63. Troldborg, M.; Heslop, S.; Hough, R.L. Assessing the sustainability of renewable energy technologies using multi-criteria analysis: Suitability of approach for national-scale assessments and associated uncertainties. *Renew. Sustain. Energy Rev.* **2014**, *39*, 1173–1184. [CrossRef]
64. Büyüközkan, G.; Karabulut, Y.; Mukul, E. A novel renewable energy selection model for United Nations' sustainable development goals. *Energy* **2018**, *165*, 290–302. [CrossRef]
65. Büyüközkan, G.; Güleryüz, S. An integrated DEMATEL-ANP approach for renewable energy resources selection in Turkey. *Int. J. Prod. Econ.* **2016**, *182*, 435–448. [CrossRef]
66. Wang, J.J.; Jing, Y.Y.; Zhang, C.F.; Zhao, J.H. Review on multi-criteria decision analysis aid in sustainable energy decision-making. *Renew. Sustain. Energy Rev.* **2009**, *13*, 2263–2278. [CrossRef]
67. Pamucar, D. Normalized Weighted Geometric Dombi Bonferoni Mean Operator with Interval Grey Numbers: Application in Multicriteria Decision Making. *Rep. Mech. Eng.* **2020**, *1*, 44–52. [CrossRef]

68. Li, J.; Wang, J.Q.; Hu, J.H. Multi-criteria decision-making method based on dominance degree and BWM with probabilistic hesitant fuzzy information. *Int. J. Mach. Learn. Cybern.* **2019**, *10*, 1671–1685.

 © 2020 by the authors. Licensee MDPI, Basel, Switzerland. This article is an open access article distributed under the terms and conditions of the Creative Commons Attribution (CC BY) license (http://creativecommons.org/licenses/by/4.0/).

A Robust Algorithm for Classification and Diagnosis of Brain Disease Using Local Linear Approximation and Generalized Autoregressive Conditional Heteroscedasticity Model

Ali Hamzenejad [1], Saeid Jafarzadeh Ghoushchi [2], Vahid Baradaran [1] and Abbas Mardani [3,4,*]

1. Department of Industrial engineering, Islamic Azad University Tehran North Branch, Tehran 1477893855, Iran; ali.hamzenejad@gmail.com (A.H.); v_baradaran@iau-tnb.ac.ir (V.B.)
2. Department of Industrial engineering, Urmia University of Technology, Urmia 5716693188, Iran; s.jJafarzadeh@uut.ac.ir
3. Informetrics Research Group, Ton Duc Thang University, Ho Chi Minh City 758307, Vietnam
4. Faculty of Business Administration, Ton Duc Thang University, Ho Chi Minh City 758307, Vietnam
* Correspondence: abbas.mardani@tdtu.edu.vn

Received: 5 July 2020; Accepted: 24 July 2020; Published: 2 August 2020

Abstract: Regions detection has an influence on the better treatment of brain tumors. Existing algorithms in the early detection of tumors are difficult to diagnose reliably. In this paper, we introduced a new robust algorithm using three methods for the classification of brain disease. The first method is Wavelet-Generalized Autoregressive Conditional Heteroscedasticity-K-Nearest Neighbor (W-GARCH-KNN). The Two-Dimensional Discrete Wavelet (2D-DWT) is utilized as the input images. The sub-banded wavelet coefficients are modeled using the GARCH model. The features of the GARCH model are considered as the main property vector. The second method is the Developed Wavelet-GARCH-KNN (D-WGK), which solves the incompatibility of the WGK method for the use of a low pass sub-band. The third method is the Wavelet Local Linear Approximation (LLA)-KNN, which we used for modeling the wavelet sub-bands. The extracted features were applied separately to determine the normal image or brain tumor based on classification methods. The classification was performed for the diagnosis of tumor types. The empirical results showed that the proposed algorithm obtained a high rate of classification and better practices than recently introduced algorithms while requiring a smaller number of classification features. According to the results, the Low-Low sub-bands are not adopted with the GARCH model; therefore, with the use of homomorphic filtering, this limitation is overcome. The results showed that the presented Local Linear (LL) method was better than the GARCH model for modeling wavelet sub-bands.

Keywords: Magnetic Resonance Imaging (MRI); wavelet transform; GARCH; LLA; LDA; KNN

1. Introduction

Electromagnetic imaging techniques provide valuable information about the human body. One of these methods is the Magnetic Resonance Imaging (MRI) of the brain [1]. One major area of research that has expanded in medical engineering involves diagnostic tools by machine control for a quicker and easier inference, which can be a great help for physicians in clinical medicine. Therefore, in recent years, mathematical methods have attracted much attention to the analysis of neural network data [2]. Brain images are considered as interesting subjects in the mathematical application and diagnosis of brain disorders in a patient [3]. The MRI can be used to examine the status of the brain tissue and discover whether or not there is a disease [4]. In MRI imaging, the patient is exposed to a strong magnetic field, after which radio waves are leaked toward him. The body's tissues emit another radio wave in response to this position. By receiving these radio waves emitted from the patient's body and by analyzing these waves via a powerful computer, images are created on the device monitor that show the levels of the target organ parts. The next step involves extracting features.

The Two-Dimensional Wavelet Transform (DWT) and the Principal Component Analysis (PCA) were the methods that were used to extract the features of the images [5,6]. Then, the classification methods were used to diagnosis the disease type in the brain [7,8]. Chaplot, et al. [9] used two-dimensional DWT sub-bands to extract the features in their research on Alzheimer's Disease (AD). Additionally, Daubechies filters were used as a filtering technique. The outcome illustrated that the Support Vector Machine (SVM) with radial base function and the polynomial kernel has a higher performance than linear neural networks and SVM [10,11]. Hackmack, et al. [12] used multidimensional complex wavelet transformations, and then linear SVM, to determine multi-scale brain images. The results showed that low-band scales include more information than high-frequency values. Maitra and Chatterjee [13] presented a Slantlet deformation—developed DWT—to extract the containing features of the brain's images. The Fuzzy C-Meaning (FCM) method has been used to analyze the brain MRI, based on the characteristics of the image histogram, in order to determine a healthy subject from Alzheimer's disease. Ramathilagam, et al. [14] used the c-means fuzzy modified algorithm to divide the brain MRI image with a T1-T2 weight. Since the c-means standard factor is intensively sensitive to the noise-induced area during extraction, the authors proposed to repeat the dist-max algorithm before executing the method.

Rivest-Hénault and Cheriet [15] used a local linear representation to model the brain tissue, after which regional models were embedded in the framework of the surface set in order to control the spatial integrity of division. Hussain, et al. [16] classified the images as normal or abnormal using (Back-Propagation Neural Networks) BPNN feed-forward, with characteristics derived from dynamic statistics and 2D-DWT. Bhattacharyya and Kim [17] presented an image segmentation technique for detecting a tumor with MRI images. The existing thresholding techniques produced different results in each image. Therefore, in order to achieve a satisfactory result in the brain tumor image, they presented a methodology that found the tumor to be unique. Kim, et al. [18] studied the diagnosis of Alzheimer's disease based on the Electroencephalogram (EEG) signal of the brain using genetic algorithms and neural networks. One of the remarkable points in this study was the ability to differentiate Alzheimer's patients from the mild stage of healthy subjects with 82% accuracy using a single-channel EEG signal [19]. Additionally, in another study, the comparison of the EEG signaling disorder of healthy people with that of brain tumor patients was calculated by entropy. According to the results, in low-frequency patients, low-rhythms of EEG signals such as Delta and Theta bands have a higher power spectrum than for healthy people. Gholipour, et al. [20] described the use of a completely new automated software algorithm using the standard MRI sequence before and after Contra T1. The T1 weighs in before and after Contra, and the images are automatically interconnected and normalized. The volume of tumor growth is automatically calculated. In their study, they were able to test a method for calculating the size of the tumor when it was enlarged by the collapse of the cavity and, of course, when the enlarged tumor was covered with semi-autogenous blood in a cutaneous cavity. It detected an increase in tumor volume among blood products, which rarely reduced measurements when using other techniques. Their approach seems to overcome many challenges by assessing the response to increased brain tumors and leading to more validation. Zacharaki, et al. [21] studied machine-learning algorithms that automatically identify the relevant features and are desirable for brain tumor differentiation. They studied various machine-learning techniques for classifying the brain tumor based on the features extracted from conventional MRI and perfusion. Their study was performed by mutual validation of Leave-One-Out (LOO) exodus on 101 brain tumors, obtained using a pack evaluation in combination with the best first-order algorithm and K-Nearest Neighbour (KNN) algorithm classification, reaching 96.9%. When differentiated, it became Glimatic and 94.5% when distinguished from a low-grade neoplasm. Fritzsche, et al. [22] completed a study of 15 patients with brain tumors and 18 patients with Mild Cognitive Impairment (MCI); eight remained stable in a three-year follow-up, and 15 were healthy individuals. The classification was also improved by limiting the analysis to the left-brain hemisphere. Devanand, et al. [23], using morphometric mapping of MRI, evaluated the local changes of the hippocampus grains and entorhinal cortex in predicting the transformation from a MCI cognitive impairment to an AD brain tumor. In the MCI model, Cox regression models for the conversion time to conversion converters were made for AD (n = 31) and 99 non-converted controls for age, sex, and education. In Zöllner, et al. [24], the performances of reduction features such as the Pearson correlation coefficient, principal components analysis, and independent component analysis in the classification of Glioma's disease were analyzed using a backup vector machine classifier.

Afshar, et al. [25] studied classification using CapsNets for the detection of brain tumors in order to present a developed architecture with higher accuracy. Their findings indicated that the presented method could overcome Convolutional Neural Networks (CNNs) successfully. Mohan and Subashini [26] provided a clinical study of brain tumor imaging related to gliomas. They used related methods of segmentation and classification. Huang, et al. [27] proposed an algorithm based on the rough set method. They presented a hybrid method with the use of FCM. Initially, the feature table was set based on FCM clustering amounts. Then, the relationship among features showed similarity criteria in each cluster.

In this paper, we presented three algorithms, named WGK, D-WGK, and WLK. The first presented method is Wavelet-GARCH-KNN (WGK). In this method, we first used a two-stage 2D-DWT to decompose the input images into sub-bands of wavelets. The reached wavelet coefficients were features of classification. Then, the GARCH model was used for feature extraction with the use of HH1, HL1, LH1, and second stage HH2, HL2, LH2. Because of the incompatibility of Local Linear (LL) with the GARCH model, this sub-band was ignored [28]. To reduce the number of features, the PCA and PCA + LDA method was then used with the extracted feature brain lesion being classified via KNN methods. The results are illustrated in the results section. The second presented method is named Developed Wavelet-GARCH-KNN (D-WGK). In the second method, we overcame the limitation of the WGK algorithm using homomorphic filtering before a wavelet transformation. Therefore, the LL2 sub-band participated in the GARCH model. Then, similarly to the WGK method, the KNN method was designated for the classification of brain tumors. The third method was Wavelet-LLA-KNN (WLK). In this method, all sub-bands of the wavelet decomposition were used for modeling with the LLA algorithm. The remaining part of the third method was also similar to the WGK and D-WGK method.

2. Methods and Materials

2.1. Image Processing

The modern world of today allows digital images to be analyzed and stored [29]. To get better results, it is sometimes necessary to make changes to these images. These changes have three main purposes: processing, analysis, and image perception. For this reason, computer image processing systems have been developed to perform these operations with better speed and accuracy. In these systems, four major processes occur pre-processing, image quality enhancement, image transformation, and classification and segmentation. In these methods, using mathematical science, rules have been created by computers to simulate human visual elements, and this is an aspect of image analysis that is used for specific purposes. Computer Vision is the analysis of scientific images in various scientific branches such as medicine, engineering, molecular imaging, astronautics, security, etc. Modern digital technology has made it possible to manipulate multidimensional signals from systems ranging from simple digital circuits to multiple parallel computers [30,31].

2.2. Discrete Wavelet Transform (DWT)

Let $f(x) \in L^2(R)$ be the function wavelet expansion related to the wavelet $\psi(x)$ and scaling $\varphi(x)$ function [20]; we then have:

$$f(x) = \frac{1}{\sqrt{M}} \sum_k W_\varphi(j_0, k) \phi_{j_0,k}(x) + \frac{1}{\sqrt{M}} \sum_{j=j_0}^{J} \sum_k W_\psi(j, k) \psi_{j,k}(x) \quad (1)$$

$$W_\varphi(j_0, k) = \frac{1}{\sqrt{M}} \sum_{x=0}^{M-1} f(x) \phi_{j_0,k}(x) \quad (2)$$

$$W_\psi(j, k) = \frac{1}{\sqrt{M}} \sum_{x=0}^{M-1} f(x) \psi_{j,k}(x) \qquad j \geq j_0 \quad (3)$$

$$\phi_{j,k}(x) = 2^{\frac{j}{2}} \phi(2^j x - k) \quad (4)$$

$$\psi_{j,k}(x) = 2^{\frac{j}{2}} \psi(2^j x - k) \quad (5)$$

where $f(x)$ is the input variable as a vector, and $\varphi_{j_0,k}(x)$ and $\psi_{j,k}(x)$ are the scaling coefficient and wavelet coefficient, respectively. $x = 0, 1, \ldots, M-1, j = 0, 1, \ldots, J-1, k = 0, 1, 2, \ldots, M-1$, where M is the number of samples to be transformed that is equal to 2^J, J is the number of transformation levels, and j_0 is a random starting scale. The expansion function is a series of crisp numbers; it is also called the discrete wavelet transform of $f(x)$. The representation of the discrete function of $f(x)$ can be written as a weighted summation of wavelet $\psi_{j,k}(x)$ and the scaling coefficient $\varphi_{j_0,k}(x)$, as shown in Equation (1). In this equation, $W_\phi(j_0, k)$ and $W_\psi(j_0, k)$ are the approximation coefficient and detail coefficient, respectively. The expansion coefficients are shown as follows.

Figure 1 shows a two-step wavelet transformation that generates four sub-bands, where ψ^H, ψ^V and ψ^D indicate deviations along the horizontal, vertical, and diagonals edges, respectively. In this diagram, $2 \downarrow$ shows a down stampeding indicator. 2D-DWT can be executed with digital filtration and down samplers. The other sub-bands are generated with discrete 2D scaling functions, with the use of 1D-FWT on $f(x, y)$ [32]. For the computation of the DWT coefficients, we should consider the multiresolution refinement equation, as shown in Equations (6) and (7):

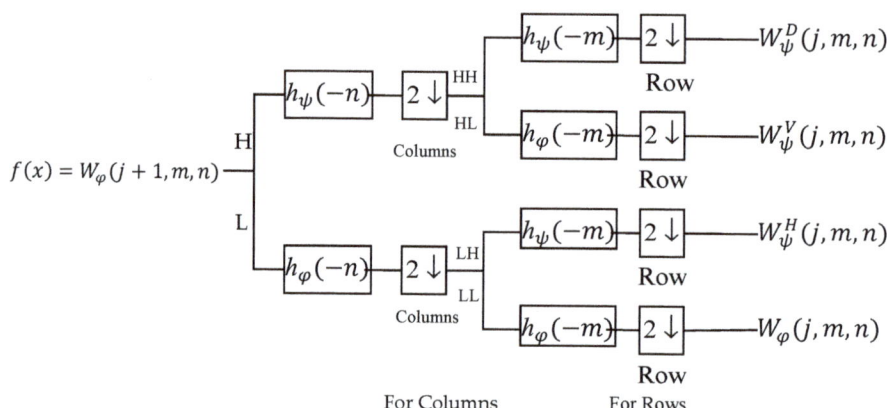

Figure 1. The two-dimensional DWT diagram.

$$\phi_{j,k}(x) = \sum_n 2^{\frac{j}{2}} \phi(2^j x - n) \cdot h_\phi(n) \quad (6)$$

$$\psi_{j,k}(x) = \sum_n 2^{\frac{j}{2}} \psi(2^j x - n) \cdot h_\psi(n) \tag{7}$$

where h_ϕ and h_ψ are the scaling vector and wavelet vector, respectively. h_ϕ and h_ψ may be considered as weights for the summation of Equations (6) and (7). With the inclusion of Equations (6) and (7) into Equations (2) and (3), the following questions result.

$$W_\phi(j,k) = h_\phi(-n) W_\phi(j+1,n), \quad (n = 2k,\ k \geq 0) \tag{8}$$

$$W_\psi(j,k) = h_\psi(-n) W_\psi(j+1,n) \quad j \geq j_0 \tag{9}$$

The scaling and wavelet coefficient of a certain scale j may be obtained via the convolution of the scaling coefficients of the next scale $j+1$ (with finer detail) with the order-reversed scaling and wavelet vectors $h_\phi(-n)$ and $h_\psi(-n)$. Based on Figure 1, the results of the first level of transformation for the column of an input image are as follows:

$$\begin{aligned} W_\phi(j+1,m,n) &= h_\phi(-n) * \left(h_\phi(-m) * W_\phi^{2\uparrow}(j,m) + h_\psi(-m) * W_\psi^{2\uparrow}(j,m) \right) \\ &+ h_\psi(-n) * \left(h_\phi(-m) * W_\phi^{2\uparrow}(j,m) + h_\psi(-m) * W_\psi^{2\uparrow}(j,m) \right), \quad (k \geq 0) \end{aligned} \tag{10}$$

$$\begin{aligned} W_\phi(j+1,m,n) &= h_\phi(-n) h_\phi(-m) * W_\phi^{2\uparrow}(j,m) + h_\phi(-n) h_\psi(-m) * W_\psi^{2\uparrow}(j,m) \\ &+ h_\psi(-n) h_\phi(-m) * W_\phi^{2\uparrow}(j,m) + h_\psi(-n) h_\psi(-m) * W_\psi^{2\uparrow}(j,m), \quad (k \geq 0) \end{aligned} \tag{11}$$

$$\begin{aligned} W_\phi(j+1,m,n) &= h_\phi(-n) h_\phi(-m) * W_\phi^{2\uparrow}(j,m) + h_\phi(-n) h_\psi(-m) * W_\psi^{2\uparrow}(j,m) \\ &+ h_\psi(-n) h_\phi(-m) * W_\phi^{2\uparrow}(j,m) + h_\psi(-n) h_\psi(-m) * W_\psi^{2\uparrow}(j,m), \quad (k \geq 0) \end{aligned} \tag{12}$$

Generally, 2D- $\varphi(x,y)$, and 3D- $\psi^H(x,y)$, $\psi^V(x,y)$, and $\psi^D(x,y)$ are required to generate a 1D scaling function φ and related wavelet ψ [20].

$$\phi(x,y) = \phi(x)\phi(y) \tag{13}$$

$$\psi^H(x,y) = \psi(x)\phi(y) \tag{14}$$

$$\psi^V(x,y) = \phi(y)\phi(x) \tag{15}$$

$$\psi^D(x,y) = \psi(x)\psi(y) \tag{16}$$

2.3. Generalized Autoregressive Conditional Heteroscedasticity

Bollerslev was the first researcher who developed the GARCH method [33]. It can be considered as being the variance of the time variable, for example, an oscillation. Conditional requires immediate dependence on past observations, and self-control combines past data at the present time. GARCH models are statistical methods that are more common in the economy. Engle [34] presented the process of Autoregressive Conditional Heteroscedasticity (ARCH) to change the conditional variance over time as a factor of past mistakes that remain based on the conditional constant variance. The GARCH process (Algorithm 1) is a general form of ARCH and is a time series modeling technique that uses the last variance to predict future variances.

Algorithm 1. GARCH

1: **Input:** $y_t, P, Q, dist$
2: **Output:** a_i, ϵ_t
3: Step 1: Estimate AR(q):
4: $y_t = a_0 + a_1 y_{t-1} + \cdots + a_q y_{t-q} + \epsilon_t$
5: $\hat{\epsilon}_t^2 = \hat{a}_0 + \sum_{i=1}^{q} \hat{a}_i \hat{\epsilon}_{t-i}^2$
6: Step 2: Compute and plot the autocorrelations of ϵ^2 by:
7: $\rho = \frac{\sum_{t=i+1}^{T}\left(\hat{\epsilon}_t^2 - \hat{\sigma}_t^2\right)\left(\hat{\epsilon}_{t-1}^2 - \hat{\sigma}_{t-1}^2\right)}{\sum_{t=1}^{T}\left(\hat{\epsilon}_t^2 - \hat{\sigma}_t^2\right)^2}$
8: Step 3: null hypothesis states that there are no ARCH or GARCH errors

2.4. Local Linear Approximation

The Local Linear Approximation is calculated via [35]. In this method, the first and second derivatives are determined so as to generate a fitting function with the observation data.

Let x have three value $x(1)$, $x(2)$, and $x(3)$. An LLA for the derivative of x at the $x(2)$ is calculated via the mean of the two slopes between $x(1)$–$x(2)$ and between $x(2)$–$x(3)$, which can now be calculated from $x(3)$ and stored in the matrix y of the same order as $x(3)$ where the kth row of y is:

$$y_{k1} = x_{k2}, \tag{17}$$

$$y_{k2} = \frac{x_{k3} - x_{k1}}{2\tau \Delta t}, \tag{18}$$

$$y_{k3} = \frac{x_{k1} - 2x_{k2} + x_{k3}}{(\tau \Delta t)^2}. \tag{19}$$

$$\frac{dx(1-\tau)}{dt} \approx \frac{x(1+2\tau) - x(1)}{2\tau \Delta t} \tag{20}$$

where the first column of y is the value of x at the moment of measurement indexed in the second column of $x(3)$, and the second and third columns of y are the approximated first and second derivatives, respectively, at that same moment of measurement. In this case, $\tau = 1$ since $x(1)$, $x(2)$, and $x(3)$ are successive measures, and Δt is the time interval among the measures. The others (for instance $x(1)$, $x(3)$, and $x(5)$) can be calculated with $\tau = 2$ being substituted into Equation (20).

2.5. K-Nearest Neighbour Algorithm

KNN is a simple form of machine learning [31,36]. In this algorithm, an article is classified by the values of its neighbors, which are allocated to k ($\in \mathbb{N}^+$) nearest neighbors [37]. The similarity of each object in a class is utilized as the weight of the class. In the case of a few of the k nearest neighbors sharing a category, the per-neighbor weights of that category are included together at that point, and the obtained weighted entirety is utilized as the probability score of the candidate categories. A positioned list is obtained for the test archive. By thresholding these scores, twofold category assignments are obtained.

2.6. Proposed Method

In this paper, we aim to use mathematical methods to diagnose brain diseases. We implemented three methods for the classification and diagnosis of brain tumors (Algorithm 2). The first presented method is Wavelet-GARCH-KNN (WGK). In this method, we first used two-stage 2D-DWT to decompose input images into sub-bands of wavelets. The obtained wavelet coefficients are features of classification. Then, the GARCH model was used for feature extraction with the use of HH1, HL1, LH1, and second-stage HH2, HL2, LH2. Because of the incompatibility of LL with the GARCH model, this sub-band was ignored. To reduce the number of features, the PCA and PCA + LDA method was then used, with extracted feature brain lesions being classified with the use of KNN methods. The results are illustrated in the results section.

The second presented method is named Developed Wavelet-GARCH-KNN (D-WGK). In the second method, we overcame the limitation of the WGK algorithm by using homomorphic filtering before a wavelet transformation. Therefore, the LL2 sub-band participated in the GARCH model. Then, similarly to the WGK method, the KNN method was designated for the classification of brain tumors.

The third method is Wavelet-LLA-KNN (WLK). In this method, all sub-bands of wavelet decomposition were used for modeling with the LLA algorithm. The remaining part of the third method was also similar to the WGK and D-WGK method. The results of each algorithm are depicted in the below sections. The structure and proposed model in this study are shown in Figure 2.

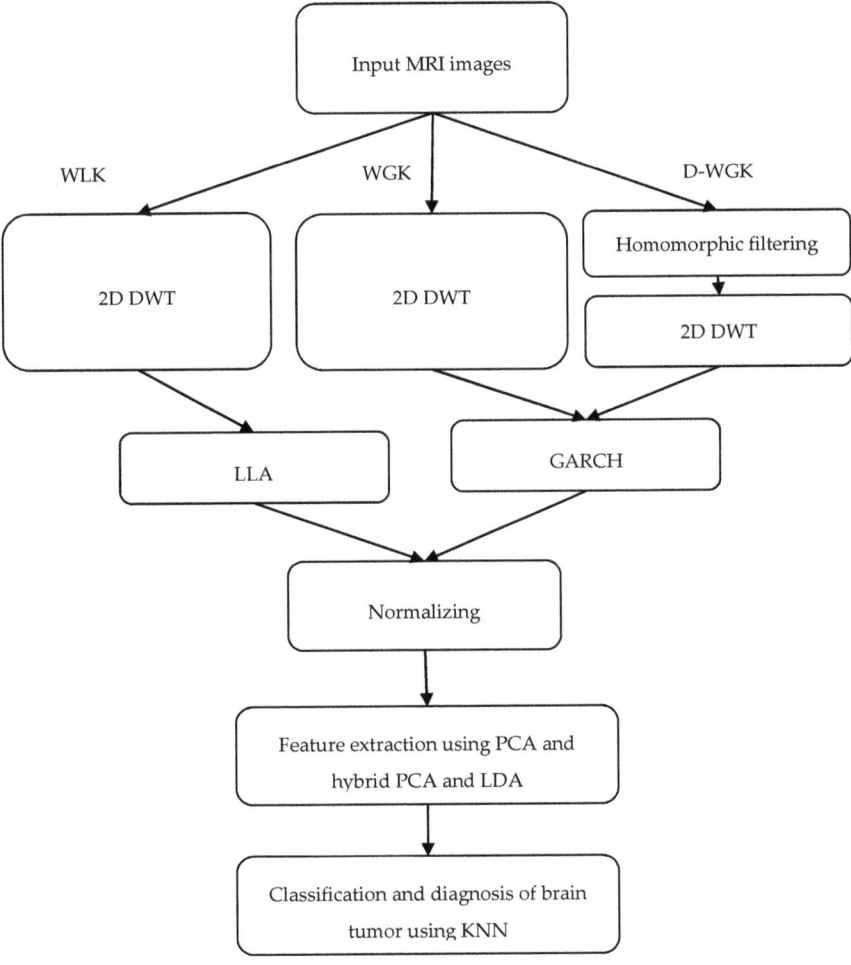

Figure 2. The block diagram of the proposed method.

Algorithm 2. Presented
1: **Input:** $y_{m \times m} = \{m \times m\} \in R^2$
2: **Switch:**
3: **Case 1:** WGK
4: Step 1: Wavelet decomposition for all images
5: Step 2: Calculate GARCH parameters for sub-bands of high-frequency detail of (HH1, HL1, LH1, HL2, LH2)
6: Step 3: Normalization of features
7: Step 4: Feature reduction using PCA and PCA+LDA
8: Step 5: Classification of Features using KNN
9: **Case 2:** D-WGK
10: Step 1: Apply homomorphic filtering for all images
11: Step 2: Wavelet decomposition for all images
12: Step 2: Calculate GARCH parameters for all sub-bands of high-frequency detail of (HH1, HL1, LH1, HL2, LH2, LL2)
13: Step 3: Normalization of features
14: Step 4: Feature reduction using PCA and PCA+LDA
15: Step 5: Classification of Features using KNN
16: **Case 3:** WLK
17: Step 1: Wavelet decomposition for all images
18: Step 2: Calculate LLA parameters
19: Step 3: Normalization of features
20: Step 4: Feature reduction using PCA and PCA+LDA
21: Step 5: Classification of Features using KNN
22: **Comparison and analysis**

3. Results and Discussion

3.1. Datasets

In this paper, we used seven brain diseases to implement and test the presented methods. They consist of Alzheimer's, Alzheimer plus visual agnosia, Glioma, Huntington, Meningioma, Pick, and Sarcoma. These diseases, in conjunction with normal brain images, include 240 MRI images from the Harvard medical school website. All images are from T2-weighted MR brain images in the axial plane and have 256×256 pixels. These images were saved in different folders and studied separately. Therefore, after feature extraction, they were aggregated into a single code folder.

3.2. Two-dimensional Discrete Wavelet Transforms (2D-DWT)

In this paper, we used 2D-DWT to separate the sub-bands of images. In this transformation, we input images from 256×256 pixels to 131×131 first-stage sub-bands and 69×69 sub-bands. The example of a wavelet transformation is shown in Figure 3. Additionally, for the second aforementioned method, we needed homomorphic filtering.

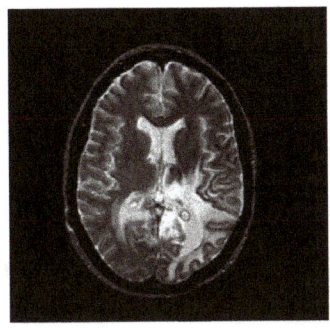

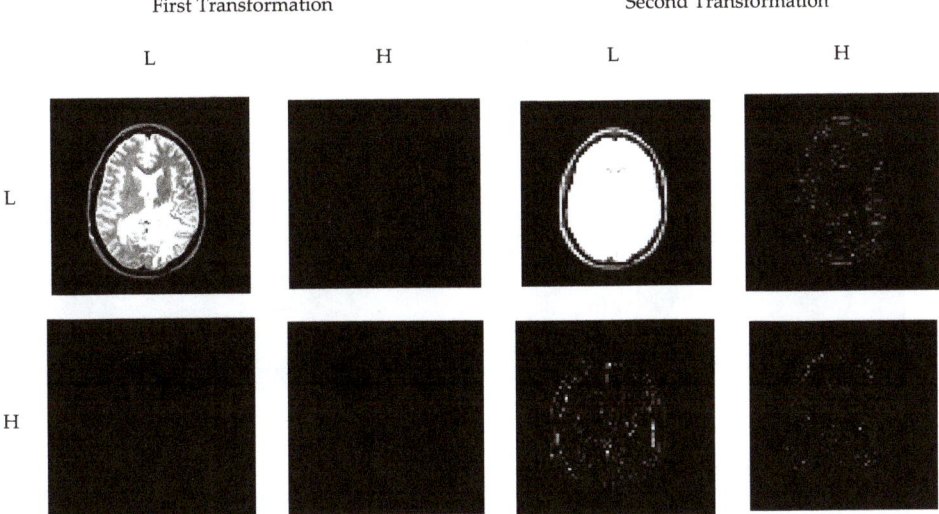

Figure 3. The sub-bands of the wavelet transformation.

The results of the wavelet discretization when using homomorphic filtering ($\sigma = 5$) are shown in Figure 4. The top images show the original image without (with) the filtration, and the first and second transformation are shown on the left and right sides of the images, respectively. Regarding the literature studies, the GARCH model was not compatible with LL2 sub-bands [38]. This situation is obviously shown in Figure 3 (LL2). Because all the brain sections of the images were almost within the GARCH model in (1, 1), we did not find the model coefficient to be significant for the GARCH (1, 1) model. In this paper, we overcame this limitation and made the LL2 model be compatible with the GARCH (1, 1) model. To overcome this condition, we used homomorphic filtration for the main image, and then the 2D-DWT was performed on it. With this method, we increased the contrast of the LL2 sub-band, as can be seen in Figure 4 (LL2).

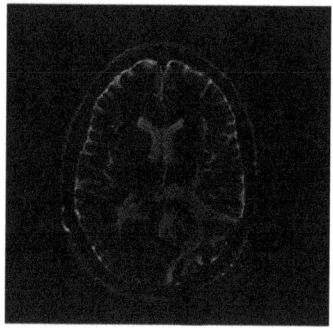

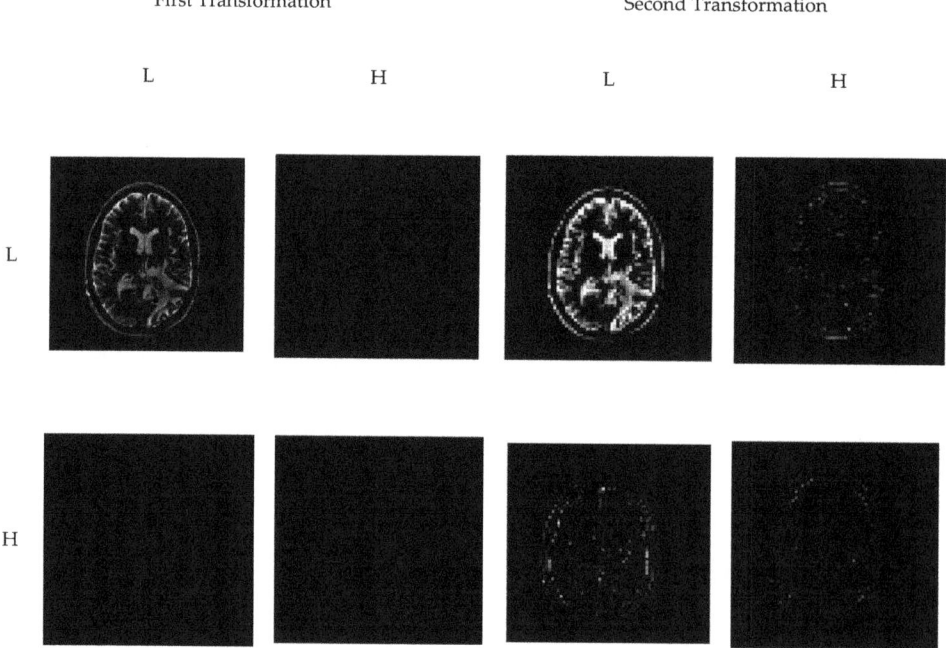

Figure 4. The sub-bands of the wavelet transformation using homomorphic filtering.

3.3. Feature Reduction

In this section, we used nonconvulsive status epilepticus (NCSE) to extract features and classify them. Via this method, we can classify the features into two classification states: two-classes and eight-classes. In the two-class state, we classify the features into two classes to diagnosis the normal and abnormal MRI images. Using this state, we can find patient and inpatient brain images. Moreover, using the eight-class state, we can classify the brain images into seven different classes in conjunction with normal brain images.

In this paper, we studied different methods to reduce features, consisting of:

WGK: Using GARCH without LL2 + PCA
WGK: Using GARCH without LL2 + PCA + LDA
D-WGK: Using Homomorphic filtering + GARCH with LL2 + PCA

WLK: Using LLA + PCA
WLK: Using LLA + PCA + LDA

The results are depicted in Figures 5–8. Figure 5 shows the feature reduction plots used to find the best number of classes. In this figure, we used two methods, 2D-DWT and GARCH (1, 1), used with and without LL2 sub-bands. The result shows that with the addition of LL2 to the GARCH method, the model is developed. Furthermore, the results of the PCA method show that we can use 14 features for the classification of images.

Furthermore, this enhancement is shown in Figure 6 for the two-class state. Additionally, in this state, the method is developed, and a number of features are decremented from 6 to 5. This can speed up the classification method and increase the accuracy of the methods because we used all sub-bands of the 2D-DWT method for classification with fewer features.

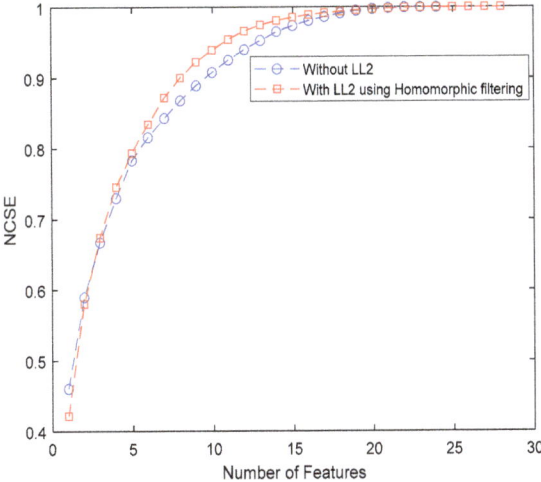

Figure 5. Normalized cumulative summation of eigenvalues of training data for GARCH (1, 1) with and without LL2 (Eight-classes).

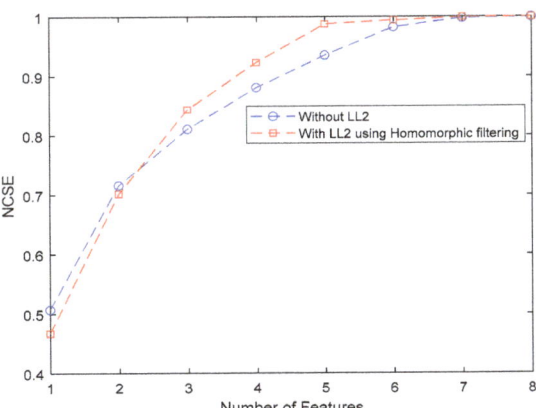

Figure 6. Normalized cumulative summation of eigenvalues of training data for GARCH (1, 1) with and without LL2 (two-classes).

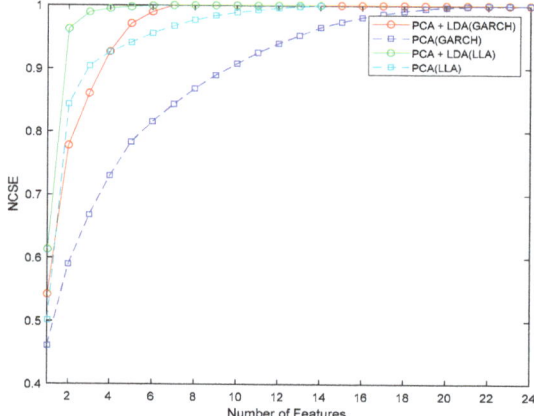

Figure 7. Normalized cumulative summation of eigenvalues of training data for the GARCH and LLA methods for different PCA and PCA + LDA methods (eight-classes).

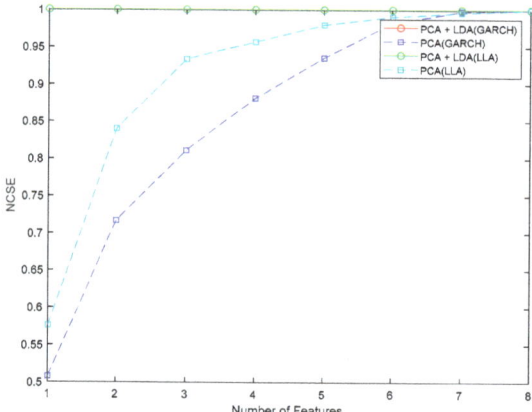

Figure 8. Normalized cumulative summation of eigenvalues of training data for the GARCH and LLA methods for different PCA and PCA + LDA methods (two-classes).

Figures 7 and 8 show the feature reduction results for the presented LLA and GARCH model using the PCA and PCA + LDA methods. In the eight-class method (Figure 7), the best number of features for the GARCH and PCA method was 20, which for GARCH + PCA + LLDA decreased to 10 features. Using the presented method, the LLA + PCA method's number of features decreased to 7 features. Furthermore, for the LLA + PCA + LDA method, the best number of features should be three features. The results showed that the last presented method decreased the number of features to 3 so that it would be great for feature reduction.

For a two-class state (Figure 8), this reduction is conspicuously shown. The resolution between the classes is high, which indicates the ability of LLA + PCA + LDA in incremental inter-class distances and decremental intra-class distances.

3.4. The Classification Results

In this paper, we used the k-Nearest Neighborhood (KNN) method to classify the input features. KNN is a non-parametric method used in data mining, machine learning, and pattern recognition. The KNN algorithm is one of the ten most used algorithms in various machine learning and data mining projects in the industry. The KNN algorithm can be used for classification and regression issues. However, it is often used for classification issues.

The value of K in the KNN method is one of the effective parameters in classification. The mean classification accuracy was determined for different values of K, which was increased from 1 to 11 in steps of two for both states. The results are depicted in Figure 9. The results show that, for K ≤ 5, the classifier has good efficiency. Furthermore, the accuracy of the LLA method in the KNN classifier is greater than the GARCH method.

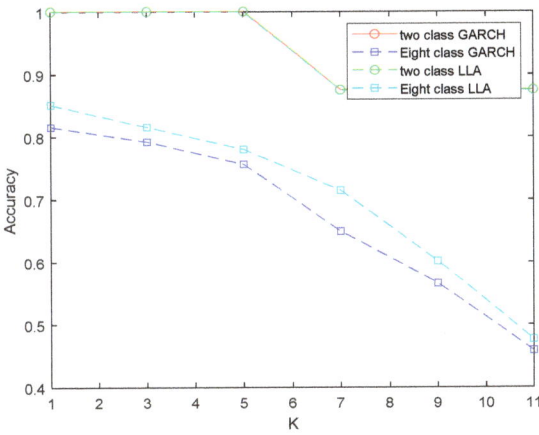

Figure 9. The plots of the accuracy of the two- and eight-class methods for different K values.

In the statistics, indicators of sensitivity and specificity are utilized to evaluate the result of the binary classification (two-class). When the data can be divided into positive and negative groups, the accuracy of the results of a test that divides the information into these two categories is measurable and describable using sensitivity and attribute indicators. Sensitivity means a proportion of positive cases that will test them correctly as being positive. Specificity means the proportion of negative cases that mark them correctly as being negative.

True Positive (TP): The disease is diagnosed correctly.
False Positive (FP): A healthy person is diagnosed with mistakes.
True Negative (TN): A healthy person is diagnosed correctly.
False Negative (FN): The disease is diagnosed with mistakes.

The sensitivity parameter is calculated by dividing the numbers of TP cases by the sum of TP cases and FN cases.

$$sensitivity, \text{TPR} = \frac{\text{TP}}{\text{TP} + \text{FN}} \qquad (21)$$

In a similar way, the specificity results are the division of TN cases by the sum of FP and TN cases.

$$specificity, \text{TNR} = \frac{\text{TN}}{\text{TN} + \text{FP}} \qquad (22)$$

Other classification criteria, such as precision, accuracy, and fall-out, are defined as following Equations (23)–(25).

$$precision, \text{PPV} = \frac{\text{TP}}{\text{TP} + \text{FP}} \qquad (23)$$

$$accuracy(\text{ACC}) = \frac{TP + TN}{TP + TN + FP + FN} \tag{24}$$

$$fall-out(\text{FPR}) = \frac{FP}{FP + FN} \tag{25}$$

The results of the classification using the LLA method are shown in Tables 1 and 2. Table 1 shows the results of the classification using the presented methods. The results show that the maximum accuracy belongs to the presented LLA method that conducted the extraction using the combination of the PCA and LDA methods. Moreover, the minimum one belongs to the GARCH method that used the PCA feature extraction method.

Table 1. The comparison between the presented methods.

Method	Class	Images	Features	Accuracy
Ref. *	6	56	6	91.5
PCA + LDA (WGK) **	8	80	10	89.4
PCA (WGK) **	8	80	22	90.1
Proposed PCA + LDA (D-WGK)	8	240	10	90.2
Proposed PCA (D-WGK)	8	240	20	89.3
Proposed PCA + LDA (WLK)	8	240	3	92.5
Proposed PCA (WLK)	8	240	7	91.3

* Marti nez, et al. [39]; ** Kalbkhani, Shayesteh and Zali-Vargahan [38].

Table 2. The results of the classification for eight-class states using PCA + LDA (WLK).

Diseases	TPR	TNR	PPV	ACC	FPR
Alzheimer	0.933	1	0.903	0.967	0
Alzheimer+	0.933	1	0.875	0.967	0
Glioma	0.900	1	1	0.950	0
Huntington	0.967	1	0.906	0.983	0
Meningioma	0.967	1	1	0.983	0
Pick	0.867	1	0.839	0.933	0
Sarcoma	0.833	1	0.926	0.917	0

Therefore, we can prioritize the presented methods that follow a maximum sensitivity and minimum fall-out as PCA + LDA (WLK), PCA (WLK), PCA + LDA (WGK), and PCA (WGK) (see Figure 10). This shows that the LLA method is better than the GARCH model in terms of robustness, sensitivity, and accuracy. Moreover, the combination of PCA and LDA produces better results than single PCA. One of the main reasons that the GARCH model has not produced a good model is the incompatibility of this method with some images. Table 2 also shows the results of a classification in the eight-class state, and the results show the acceptable outperformance of most diseases. The diagnosis of Pick and Sarcoma is somewhat more inaccurate than that of others; this is because of the complex images of these diseases.

Figure 11 shows the confusion matrix of the presented model of the hybrid PCA, LDA, and LLA methods for the diagnosis of normal and abnormal images. The main diameter of the matrix shows the number of images detected correctly. From 210 abnormal images, 18 (8.57%) were recognized as normal lesions. However, 192 (91.43%) of the abnormal images were diagnosed correctly. Nevertheless, all the normal images were detected, and 92.5% (accuracy) of all images are were correctly classified, while 7.5% were incorrectly classed.

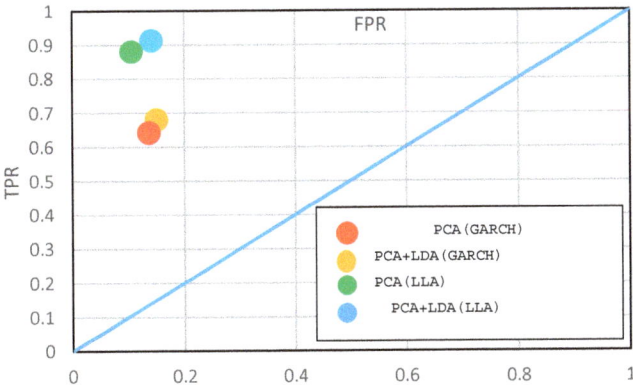

Figure 10. The Receiver Operating Characteristic (ROC) curve of the presented method.

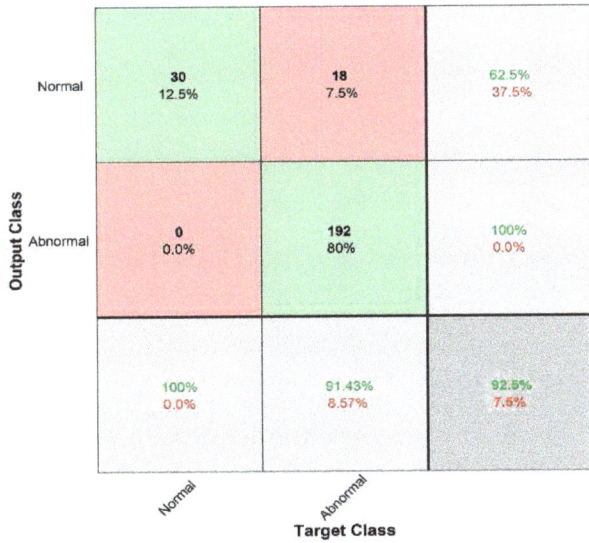

Figure 11. The confusion matrix for two-classes states using PCA-LDA (LLA).

Figure 12 also shows the confusion matrix of the presented method for the classification in eight classes. The lower row of the matrix shows the percentages of each disease that were detected correctly (sensitivity). The maximum detection percentage belonged to normal images, and then Huntington and Meningioma came second. However, only 93.3% of Sarcomas were diagnosed correctly. In the end, 92.5% (accuracy) of all images were classified in the proper class, while 7.3% of them could not be recognized and were incorrectly classed. The red cells show incorrect choices or false ones. In each column, the sum of the elements equals the number of images of each disease. For example, for Alzheimer's (first column), 28 images (from 30) were diagnosed correctly; however, two images were classified into the Alzheimer plus category.

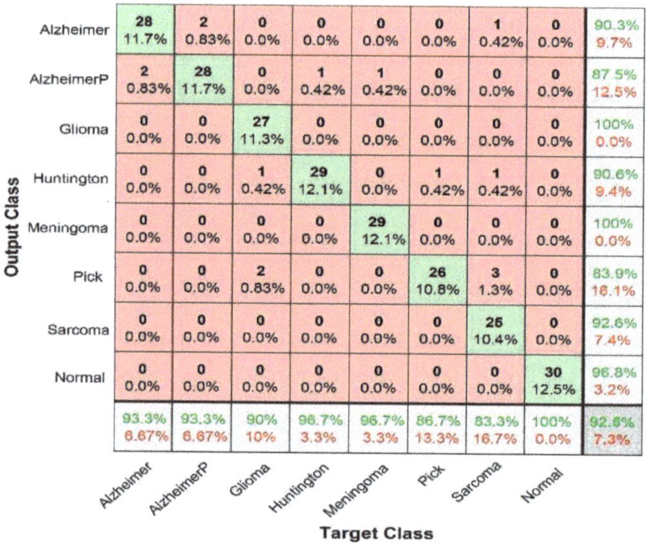

	Alzheimer	AlzheimerP	Glioma	Huntington	Meningoma	Pick	Sarcoma	Normal	
Alzheimer	**28** / 11.7%	2 / 0.83%	0 / 0.0%	0 / 0.0%	0 / 0.0%	0 / 0.0%	1 / 0.42%	0 / 0.0%	90.3% / 9.7%
AlzheimerP	2 / 0.83%	**28** / 11.7%	0 / 0.0%	1 / 0.42%	1 / 0.42%	0 / 0.0%	0 / 0.0%	0 / 0.0%	87.5% / 12.5%
Glioma	0 / 0.0%	0 / 0.0%	**27** / 11.3%	0 / 0.0%	0 / 0.0%	0 / 0.0%	0 / 0.0%	0 / 0.0%	100% / 0.0%
Huntington	0 / 0.0%	0 / 0.0%	1 / 0.42%	**29** / 12.1%	0 / 0.0%	1 / 0.42%	1 / 0.42%	0 / 0.0%	90.6% / 9.4%
Meningoma	0 / 0.0%	0 / 0.0%	0 / 0.0%	0 / 0.0%	**29** / 12.1%	0 / 0.0%	0 / 0.0%	0 / 0.0%	100% / 0.0%
Pick	0 / 0.0%	0 / 0.0%	2 / 0.83%	0 / 0.0%	0 / 0.0%	**26** / 10.8%	3 / 1.3%	0 / 0.0%	83.9% / 16.1%
Sarcoma	0 / 0.0%	0 / 0.0%	0 / 0.0%	0 / 0.0%	0 / 0.0%	0 / 0.0%	**25** / 10.4%	0 / 0.0%	92.6% / 7.4%
Normal	0 / 0.0%	0 / 0.0%	0 / 0.0%	0 / 0.0%	0 / 0.0%	0 / 0.0%	0 / 0.0%	**30** / 12.5%	96.8% / 3.2%
	93.3% / 6.67%	93.3% / 6.67%	90% / 10%	96.7% / 3.3%	96.7% / 3.3%	86.7% / 13.3%	83.3% / 16.7%	100% / 0.0%	**92.6% / 7.3%**

Figure 12. The confusion matrix for eight-classes states using PCA-LDA (WLK).

4. The Complexity Analysis

In the proposed method, we used five major approaches. Therefore, we should calculate their complexity. The complexity of PCA is $O(min(p^3, n^3))$, where p shows the number of features, and n is the data abundance (image size 256 × 256) [40]. Additionally, the complexity of the LDA method for feature extraction is $O(np^2)$ if $n > p$. Otherwise, it is $O(p^3)$. The complexity of 2D-DWT is $O(4Mn^2 log2n)$, where M is the number of vanishing moments of the mother wavelets that are used. The complexity of the GARCH (1, 1) method depends on the autocorrelation complexity and is $O(n)$, where, in this case, n is 256 × 256. Regarding the complexity of the LLA method, we can calculate this as $O(n'n)$, where n' is of the order of the derivative in the method and where, in this case, $n' = 2$. The complexity of the KNN method is $O(npk)$, where, in this case, $k = 1$. Therefore, the complexity of the presented method is as follows: PCA (GARCH) is $O(min(p^3, n^3) + n)$, PCA + LDA (GARCH) is $O(min(p^3, n^3) + np^2 + n)$, PCA (LLA) is $O(min(p^3, n^3) + 2n)$, and PCA + LDA (LLA) is $O(min(p^3, n^3) + np^2 + 2n)$; therefore, the group of the LLA method is somewhat more complex than that of the GARCH group; however, the result is remarkable and compatible with all of the images.

5. Conclusions

In this paper, a hybrid algorithm for determining the diagnosis of brain disease in MRIs is presented. Initially, the two-level transformation of the 2D-DWT was calculated as the input images. The sub-banded wavelet coefficients could be modeled using the GARCH and LLA models. We used five studies in this paper. After using the 2D-DWT method and the separation of the image into six sub-bands to model the sub-bands, we used GARCH (1, 1) without using the Low-Low sub-band in the second wavelet level (use of WGK). Because this sub-band was incompatible with the GARCH (1, 1) method in terms of overcoming this condition, we used homomorphic filtering before 2D-DWT (use of D-WGK). The results showed that, by using Homomorphic filtering, the LL2 sub-band with the maximum image data could be utilized in the GARCH (1, 1) method with high performance. Moreover, we used the LLA method to model the 2D-DWT sub-bands. In this method, we used all of the sub-bands to model features (use of WLK). The results showed that using the LLA method, we could reduce the number of features from 20 to 3. Then, we classified the images using the KNN method. The results demonstrated the high accuracy and robustness of the presented methods. The results showed that the WLK method was better than the WGK and D-WGL models in terms of robustness, sensitivity, and accuracy. Furthermore, the hybrid of PCA and LDA produced better results than PCA. One of the main reasons why the GARCH model has not produced a good model relates to the incompatibility of this method with some images. We overcame this problem in D-WGT with the use of homomorphic filtering. The results of an eight-class classification (diagnosis of disease type) showed an acceptable outperformance for most diseases. The diagnosis of Pick and Sarcoma was somewhat more inaccurate than that of the others; this is because of the complex images of these diseases. Out of the abnormal images, 8.57% were recognized as normal lesions. However, 91.43% of abnormal images were diagnosed correctly. Nevertheless, all the normal images were detected with 92.5% accuracy. The maximum detection percentage belonged to normal images, and then Huntington and Meningioma came second. However, 93.3% of sarcomas were classified correctly. In the end, 92.5% of all images were classified in their proper class, with a 7.3% error. Future work should focus on increasing the dataset volume for the diagnosis of brain tumors. Furthermore, it could be implemented for other MRI images, like breast cancer, prostate cancer, and so on. The novel methods of deep learning could also be enriched with this feature extraction method, which increases process speed and accuracy.

Author Contributions: Conceptualization, A.H.; Formal analysis, A.H. and S.J.G.; Methodology, A.H. and V.B.; Project administration, S.J.G. and V.B.; Resources, A.H. and A.M.; Software, A.H.; Supervision, S.J.G.; Validation, A.H.; Visualization, S.J.G. and V.B.; Writing—original draft, A.M.; Writing—review & editing, A.M. All authors have read and agreed to the published version of the manuscript.

Funding: The funding sources had no involvement in the study design, collection, analysis or interpretation of data, writing of the manuscript or in the decision to submit the manuscript for publication.

Conflicts of Interest: The authors declare no conflict of interest.

Ethical Approval: This article does not contain any studies with human participants or animals performed by any of the authors.

References

1. Herszterg, I.; Poggi, M.; Vidal, T. Two-Dimensional Phase Unwrapping via Balanced Spanning Forests. *INFORMS J. Comput.* **2019**, *31*, 527–543. [CrossRef]
2. Won, D.; Manzour, H.; Chaovalitwongse, W. Convex Optimization for Group Feature Selection in Networked Data. *INFORMS J. Comput.* **2020**, *32*, 182–198. [CrossRef]
3. Zhang, Y.; Dong, Z.; Wu, L.; Wang, S. A hybrid method for MRI brain image classification. *Expert Syst. Appl.* **2011**, *38*, 10049–10053. [CrossRef]
4. Abdullah, N.; Ngah, U.K.; Aziz, S.A. Image classification of brain MRI using support vector machine. In Proceedings of the 2011 IEEE International Conference on Imaging Systems and Techniques, Penang, Malaysia, 17–18 May 2011; pp. 242–247.
5. Gillis, N.; Vavasis, S.A. On the Complexity of Robust PCA and ℓ1-Norm Low-Rank Matrix Approximation. *Math. Oper. Res.* **2018**, *43*, 1072–1084. [CrossRef]
6. Abdulkareem, M.; Bakhary, N.; Vafaei, M.; Noor, N.M.; Mohamed, R.N. Application of two-dimensional wavelet transform to detect damage in steel plate structures. *Measurement* **2019**, *146*, 912–923. [CrossRef]
7. Talo, M.; Baloglu, U.B.; Yıldırım, Ö.; Rajendra Acharya, U. Application of deep transfer learning for automated brain abnormality classification using MR images. *Cogn. Syst. Res.* **2019**, *54*, 176–188. [CrossRef]
8. Abdelaziz Ismael, S.A.; Mohammed, A.; Hefny, H. An enhanced deep learning approach for brain cancer MRI images classification using residual networks. *Artif. Intell. Med.* **2020**, *102*, 101779. [CrossRef]
9. Chaplot, S.; Patnaik, L.M.; Jagannathan, N.R. Classification of magnetic resonance brain images using wavelets as input to support vector machine and neural network. *Biomed. Signal. Process. Control* **2006**, *1*, 86–92. [CrossRef]
10. Hackmack, K.; Paul, F.; Weygandt, M.; Allefeld, C.; Haynes, J.D. Multi-scale classification of disease using structural MRI and wavelet transform. *Neuroimage* **2012**, *62*, 48–58. [CrossRef]
11. Maitra, M.; Chatterjee, A. Hybrid multiresolution Slantlet transform and fuzzy c-means clustering approach for normal-pathological brain MR image segregation. *Med. Eng. Phys.* **2008**, *30*, 615–623. [CrossRef]

12. Ramathilagam, S.; Pandiyarajan, R.; Sathya, A.; Devi, R.; Kannan, S.R. Modified fuzzy c-means algorithm for segmentation of T1–T2-weighted brain MRI. *J. Comput. Appl. Math.* **2011**, *235*, 1578–1586. [CrossRef]
13. Rivest-Hénault, D.; Cheriet, M. Unsupervised MRI segmentation of brain tissues using a local linear model and level set. *Magn. Reson. Imaging* **2011**, *29*, 243–259. [CrossRef] [PubMed]
14. Hussain, S.J.; Savithri, A.S.; Devi, P.V.S. Segmentation of brain MRI with statistical and 2D wavelet features by using neural networks. In Proceedings of the 3rd International Conference on Trendz in Information Sciences & Computing (TISC2011), Chennai, India, 8–9 December 2011; pp. 154–159.
15. Bhattacharyya, D.; Kim, T.-H. *Brain Tumor Detection Using MRI Image Analysis*; Springer: Berlin/Heidelberg, Germany, 2011; pp. 307–314.
16. Kim, H.T.; Kim, B.Y.; Park, E.H.; Kim, J.W.; Hwang, E.W.; Han, S.K.; Cho, S. Computerized recognition of Alzheimer disease-EEG using genetic algorithms and neural network. *Future Gener. Comput. Syst.* **2005**, *21*, 1124–1130. [CrossRef]
17. Abásolo, D.; Hornero, R.; Espino, P.; Poza, J.; Sánchez, C.I.; de la Rosa, R. Analysis of regularity in the EEG background activity of Alzheimer's disease patients with Approximate Entropy. *Clin. Neurophysiol.* **2005**, *116*, 1826–1834. [CrossRef] [PubMed]
18. Gholipour, A.; Estroff, J.A.; Barnewolt, C.E.; Connolly, S.A.; Warfield, S.K. Fetal brain volumetry through MRI volumetric reconstruction and segmentation. *Int. J. Comput. Assist. Radiol. Surg.* **2011**, *6*, 329–339. [CrossRef]
19. Zacharaki, E.I.; Kanas, V.G.; Davatzikos, C. Investigating machine learning techniques for MRI-based classification of brain neoplasms. *Int. J. Comput. Assist. Radiol. Surg.* **2011**, *6*, 821–828. [CrossRef] [PubMed]
20. Fritzsche, K.H.; Stieltjes, B.; Schlindwein, S.; van Bruggen, T.; Essig, M.; Meinzer, H.P. Automated MR morphometry to predict Alzheimer's disease in mild cognitive impairment. *Int. J. Comput. Assist. Radiol. Surg.* **2010**, *5*, 623–632. [CrossRef] [PubMed]
21. Devanand, D.P.; Bansal, R.; Liu, J.; Hao, X.; Pradhaban, G.; Peterson, B.S. MRI hippocampal and entorhinal cortex mapping in predicting conversion to Alzheimer's disease. *Neuroimage* **2012**, *60*, 1622–1629. [CrossRef] [PubMed]
22. Zöllner, F.G.; Emblem, K.E.; Schad, L.R. SVM-based glioma grading: Optimization by feature reduction analysis. *Z. Med. Phys.* **2012**, *22*, 205–214. [CrossRef] [PubMed]
23. Afshar, P.; Mohammadi, A.; Plataniotis, K.N. Brain Tumor Type Classification via Capsule Networks. In Proceedings of the 2018 25th IEEE International Conference on Image Processing (ICIP), Athens, Greece, 7–10 October 2018; pp. 3129–3133.
24. Mohan, G.; Subashini, M.M. MRI based medical image analysis: Survey on brain tumor grade classification. *Biomed. Signal Process. Control* **2018**, *39*, 139–161. [CrossRef]
25. Huang, H.; Meng, F.; Zhou, S.; Jiang, F.; Manogaran, G. Brain Image Segmentation Based on FCM Clustering Algorithm and Rough Set. *IEEE Access* **2019**, *7*, 12386–12396. [CrossRef]
26. Breton, M.; Frutos, J.d. Option Pricing Under GARCH Processes Using PDE Methods. *Oper. Res.* **2010**, *58*, 1148–1157. [CrossRef]
27. Zhao, Y.-B.; Luo, Z.-Q. Constructing New Weighted ℓ_1-Algorithms for the Sparsest Points of Polyhedral Sets. *Math. Oper. Res.* **2016**, *42*, 57–76. [CrossRef]
28. Milstein, A.; Topol, E.J. Computer vision's potential to improve health care. *Lancet* **2020**, *395*, 1537. [CrossRef]
29. Liu, D.; Oczak, M.; Maschat, K.; Baumgartner, J.; Pletzer, B.; He, D.; Norton, T. A computer vision-based method for spatial-temporal action recognition of tail-biting behaviour in group-housed pigs. *Biosyst. Eng.* **2020**, *195*, 27–41. [CrossRef]
30. Burrus, C.S.; Gopinath, R.A. *Introduction to Wavelets and Wavelet Transforms: A Primer*; Pearson Prentice Hall: Upper Saddle River, NJ, USA, 1998.
31. Bollerslev, T. Generalized autoregressive conditional heteroskedasticity. *J. Econom.* **1986**, *31*, 307–327. [CrossRef]
32. Engle, R.F. Autoregressive Conditional Heteroscedasticity with Estimates of the Variance of United Kingdom Inflation. *Econometrica* **1982**, *50*, 987–1007. [CrossRef]
33. Boker, S.M. Differential Models and "Differential Structural Equation Modeling of Intraindividual Variability"; American Psychological Association: 2001. Available online: https://psycnet.apa.org/record/2001-01077-006 (accessed on 2 June 2020).
34. Lutu, P.E.N.; Engelbrecht, A.P. Base Model Combination Algorithm for Resolving Tied Predictions for K-Nearest Neighbor OVA Ensemble Models. *INFORMS J. Comput.* **2012**, *25*, 517–526. [CrossRef]

35. Fukunaga, K.; Narendra, P.M. A Branch and Bound Algorithm for Computing k-Nearest Neighbors. *IEEE Trans. Comput.* **1975**, *C-24*, 750–753. [CrossRef]
36. Kalbkhani, H.; Shayesteh, M.G.; Zali-Vargahan, B. Robust algorithm for brain magnetic resonance image (MRI) classification based on GARCH variances series. *Biomed. Signal. Process. Control* **2013**, *8*, 909–919. [CrossRef]
37. Marti-nez, J.M.P.; Berlanga, R.; Aramburu, M.J.; Pedersen, T.B. Integrating Data Warehouses with Web Data: A Survey. *IEEE Trans. Knowl. Data Eng.* **2008**, *20*, 940–955. [CrossRef]
38. Johnstone, I.M.; Lu, A.Y. On Consistency and Sparsity for Principal Components Analysis in High Dimensions. *J. Am. Stat. Assoc.* **2009**, *104*, 682–693. [CrossRef] [PubMed]
39. Shi, Q.; Zhang, H. Fault diagnosis of an autonomous vehicle with an improved SVM algorithm subject to unbalanced datasets. *IEEE Trans. Ind. Electron.* **2020**. [CrossRef]
40. Qi, Z.; Shi, Q.; Zhang, H. Tuning of digital PID controllers using particle swarm optimization algorithm for a CAN-based DC motor subject to stochastic delays. *IEEE Trans. Ind. Electron.* **2019**, *67*, 5637–5646. [CrossRef]

© 2020 by the authors. Licensee MDPI, Basel, Switzerland. This article is an open access article distributed under the terms and conditions of the Creative Commons Attribution (CC BY) license (http://creativecommons.org/licenses/by/4.0/).

Article

Eliminating Rank Reversal Problem Using a New Multi-Attribute Model—The RAFSI Method

Mališa Žižović [1], Dragan Pamučar [2,*], Miloljub Albijanić [3], Prasenjit Chatterjee [4] and Ivan Pribićević [5]

1. Faculty of Technical Sciences in Čačak, University of Kragujevac, Svetog Save 65, 32102 Čačak, Serbia; zizovic@gmail.com
2. Department of Logistics, Military academy, University of Defence in Belgrade, Pavla Jurišića Šturma 33, 11000 Belgrade, Serbia
3. Faculty of Economics, Finance and Administration, Metropolitan University, 11000 Belgrade, Serbia; albijanicm@fefa.edu.rs
4. Department of Mechanical Engineering, MCKV Institute of Engineering, West Bengal, Howrah 711204, India; prasenjit2007@gmail.com
5. Simplify Outsourcing d.o.o. Belgrade, 11000 Belgrade, Serbia; ivanp@simplify.rs
* Correspondence: dragan.pamucar@va.mod.gov.rs

Received: 16 May 2020; Accepted: 19 June 2020; Published: 21 June 2020

Abstract: Multi-attribute decision-making (MADM) methods represent reliable ways to solve real-world problems for various applications by providing rational and logical solutions. In reaching such a goal, it is expected that MADM methods would eliminate inconsistencies like rank reversal issues in a given solution. In this paper, an endeavor is taken to put forward a new MADM method, called RAFSI (Ranking of Alternatives through Functional mapping of criterion sub-intervals into a Single Interval), which successfully eliminates the rank reversal problem. The developed RAFSI method has three major advantages that recommend it for further use: (i) its simple algorithm helps in solving complex real-world problems, (ii) RAFSI method has a new approach for data normalization, which transfers data from the starting decision-making matrix into any interval, suitable for making rational decisions, (iii) mathematical formulation of RAFSI method eliminates the rank reversal problem, which is one of the most significant shortcomings of existing MADM methods. A real-time case study that shows the advantages of RAFSI method is presented. Additional comprehensive analysis, including a comparison with other three traditional MADM methods that use different ways for data normalization and testing the resistance of RAFSI method and other MADM methods to rank the reversal problem, is also carried out.

Keywords: multi-criteria optimization; RAFSI method; performance comparison; rank reversal

1. Introduction

Multi-criteria optimization (MCO) methods represent powerful tools for making rational decisions while being engaged in various types of activities. Studies in MCO problems have particularly been prevalent in recent decades [1]. The reasons for such developments lie both in theoretical and practical points of view. In a theoretical sense, MCO is attractive as it studies insufficiently structured problems, while, in a practical sense, MCO represents a powerful way for choosing adequate actions. Furthermore, MCO methods are unavoidable for designing appropriate tools to explore diverse systems.

MCO methods can be classified into five groups [2]: (1) methods for determining non-inferior solutions that determine the set of non-inferior solutions, while it depends on the decision-makers (DMs) to adopt the final solution based on their preferences. The following methods belong to this group: weighting coefficient methods (the restriction method in the criteria functions environment, as well as the Simplex method), (2) methods with a predetermined preference, which are used to form synthesizing (resultant) criterion function (it includes almost all multi-attribute decision-making (MADM) methods, (3) interactive methods in which DMs express their preferences interactively, (4) stochastic methods where indicators of uncertainty are included in the optimization model, and (5) methods for emphasizing a subset of non-inferior solutions that narrow down the subset of non-inferior results, which are achieved by introducing additional elements for making rational decisions.

MADM methods involve sound mathematical steps for processing information to evaluate alternatives concerning a predetermined set of criteria, which is the main focus of this paper. It is performed to establish a ranking of solutions and the best choice. Some of the most predominant representative methods of this group are

- Preference Ranking Organization Method for Enrichment Evaluation (PROMETHEE) [3],
- Više Kriterijumska optimizacija i Kompromisno Rešenje (VIKOR) [4,5],
- Technique for Order Preference by Similarity to Ideal Solution (TOPSIS) [6],
- Analytical Hierarchy Process (AHP) [7],
- Elimination Et Choice Translating Reality (ELECTRE) [8],
- Multi-Attributive Border Approximation Area Comparison (MABAC) [9],
- Complex Proportional Assessment (COPRAS) [10],
- Combinative Distance-based Assessment (CODAS) [11],
- lattice MADM methods [12].

MADM methods play a significant role in solving real-world problems in several areas. Let us mention some interesting studies, which show the diversity of applications of MADM methods. Orji and Wei [13] applied a hybrid decision-making trial and evaluation laboratory (DEMATEL)-TOPSIS model for sustainable supplier selection. Rabbani et al. [14] modified traditional MADM methods using fuzzy sets and demonstrated their application in logistics. Mahdi Paydar et al. [15] applied the fuzzy Multi-Objective Optimization Method by Ratio Analysis (MOORA) and Failure Mode and Effects Analysis (FMEA) methods in the Iranian chemical industry application. Zhou and Xu [16] used DEMATEL, Analytic Network Process (ANP), and VIKOR methods in sustainable supplier selection. Lu et al. [17] extended the ELECTRE method using a rough set theory. Si et al. [18] showed the possibilities of applying picture fuzzy numbers in MADM. Noureddine and Ristic [19] combined the Full Consistency Method (FUCOM), TOPSIS, and MABAC with the Dijkstra algorithm for optimizing the transport of dangerous cargo. Badi et al. [20] used a gray-based assessment model to evaluate healthcare waste treatment alternatives in Libya. Krmac and Djordjevic [21] applied the TOPSIS method for evaluating the influence of the Train Control Information System on capacity utilization.

One of the most important problems that occur in most MADM methods with predetermined preferences is the lack of resistance to rank reversal problems. If unexpected changes in the ranking of alternatives occur when any non-optimal alternative is added or deleted from the existing set of alternatives, this indicates serious mathematical issues in the applied MADM method. This problem can be illustrated with the following example in which three candidates are examined (candidates A, B, and C) who applied for the same work position. A MADM method is used to rank the candidate alternatives and the method suggested the following ranking of the candidates: A > B > C. Furthermore, it is assumed that candidate B (with the second rank) is replaced with a poor candidate D, which kept candidates A and C unchanged. If this new set of alternatives (A, D, and C) is now ranked by the same method under the same criteria weights, it is expected that the applied MADM method would again suggest candidate A as the best solution under the new conditions. However, in actual practice, some unwanted changes in the ranking order of the alternatives occur for the majority of the MADM methods [22].

The rank reversal problem was noticed and presented for the first time by Belton and Gear [22], who analyzed the use of Analytic Hierarchy Process (AHP) for ranking alternatives. In their research, they conducted a simple experiment in which three alternatives and two criteria were analyzed. After the initial ranking of the alternatives, they formed a new set of alternatives by introducing a copy of the non-optimal alternative. After evaluating this new set of alternatives while keeping the same criteria weights, inconsistencies were observed as the ranking order of the best alternative was changed. Thus, they concluded that AHP suffers from rank reversal phenomena. A few years later, Triantaphyllou and Mann [23] noticed the same problem again in AHP when the worst alternative was replaced by a non-optimal alternative. Triantaphyllou and Mann [23] also conducted the same experiment on two other methods, which included the Weighted Sum Model (WSM) and Weighted Product Model (WPM), and concluded that none of these methods were efficient in solving the rank reversal problem. Afterward, Triantaphyllou and Lin [24] further tested five MADM methods, including WSM, WPM, AHP, revised AHP, and TOPSIS in terms of the same two evaluative criteria in the fuzzy environment and came to the same conclusions. Then, many authors pointed out the rank reversal problem in many other MADM methods [25–30].

Furthermore, there is a large number of MADM methods already developed in the past few years, which give successful results for solving practical problems [31]. Nevertheless, most of these methods are not able to successfully eliminate the rank reversal problem. Among such methods, only the lattice MADM method can successfully eliminate the rank reversal problem [12]. However, this method has a complex mathematical algorithm and requires profound knowledge in net theory [32]. The complexity of the lattice algorithm significantly limits its broader use [33]. Moreover, several studies have shown that the rank reversal problem can be solved when traditional methods are substantially modified [34–36]. Keeping in mind that MADM methods are often used in the condition of dynamic changes in the initial decision matrix, authors of this research have paid attention to the development of a new MADM method, called Ranking of Alternatives through Functional mapping of criterion sub-intervals into a Single Interval (RAFSI) method that eliminates rank reversal problems. Besides eliminating the rank reversal problem, RAFSI method is also characterized by simple mathematical formulations that can be easily used for solving complex problems. RAFSI method integrates three starting points for making consistent decisions, which encompass (1) defining referential criteria points including ideal and anti-ideal criteria values, (2) defining relations between the considered alternatives and ideal/anti-ideal values, and (3) using a new technique for data normalization, based on defining criteria functions that map criteria sub-intervals into a unique criteria interval.

According to the results shown in this paper, three main advantages of the RAFSI method distinguish it from the other traditional MADM methods, which include (1) a simple algorithm of RAFSI method that enables DMs to solve complex problems, (2) use a new data normalization technique that converts an initial decision matrix into a unique criterion interval, and (3) resistance of the RAFSI method to rank reversal problems. We are emphasizing this phenomenon since it can be especially seen in dynamic conditions of decision-making where some alternatives often change during the process of making decisions, and MADM methods are often used in such conditions. Based on these advantages of RAFSI method, one of the most important contributions of this paper is to enrich the MADM research domain by developing a new method, which enables the DMs to make stable and coherent decisions in dynamic and uncertain environments.

After the introductory discussion on motivation, goals, and contributions, the content of the paper is presented as follows. In Section 2, the mathematical formulation of the RAFSI method is presented. Section 3 covers the application of RAFSI method for a real-time case study by considering six alternatives and five criteria. Results' validation and performance comparisons are presented in Section 4. Lastly, Section 5 concludes the paper with future research directions.

2. RAFSI Method

Let us assume that the DMs have to rank m alternatives on the basis of n criteria $C_1, C_2, \ldots, C_n$. Criteria weights $(w_j, j = 1, 2, \ldots, n)$ meet the following condition $\sum_{j=1}^{n} w_j = 1$. Criteria $C_1, C_2, \ldots, C_n$ can be maximizing type (*max*) or minimizing type (*min*). Alternatives $A_i (i = 1, 2, \ldots, m)$ are defined by their respective values (a_{ij}) on each criterion (c_j). The initial decision matrix is shown as follows.

$$N = \begin{array}{c} \\ A_1 \\ A_2 \\ \vdots \\ A_m \end{array} \begin{array}{cccc} C_1 & C_2 & \cdots & C_n \\ \left[\begin{array}{cccc} n_{11} & n_{12} & \cdots & n_{1n} \\ n_{21} & n_{22} & \cdots & n_{2n} \\ \vdots & \vdots & \ddots & \vdots \\ n_{m1} & n_{m2} & \cdots & n_{mn} \end{array} \right] \end{array} \quad (1)$$

The RAFSI method has the following steps.

Step 1: Define ideal and anti-ideal values. For each criterion $C_j (j = 1, 2, \ldots, n)$, the DM defines two values a_{I_j} and a_{N_j}, where a_{I_j} represents the ideal value of criterion C_j, while a_{N_j} represents an anti-ideal value of criterion C_j. It is clear that $a_{I_j} > a_{N_j}$ for max criteria and $a_{I_j} < a_{N_j}$ for min criteria.

Step 2: Mapping of elements of the initial decision matrix into criteria intervals. In the previous part, criteria intervals are defined below.

(a) $C_j \in [a_{N_j}, a_{I_j}]$, when C_j belongs to *max* type criteria and
(b) $C_j \in [a_{I_j}, a_{N_j}]$, when C_j belongs to *min* type criteria.

In order to make all criteria of the initial decision matrix equal or transfer them into the criteria interval $[n_1, n_{2k}]$, we are forming a sequence of numbers from the k interval in the way where $k-1$ points are inserted between the highest and the lowest values of the criteria interval.

$$n_1 < n_2 \leq n_3 < n_4 \leq n_5 < n_6 \ldots \leq n_{2k-1} < n_{2k} \quad (2)$$

The criteria interval is constant for all criteria and it has n_1 and n_{2k} fixed points. Then we can map sub-intervals of the criteria into criteria intervals using functions f_1, f_2, f_3, that is f_s, as shown in Figure 1.

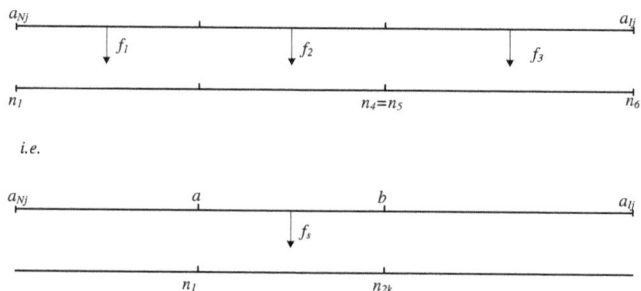

Figure 1. Mapping of sub-intervals into the criteria interval.

The map of minimum value a_{N_j} (for *max* criteria) and a_{I_j} (for *min* criteria) is n_1. Additionally, the map of maximum value a_{I_j} (for *max* criteria) and a_{N_j} (for *min* criteria) is n_{2k}. It is suggested that the ideal value is at least six times better than the anti-ideal (barely acceptable value), or $n_1 = 1$ and $n_{2k} = 6$. However, the DM can use other preferred values such as $n_1 = 1$ and $n_{2k} = 9$.

We define a function $f_s(x)$, which maps sub-intervals into the criteria interval $[n_1, n_{2k}]$ by Formula (3) below. The endpoints of the interval $[n_1, n_{2k}]$ determine the ratio of a barely acceptable alternative to the ideal alternative. This ratio is set up by the DM.

$$f_s(x) = \frac{n_{2k} - n_1}{a_{I_j} - a_{N_j}} x + \frac{a_{I_j} \cdot n_1 - a_{N_j} \cdot n_{2k}}{a_{I_j} - a_{N_j}} \quad (3)$$

where n_{2k} and n_1 represent the relation that shows the extent to which the ideal value is preferred over the anti-ideal value, and where a_{I_j} and a_{N_j} represent ideal and anti-ideal values of criteria C_j, respectively.

Expression (3), as a function, can be part of the function, which maps a part of the interval $[a_{N_j}, a_{I_j}]$ into interval $[n_1, n_{2k}]$. In this case, all these parts, that is, all functions $f_1(x), f_2(x)...,f_n(x)$, represent a function $f_s(x)$ that maps the entire criterion interval into a defined numerical interval. Thus, Expression (3) can represent a function that maps a part of an interval, but can also map a complete criterion interval into the corresponding numerical interval. Therefore, the numbers a_{I_j} and a_{N_j} can represent: (1) values from inside the criterion interval or (2) endpoints of the criterion interval. The second possibility is used in this paper.

In this way, the standardized decision matrix $S = [s_{ij}]_{m \times n}$ $(i = 1, 2, \ldots, m, \; j = 1, 2, \ldots, n)$ is obtained in which all elements of the matrix are mapped into the interval $[n_1, n_{2k}]$. After functional mapping of the elements of the initial decision matrix into criteria interval N $[n_1, n_{2k}]$, the condition $n_1 \leq s_{ij} \leq n_{2k}$ is achieved for every I, j.

$$S = \begin{array}{c} \\ A_1 \\ A_2 \\ \vdots \\ A_m \end{array} \begin{array}{c} C_1 \; C_2 \; \ldots \; C_n \\ \left[\begin{array}{cccc} s_{11} & s_{12} & \cdots & s_{1n} \\ s_{21} & s_{22} & \cdots & s_{2n} \\ \vdots & \vdots & \ddots & \vdots \\ s_{m1} & s_{m2} & \cdots & s_{mn} \end{array} \right] \end{array} \quad (4)$$

In the above formula, the elements of the matrix s_{ij} are obtained by using expression (3), that is, $s_{ij} = f_{A_i}(C_j)$.

Note the following:

(a) for *max* type criteria, if there is a_{x_j} where $a_{x_j} > a_{I_j}$, then we have equality $f(a_{x_j}) = f(a_{I_j})$

(b) for *min* type criteria, if there is a_{x_j} where $a_{x_j} < a_{I_j}$, then we have equality $f(a_{x_j}) = f(a_{I_j})$

Step 3: Calculate arithmetic and harmonic means. Using expressions (5) and (6), arithmetic and harmonic means are calculated for minimum and maximum sequence of the elements n_1 and n_{2k}.

$$A = \frac{n_1 + n_{2k}}{2} \quad (5)$$

$$H = \frac{2}{\frac{1}{n_1} + \frac{1}{n_{2k}}} \quad (6)$$

Step 4: Form normalized decision matrix $\hat{S} = [\hat{s}_{ij}]_{m \times n}$ $(i = 1, 2, \ldots, m, \; j = 1, 2, \ldots, n)$. Using expressions (7) and (8), elements of the matrix S are normalized, and transferred into the interval $[0,1]$.

(a) for the criteria C_j $(j = 1, 2, \ldots, n)$ max type:

$$\hat{s}_{ij} = \frac{s_{ij}}{2A} \quad (7)$$

(b) for the criteria C_j ($j = 1, 2, \ldots, n$) min type:

$$\hat{s}_{ij} = \frac{H}{2s_{ij}} \qquad (8)$$

In this way, a new normalized decision matrix is created, as shown below.

$$\hat{S} = \begin{array}{c} \\ A_1 \\ A_2 \\ \vdots \\ A_m \end{array} \begin{bmatrix} C_1 & C_2 & \cdots & C_n \\ \hat{s}_{11} & \hat{s}_{12} & \cdots & \hat{s}_{1n} \\ \hat{s}_{21} & \hat{s}_{22} & \cdots & \hat{s}_{2n} \\ \vdots & \vdots & \ddots & \vdots \\ \hat{s}_{m1} & \hat{s}_{m2} & \cdots & \hat{s}_{mn} \end{bmatrix} \qquad (9)$$

where $\hat{s}_{ij} \in [0, 1]$ represents normalized elements of $\hat{S}$.

For the elements of the normalized decision matrix $\hat{S} = [\hat{s}_{ij}]_{m \times n}$, which are defined using Expressions (7) and (8), the following relations can apply.

(a) For max type criteria C_j ($j = 1, 2, \ldots, n$), we have the following condition.

$$0 < \frac{n_1}{2A} \leq \hat{s}_{ij} \leq \frac{n_{2k}}{2A} < 1 \qquad (10)$$

Proof of (10):

$$\frac{n_{2k}}{2A} = \frac{n_{2k}}{2\frac{n_1 + n_{2k}}{2}} = \frac{n_{2k}}{n_1 + n_{2k}} < \frac{n_{2k} + n_1}{n_1 + n_{2k}} = 1$$

(b) for min type criteria C_j ($j = 1, 2, \ldots, n$), we have the following condition.

$$0 < \frac{H}{2n_{2k}} \leq \hat{s}_{ij} \leq \frac{H}{2n_1} < 1 \qquad (11)$$

Proof of (11):

$$\frac{H}{2n_1} = \frac{\frac{2}{\frac{1}{n_{2k}} + \frac{1}{n_1}}}{2n_1} = \frac{1}{n_1\left(\frac{1}{n_{2k}} + \frac{1}{n_1}\right)} = \frac{1}{1 + \frac{n_1}{n_{2k}}} < 1$$

Additionally, for the boundary values of criteria intervals n_1 and n_{2k}, we have the following equality (12) and (13).

$$\frac{n_1}{2A} = \frac{H}{2n_{2k}} \qquad (12)$$

Proof of (12):

$$\frac{n_1}{2A} = \frac{H}{2n_{2k}} \Rightarrow \frac{n_1}{A} = \frac{H}{n_{2k}}$$

$$\frac{n_1}{A} = \frac{n_1}{\frac{n_1 + n_{2k}}{2}} = \frac{2}{\frac{n_1 + n_{2k}}{n_1}} = \frac{2}{1 + \frac{n_{2k}}{n_1}}$$

$$= \frac{2}{\frac{n_{2k}}{n_{2k}} + \frac{n_{2k}}{n_1}} = \frac{2}{n_{2k}\left(\frac{1}{n_{2k}} + \frac{1}{n_1}\right)} = \frac{\frac{1}{n_{2k}} + \frac{1}{n_1}}{n_{2k}} = \frac{H}{n_{2k}}$$

$$\frac{n_{2k}}{2A} = \frac{H}{2n_1} \qquad (13)$$

Proof of equality (13):

$$\frac{n_{2k}}{2A} = \frac{H}{2n_1} \Rightarrow \frac{n_{2k}}{A} = \frac{H}{n_1}$$

$$\frac{n_{2k}}{A} = \frac{n_{2k}}{\frac{n_1+n_{2k}}{2}} = \frac{2}{\frac{n_1+n_{2k}}{n_{2k}}} = \frac{2}{\frac{n_1}{n_{2k}}+1}$$
$$= \frac{2}{\frac{n_1}{n_{2k}}+\frac{n_1}{n_1}} = \frac{2}{n_1\left(\frac{1}{n_{2k}}+\frac{1}{n_1}\right)} = \frac{1}{n_1}\cdot\frac{2}{\frac{1}{n_{2k}}+\frac{1}{n_1}} = \frac{H}{n_1}$$

Step 5: Calculate criteria functions of the alternatives $V(A_i)$. Criteria functions of the alternatives ($V(A_i)$) are calculated according to Equation (14) below. Alternatives are then ranked according to the descending order of the calculated ($V(A_i)$) values.

$$V(A_i) = w_1\hat{s}_{i1} + w_2\hat{s}_{i2} + \ldots + w_n\hat{s}_{in} \tag{14}$$

3. Case Study and Results

In this section, the application of the newly developed RFIS method is presented by giving an example that considers the evaluation of six alternatives A_i ($i = 1, 2, \ldots, 6$) in relation to five criteria C_j ($j = 1, 2, \ldots, 5$). Suppose that the alternatives represent researchers who applied for a job at a scientific research center. Evaluation of the researchers is performed using five criteria. The criteria are arranged in two groups: 1) criteria of maximizing type (max): C1, C2, and C5, and 2) criteria of minimizing type (min): C3 and C4. Criteria weights are estimated by the Level-Based Weight Assessment (LBWA) model [26] as w_j = (0.35, 0.25, 0.15, 0.15, 0.1). The initial decision matrix ($N = [n_{ij}]_{m \times n}, i = 1, 2, \ldots, m, j = 1, 2, \ldots, n$) is given below.

	C1	C2	C3	C4	C5
A1	180	10.5	15.5	160	3.7
A2	165	9.2	16.5	131	5
A3	160	8.8	14	125	4.5
A4	170	9.5	16	135	3.4
A5	185	10	14.5	143	4.3
A6	167	8.9	15.1	140	4.1
	max	max	min	min	max

Application of RAFSI method is illustrated by following the steps described in Section 2.

Step 1: In the first step, DM defines the set of ideal (a_{I_j}) and anti-ideal values (a_{N_j}) for the considered criteria. In this example, the following ideal and anti-deal points are defined by consensus.

$$a_{I_j} = \{200, 12, 10, 100, 8\}$$

$$a_{N_j} = \{120, 6, 20, 200, 2\}$$

Step 2: Based on the defined ideal and anti-ideal points, criteria intervals are formed.

(a) for max type criteria: $C_1 \in [120, 200]$; $C_2 \in [6, 12]$ i $C_5 \in [2, 8]$,
(b) for min type criteria: $C_3 \in [10, 20]$ i $C_4 \in [100, 200]$.

To transfer the values of all criteria into a unique interval, a sequence of numbers is chosen where $n_1 < n_2 \leq n_3 < n_4 \leq n_5 < n_6 \ldots \leq n_{2k-1} < n_{2k}$. The final points of the sequence n_1 and n_{2k} define the values determining the number of times the ideal value is better than the anti-ideal value. In other words, points n_1 and n_{2k} determine the boundary values of the interval in which all values of the initial decision matrix are transferred. In this paper, it is assumed that the ideal value is six times better than the barely acceptable value (anti-ideal value). Now, the functions for criteria standardization are defined using expression (3). It helps to transfer the values of the initial decision matrix into the interval $[1, 6]$. Therefore, we consider the following functions.

$$f_{A_i}(C_1) = \frac{6-1}{200-120}C_1 + \frac{200 \cdot 1 - 120 \cdot 6}{200-120} = 0.06 \cdot C_1 - 6.50$$

$$f_{A_i}(C_2) = \frac{6-1}{12-6}C_2 + \frac{12 \cdot 1 - 6 \cdot 6}{12-6} = 0.83 \cdot C_2 - 4.00$$

$$f_{A_i}(C_3) = \frac{6-1}{20-10}C_3 + \frac{20 \cdot 1 - 10 \cdot 6}{20-10} = 0.50 \cdot C_3 - 4.00$$

$$f_{A_i}(C_4) = \frac{6-1}{200-10}C_4 + \frac{200 \cdot 1 - 100 \cdot 6}{200-100} = 0.05 \cdot C_4 - 4.00$$

$$f_{A_i}(C_5) = \frac{6-1}{8-2}C_5 + \frac{8 \cdot 1 - 2 \cdot 6}{8-2} = 0.83 \cdot C_5 - 0.67$$

Based on the defined functions, the elements of the initial decision matrix are mapped into the interval $[1, 6]$ and the standardized decision matrix ($S = [s_{ij}]_{6 \times 5}, i = 1, 2, \ldots, 6, j = 1, 2, \ldots, 5$) is obtained in which all elements are transferred into the interval $[1, 6]$.

$$S = \begin{array}{c} \\ A1 \\ A2 \\ A3 \\ A4 \\ A5 \\ A6 \\ \end{array} \begin{array}{c} \begin{array}{ccccc} C1 & C2 & C3 & C4 & C5 \end{array} \\ \left[\begin{array}{ccccc} 4.75 & 4.75 & 3.75 & 4.00 & 2.42 \\ 3.81 & 3.67 & 4.25 & 2.55 & 3.50 \\ 3.50 & 3.33 & 3.00 & 2.25 & 3.08 \\ 4.13 & 3.92 & 4.00 & 2.75 & 2.17 \\ 5.06 & 4.33 & 3.25 & 3.15 & 2.92 \\ 3.94 & 3.42 & 3.55 & 3.00 & 2.75 \end{array} \right] \\ \begin{array}{ccccc} max & max & min & min & max \end{array} \end{array}$$

The elements of the position A_i-C_1 are obtained using the functions $f_{A_i}(C_1) = 0.06 \cdot C_1 - 6.50$:

$$f_{A_1}(180) = 0.06 \cdot 180 - 6.50 = 4.75, \quad f_{A_2}(165) = 0.06 \cdot 165 - 6.50 = 3.81$$

$$f_{A_3}(160) = 0.06 \cdot 160 - 6.50 = 3.50, \quad f_{A_4}(170) = 0.06 \cdot 170 - 6.50 = 4.13$$

$$f_{A_5}(185) = 0.06 \cdot 185 - 6.50 = 5.06, \quad f_{A_6}(167) = 0.06 \cdot 167 - 6.50 = 3.94$$

Replacing the values from the initial matrix into functions $f_{A_i}(C_2)$, $f_{A_i}(C_3)$, $f_{A_i}(C_4)$, and $f_{A_i}(C_5)$, we get the remaining values of elements of s_{ij}.

Step 3: Calculating the arithmetic and harmonic means of minimum and maximum elements $n_1 = 1$ and $n_{2k} = 6$.

$$A = (n_1 + n_{2k})/2 = (1 + 6)/2 = 3.5$$

$$H = \frac{2}{\frac{1}{n_1} + \frac{1}{n_{2k}}} = \frac{2}{\frac{1}{1} + \frac{1}{6}} = 1.71$$

The arithmetic mean for $n_1 = 1$ and $n_{2k} = 6$ is 3.5, while the harmonic mean is 1.71.

Step 4: Using expressions (7) and (8) elements of matrix S are normalized and transformed, depending on whether they belong to min or max type criteria. In this way, we get a new matrix $\hat{S} = \left[\hat{s}_{ij}\right]_{6\times5}$ ($i = 1, 2, \ldots, 6, j = 1, 2, \ldots, 5$).

$$\hat{S} = \begin{array}{c} \\ A1 \\ A2 \\ A3 \\ A4 \\ A5 \\ A6 \\ \end{array} \begin{array}{ccccc} C1 & C2 & C3 & C4 & C5 \\ \left[\begin{array}{ccccc} 0.68 & 0.68 & 0.23 & 0.21 & 0.35 \\ 0.54 & 0.52 & 0.20 & 0.34 & 0.50 \\ 0.50 & 0.48 & 0.29 & 0.38 & 0.44 \\ 0.59 & 0.56 & 0.21 & 0.31 & 0.31 \\ 0.72 & 0.62 & 0.26 & 0.27 & 0.42 \\ 0.56 & 0.49 & 0.24 & 0.29 & 0.39 \\ \end{array}\right] \\ max & max & min & min & max \end{array}$$

For example, the element of the matrix $\hat{S}$ in position A1–C1 is $\hat{s}_{11} = \frac{4.75}{2\cdot3.5} = 0.68$. Moreover, for the min type criteria, A1–C3 is $\hat{s}_{13} = \frac{1.71}{2\cdot3.75} = 0.23$.

Step 5: Using expression (14), criteria functions $V(A_i)$ of the alternatives are calculated, as exhibited in Table 1. Ranking pre-order of the alternatives is derived as per the descending order of $V(A_i)$ values, where the alternative with higher $V(A_i)$ values are always preferred.

Table 1. The function criteria and the final ranking of the researchers/alternatives.

Alternative	$V(A_i)$	Rank
A1	0.5081	2
A2	0.4522	4
A3	0.4381	5
A4	0.4560	3
A5	0.5299	1
A6	0.4373	6

Based on the above findings, the researcher A5 is selected as the best alternative candidate for the considered case study.

4. Validation of the Results

4.1. Comparing the Results with Other MADM Methods

For validation, the results of RFIS method are now compared with other traditional MADM methods like TOPSIS [6], VIKOR [4,5], and COPRAS [10]. The same decision matrix and criteria weights are used for this performance comparison. The results of this comparison are shown in Figure 2.

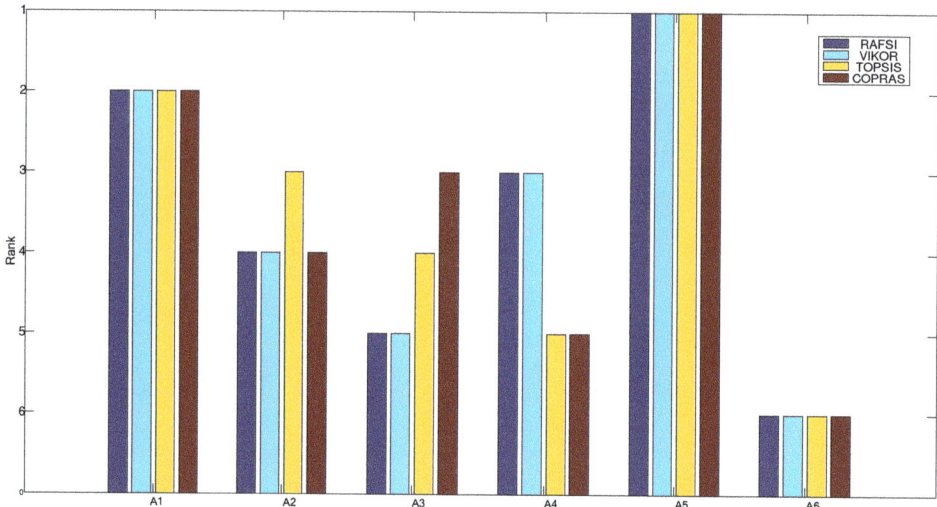

Figure 2. Comparing RAFSI method with other MADM methods.

The ranking orders as obtained by VIKOR and RAFSI methods are in complete agreement, whereas, in COPRAS and TOPSIS methods, the rank similarity is observed only for the first two alternatives {A5, A1}, and the last ranked alternative (A6). For the remaining three alternatives (A2, A3, and A4), COPRAS and TOPSIS methods suggested different rankings. Such a result is a consequence of using different data normalization techniques, such as vector normalization (in TOPSIS method) and additive normalization (in the COPRAS method). To confirm this fact, an experiment is further conducted, which was comprised of the following two stages.

(1) In the first stage, the COPRAS and TOPSIS methods were slightly modified through the use of additive data normalization techniques in both methods. It was observed that both methods gave the same ranking order (Figure 2) for the considered alternatives under additive data normalization.

(2) In the second stage, data normalization, as suggested in RAFSI method, was also used for TOPSIS, VIKOR, and COPRAS methods. After using the new normalization technique, identical rankings were obtained by all the methods. Based on these results, it can be concluded that the RAFSI method gives credible and reliable results.

4.2. Rank Reversal Problem

One of the ways to check the stability of MADM methods is by introducing new alternatives in the original set or by eliminating poor alternatives from the set. In such conditions, it is expected that the MADM method will not show any drastic change in the ranking of the alternatives. This phenomenon is called the well popular rank reversal problem [13], and considerable attention has already been paid to it in the literature [21,25]. The resistance of the developed RAFSI method to the rank reversal problem is now tested through two experiments. In the first experiment, five scenarios are considered. In each scenario, the worst alternative is eliminated from the set of alternatives, and the impact of this change on ranking and criteria functions of the alternatives are analyzed. In the second experiment, the set of alternatives is further expanded by introducing a new alternative, and the impact of such inclusion on alternatives' rank is analysed.

The first experiment: After applying RAFSI method, the researchers are ranked according to the results shown in scenario S0 (the original rank). In the next scenario (S1), the researcher who achieved the least rank is eliminated. After that, the remaining five candidates are again ranked. Thus, a total of five scenarios (S1–S5) are formed, whereby, in each subsequent scenario, the worst-ranked researcher from the set is eliminated. At the same time, we also analyzed the possibility of any changes in criteria function values and rankings of the remaining alternatives for each of the newly formed scenarios. The rankings of the alternatives in all five scenarios are shown in Table 2.

Table 2. The ranking of the alternatives in scenarios.

Alternative	S0	S1	S2	S3	S4	S5
A5	1	1	1	1	1	1
A1	2	2	2	2	2	
A4	3	3	3	3		
A2	4	4	4			
A3	5	5				
A6	6					

From Table 2, it is easy to observe that RAFSI method gives valid results in a dynamic environment. This is also confirmed by criteria function values of the alternatives $(f(A_i))$. In all these scenarios, the criteria functions of the alternatives remained unchanged. TOPSIS, VIKOR, and COPRAS methods are used in the same condition. All these methods also showed stability and resistance to rank reversal. However, changes in criteria function values are observed in these methods.

The second experiment: In the second experiment, among the six existing candidates, another candidate (A7) is added who achieved the same test results as compared to candidate A6. The new decision matrix is shown below.

$$N = \begin{array}{c} \\ A1 \\ A2 \\ A3 \\ A4 \\ A5 \\ A6 \\ A7 \\ \\ \end{array} \begin{bmatrix} C1 & C2 & C3 & C4 & C5 \\ 180 & 10.5 & 15.5 & 160 & 3.7 \\ 165 & 9.2 & 16.5 & 131 & 5 \\ 160 & 8.8 & 14 & 125 & 4.5 \\ 170 & 9.5 & 16 & 135 & 3.4 \\ 185 & 10 & 14.5 & 143 & 4.3 \\ 167 & 8.9 & 15.1 & 140 & 4.1 \\ 165 & 8.9 & 11 & 120 & 3.5 \\ max & max & min & min & max \end{bmatrix}$$

After evaluating the new set of candidates by RAFSI, TOPSIS, VIKOR, and COPRAS methods with the same criteria weights, it was observed that the rankings and criteria functions of certain alternatives are changed, as shown in Table 3. To compare the results more comprehensively, a parallel presentation of the results is given using RAFSI, TOPSIS, VIKOR, and COPRAS methods on the new and old set of alternatives.

Table 3. Ranking pre-orders for the old and new set of the alternatives.

		A1	A2	A3	A4	A5	A6	A7
	$f(Ai)$							
RAFSI	Original $f(Ai)$	$f(A1) = 0.508$	$f(A2) = 0.452$	$f(A3) = 0.438$	$f(A4) = 0.456$	$f(A5) = 0.530$	$f(A6) = 0.437$	
	Original rank	2	4	5	3	1	6	
	New $f(Ai)$	$f(A1) = 0.508$	$f(A2) = 0.452$	$f(A3) = 0.438$	$f(A4) = 0.456$	$f(A5) = 0.530$	$f(A6) = 0.437$	$f(A7) = 0.495$
	New rank	2	5	6	4	1	7	3
VIKOR	Original $f(Ai)$	$f(A1) = 0.350$	$f(A2) = 0.901$	$f(A3) = 0.924$	$f(A4) = 0.801$	$f(A5) = 0.00$	$f(A6) = 0.928$	
	Original rank	2	4	5	3	1	6	
	New $f(Ai)$	$f(A1) = 0.274$	$f(A2) = 0.817$	$f(A3) = 1.000$	$f(A4) = 0.738$	$f(A5) = 0.00$	$f(A6) = 0.920$	$f(A7) = 0.718$
	New rank	2	5	7	4	1	6	3
TOPSIS	Original $f(Ai)$	$f(A1) = 0.542$	$f(A2) = 0.464$	$f(A3) = 0.431$	$f(A4) = 0.396$	$f(A5) = 0.704$	$f(A6) = 0.351$	
	Original rank	2	3	4	5	1	6	
	New $f(Ai)$	$f(A1) = 0.468$	$f(A2) = 0.400$	$f(A3) = 0.410$	$f(A4) = 0.340$	$f(A5) = 0.593$	$f(A6) = 0.311$	$f(A7) = 0.507$
	New rank	3	5	4	6	1	7	2
COPRAS	Original $f(Ai)$	$f(A1) = 0.964$	$f(A2) = 0.950$	$f(A3) = 0.951$	$f(A4) = 0.932$	$f(A5) = 1.00$	$f(A6) = 0.930$	
	Original rank	2	4	3	5	1	6	
	New $f(Ai)$	$f(A1) = 0.962$	$f(A2) = 0.952$	$f(A3) = 0.957$	$f(A4) = 0.933$	$f(A5) = 1.00$	$f(A6) = 0.933$	$f(A7) = 0.998$
	New rank	3	5	4	6	1	7	2

After analyzing the results of Table 3, we can conclude the following

(1) COPRAS method: The new candidate A7 was ranked second in the ranking order, so it is clear that all the candidates (except the first ranked) moved one place down in the ranking order. Furthermore, it is expected that the values of criteria functions $f(Ai)$ for an old set of the alternatives $f(A1), f(A2), \ldots, f(A6)$ would not change, which signifies the function of an $f(A7)$ of the new alternative would be ranked based on the old values of $f(Ai)$. However, from Table 3, after introducing the new alternative, a change in $f(Ai)$ values are observed for the COPRAS method. This fact can cause inconsistencies in ranking order of the alternatives.

(2) TOPSIS method: The introduction of the new alternative resulted in a significant change in the ranking order as well as changes in $f(Ai)$ values that are also observed. Alternative A7 is placed in the second position. Therefore, it is clear that the ranks of the other alternatives moved one place down. However, the same did not happen for alternative A3 as it remained in the fourth position in both new and old sets of alternatives. Additionally, alternative A2 was third in the old set, while, in the new set, it is in the fifth position instead of the fourth. These kinds of changes in alternatives' ranking are observed with changes in $f(Ai)$ values.

(3) VIKOR method: In this method, similar changes happened as in the previous two methods. The new alternative A7 is placed in the third position. It is expected that, in the new set of alternatives, all the alternatives below the third rank would move one place down. However, some more drastic changes are noticed in the VIKOR method. For example, alternative A3 was in the fifth rank in the old set, but, in the new set, it is ranked last. Moreover, alternative A6 was last in the old set of alternatives, while it is in the second to last in the new set of alternatives. These changes in the ranking order also followed with the changes in $f(Ai)$ values.

(4) RAFSI method: This method showed stability in both sets of alternatives. All the alternatives kept the same $f(Ai)$ values in both sets. Thus, it can be concluded that the RAFSI method has shown logical results following the new set of alternatives.

Based on these analyses, we can conclude that rank reversal problems exist in COPRAS, TOPSIS, and VIKOR methods can lead to irrational results in conditions where we have changeable initial parameters in the decision matrix. At the same time, we can conclude that the developed RAFSI method is resistant to rank reversal problems, which contributes to achieving stable and reliable evaluation results while solving complex real-world problems.

5. Discussion and Conclusions

In this paper, a new MADM method, called RAFSI, is suggested, which shows a high level of reliability in results. This makes this method suitable for solving real-time MADM problems in different areas. The mathematical formulation of the RAFSI method does not use traditional data normalization expression. Instead, a new technique for standardization is suggested that enables data transformation from the initial decision matrix into any interval, which makes this method suitable for rational decision making. The mapping of criteria sub-intervals from the initial decision matrix into a unique criteria interval is done by using criteria functions. After forming a unique criteria interval, using arithmetic and harmonic means, the criteria interval is transformed into a normalized criteria interval. This mapping is done depending on the criteria type. Therefore, we can highlight the following contributions of this paper: (1) the development of a new MADM method for solving real problems in the business world, (2) presentation of the new method that is based on coherent defining relations between ideal and anti-ideal criteria values, (3) it eliminates the rank reversal problem and offers reliable results for making rational decisions, (4) development of a new method for the data normalization, which can be used in various areas, from MADM to heuristic algorithms and artificial intelligence-based methods.

The RAFSI method is validated through a comparison of the results with traditional MADM methods and by checking resistance to rank reversal problems. The performance comparison of the results of the RAFSI method is done with TOPSIS, COPRAS, and VIKOR methods. These methods are chosen because they use different ways of data normalization like vector, linear normalization, and additive normalization. The goal of comparison with different methods is to confirm the validity of the new method by concerning traditional MADM methods that have already shown high efficiency in solving real-world problems. The performance comparison results showed a very high level of a positive correlation between the results of the RAFSI method and other widely used MCO methods.

After comparing the ranks in the second phase, the validity of resistance of RAFSI, TOPSIS, COPRAS, and VIKOR methods to rank reversal problem is executed. In these experiments, the change in the number of alternatives is simulated. In the first experiment, the number of alternatives is reduced in five scenarios, while, in the second experiment, a set of alternatives is expanded by introducing one non-optimal alternative. The results showed that the RAFSI method is resistant to the rank reversal problem. On the other hand, the conventional TOPSIS, COPRAS, and VIKOR methods did not show satisfying results. The achieved results confirm the validity of RAFSI methods and can be recommended for using in future research for solving different multi-criteria problems.

The goals of future research should be aimed into the direction of using the RAFSI method for other real problems as well as combining with objective and subjective criteria weighting techniques. Furthermore, one of the goals of future research also lies in expanding RAFSI method by using different uncertainty theories. Using uncertainty theories, it would enable the use of linguistic variables for rational expression of human preferences. In addition, the use of new data normalization techniques in heuristic algorithms and other MADM methods can be a future research scope.

Author Contributions: Conceptualization, M.Ž. and D.P. Methodology, M.Ž. and D.P. Validation, M.Ž. and D.P. Writing—original draft preparation, M.Ž. and D.P. Review and editing, M.A., P.C., and I.P. All authors have read and agreed to the published version of the manuscript.

Funding: This research received no external funding.

Conflicts of Interest: The authors declare no conflict of interest.

References

1. Kahraman, C.; Büyüközkan, G.; Ates, N.Y. A two phase multi-attribute decision-making approach for new product introduction. *Inf. Sci.* **2007**, *177*, 1567–1582. [CrossRef]
2. Nassiri, P.; Dehrashid, S.A.; Hashemi, M.; Shalkouhi, P.J. Traffic Noise Prediction and the Influence of Vehicle Horn Noise. *J. Low Freq. Noise, Vib. Act. Control.* **2013**, *32*, 285–291. [CrossRef]
3. Brans, J.P. L'ingénierie de la Décision: Élaborationd'instrumentsd'aide à la Décision. La Méthode Promethee; Presses de l'Université Laval: Quebec City, QC, Canada, 1982.
4. Duckstein, L.; Opricovic, S. Multiobjective optimization in river basin development. *Water Resour. Res.* **1980**, *16*, 14–20. [CrossRef]
5. Opricovic, S.; Tzeng, G.-H. Compromise solution by MCDM methods: A comparative analysis of VIKOR and TOPSIS. *Eur. J. Oper. Res.* **2004**, *156*, 445–455. [CrossRef]
6. Hwang, C.-L.; Yoon, K. *Multiple Attribute Decision Making: Methods and Applications*; Springer: New York, NY, USA, 1981.
7. Saaty, T.L. *The Analytic Hierarchy Process*; McGraw-Hill: New York, NY, USA, 1980.
8. Bernard, R. Classementetchoixenprésence de points de vue multiples (la méthode ELECTRE). *La Revue d'Informatiqueet de RechercheOpérationelle (RIRO)* **1968**, *8*, 57–75.
9. Pamucar, D.; Cirovic, G. The selection of transport and handling resources in logistics centres using Multi-Attributive Border Approximation area Comparison (MABAC). *Expert Syst. Appl.* **2015**, *42*, 3016–3028. [CrossRef]
10. Zavadskas, E.K.; Kaklauskas, A.; Sarka, V. The new method of multicriteria complex proportional assessment of projects. *Technol. Econ. Dev. Econ.* **1994**, *1*, 131–139.
11. Keshavarz Ghorabaee, M.; Zavadskas, E.K.; Turskis, Z.; Antucheviciene, J. A new combinative distance-based assessment (CODAS) method for multi-criteria decision-making. *Econ. Comput. Econ. Cybern. Stud. Res.* **2016**, *50*, 25–44.

12. Zizovic, M.; Damljanovic, N.; Lazarevic, V.; Deretic, N. New method for multicriteria analysis. *UPB Sci. Bull. Ser. A Appl. Math. Phys.* **2011**, *73*, 13–22.
13. Orji, I.; Wei, S. A decision support tool for sustainable supplier selection in manufacturing firms. *J. Ind. Eng. Manag.* **2014**, *7*, 1293–1315. [CrossRef]
14. Rabbani, M.; Foroozesh, N.; Mousavi, S.M.; Farrokhi-Asl, H. Sustainable supplier selection by a new decision model based on interval-valued fuzzy sets and possibilistic statistical reference point systems under uncertainty. *Int. J. Syst. Sci. Oper. Logist.* **2017**, *6*, 162–178. [CrossRef]
15. Paydar, M.M.; Arabsheybani, A.; SattarSafaei, A. A new approach for sustainable supplier selection. *Int. J. Ind. Eng. Prod. Res.* **2017**, *28*, 47–59. [CrossRef]
16. Zhou, X.; Xu, Z. An Integrated Sustainable Supplier Selection Approach Based on Hybrid Information Aggregation. *Sustainability* **2018**, *10*, 2543. [CrossRef]
17. Lu, H.; Jiang, S.; Song, W.; Ming, X. A Rough Multi-Criteria Decision-Making Approach for Sustainable Supplier Selection under Vague Environment. *Sustainability* **2018**, *10*, 2622. [CrossRef]
18. Si, A.; Das, S.; Kar, S. An Approach to Rank Picture Fuzzy Numbers for Decision Making Problems. *Decis. Making: Appl. Manag. Eng.* **2019**, *2*, 54–64. [CrossRef]
19. Noureddine, M.; Ristic, M. Route planning for hazardous materials transportation: Multi-criteria decision-making approach. *Decis. Mak. Appl. Manag. Eng.* **2019**, *2*, 66–84. [CrossRef]
20. Badi, I.; Shetwan, A.; Hemeda, A. A grey-based assessment model to evaluate health-care waste treatment alternatives in Libya. *Oper. Res. Eng. Sci. Theory Appl.* **2019**, *2*, 92–106. [CrossRef]
21. Krmac, E.; Djordjević, B. Evaluation of the TCIS Influence on the capacity utilization using the TOPSIS method: Case studies of Serbian and Austrian railways. *Oper. Res. Eng. Sci. Theory Appl.* **2019**, *2*, 27–36. [CrossRef]
22. Belton, V.; Gear, T. On a Short-Coming of Saaty's Method of Analytic Hierarchies. *Omega* **1983**, *11*, 228–230. [CrossRef]
23. Triantaphyllou, E.; Mann, S.H. An examination of the effectiveness of multi-dimensional decision-making methods: A decision-making paradox. *Decis. Support Syst.* **1989**, *5*, 303–312. [CrossRef]
24. Triantaphyllou, E.; Lin, C.-T. Development and evaluation of five fuzzy multiattribute decision-making methods. *Int. J. Approx. Reason.* **1996**, *14*, 281–310. [CrossRef]
25. Triantaphyllou, E. *Multi-Criteria Decision Making: A Comparative Study*; Springer: Dordrecht, The Netherlands, 2000; Volume 44, pp. 241–262.
26. Saaty, T. Making and validating complex decisions with the AHP/ANP. *J. Syst. Sci. Syst. Eng.* **2005**, *14*, 1–36. [CrossRef]
27. Kujawski, E. A reference-dependent regret model for deterministic tradeoff studies. *Syst. Eng.* **2005**, *8*, 119–137. [CrossRef]
28. Leskinen, P.; Kangas, J. Rank reversals in multi-criteria decision analysis with statistical modelling of ratio-scale pairwise comparisons. *J. Oper. Res. Soc.* **2005**, *56*, 855–861. [CrossRef]
29. Pamucar, D.; Božanić, D.; Randjelovic, A. Multi-criteria decision making: An example of sensitivity analysis. *Serbian J. Manag.* **2017**, *12*, 1–27. [CrossRef]
30. Mukhametzyanov, I.; Pamucar, D. A Sensitivity analysis in MCDM problems: A statistical approach. *Decis. Making: Appl. Manag. Eng.* **2018**, *1*, 51–80. [CrossRef]
31. Stević, Z.; Pamucar, D.; Puška, A.; Chatterjee, P. Sustainable supplier selection in healthcare industries using a new MCDM method: Measurement of alternatives and ranking according to Compromise solution (MARCOS). *Comput. Ind. Eng.* **2020**, *140*, 106231. [CrossRef]
32. Zizovic, M.; Damljanovic, N. Main advantage of lattice MCD-method. In Proceedings of the 13th Conference on Mathematics and its Applications, Timisoara, Romania, 1–3 November 2012; pp. 315–320.
33. Damljanovic, N.; Petojevic, A.; Zizovic, M. Comparative application of lattice MCD-method with Promethee-method. In Proceedings of the 13th Conference on Mathematics and its Applications, Timisoara, Romania, 1–3 November 2012; pp. 205–210.
34. Petrović, G.; Mihajlović, J.; Ćojbašić, Ž.; Madić, M.; Marinković, D. Comparison of three fuzzy MCDM methods for solving the supplier selection problem. *Facta Univ. Ser. Mech. Eng.* **2019**, *17*, 455–469. [CrossRef]

35. Diyaley, S.; Chakraborty, S. Optimization of multi-pass face milling parameters using metaheuristic algorithms. *Facta Univ. Ser. Mech. Eng.* **2019**, *17*, 365–383. [CrossRef]
36. Žižović, M.; Pamučar, D. New model for determining criteria weights: Level Based Weight Assessment (LBWA) model. *Decis. Mak. Appl. Manag. Eng.* **2019**, *2*, 126–137. [CrossRef]

© 2020 by the authors. Licensee MDPI, Basel, Switzerland. This article is an open access article distributed under the terms and conditions of the Creative Commons Attribution (CC BY) license (http://creativecommons.org/licenses/by/4.0/).

Article

Novel Extension of DEMATEL Method by Trapezoidal Fuzzy Numbers and D Numbers for Management of Decision-Making Processes

Ivan Pribićević [1], Suzana Doljanica [2], Oliver Momčilović [3], Dillip Kumar Das [4], Dragan Pamučar [5,*]  and Željko Stević [6]

1. Simplify Outsourcing d.o.o. Belgrade, 11000 Belgrade, Serbia; ivan@simplify.rs
2. Faculty of Applied Management, Economics and Finance, University Business Academy in Novi Sad, Jevrejska 24, 11000 Belgrade, Serbia; suzana.doljanica@mef.edu.rs
3. Faculty of Information Technologies and Engineering, University Union-Nikola Tesla, Jurija Gagarina 149a, 11070 Belgrade, Serbia; oliver.momcilovic@fiti.edu.rs
4. Civil Engineering, School of Engineering, University of Kwazulu Natal, Durban 4041, South Africa; dasd@ukzn.ac.za
5. Department of Logistics, University of Defence in Belgrade, Pavla Jurisica Sturma 33, 11000 Belgrade, Serbia
6. Faculty of Transport and Traffic Engineering, University of East Sarajevo, Vojvode Mišića 52, 74000 Doboj, Bosnia and Herzegovina; zeljkostevic88@yahoo.com or zeljko.stevic@sf.ues.rs.ba
* Correspondence: dragan.pamucar@va.mod.gov.rs

Received: 8 April 2020; Accepted: 14 May 2020; Published: 17 May 2020

Abstract: The decision-making trial and evaluation laboratory (DEMATEL) method is one of the most significant multi-criteria techniques for defining the relationships among criteria and for defining the weight coefficients of criteria. Since multi-criteria models are very often used in management and decision-making under conditions of uncertainty, the fuzzy DEMATEL model has been extended in this paper by D numbers (fuzzy DEMATEL-D). The aim of this research was to develop a multi-criteria methodology that enables the objective processing of fuzzy linguistic information in the pairwise comparison of criteria. This aim was achieved through the development of the fuzzy DEMATEL-D method. Combining D numbers with trapezoidal fuzzy linguistic variables (LVs) allows for the additional processing of uncertainties and ambiguities that exist in experts' preferences when comparing criteria with each other. In addition, the fuzzy DEMATEL-D methodology has a unique reasoning algorithm that allows for the rational processing of uncertainties when using fuzzy linguistic expressions for pairwise comparisons of criteria. The fuzzy DEMATEL-D methodology provides an original uncertainty management framework that is rational and concise. In order to illustrate the effectiveness of the proposed methodology, a case study with the application of the proposed multi-criteria methodology is presented.

Keywords: D numbers; fuzzy sets; DEMATEL; multi-criteria decision-making; criteria weights

1. Introduction

A dynamic environment in which almost all scientific and professional fields operate requires the timely and precise management of processes, which involves decision-making at its each stage. The decisions are made on the basis of a number of inputs that are an integration of qualitative and quantitative criteria. If a certain number of experts with their different preferences in group decision-making are added, the problem is complicated in multiple ways. Therefore, it is necessary to take into account all possible uncertainties that arise in group decision-making in order to gain better and more accurate output. Certainly, an extremely important stage in a decision-making process is determining the significance of the criteria by which the most acceptable solution or ranking of solutions is defined in a further process of solving multi-criteria problems. Therefore, the aim of this paper was to develop a new methodology for determining the significance of criteria that takes aspects of uncertainty and diversity in decision-makers' preferences into account. Accordingly, an extension of the fuzzy decision-making trial and evaluation laboratory (DEMATEL) model is performed by D numbers (fuzzy DEMATEL-D), which is explained in detail in the following section. The DEMATEL method was developed by Gabus and Fontel [1], and it has thus far been widely applied in its basic or extended form, as confirmed in the study [2]. The authors carried out a comprehensive review of the literature published in a period of a decade in terms of developing various extensions of this method and its applications in different decision-making areas. Taking into account the evident wide application of this method and the need to adequately handle uncertain situations and determine the precise weights of criteria, fuzzy set theory is integrated with D numbers. In that way, an overall synergistic effect is achieved in decision-making processes.

Dempster–Shafer evidence theory [3,4] is an area of artificial intelligence because it processes and analyzes uncertainties and inaccuracies in information. It is also a convenient algorithm for reasoning in a dynamic and uncertain environment, which is recommended for use in expert systems. Since Dempster–Shafer evidence theory (DST) allows for the processing of nonspecific, ambiguous, and juxtaposed information, numerous researchers favor DST over traditional approaches, such as Bayesian probability theory [5,6]. In addition to the benefits that DST possesses for solving various real-world problems, such as network problems [7], decision-making problems [8–10], and risk theory [11], there are also limitations to DST that represent a kind of barrier to its wider application for solving real-world problems. One of the most well-known limitations that restricts the wider practical application of DST is the exclusivity of elements when parsing elements of a subset [12,13]. This limitation is shown through the following example. Giving a diagnosis in medicine is a typical area that includes different types of uncertainties [12]. Say there is patient with the symptoms of fever, polypnea, and cough; taking into account the mentioned cases, they are likely caused by the flu (F), bacterial (B) infection, or an upper respiratory infection (U). There are two independent diagnostic reports that were submitted by two doctors. The first doctor made a diagnosis that the patient got F with a possibility of 0.7 and B or U with a possibility of 0.2. The reminder 0.1 possibility is for an unknown diagnosis: $m_1(F) = 0.7$; $m_1(B, U) = 0.2$ and $m_1(F, B, U) = 0.1$. The second doctor made a diagnosis which showed: $m_2(F) = 0.5$; $m_2(B) = 0.3$ and $m_2(F, B, U) = 0.2$. The questions is: What disease does the patient have? The DST in this scenario would show following results: $m(B) = 0.1304$; $m(B, U) = 0.058$, and $m(F, B, U) = 0.0290$. It can be seen that there is an invisible hypothesis that the possibility of the unknown is equal to that of $\{F, B, U\}$. Based on the presented results, it can be concluded that the set of all diseases, which are manifested through the considered symptoms, can be presented as a set $\{F, B, U\}$. However, the set $\{F, B, U\}$ contains only three types of diseases that are considered in this example. Obviously, this unseen hypothesis is not reasonable. Such a problem cannot be addressed by applying DST (Figure 1a) because DST implies the exclusivity of the elements, in our case being diagnosed diseases. This problem can be successfully eliminated by D numbers [12,13]. After the application of D numbers, $D(F) = 0.6147$ and $D(B) = 0.1054$ are obtained. The result shows that the patient having the flu is the highest probability. In comparison to DST, in the D numbers theory, the unknown is inherited during the reasoning.

D numbers, as a reliable and effective expression of uncertain information (and according to Xiao [14]), are good at handling these types of uncertainties. Deng and Jiang [15] developed a decision-making model to solve the adversarial problem under uncertainty with D numbers. Their model integrated fuzzy set theory, game theory, and D number theory (DNT). The same authors in [16] showed the advantages of using D numbers in green supply chain management in a fuzzy environment.

Overcoming the problem was recognized by Zhou et al. [17], who performed an integration of crisp DEMATEL and D numbers to identify the critical success factors (CSFs) in emergency management.

The same method was applied in [18] for the risk identification and analysis of an energy power system. The advantages of the D-DEMATEL method are reflected when simultaneously considering ambiguities and subjectivity, which is impossible with classical approaches, as stated by Zhou et al. [17]. By developing an extension of the DEMATEL method with trapezoidal fuzzy numbers (TrFN) and D numbers in this paper, uncertainties are considered at a higher level with input parameters manifested through output functions.

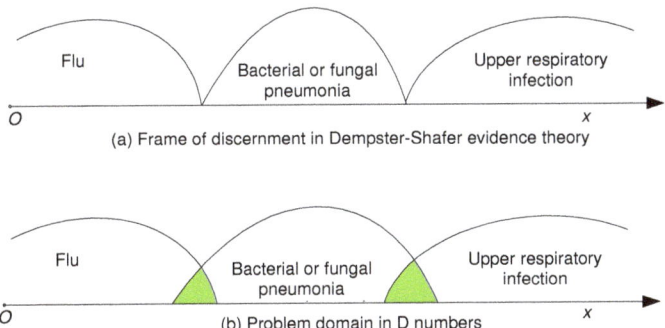

Figure 1. The frame of discernment in Dempster–Shafer evidence theory (DST) and in D numbers.

In addition to the needs and aims presented in the introduction, the paper is has several other sections. Section 2 presents the preliminaries that outline the basics of D numbers and fuzzy theory. Section 3 is an extension of TrFN DEMATEL with D numbers, while Section 4 shows the application of the developed methodology with a specific example. Section 5 summarizes the contributions of the paper, with an overview of further research related to this paper.

2. Background

2.1. D Numbers

D numbers represent an extension of DST with the aim to present more effectively uncertainties in the information being processed. As shown in Figure 1b, D numbers do not require the exclusivity of the elements of a set, which significantly broadens the domain of the practical application of D numbers.

Definition 1 ([12]). *Let Y be a finite nonempty set, and a D number is a mapping that $D : Y \rightarrow [0,1]$, with:*

$$\sum_{A \subseteq Y} D(A) \leq 1 \text{ and } D(\varnothing) = 0 \tag{1}$$

where $\varnothing$ is an empty set and A is any subset of Y. As stated in the previous section of the paper, the theory of D numbers does not require the elements of a set Y to be mutually exclusive. The information presented by D numbers is called complete information if the condition of $\sum_{A \subseteq Y} D(A) = 1$ is filled. If $\sum_{A \subseteq Y} D(A) < 1$, the information is incomplete.

If Y is a discrete set of elements $Y = \{b_1, b_2, \ldots, b_i, b_j, \ldots, b_n\}$, where $b_i \in R$ and $b_i \neq b_j$ (when $i \neq j$), then we can express D numbers by:

$$D(b_1) = v_1, D(b_2) = v_2, \ldots D(b_i) = v_i, D(b_j) = v_j, \ldots D(b_n) = v_n. \tag{2}$$

in addition to expressing D numbers using Equation (2), there is another simplified way to express D numbers: $D = \{(b_1, v_1), (b_2, v_2) \ldots (b_i, v_i), (b_j, v_j) \ldots (b_n, v_n)\}$. This presentation also satisfies the condition that $v_i > 0$ and $\sum_{i=1}^{n} v_i \leq 1$.

Definition 2 ([12]). *Let two D numbers $D_1 = \{(b_1, v_1), \ldots, (b_i, v_i), \ldots, (b_n, v_n)\}$ and $D_2 = \{(b_n, v_n), \ldots, (b_i, v_i), \ldots, (b_1, v_1)\}$ $(b_i, v_i), (b_j, v_j) \ldots (b_n, v_n)\}$ be given. Then, we can define the rule for the combination of D numbers $D = D_1 \odot D_2$ as follows:*

$$\begin{cases} D(\emptyset) = 0 \\ D(B) = \frac{1}{1-K_D} \sum_{B_1 \cap B_2 = B} D_1(B_1) D_2(B_2), B \neq \emptyset \end{cases}$$
with
$$K_D = \frac{1}{Q_1 Q_2} \sum_{B_1 \cap B_2 = \emptyset} D_1(B_1) D_2(B_2)$$
$$Q_1 = \sum_{B_1 \subseteq \Theta} D_1(B_1)$$
$$Q_2 = \sum_{B_2 \subseteq \Theta} D_2(B_2)$$
(3)

Rule (3) is a generalization of Dempster's rule [8]. If D_1 and D_2 are defined in the frame of discernment and if $Q_1 = 1$ and $Q_2 = 1$, then the rule of combining D numbers (Rule (3)) is transformed into Dempster's rule. Rule (3) of numbers is an algorithm for the combination and fusion of uncertain information presented in D numbers.

For a discrete D number $D = \{(b_1, v_1), (b_2, v_2) \ldots (b_i, v_i), (b_j, v_j) \ldots (b_n, v_n)\}$, we can define the integration operator as follows:

$$I(D) = \sum_{i=1}^{n} d_i v_i \quad (4)$$

where $d_i \in R^+, v_i > 0$ i $\sum_{i=1}^{n} v_i \leq 1$.

2.2. Fuzzy Set Theory

Fuzzy set theory is widely used to model uncertainties [19–23]. In some decision-making models, qualitative assessments are given in natural language. These linguistic variables (LVs) can be presented by linguistic expressions [24–26].

Definition 3. *Let X crisp be a universe of generic elements containing a fuzzy set $\widetilde{A}$ as a subset. For each element, let $x \in X$ be a number $\mu_{\widetilde{A}}(x) \in [0, 1]$; then, we can call the number the grade of membership of x in $\widetilde{A}$ [27].*

Definition 4. *A fuzzy set $\widetilde{A}$ of the universe of discourse X is convex if and only if for every element, $x_1, x_2 \in X$, thus implying that:*

$$\mu_{\widetilde{A}}(\lambda x_1 + (1-\lambda) x_2) \geq \min(\mu_{\widetilde{A}}(x_1), \mu_{\widetilde{A}}(x_2)) \quad (5)$$

where $\lambda \in [0, 1]$.

Definition 5. *The trapezoidal fuzzy number $\widetilde{A}$ can be defined as $\widetilde{A} = (a_1, a_2, a_3, a_4)$, as shown in Figure 2.*

$$\mu_{\widetilde{A}}(x) = \begin{cases} \frac{x - a_1}{a_2 - a_1} & a_1 \leq x \leq a_2 \\ 1 & a_2 \leq x \leq a_3 \\ \frac{a_4 - x}{a_4 - a_3} & a_3 \leq x \leq a_4 \\ 0 & \text{otherwise} \end{cases} \quad (6)$$

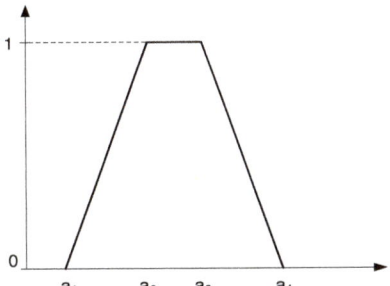

Figure 2. Trapezoidal number membership function.

The concept of an LV is very appropriate in activities where the processing of complex or poorly defined information that cannot be well described by traditional quantitative formulations is needed. The LVs are expressed by words, sentences, or artificial languages. Each linguistic value can be presented by a fuzzy set [28]. Linguistic modelling permits experts to express themselves by labels belonging to a specific linguistic label set [29]. In this paper, experts' preferences, according to different criteria, were considered as linguistic variables. LVs can be expressed by positive TrFN, shown in Table 1, as was the case in our study.

Table 1. Linguistic variables.

Linguistic Variables	Trapezoidal Fuzzy Number
Extremely low (EL)	(0, 1, 2, 3)
Very low (VL)	(1, 2, 3, 4)
Low (L)	(2, 3, 4, 5)
Medium low (ML)	(3, 4, 5, 6)
Medium (M)	(4, 5, 6, 7)
Medium high (MH)	(5, 6, 7, 8)
High (H)	(6, 7, 8, 9)
Very high (VH)	(7, 8, 9, 10)
Extremely high (EH)	(8, 9, 10, 10)

Basic arithmetic operations with TrFN $\widetilde{A}_1 = (a_1, a_2, a_3, a_4)$ and $\widetilde{A}_2 = (b_1, b_2, b_3, b_4)$ are presented in the next section [30,31]:

(1) Addition:

$$\widetilde{A}_1 \oplus \widetilde{A}_2 = (a_1, a_2, a_3, a_{41}) + (b_1, b_2, b_3, b_4) = (a_1 + b_1, a_2 + b_2, a_3 + b_3, a_4 + b_4) \quad (7)$$

(2) Multiplication:

$$\widetilde{A}_1 \otimes \widetilde{A}_2 = (a_1, a_2, a_3, a_{41}) \otimes (b_1, b_2, b_3, b_4) = (a_1 \times b_1, a_2 \times b_2, a_3 \times b_3, a_4 \times b_4) \quad (8)$$

(3) Subtraction:

$$\widetilde{A}_1 - \widetilde{A}_2 = (a_1, a_2, a_3, a_{41}) - (b_1, b_2, b_3, b_4) = (a_1 - b_4, a_2 - b_3, a_3 - b_2, a_4 - b_1) \quad (9)$$

(4) Division:

$$\widetilde{A}_1 \div \widetilde{A}_2 = (a_1, a_2, a_3, a_{41}) \div (b_1, b_2, b_3, b_4) = (a_1 \div b_4, a_2 \div b_3, a_3 \div b_2, a_4 \div b_1) \quad (10)$$

(5) Reciprocal values:

$$\widetilde{A}_1^{-1} = (a_1, a_2, a_3, a_4)^{-1} = (\frac{1}{a_4}, \frac{1}{a_3}, \frac{1}{a_2}, \frac{1}{a_1}) \tag{11}$$

3. TrFN DEMATEL-D Methodology

Due to the imprecision and subjectivity evident in group decision-making, an extension of the fuzzy DEMATEL methodology was made using D numbers. The use of D numbers makes it possible to: (1) take the uncertainties that exist in experts' comparisons of criteria into account and (2) define the intervals of fuzzy linguistic expressions on the basis of uncertainties and inaccuracies that exist in experts' judgment. Numerous multi-criteria models imply the introduction of fuzzy numbers to express the uncertainties that exist in group decision-making [32–37]. The introduction of D numbers makes it possible to take additional uncertainties that arise when selecting fuzzy linguistic variables from a predefined set into account. In addition to fuzzy linguistic variables, D numbers introduce the probability of choosing a fuzzy linguistic variable, thus increasing the objectivity and quality of existing data in group decision-making. Since it is a new extension of the fuzzy DEMATEL methodology by D numbers, the following section details the algorithm which includes six steps:

Step 1: Experts' analysis of factors: Suppose that there are m experts divided into two homogeneous expert groups EG1 and EG2, and there are n criteria considered in a comparison matrix. Let the fuzzy linguistic variables used to compare the criteria be expressed by trapezoidal fuzzy numbers $l = \{l_b, b = 1, 2, \ldots, t\}$, where t represents the total number of fuzzy linguistic variables.

Each expert group defines the degree of influence of the criterion i on the criterion j. The comparative analysis of the pair of ith and jth criterion by the expert group is denoted by the D number

$$D_{ij}^1 = \left\{(l_{ij(1)}^1, v_{ij(1)}^1), \ldots, (l_{ij(i)}^1, v_{ij(i)}^1), \ldots, (l_{ij(t)}^1, v_{ij(t)}^1)\right\} \text{ and } D_{ij}^2 = \left\{(l_{ij(1)}^2, v_{ij(1)}^2), \ldots, (l_{ij(i)}^2, v_{ij(i)}^2), \ldots, (l_{ij(t)}^2, v_{ij(t)}^2)\right\}, \tag{12}$$

where D_{ij}^1 and D_{ij}^2 represent the D numbers used to express the preferences of EG1 and EG2, respectively, and t represents the number of fuzzy linguistic variables used to compare the criteria. As a result of the comparison, two nonnegative matrices of rank $n \times n$ are obtained, and each element of the matrix $X^1 = \left[D_{ij}^1\right]_{n \times n}$ and $X^2 = \left[D_{ij}^2\right]_{n \times n}$ represents a D number. The diagonal elements of the matrices X^1 and X^2 have a value of zero because the same factors have no effect. Thus, we can get one matrix $X^1 = \left[D_{ij}^1\right]_{n \times n}$ and $X^2 = \left[D_{ij}^2\right]_{n \times n}$ for each expert group.

Step 2: Forming a single fuzzy direct-relation matrix $\widetilde{X}$: The transformation of D matrices into a single matrix of fuzzy linguistic values is carried out through three phases.

Phase 1: In the first phase, the uncertainties presented in the initial experts' preferences are fused. Accordingly, applying the rules for the combination of D numbers $D_{ij} = D_{ij}^1 \odot D_{ij}^2$, (Equation (3)), the analysis and synthesis of the data provided by D numbers in expert matrices $X^1 = \left[D_{ij}^1\right]_{n \times n}$ and $X^2 = \left[D_{ij}^2\right]_{n \times n}$ are performed.

Phase 2: After implementing the rules for the combination of D numbers, the uncertainties presented at the intersection of fuzzy linguistic variables (FLVs) (Figure 3) are transformed into unique fuzzy linguistic variables.

We can define FLVs as the term-set $L = \{l_b | b = (0, \ldots, B)\}$, where l_b is an FLV presented in D_{ij}^1 and D_{ij}^2. Each term l_b is presented as trapezoidal fuzzy number $\widetilde{z}$, i.e., $\widetilde{z} = \left(z^{(l)}, z^{(m_1)}, z^{(m_2)}, z^{(u)}\right)$, where $z^{(m_1)}$ and $z^{(m_2)}$ represent the middle points of the trapezoidal fuzzy number (TrFN), and $z^{(l)}$ and $z^{(u)}$ are the lower and upper limits, respectively, of the fuzzy interval.

FLV transformation is performed on the basis of the ratio of the surfaces located at the intersection $S_{i,i+1}$ and the corresponding area of the FLVs.

$$D_{FLVT}(H_i) = D(H_i) + D(H_i, H_{i+1}) \frac{\frac{S_{i,i+1}}{S_i}}{\frac{S_{i,i+1}}{S_i} + \frac{S_{i,i+1}}{S_{i+1}}} \quad (13)$$

$$D_{FLVT}(H_{i+1}) = D(H_{i+1}) + D(H_i, H_{i+1}) \frac{\frac{S_{i,i+1}}{S_{i+1}}}{\frac{S_{i,i+1}}{S_i} + \frac{S_{i,i+1}}{S_{i+1}}} \quad (14)$$

where $S_{i,i+1}$ represents the intersection between the linguistic variable l_i and the linguistic variable l_{i+1}, while S_i and S_{i+1} represent the area of the linguistic variable l_i and l_{i+1}, respectively.

After the FLV transformation, we can obtain a single D matrix $X = [D_{ij}]_{n \times n}$.

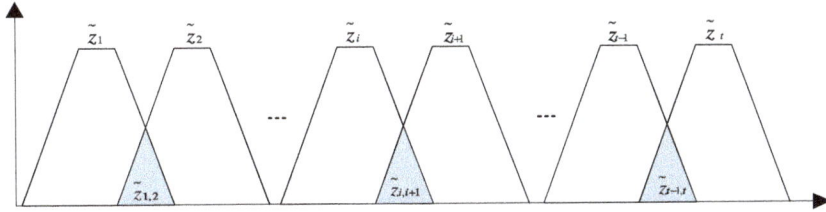

Figure 3. Fuzzy linguistic variables.

Phase 3: The elements of the D matrix $X = [D_{ij}]_{n \times n}$ are transformed into a single fuzzy direct-relation matrix $\widetilde{X} = [\widetilde{x}_{ij}]_{n \times n}$, where $\widetilde{x}_{ij} = (x_{ij1}, x_{ij2}, x_{ij3}, x_{ij4})$ represents the elements of the matrix $\widetilde{X}$ expressed by trapezoidal fuzzy numbers. The elements of the matrix $\widetilde{X} = [\widetilde{x}_{ij}]_{n \times n}$ are obtained by applying the operator of integration of D numbers (Equation (4)), i.e., $\widetilde{x}_{ij} = \sum_{i=1}^{e} l_i v_i$, where e represents the number of FLVs contained in the D number.

Step 3: Computing the elements of a normalized fuzzy direct-relation matrix: After forming a single fuzzy direct-relation matrix $\widetilde{X} = [\widetilde{x}_{ij}]_{n \times n}$ by applying Equations (16) and (17), we can obtain the elements of the normalized fuzzy direct-relation matrix (Equation (15)).

$$N = \begin{bmatrix} 0 & \widetilde{d}_{12} & \cdots & \widetilde{d}_{1n} \\ \widetilde{d}_{21} & 0 & \cdots & \widetilde{d}_{2n} \\ \vdots & \vdots & \ddots & \vdots \\ \widetilde{d}_{n1} & \widetilde{d}_{n2} & \cdots & 0 \end{bmatrix} \quad (15)$$

where $\widetilde{d}_{ij} = (d_{ij}^L, d_{ij}^M, d_{ij}^U)$ represents the normalized values of the matrix $\widetilde{X} = [\widetilde{x}_{ij}]_{n \times n}$, which are obtained by applying Equations (16) and (17):

$$\widetilde{d}_{ij} = \frac{\widetilde{x}_{ij}}{\widetilde{s}} = \left(\frac{x_{ij1}}{s_4}, \frac{x_{ij2}}{s_3}, \frac{x_{ij3}}{s_2}, \frac{x_{ij4}}{s_1}\right) \quad (16)$$

$$\begin{aligned} \widetilde{s} = \max(\textstyle\sum_{j=1}^{n} \widetilde{x}_{ij}) &= \max\left(\textstyle\sum_{j=1}^{n} x_{ij1}, \sum_{j=1}^{n} x_{ij2}, \sum_{j=1}^{n} x_{ij3}, \sum_{j=1}^{n} x_{ij4}\right) \\ &= \left(\max(\textstyle\sum_{j=1}^{n} x_{ij1}), \max(\sum_{j=1}^{n} x_{ij2}), \max(\sum_{j=1}^{n} x_{ij3}), \max(\sum_{j=1}^{n} x_{ij4})\right) \end{aligned} \quad (17)$$

Step 4: Determining the fuzzy number-based total relation matrices: By applying Equations (18)–(20), we can obtain a total influence matrix $T = [\widetilde{t}_{ij}]_{n \times n}$, where I is an $n \times n$ identity matrix.

Since the matrix $N = [\tilde{d}_{ij}]_{n\times n}$ is presented by trapezoidal fuzzy numbers, we can form four submatrices $N = (N_1, N_2, N_3, N_4)$, where $N_1 = [d_{ij1}]_{n\times n}$, $N_2 = [d_{ij2}]_{n\times n}$, $N_3 = [d_{ij3}]_{n\times n}$, and $N_4 = [d_{ij4}]_{n\times n}$. In addition, $\lim_{m\to\infty}(N_1)^m = O$, $\lim_{m\to\infty}(N_2)^m = O$, $\lim_{m\to\infty}(N_3)^m = O$, and $\lim_{m\to\infty}(N_4)^m = O$, where O represents the zero matrix.

$$\left.\begin{array}{l} \lim_{m\to\infty}(I + N_1 + N_1^2 + \ldots + N_1^m) = (I - N_1)^{-1} \\ \lim_{m\to\infty}(I + N_2 + N_2^2 + \ldots + N_2^m) = (I - N_2)^{-1} \\ \lim_{m\to\infty}(I + N_3 + N_3^2 + \ldots + N_3^m) = (I - N_3)^{-1} \\ \text{and} \\ \lim_{m\to\infty}(I + N_4 + N_4^2 + \ldots + N_4^m) = (I - N_4)^{-1} \end{array}\right\} \quad (18)$$

The total relation fuzzy matrix T is obtained by computing each of the sub-elements:

$$\left.\begin{array}{l} T_1 = \lim_{m\to\infty}(I + N_1 + N_1^2 + \ldots + N_1^m) = (I - N_1)^{-1} = [t_{ij1}]_{n\times n} \\ T_2 = \lim_{m\to\infty}(I + N_2 + N_2^2 + \ldots + N_2^m) = (I - N_2)^{-1} = [t_{ij2}]_{n\times n} \\ T_3 = \lim_{m\to\infty}(I + N_3 + N_3^2 + \ldots + N_3^m) = (I - N_3)^{-1} = [t_{ij3}]_{n\times n} \\ \text{and} \\ T_4 = \lim_{m\to\infty}(I + N_4 + N_4^2 + \ldots + N_4^m) = (I - N_4)^{-1} = [t_{ij4}]_{n\times n} \end{array}\right\} \quad (19)$$

where $N_1 = [d_{ij1}]_{n\times n}$, $N_2 = [d_{ij2}]_{n\times n}$, $N_3 = [d_{ij3}]_{n\times n}$, and $N_4 = [d_{ij4}]_{n\times n}$. Submatrices T_1, T_2, T_3, and T_4 form the single fuzzy total relation matrix $T = (T_1, T_2, T_3, T_4)$, which is presented as follows:

$$T = \begin{bmatrix} \tilde{t}_{11} & \tilde{t}_{12} & \cdots & \tilde{t}_{1n} \\ \tilde{t}_{21} & \tilde{t}_{22} & \cdots & \tilde{t}_{2n} \\ \vdots & \vdots & \ddots & \vdots \\ \tilde{t}_{n1} & \tilde{t}_{n2} & \cdots & \tilde{t}_{nn} \end{bmatrix}_{n\times n} \quad (20)$$

where $\tilde{t}_{ij} = (\tilde{t}_{ij1}, \tilde{t}_{ij2}, \tilde{t}_{ij3}, \tilde{t}_{ij4})$ is the total assessment of experts' effect for each criterion i and criterion j, thus expressing their mutual influence and dependence.

Step 5: Computing the sum of rows and columns of the total relation matrix: Presented by vectors R and C of rank $n \times 1$, Equations (21) and (22) are:

$$R = \left[\sum_{j=1}^{n} \tilde{t}_{ij}\right]_{n\times 1} = \left[\left(\sum_{j=1}^{n} t_{ij1}, \sum_{j=1}^{n} t_{ij2}, \sum_{j=1}^{n} t_{ij3}, \sum_{j=1}^{n} t_{ij4}\right)\right]_{n\times 1} \quad (21)$$

$$C = \left[\sum_{i=1}^{n} \tilde{t}_{ij}\right]_{1\times n} = \left[\left(\sum_{i=1}^{n} t_{ij1}, \sum_{i=1}^{n} t_{ij2}, \sum_{i=1}^{n} t_{ij3}, \sum_{i=1}^{n} t_{ij4}\right)\right]_{1\times n} \quad (22)$$

The value R_i represents the sum of the ith raw of the matrix T. The determined value presents the total direct and indirect effects that the criterion i provides for the other criteria. Meanwhile, the value of C_i represents the sum of the jth column of the matrix T and shows the effects that the criterion j receives from the other criteria [37].

Step 6. Determining the weight coefficients of the criterion (w_j): This is achieved via Equation (23):

$$\widetilde{W}_j = \sqrt{(\widetilde{R}_i + \widetilde{C}_i)^2 + (\widetilde{R}_i - \widetilde{C}_i)^2} \quad (23)$$

where the values $\widetilde{R}_i + \widetilde{C}_i$ and $\widetilde{R}_i - \widetilde{C}_i$ are obtained using Equations (24) and (25):

$$\widetilde{R}_i + \widetilde{C}_i = \begin{pmatrix} \sum_{j=1}^n t_{ij1} + \sum_{i=1}^n t_{ij1}, \sum_{j=1}^n t_{ij2} + \sum_{i=1}^n t_{ij2}, \\ \sum_{j=1}^n t_{ij3} + \sum_{i=1}^n t_{ij3}, \sum_{j=1}^n t_{ij4} + \sum_{i=1}^n t_{ij4} \end{pmatrix} \quad (24)$$

$$\widetilde{R}_i - \widetilde{C}_i = \begin{pmatrix} \sum_{j=1}^n t_{ij1} - \sum_{i=1}^n t_{ij1}, \sum_{j=1}^n t_{ij2} - \sum_{i=1}^n t_{ij2}, \\ \sum_{j=1}^n t_{ij3} - \sum_{i=1}^n t_{ij3}, \sum_{j=1}^n t_{ij4} - \sum_{i=1}^n t_{ij4} \end{pmatrix} \quad (25)$$

The normalization of the weight coefficients is carried out by Equation (26):

$$w_j = \frac{\widetilde{W}_j}{\sum_{j=1}^n \widetilde{W}_j} \quad (26)$$

where n is the number of criteria and $\widetilde{w}_j$ is the fuzzy values of the criteria weight. The values of the criteria weight are in the interval $\widetilde{w}_j = (w_{j1}, w_{j2}, w_{j3}, w_{j4})$, where the condition $0 \leq w_{j1} \leq w_{j2} \leq w_{j3} \leq w_{j4} \leq 1$ is fulfilled for each evaluation criterion. However, the requirement that the sum of the weight coefficients of the criteria be generally equal to one must be fulfilled. Since these are fuzzy coefficients of criteria, using Equation (26) allows for the obtainment of the weight coefficients for which $0 \leq \sum_{j=1}^n w_{j1} \leq \sum_{j=1}^n w_{j2} \leq \sum_{j=1}^n w_{j3} \leq 1$ and $\sum_{j=1}^n w_{j4} \geq 1$. This fulfills the condition that the criteria weight are in the interval $w_j \in [0, 1], (j = 1, 2, \ldots, n)$.

4. Application of TrFN D-DEMATEL Method

This section describes the application of the TrFN D-DEMATEL method for determining the quality of logistics services in order to obtain an adequate insight into the management processes of the service provider. The research by Prentkovskis et al. [38] was used to test the methodology presented. The dimensions that affect the measurement of logistics service quality were taken from the study [38], and they were evaluated using the TrFN D-DEMATEL methodology. There were five defined dimensions: reliability (C1), assurance (C2), tangibles (C3), empathy (C4), and responsiveness (C5). The study involved six experts who evaluated the dimensions. A detailed description of applying the TrFN D-DEMATEL methodology is presented in the following section.

Step 1: Experts' analysis of factors.

Six experts participated in the study, and they were divided into two homogenous expert groups: EG1 and EG2. Expert groups expressed their preferences when comparing dimensions using a nine-degree fuzzy linguistic scale; see Table 1. Each expert group defined the mutual degree of influence of the criteria by D numbers; see Table 2.

Table 2 shows the experts' comparisons of dimensions using D numbers, where the D number D_1 represents the experts' preferences of the EG1 expert group and D_2 represents the experts' preferences of the EG2 expert group.

Step 2: Forming a single fuzzy direct-relation matrix.

Phase I: In order to obtain aggregated experts' preferences, a fusion of the uncertainties expressed in the group experts' preferences D_1 and D_2 is performed. For the uncertainty fusion, the rule for the combination of D numbers $D_{ij} = D_{ij}^1 \odot D_{ij}^2$ (Equation (3)) is used. Thus, an aggregated D matrix of experts' preferences is obtained; see Table 3.

In order to clarify the application of the rules for combining D numbers, the following section shows the application of the rules for the combination of D numbers for position C2–C1 in the experts' analysis of dimensions (Table 2).

Based on the data in Table 2, for position C2–C1, we can distinguish two D numbers that represent the experts' preferences of homogeneous expert groups: D_1 = {(VH,0.2), (VH;EH,0.35), (EH,0.4)} (where VH is 'very high' and EH is 'extremely high') and D_2 = {(VH,0.25), (VH;EH,0.45),

(EH,0.1)}. Table 4 provides an analysis of the data on D numbers whose combination was considered, $D = D^1_{C2-C1} \odot D^2_{C2-C1}$.

Table 2. Experts' analysis of dimensions.

Dim.	C1	C2
C1	D_1 = {(0,0.00)}; D_2 = {(0,0.00)}	D_1 = {(H,0.3),(H;VH,0.25),(H,0.4)}; D_2 = {(VH,0.3),(VH;EH,0.4),(EH,0.3)}
C2	D_1 = {(VH,0.2),(VH;EH,0.35),(EH,0.4)}; D_2 = {(VH,0.25),(VH;EH,0.45),(EH,0.1)}	D_1 = {(0,0.00)}; D_2 = {(0,0.00)}
C3	D_1 = {(L,0.2),(ML,0.6),(M,0.15)}; D_2 = {(ML,0.35),(ML;M,0.45)}	D_1 = {(ML,0.2),(ML;M,0.2),(M,0.55)}; D_2 = {(ML;M,0.3),(M,0.3),(M;MH,0.4)}
C4	D_1 = {(EL,0.4),(EL;VL,0.3),(VL,0.3)}; D_2 = {(EL;VL,0.25),(VL,0.35),(VL;L,0.35)}	D_1 = {(EL,0.4),(EL;VL,0.4),(VL,0.1)}; D_2 = {(EL;VL,0.5),(VL,0.25),(L,0.2)}
C5	D_1 = {(EL,0.25),(VL,0.55),(VL;L,0.15)}; D_2 = {(EL,0.2),(EL;VL,0.5),(VL,0.25)}	D_1 = {(L,0.4),(ML,0.25),(ML;M,0.35)}; D_2 = {(ML,0.3),(ML;M,0.35),(M,0.3)}
	C3	C4
C1	D_1 = {(H,0.4),(VH,0.3),(VH;EH,0.3)} D_2 = {(VH,0.3),(VH;EH,0.3),(EH,0.4)}	D_1 = {(MH;H,0.3),(H,0.6),(VH,0.1)} D_2 = {(M,0.3),(MH,0.45),(H,0.25)}
C2	D_1 = {(MH,0.3),(MH;H,0.35),(H,0.3)} D_2 = {(MH,0.45),(H,0.45)}	D_1 = {(VH,0.3),(VH;EH,0.4),(EH,0.25)} D_2 = {(VH,0.3),(EH,0.4),(H,0.15)}
C3	D_1 = {(0,0.00)}; D_2 = {(0,0.00)}	D_1 = {(MH,0.6),(MH;H,0.2),(H,0.2)} D_2 = {(M,0.25),(MH,0.35),(H,0.4)}
C4	D_1 = {(L,0.1),(ML,0.55),(M,0.3)}; D_2 = {(VL,0.35),(L,0.45),(ML,0.2)}	D_1 = {(0,0.00)}; D_2 = {(0,0.00)}
C5	D_1 = {(MH,0.3),(H,0.25),(H;VH,0.45)}; D_2 = {(H,0.3),(H;VH,0.25),(VH,0.45)}	D_1 = {(ML,0.2),(ML;M,0.35),(M,0.4)}; D_2 = {(ML,0.25),(ML;M,0.3),(M,0.4)}
	C5	
C1	D_1 = {(VH,0.5),(VH;EH,0.1),(EH,0.35)}; D_2 = {(VH,0.35),(VH;EH,0.2),(EH,0.45)}	
C2	D_1 = {(MH,0.1),(MH;H,0.3),(H,0.4),(VH,0.15)}; D_2 = {(MH;H,0.35),(H,0.25),(VH,0.3)}	
C3	D_1 = {(MH,0.15),(MH;H,0.2),(H,0.55)}; D_2 = {(MH,0.25),(MH;H,0.35),(H,0.35)}	
C4	D_1 = {(EL,0.4),(EL;VL,0.4),(VL,0.2)}; D_2 = {(EL,0.25),(EL;VL,0.35),(VL,0.3)}	
C5	D_1 = {(0,0.00)}; D_2 = {(0,0.00)}	

By applying Equation (4), we can calculate the relationships defined by the rule for the combination of D numbers.

$$K_D = \frac{1}{Q_1 Q_2} \left(D^1_{C2-C1}(\text{VH}) \cdot D^2_{C2-C1}(\text{EH}) + D^1_{C2-C1}(\text{EH}) \cdot D^2_{C2-C1}(\text{VH}) \right) = 0.158$$

$$Q_1 = D^1_{C2-C1}(\text{VH}) + D^1_{C2-C1}(\text{VH;EH}) + D^1_{C2-C1}(\text{EH}) = 0.2 + 0.35 + 0.4 = 0.95$$

$$Q_2 = D^2_{C2-C1}(\text{VH}) + D^2_{C2-C1}(\text{VH;EH}) + D^2_{C2-C1}(\text{VH}) = 0.25 + 0.45 + 0.1 = 0.80$$

Thus, we can obtain:

$$D_{C2-C1}(\text{VH}) = \frac{1}{1-K_D} \left(\begin{array}{l} D^1_{C2-C1}(\text{VH}) D^2_{C2-C1}(\text{VH}) + D^1_{C2-C1}(\text{VH}) D^2_{C2-C1}(\text{VH;EH}) + \\ D^1_{C2-C1}(\text{VH;EH}) D^2_{C2-C1}(\text{VH}) \end{array} \right) = 0.270$$

$$D_{C2-C1}(\text{VH;EH}) = \frac{1}{1-K_D} \left(D^1_{C2-C1}(\text{VH;EH}) D^2_{C2-C1}(\text{VH;EH}) \right) = 0.187$$

$$D_{C2-C1}(\text{EH}) = \frac{1}{1-K_D} \left(\begin{array}{l} D^1_{C2-C1}(\text{VH;EH}) D^2_{C2-C1}(\text{EH}) + D^1_{C2-C1}(\text{EH}) D^2_{C2-C1}(\text{VH;EH}) + \\ D^1_{C2-C1}(\text{EH}) D^2_{C2-C1}(\text{EH}) \end{array} \right) = 0.303$$

Table 3. Aggregated D matrix of experts' preferences.

Dim.	C1	C2
C1	$D = \{(0,0.00)\}$	$D = \{(VH,0.95)\}$
C2	$D = \{(VH,0.27),(VH;EH,0.19),(EH,0.3)\}$	$D = \{(0,0.00)\}$
C3	$D = \{(ML,0.67),(M,0.09)\}$	$D = \{(ML,0.07),(ML;M5,0.07),(M,0.72)\}$
C4	$D = \{(EL,0.14),(EL;L,0.11),(2,0.7)\}$	$D = \{(EL,0.3),(EL;L,0.3),(L,0.26)\}$
C5	$D = \{(EL,0.23),(VL,0.68)\}$	$D = \{(ML,0.51),(ML;M,0.24),(M,0.2)\}$
	C3	**C4**
C1	$D = \{(VH,0.56),(VH;EH,0.19),(EH,0.25)\}$	$D = \{(MH,0.38),(H,0.63)\}$
C2	$D = \{(MH,0.43),(H,0.43)\}$	$D = \{(VH,0.36),(EH,0.45)\}$
C3	$D = \{(0,0.00)\}$	$D = \{(MH,0.64),(H,0.36)\}$
C4	$D = \{(L,0.28),(ML,0.67)\}$	$D = \{(0,0.00)\}$
C5	$D = \{(H,0.46),(H;VH,0.19),(VH,0.34)\}$	$D = \{(ML,0.25),(ML;M,0.13),(M,0.52)\}$
	C5	
C1	$D = \{(VH,0.49),(VH;EH,0.03),(EH,0.43)\}$	
C2	$D = \{(MH,0.06),(MH;H,0.18),(H,0.54),(VH,0.08)\}$	
C3	$D = \{(MH,0.18),(MH;H,0.09),(H,0.59)\}$	
C4	$D = \{(EL,0.42),(EL;VL,0.17),(VL,0.31)\}$	
C5	$D = \{(0,0.00)\}$	

Table 4. Intersection table to combine D^1_{C2-C1} and D^2_{C2-C1}.

$D = D^1_{C2-C1} \odot D^2_{C2-C1}$	$D_{C2-C1}{}^2(VH) = 0.25$	$D_{C2-C1}{}^2(VH;EH) = 0.45$	$D_{C2-C1}{}^2(EH) = 0.1$
$D_{C2-C1}{}^1(VH) = 0.2$	{VH} (0.05)	{VH} (0.09)	∅ (0.02)
$D_{C2-C1}{}^1(VH;EH) = 0.35$	{VH} (0.0875)	{VH;EH} (0.1575)	{EH} (0.035)
$D_{C2-C1}{}^1(EH) = 0.4$	∅ (0.1)	{EH} (0.18)	{EH} (0.04)

Phase II: After applying the rule for the combination of D numbers, we can obtain a D number located between the fuzzy linguistic variables VH and EH, and so it is necessary to transform the uncertainty found between the fuzzy variables VH and EH into unique FLVs. The transformation of uncertainty is performed by applying Equations (13) and (14). The following section presents the procedure for the transformation of uncertainty between the fuzzy variables VH and EH. A graphical display of the fuzzy linguistic variables VH and EH is given in Figure 4.

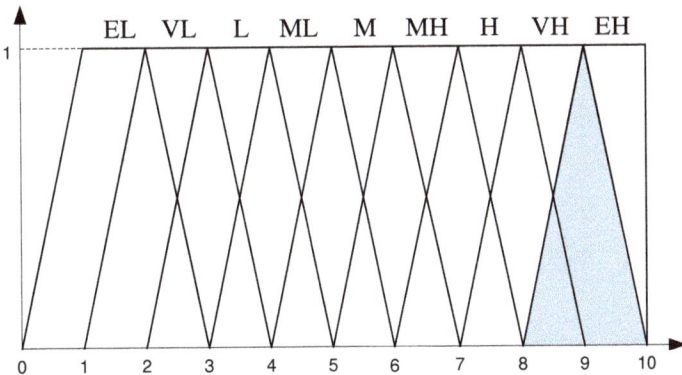

Figure 4. Fuzzy linguistic variables VH (very high) and EH (extremely high).

The transformation of FLVs is performed on the basis of the ratio of the surfaces located at the intersection $S_{VH,EH}$ and the area that covers the fuzzy variables VH and EH, i.e., $S_{VH,EH} = 0.5 \times 2 \times 1 =$

1.00 and $S_{EH} = 0.5 \times 3 \times 1 = 1.50$. Using Equations (13) and (14), we can obtain finite values of D numbers for the fuzzy variables VH and EH:

$$D_{C2-C1}(\text{VH}) = 0.270 + 0.187 \frac{1/2}{1/2 + 1.5/2} = 0.350$$
$$D_{C2-C1}(\text{EH}) = 0.303 + 0.187 \frac{1/1.5}{1/2 + 1.5/2} = 0.410$$

$$D_{B1}(\text{MH}) = 0.461 + 0.154 \frac{1.125/2}{1.125/2 + 1.125/2} = 0.538$$

Thus, we can obtain D number D_{C2-C1} = {(VH,0.350), (EH,0.410)} which is in the first position C2–C1. The remaining values of the aggregated D matrix of experts' preferences are obtained in a similar way (Table 3).

Phase III: Using Equation (4), the values of the aggregated D matrix of experts' preferences are integrated into the corresponding fuzzy values; see Table 5. By this procedure, the uncertainties expressed by D numbers are transformed into unique trapezoidal fuzzy numbers.

Table 5. Single fuzzy direct-relation matrix.

Dim.	C1	C2	C3
C1	(0.00, 0.00, 0.00, 0.00)	(6.65, 7.6, 8.55, 9.5)	(7.36, 8.36, 9.36, 10)
C2	(5.73, 6.49, 7.25, 7.6)	(0.00, 0.00, 0.00, 0.00)	(4.7, 5.56, 6.41, 7.27)
C3	(2.37, 3.13, 3.89, 4.65)	(3.32, 4.18, 5.03, 5.89)	(0.00, 0.00, 0.00, 0.00)
C4	(0.76, 1.71, 2.66, 3.61)	(0.41, 1.26, 2.12, 2.97)	(2.57, 3.52, 4.47, 5.42)
C5	(0.68, 1.58, 2.48, 3.38)	(3.17, 4.12, 5.07, 6.02)	(6.44, 7.44, 8.44, 9.44)

	C4	C5
C1	(5.63, 6.63, 7.63, 8.63)	(7.36, 8.31, 9.26, 9.5)
C2	(6.1, 6.91, 7.71, 8.08)	(5.06, 5.91, 6.77, 7.62)
C3	(5.36, 6.36, 7.36, 8.36)	(4.91, 5.76, 6.62, 7.47)
C4	(0.00, 0.00, 0.00, 0.00)	(0.39, 1.29, 2.19, 3.09)
C5	(3.3, 4.2, 5.1, 6.01)	(0.00, 0.00, 0.00, 0.00)

Using Equations (4), (7), and (8), the element C2–C1 of the single fuzzy direct-relation matrix (Table 5) is obtained as follows:

$$\widetilde{x}_{21} = 0.350 \cdot (7, 8, 9, 10) + 0.410 \cdot (8, 9, 10, 10) = (5.73, 6.49, 7.25, 7.60)$$

Similarly, we can obtain the remaining elements of the single fuzzy direct-relation matrix (Table 5).

Steps 3 and 4: Computing the elements of the normalized fuzzy direct-relation matrix and total fuzzy influence matrix.

By applying Equations (16) and (17), we can obtain the elements of the normalized fuzzy direct-relation matrix; see Table 6.

In the next step, by using Equations (18)–(20), we can obtain the total influence matrix $T = \left[\widetilde{t}_{ij}\right]_{5 \times 5}$; see Table 7.

Steps 5 and 6: Computing the sum of rows and columns of the fuzzy total relation matrix and determining the optimal values of the weight coefficients of dimensions.

The optimal values of the weight coefficients of dimensions are defined on the basis of the total direct/indirect effects that the criterion i provides for other criteria (R_i) and the total direct/indirect effects that the criterion j receives from other criteria (C_i). The values of R_i and C_i are obtained by using Equations (21) and (22). After calculating the values of R_i and C_i (Table 8), we can obtain the optimal values of the dimensions by using Equations (23)–(26).

Table 6. Normalized fuzzy direct-relation matrix.

Dim.	C1	C2	C3
C1	(0.00, 0.00, 0.00, 0.00)	(0.25, 0.25, 0.25, 0.25)	(0.27, 0.27, 0.27, 0.27)
C2	(0.21, 0.21, 0.21, 0.20)	(0.00, 0.00, 0.00, 0.00)	(0.17, 0.18, 0.18, 0.19)
C3	(0.09, 0.10, 0.11, 0.12)	(0.12, 0.14, 0.14, 0.16)	(0.00, 0.00, 0.00, 0.00)
C4	(0.03, 0.06, 0.08, 0.10)	(0.02, 0.04, 0.06, 0.08)	(0.10, 0.11, 0.13, 0.14)
C5	(0.03, 0.05, 0.07, 0.09)	(0.12, 0.13, 0.15, 0.16)	(0.24, 0.24, 0.24, 0.25)

Dim.	C4	C5
C1	(0.21, 0.21, 0.22, 0.23)	(0.27, 0.27, 0.27, 0.25)
C2	(0.23, 0.22, 0.22, 0.21)	(0.19, 0.19, 0.19, 0.20)
C3	(0.20, 0.21, 0.21, 0.22)	(0.18, 0.19, 0.19, 0.20)
C4	(0.00, 0.00, 0.00, 0.00)	(0.01, 0.04, 0.06, 0.08)
C5	(0.12, 0.14, 0.15, 0.16)	(0.00, 0.00, 0.00, 0.00)

Table 7. Total fuzzy influence matrix.

Dim.	C1	C2	C3
C1	(0.16, 0.22, 0.28, 0.35)	(0.42, 0.48, 0.54, 0.62)	(0.56, 0.62, 0.67, 0.75)
C2	(0.30, 0.35, 0.40, 0.46)	(0.18, 0.23, 0.28, 0.35)	(0.42, 0.48, 0.53, 0.61)
C3	(0.17, 0.23, 0.28, 0.36)	(0.23, 0.29, 0.35, 0.43)	(0.20, 0.25, 0.30, 0.38)
C4	(0.06, 0.11, 0.17, 0.24)	(0.05, 0.12, 0.19, 0.26)	(0.14, 0.21, 0.28, 0.37)
C5	(0.11, 0.18, 0.24, 0.32)	(0.21, 0.27, 0.34, 0.42)	(0.37, 0.43, 0.48, 0.57)

Dim.	C4	C5
C1	(0.51, 0.57, 0.63, 0.72)	(0.51, 0.56, 0.61, 0.67)
C2	(0.46, 0.51, 0.56, 0.62)	(0.39, 0.44, 0.49, 0.56)
C3	(0.36, 0.42, 0.48, 0.56)	(0.31, 0.37, 0.42, 0.50)
C4	(0.06, 0.12, 0.17, 0.24)	(0.07, 0.14, 0.21, 0.29)
C5	(0.28, 0.35, 0.41, 0.50)	(0.14, 0.19, 0.25, 0.32)

Table 8. Ranking the weight coefficients of the dimensions.

Dim.	R_i	C_i	$R_i + C_i$	$R_i - C_i$
C1	(2.16, 2.45, 2.73, 3.11)	(0.80, 1.09, 1.37, 1.73)	(4.84, 0.43, −3.01, −2.17)	(−1.23, 3.84, −2.15, 4.40)
C2	(1.75, 2.01, 2.26, 2.61)	(1.10, 1.40, 1.69, 2.09)	(4.70, −0.33, −2.55, −1.72)	(−0.76, 3.70, −1.82, 4.12)
C3	(1.28, 1.56, 1.84, 2.23)	(1.69, 1.99, 2.28, 2.69)	(4.92, −1.41, −2.13, −1.27)	(−0.28, 3.85, −1.53, 4.14)
C4	(0.38, 0.71, 1.02, 1.40)	(1.68, 1.97, 2.25, 2.64)	(4.05, −2.27, −1.30, −0.42)	(0.59, 2.99, −0.86, 3.11)
C5	(1.11, 1.42, 1.73, 2.14)	(1.41, 1.70, 1.98, 2.35)	(4.49, −1.23, −2.01, −1.14)	(−0.18, 3.44, −1.40, 3.71)

Dim.	W_j	w_j	Rank
C1	4.404	0.226	1
C2	4.122	0.211	3
C3	4.144	0.213	2
C4	3.110	0.160	5
C5	3.712	0.190	4

The final values of the weight coefficients of the dimensions are: reliability ($w_1 = 0.226$), assurance ($w_2 = 0.211$), tangibles ($w_3 = 0.213$), empathy ($w_4 = 0.160$), and responsiveness ($w_5 = 0.190$). Based on presented results, we can define the final ranking as C1 > C3 > C2 > C5 > C4.

Compared to crisp DEMATEL, the proposed method has two main advantages. The first advantage of proposed model is the elimination of disadvantage in the DST where the elements in the frame of discernment are required to be independent. While both evidence DEMATEL [39] and DEMATEL-D can decrease the subjectivity of expert preferences, the DST is not very applicable for the presentation of linguistic estimates in conditions where it is required that the elements within the distinction must be mutually exclusive. As shown In Figure 1a, the variables must have boundaries in DST. However, it was found that this demand is difficult to be satisfied for LVs such as "F", "B", and "U". As shown in Figure 1b, the D numbers theory overcomes this poorness and permit overlap between

LVs, which makes it more applicable for linguistic assessments. Furthermore, in DST, the sum of basic probability assignment must present the complete information, i.e., the sum of probability must be 1. However, in the D numbers theory, the information can be incomplete, which is more practical and realistic.

The second advantage of proposed DEMATEL-D model is related to reducing experts subjectivity. Even though both fuzzy DEMATEL [40] and the TrFN DEMATEL consider fuzziness, the developed method is more objective than fuzzy DEMATEL because it can reduce the impact of expert subjectivity by fusing group opinions.

The precedence of the D numbers theory is the ability to integrate group information. Therefore, in order to perform the verification and validity of the developed method, this study computed the result in each expert group and compared the opinions of these two expert groups with the final result, as shown in Table 8. In these three cases (the first group, the second group, and the aggregated values), C1 was the most significant element but the ranking of the other elements was quite various, thus showing that the final rank was sensitive to the knowledge of experts. Consequently, the need for the integration of expert information in various fields using the D numbers theory has been shown.

The D numbers theory is used to fuse the expert preferences in decision-making processes. Therefore, it is reasonable to expect the aggregate values to be close to the values represented by the expert preferences. The final values of the criteria obtained using the DEMATEL-D model in this study were between the results that have been proposed through expert evaluations. This shows us that the proposed model respects the uncertainties that exist in group decision-making and that the model gives results that are valid and reasonable.

5. Conclusions

In this paper, the fuzzy DEMATEL methodology was expanded by D numbers to overcome uncertainties and subjectivities that are inevitable in group decision-making processes, especially with numerous decision-makers. The integration of fuzzy DEMATEL with D numbers allows for the consideration of uncertainties that exist in experts' comparisons of criteria, and that the intervals of fuzzy linguistic expressions are defined based on the uncertainties and imprecision that exist in experts' judgment. The introduction of D numbers makes it possible to take the additional uncertainties that arise when selecting fuzzy linguistic variables from a predefined set into account. D numbers, in addition to fuzzy linguistic variables, introduce the probability of choosing a fuzzy linguistic variable, thus increasing the objectivity and quality of existing data in group decision-making. This can be proven, for example, by determining the quality of logistics services in order to obtain an adequate insight into the management processes. Considering that this is a new extension of the fuzzy DEMATEL method by D numbers, which was demonstrated on a real study, it can be concluded that there is a justification for the development of the presented methodology. Future research may be based on the greater application of MCDM methods and D numbers. In addition, it is possible to integrate rough numbers with D numbers, which could provide a more comprehensive concept for managing decision-making processes.

Author Contributions: Conceptualization, I.P. and Ž.S.; methodology, I.P.; D.P., and Ž.S.; validation, S.D. and D.K.D.; writing—original draft preparation, D.P and O.M.; writing—review and editing, D.K.D. and S.D.; supervision, Ž.S. All authors have read and agreed to the published version of the manuscript.

Funding: This research received no external funding.

Conflicts of Interest: The authors declare no conflict of interest.

References

1. Gabus, A.; Fontela, E. *World Problems, an Invitation to Further Thought within the Framework of DEMATEL*; Battelle Geneva Research Centre: Geneva, Switzerland, 1972.

2. Si, S.L.; You, X.Y.; Liu, H.C.; Zhang, P. DEMATEL technique: A systematic review of the state-of-the-art literature on methodologies and applications. *Math. Probl. Eng.* **2018**, *1*, 1–33. [CrossRef]
3. Dempster, A.P. Upper and lower probabilities induced by a multivalued mapping. *Ann. Math. Stat.* **1967**, *38*, 325–339. [CrossRef]
4. Shafer, G. A mathematical theory of evidence. *Technometrics* **1978**, *20*, 242.
5. Yang, J.; Huang, H.-Z.; He, L.-P.; Zhu, S.-P.; Wen, D. Risk evaluation in failure mode and effects analysis of aircraft turbine rotor blades using Dempster-Shafer evidence theory under uncertainty. *Eng. Fail. Anal.* **2011**, *18*, 2084–2092. [CrossRef]
6. Xiao, F. A novel multi-criteria decision making method for assessing health-care waste treatment technologies based on D numbers. *Eng. Appl. Artif. Intell.* **2018**, *71*, 216–225. [CrossRef]
7. Kang, B.; Deng, Y.; Sadiq, R.; Mahadevan, S. Evidential cognitive maps. *Knowl. Based Syst.* **2012**, *35*, 77–86. [CrossRef]
8. Ju, Y.; Wang, A. Emergency alternative evaluation under group decision makers: A method of incorporating DS/AHP with extended TOPSIS. *Expert Syst. Appl.* **2012**, *39*, 1315–1323. [CrossRef]
9. Ma, W.; Xiong, W.; Luo, X. A model for decision making with missing, imprecise, and uncertain evaluations of multiple criteria. *Int. J. Intell. Syst.* **2013**, *28*, 152–184. [CrossRef]
10. Fei, L.; Deng, Y.; Hu, Y. DS-VIKOR: A new multi-criteria decision-making method for supplier selection. *Int. J. Fuzzy Syst.* **2019**, *21*, 157–175. [CrossRef]
11. Sadiq, R.; Kleiner, Y.; Rajani, B. Estimating risk of contaminant intrusion in water distribution networks using Dempster–Shafer theory of evidence. *Civ. Eng. Environ. Syst.* **2006**, *23*, 129–141. [CrossRef]
12. Deng, X.; Hu, Y.; Deng, Y.; Mahadevan, S. Environmental impact assessment based on D numbers. *Expert Syst. Appl.* **2014**, *41*, 635–643. [CrossRef]
13. Deng, X.; Hu, Y.; Deng, Y. Bridge condition assessment using D numbers. *Sci. World J.* **2014**, *2014*, 358057. [CrossRef] [PubMed]
14. Xiao, F. A multiple-criteria decision-making method based on D numbers and belief entropy. *Int. J. Fuzzy Syst.* **2019**, *21*, 1144–1153. [CrossRef]
15. Deng, X.; Jiang, W. D number theory based game-theoretic framework in adversarial decision making under a fuzzy environment. *Int. J. Approx. Reason.* **2019**, *106*, 194–213. [CrossRef]
16. Deng, X.; Jiang, W. Evaluating green supply chain management practices under fuzzy environment: A novel method based on D number theory. *Int. J. Fuzzy Syst.* **2019**, *21*, 1389–1402. [CrossRef]
17. Zhou, X.; Shi, Y.; Deng, X.; Deng, Y. D-DEMATEL: A new method to identify critical success factors in emergency management. *Saf. Sci.* **2017**, *91*, 93–104. [CrossRef]
18. Lin, S.; Li, C.; Xu, F.; Liu, D.; Liu, J. Risk identification and analysis for new energy power system in China based on D numbers and decision-making trial and evaluation laboratory (DEMATEL). *J. Clean. Prod.* **2018**, *180*, 81–96. [CrossRef]
19. Karabašević, D.; Popović, G.; Stanujkić, D.; Maksimović, M.; Sava, C. An approach for hotel type selection based on the single-valued intuitionistic fuzzy numbers. *Int. Rev.* **2019**, *1–2*, 7–14. [CrossRef]
20. Stojić, G.; Sremac, S.; Vasiljković, I. A fuzzy model for determining the justifiability of investing in a road freight vehicle fleet. *Oper. Res. Eng. Sci. Theory Appl.* **2018**, *1*, 62–75. [CrossRef]
21. Stankovic, M.; Stevic, Z.; Das, D.K.; Subotic, M.; Pamucar, D. A New Fuzzy MARCOS Method for Road Traffic Risk Analysis. *Mathematics* **2020**, *8*, 457. [CrossRef]
22. Petrović, G.; Mihajlović, J.; Ćojbašić, Ž.; Madić, M.; Marinković, D. Comparison of three fuzzy MCDM methods for solving the supplier selection problem. *Facta Univ. Ser. Mech. Eng.* **2019**, *17*, 455–469. [CrossRef]
23. Vesković, S.; Milinković, S.; Abramović, B.; Ljubaj, I. Determining criteria significance in selecting reach stackers by applying the fuzzy PIPRECIA method. *Oper. Res. Eng. Sci. Theory Appl.* **2020**, *3*, 72–88. [CrossRef]
24. Zadeh, L.A. The concept of a linguistic variable and its application to approximate reasoning I. *Inf. Sci.* **1975**, *8*, 199–249. [CrossRef]
25. Zadeh, L.A. The concept of a linguistic variable and its application to approximate reasoning II. *Inf. Sci.* **1975**, *8*, 301–357. [CrossRef]
26. Zadeh, L.A. The concept of a linguistic variable and its application to approximate reasoning-III. *Inf. Sci.* **1975**, *9*, 43–80. [CrossRef]
27. Zadeh, L.A. Fuzzy sets. *Inf. Control* **1965**, *8*, 338–353. [CrossRef]
28. Zimmermann, H. *Fuzzy Set Theory and Its Applications*; Kluwer: Boston, MA, USA, 1991.

29. Morente-Molinera, J.A.; Wu, X.; Morfeq, A.; Al-Hmouz, R.; Herrera-Viedma, E. A novel multi-criteria group decision-making method for heterogeneous and dynamic contexts using multi-granular fuzzy linguistic modelling and consensus measures. *Inf. Fusion* **2020**, *53*, 240–250. [CrossRef]
30. Wel, S.H.; Chen, S.M. A new approach for fuzzy risk analysis based on similarity. *Expert Syst. Appl.* **2009**, *36*, 589–598.
31. Rao, P.P.B.; Ravi Shankar, N. Ranking Generalized Fuzzy Numbers using Area, Mode, Spreads and Weights. *Int. J. Appl. Sci. Eng.* **2012**, *10*, 41–57.
32. Pamucar, D.; Mihajlović, M.; Obradović, R.; Atanasković, P. Novel approach to group multi-criteria decision making based on interval rough numbers: Hybrid DEMATEL-ANP-MAIRCA model. *Expert Syst. Appl.* **2017**, *88*, 58–80. [CrossRef]
33. Chatterjee, K.; Pamucar, D.; Zavadskas, E.K. Evaluating the performance of suppliers based on using the R'AMATEL-MAIRCA method for green supply chain implementation in electronics industry. *J. Clean. Prod.* **2018**, *184*, 101–129. [CrossRef]
34. Roy, J.; Adhikary, K.; Kar, S.; Pamucar, D. A rough strength relational DEMATEL model for analysing the key success factors of hospital service quality. *Decis. Mak. Appl. Manag. Eng.* **2018**, *1*, 121–142. [CrossRef]
35. Liu, F.; Aiwu, G.; Lukovac, V.; Vukic, M. A multicriteria model for the selection of the transport service provider: A single valued neutrosophic DEMATEL multicriteria model. *Decis. Mak. Appl. Manag. Eng.* **2018**, *1*, 121–130. [CrossRef]
36. Chatterjee, P.; Stević, Ž. A two-phase fuzzy AHP-fuzzy TOPSIS model for supplier evaluation in manufacturing environment. *Oper. Res. Eng. Sci. Theory Appl.* **2019**, *2*, 72–90. [CrossRef]
37. Pamučar, D.; Božanić, D.; Lukovac, V.; Komazec, N. Normalized weighted geometric Bonferroni mean operator of interval rough numbers—Application in interval rough DEMATEL-COPRAS. *Facta Univ. Ser. Mech. Eng.* **2018**, *16*, 171–191. [CrossRef]
38. Prentkovskis, O.; Erceg, Ž.; Stević, Ž.; Tanackov, I.; Vasiljević, M.; Gavranović, M. A New Methodology for Improving Service Quality Measurement: Delphi-FUCOM-SERVQUAL Model. *Symmetry* **2018**, *10*, 757. [CrossRef]
39. Li, Y.; Hu, Y.; Zhang, X.; Deng, Y.; Mahadevan, S. An evidential DEMATEL method to identify critical success factors in emergency management. *Appl. Soft Comput.* **2014**, *22*, 504–510. [CrossRef]
40. Pamučar, D.; Ćirović, G. The selection of transport and handling resources in logistics centres using Multi-Attributive Border Approximation area Comparison (MABAC). *Expert Syst. Appl.* **2015**, *42*, 3016–3028. [CrossRef]

© 2020 by the authors. Licensee MDPI, Basel, Switzerland. This article is an open access article distributed under the terms and conditions of the Creative Commons Attribution (CC BY) license (http://creativecommons.org/licenses/by/4.0/).

Article

Preview Control for MIMO Discrete-Time System with Parameter Uncertainty

Li Li [1] and Fucheng Liao [2,*]

[1] School of Information Management and Statistics, Hubei University of Economics, Wuhan 430205, China; lili@hbue.edu.cn
[2] School of Mathematics and Physics, University of Science and Technology Beijing, Beijing 100083, China
* Correspondence: fcliao@ustb.edu.cn

Received: 16 April 2020; Accepted: 6 May 2020; Published: 9 May 2020

Abstract: We consider the problems of state feedback and static output feedback preview controller (PC) for uncertain discrete-time multiple-input multiple output (MIMO) systems based on the parameter-dependent Lyapunov function and the linear matrix inequality (LMI) technique in this paper. First, for each component of a reference signal, an augmented error system (AES) containing previewed information is constructed via the difference operator and state augmentation technique. Then, for the AES, the state feedback and static output feedback are introduced, and when considering the output feedback, a previewable reference signal is utilized by modifying the output equation. The preview controllers' parameter matrices can be achieved from the solution of LMI problems. The superiority of the PC is illustrated via two numerical examples.

Keywords: AES; PC; MIMO discrete-time system; state feedback and output feedback; parameter dependence

1. Introduction

In the field of control, there are many effective control methods, for example, optimal control [1], learning control [2], tracking control [3], and repetitive control [4] and so on. In many practical problems, future information is always known completely or partially, such as a vehicle driving path, scheduled flight route of an aircraft, and machining rules of a machine tool. Preview control can fully utilize the future values of these previewed signals to improve the control performance [5,6]. The preview control was first proposed by Sheridan in 1966 [7], and Bender [8] applied preview control theory to a vehicle suspension system. The field of preview control has attracted researchers and has been studied since the 1970s (see, the papers [9–13]). For a linear constant preview control system, LQR-based design methods have been most widely studied, e.g., [14–20]. However, the presence of an unknown disturbance or uncertain system model can cause degraded performance or even loss of closed-loop stability. To deal with this problem, robust preview control has received considerable attention [21–27]. In recent years, the integration of preview control and other control methods has attracted much attention. For example, in [28,29], the analysis and design problems of preview repetitive control for discrete system have been investigated. A fault-tolerant control theory was combined with preview control in [30,31]. In [32], the preview control concept was added to the Lipschitz non-linear system to consider the preview tracking control problems. Of course, preview control has attracted researchers for its applications in varied areas, e.g., wind turbine blade-pitch control [33], autonomous vehicle guidance [34], robotics [35], and so on.

With the rapid development of computer, electronics and information technology, industrial systems are becoming larger and more complex. Therefore, it is more interesting to consider the control problem of MIMO systems. For example, the preview control problem of MIMO systems was studied in [36] by combining linear quadratic optimal theory with the AES method. However, the dimension of an AES is high and the calculation is complex. In addition, through numerical simulations, we find that the preview control effect is not ideal when the reference signal is a vector, as in [11,13,15,36,37]. The components of the reference signal influence each other, and the influence is often negative. However, for a high-dimensional reference signal, the AES constructed in [11,13,15,36,37] not only has a high dimension, but the component signals also share the same preview length.

In this paper, robust PC design methods are proposed for MIMO discrete systems. First, the construction of an AES including previewable signals is carried out. Then, sufficient conditions of closed-loop systems and the PC design methods are proposed. The main contributions of our preview control scheme are summarized as follows: (i) The AES of a MIMO uncertain discrete-time system is successfully constructed from a new perspective. It not only constructs a lower-dimensional error system, but it also provides optional preview lengths. (ii) Our desired PC design method can avoid the negative influence of reference signal components on each other, and then effectively improve the tracking performance. (iii) Our design additionally allows the system output matrices to be non-common and have uncertainties. Finally, the simulation results clearly validate the superiority of the proposed PC.

Notation. $A > 0$: symmetric and positive definite matrix A. A^T denotes the matrix transposition of A. The symbol $*$ denotes the entries of matrices implied by symmetry. $sym(A)$ means $A + A^T$. I and 0: identity matrix and zero matrix of appropriate dimensions, respectively.

2. Problem Formulation

Consider the uncertain discrete-time system

$$\begin{cases} x(k+1) = A(\theta)x(k) + B(\theta)u(k), \\ y(k) = C(\theta)x(k) + D(\theta)u(k), \end{cases} \quad (1)$$

where $x(k) \in R^n$, $u(k) \in R^m$ and $y(k) \in R^q$ are respectively the state vector, input control vector, and output vector.

$y(k) = \begin{bmatrix} y_1(k) & y_2(k) & \cdots & y_q(k) \end{bmatrix}^T$, $C^i(\theta)$, and $D^i(\theta)$ represent the i $(i = 1, 2, \cdots, q)$ row of matrices $C(\theta)$ and $D(\theta)$, respectively. Then, we can have

$$y_i(k) = C^i(\theta)x(k) + D^i(\theta)u(k) \quad (2)$$

A1: The uncertain matrices are given by

$$\begin{bmatrix} A(\theta) & B(\theta) & C(\theta) & D(\theta) \end{bmatrix} = \sum_{j=1}^{s} \theta_j \begin{bmatrix} A_j & B_j & C_j & D_j \end{bmatrix} \quad (3)$$

where A_j, B_j, C_j, and D_j $(j = 1, 2, \cdots, s)$ are matrices with appropriate dimensions. $\theta = \begin{bmatrix} \theta_1 & \theta_2 & \cdots & \theta_s \end{bmatrix}^T \in R^s$ is the parameter vector and satisfies

$$\theta \in \Theta := \left\{ \theta \in R^s \middle| \theta_j \geq 0, (j = 1, 2, \cdots, s), \sum_{j=1}^{s} \theta_j = 1 \right\} \quad (4)$$

A2: Let $r(k) = \begin{bmatrix} r_1(k) & r_2(k) & \cdots & r_q(k) \end{bmatrix}^T \in R^q$ be the reference signal. Assume that the component reference signal $r_i(k)$ $(i = 1, 2, \cdots q)$ is available from current time k to $k + h_i$. The future values are assumed not to change beyond $k + h_i$, namely,

$$r_i(k+j) = r_i(k+h_i), \ (j \geq h_i + 1)$$

where h_i is the preview length.

Remark 1. *It should be noted that A2 is an assumption about $r_i(k)$ $(i = 1, 2, \cdots, q)$ rather than $r(k)$. There are two advantages of A2: (1) Each component $r_i(k)$ can have its own preview length h_i instead of sharing one preview length h. (2) It can avoid the negative effects of other signals.*

The objective is to design preview controller such that

(i) The output tracks the reference signal without steady-state error, that is,

$$\lim_{k \to \infty} e_i(k) = 0 \tag{5}$$

where $e_i(k) = y_i(k) - r_i(k)$.

(ii) The closed-loop system is robustly stable and exhibits acceptable transient responses for all $\theta \in \Theta$.

3. Derivation of AES

Here, we derived an AES that contains previewed information. Employing the difference operator Δ as:

$$\Delta \delta(k) = \delta(k+1) - \delta(k) \tag{6}$$

and applying the difference operator to (1) and (2), one obtains:

$$\begin{cases} \Delta x(k+1) = A(\theta) \Delta x(k) + B(\theta) \Delta u(k), \\ \Delta y_i(k) = C^i(\theta) \Delta x(k) + D^i(\theta) \Delta u(k). \end{cases} \tag{7}$$

Considering (5)–(7), it is obtained that:

$$e_i(k+1) = e_i(k) + C^i(\theta) \Delta x(k) + D^i(\theta) \Delta u(k) - \Delta r_i(k) \tag{8}$$

It follows from (6) and (8) that:

$$\widetilde{x}_i(k+1) = \widetilde{A}_i(\theta) \widetilde{x}_i(k) + \widetilde{B}_i(\theta) \Delta u_i(k) + G \Delta r_i(k) \tag{9}$$

where

$$\widetilde{x}_i(k) = \begin{bmatrix} e_i(k) \\ \Delta x(k) \end{bmatrix}, \widetilde{A}_i(\theta) = \begin{bmatrix} I & C^i(\theta) \\ 0 & A(\theta) \end{bmatrix}, \widetilde{B}_i(\theta) = \begin{bmatrix} D^i(\theta) \\ B(\theta) \end{bmatrix}, G = \begin{bmatrix} -1 \\ 0 \end{bmatrix}$$

From A1, $\widetilde{A}_i(\theta)$ and $\widetilde{B}_i(\theta)$ can be given by:

$$\widetilde{A}_i(\theta) = \begin{bmatrix} I & \sum_{j=1}^{s} \theta_j C_j^i \\ 0 & \sum_{j=1}^{s} \theta_j A_j \end{bmatrix} = \sum_{j=1}^{s} \theta_j \begin{bmatrix} I & C_j^i \\ 0 & A_j \end{bmatrix} = \sum_{j=1}^{s} \theta_j \widetilde{A}_{i,j} \tag{10}$$

$$\widetilde{B}_i(\theta) = \begin{bmatrix} \sum_{j=1}^{s} \theta_j D_j^i \\ \sum_{j=1}^{s} \theta_j B_j \end{bmatrix} = \sum_{j=1}^{s} \theta_j \begin{bmatrix} D_j^i \\ B_j \end{bmatrix} = \sum_{j=1}^{s} \theta_j \widetilde{B}_{i,j} \tag{11}$$

Note that, in (10) and (11), C_j^i and D_j^i represent the i row of matrices C_j and D_j, respectively, where $i \in \{1, 2, \cdots, q\}, j \in \{1, 2, \cdots, s\}$.

From A2, $r_i(k), r_i(k+1), \cdots, r_i(k+h_i)$ are available at time k. Defining

$$x_{ri}(k) = \begin{bmatrix} \Delta r_i(k) \\ \Delta r_i(k+1) \\ \vdots \\ \vdots \\ \Delta r_i(k+h_i) \end{bmatrix}, A_{R,i} = \begin{bmatrix} 0 & 1 & & & 0 \\ 0 & \ddots & \ddots & & \\ \vdots & & \ddots & \ddots & \\ 0 & \cdots & \cdots & 0 & 1 \\ 0 & \cdots & \cdots & 0 & 0 \end{bmatrix}$$

then, it can be obtained:
$$x_{ri}(k+1) = A_{R,i} x_{ri}(k) \tag{12}$$

where $x_{ri}(k) \in R^{h_i+1}$ and $A_{R,i} \in R^{(h_i+1)\times(h_i+1)}$.

Each component $r_i(k)$ can have its own preview length h_i; therefore, h_i can be selected appropriately as needed.

Based on (8) and (12), we obtain:
$$\hat{x}_i(k+1) = \hat{A}_i(\theta)\hat{x}_i(k) + \hat{B}_i(\theta)\Delta u_i(k) \tag{13}$$

where

$$\hat{x}_i(k) = \begin{bmatrix} \widetilde{x}_i(k) \\ x_{ri}(k) \end{bmatrix}, \hat{A}_i(\theta) = \begin{bmatrix} \widetilde{A}_i(\theta) & W_i \\ 0 & A_{R,i} \end{bmatrix}, \hat{B}_i(\theta) = \begin{bmatrix} \widetilde{B}_i(\theta) \\ 0 \end{bmatrix}, W_i = \begin{bmatrix} G & 0 & \cdots & 0 \\ & & \underbrace{}_{h_i} & \end{bmatrix}$$

System (13) is the AES and the future information of $r_i(k)$ is added to System (13).
Based on (10) and (11), $\hat{A}_i(\theta)$ and $\hat{B}_i(\theta)$ are written as:

$$\hat{A}_i(\theta) = \begin{bmatrix} \sum_{j=1}^{s} \theta_j \widetilde{A}_{i,j} & W_i \\ 0 & A_{R,i} \end{bmatrix} = \sum_{j=1}^{s} \theta_j \begin{bmatrix} \widetilde{A}_{i,j} & W_i \\ 0 & A_{R,i} \end{bmatrix} = \sum_{j=1}^{s} \theta_j \hat{A}_{i,j} \tag{14}$$

$$\hat{B}_i(\theta) = \begin{bmatrix} \sum_{j=1}^{s} \theta_j \widetilde{B}_{i,j} \\ 0 \end{bmatrix} = \sum_{j=1}^{s} \theta_j \begin{bmatrix} \widetilde{B}_{i,j} \\ 0 \end{bmatrix} = \sum_{j=1}^{s} \theta_j \hat{B}_{i,j} \tag{15}$$

Remark 2. *System (13) is the so-called AES. The future information of $r_i(k)$ is added to the AES (13) rather than the future information of $r_1(k), r_2(k), \cdots, r_q(k)$. The benefits of this treatment are: (i) the size of the AES in this paper is smaller. Our proposed AES has $1 + n + (h_i + 1)$ states, whereas the AES in refs. [5,10,11,26,27] has $q + n + (h+1)q$. (ii) Based on the theoretical analysis and numerical simulations, we found that, if we added the future information of $r(k)$ to the AES as usual, the control effect of the PC is poor.*

4. PC Design

Consider the following system
$$\hat{x}_i(k) = \hat{A}_i(\theta)\hat{x}_i(k) \tag{16}$$

Lemma 1. *Lemma 1: System (16) is asymptotically stable, if there exists $P_i(\theta) > 0$ and matrices F_{1i} and F_{2i} with appropriate dimensions such that:*

$$\Omega_i(\theta) = \begin{bmatrix} -P_i(\theta) - F_{1i}\hat{A}_i(\theta) - \hat{A}_i(\theta)^T F_{1i}^T & * \\ F_{1i}^T - F_{2i}\hat{A}_i(\theta) & P_i(\theta) + F_{2i} + F_{2i}^T \end{bmatrix} < 0 \tag{17}$$
$$(i = 1, 2, \cdots, q)$$

Proof. Consider the Lyapunov function

$$V_i(k) = \hat{x}_i(k)^T P_i(\theta) \hat{x}_i(k)$$

We have

$$\Delta V_i(k) = \hat{x}_i(k+1)^T P_i(\theta) \hat{x}_i(k+1) - \hat{x}_i(k)^T P_i(\theta) \hat{x}_i(k) \tag{18}$$

From (17), the following equation holds:

$$2\left[\hat{x}_i(k)^T F_{1i} + \hat{x}_i(k+1)^T F_{2i}\right]\left[\hat{x}_i(k+1) - \hat{A}_i(\theta)\hat{x}_i(k)\right] = 0 \tag{19}$$

where F_{1i} and F_{2i} are matrices with appropriate dimensions.

Obviously, if (17) holds, then it can be concluded that $\Delta V_i(k) < 0$, which implies that System (16) is asymptotically stable. This completes the proof. □

4.1. State Feedback PC

The state feedback control is presented as follows:

$$\Delta u_i(k) = \left(\sum_{j=1}^{s} \gamma_j K_{i,j}\right) \hat{x}_i(k) \quad (i = 1, 2, \cdots, q) \tag{20}$$

where, $K_{i,j}$ and γ_j ($i = 1, 2, \cdots, s$) are matrices and adjustable variables to be determined, and $\gamma_j \geq 0$, $\sum_{j=1}^{s} \gamma_j = 1$. For convenience, we note that $K_i(\gamma) = \sum_{j=1}^{s} \gamma_j K_{i,j}$.

Substituting (20) into (13), we obtain:

$$\hat{x}_i(k+1) = \left[\hat{A}_i(\theta) + \hat{B}_i(\theta) K_i(\gamma)\right] \hat{x}_i(k) \tag{21}$$

Theorem 1. *If there exist matrices $X_i(\theta) > 0$, $Y_i(\gamma)$, and H_i and scalars α_i and β_i such that*

$$\Pi_i(\theta, \gamma) = \begin{bmatrix} -\alpha_i^2 X_i(\theta) - sym(\alpha_i \hat{A}_i(\theta) H_i + \alpha_i \hat{B}_i(\theta) Y_i(\gamma)) & * \\ -\beta_i H_i^T - \alpha_i (\hat{A}_i(\theta) H_i + \hat{B}_i(\theta) Y_i(\gamma)) & \beta_i^2 X_i(\theta) - 2\beta_i H_i \end{bmatrix} < 0, \tag{22}$$
$$(i = 1, 2, \cdots, q)$$

then System (21) is asymptotically stable.

Proof. For the closed-loop System (21), from Lemma 1 we know that, if there exists $P_i(\theta) > 0$, F_{1i} and F_{2i} with appropriate dimensions satisfies:

$$\begin{bmatrix} -P_i(\theta) - sym(F_{1i}(\hat{A}_i(\theta) + \hat{B}_i(\theta) K_i(\gamma))) & * \\ F_{1i}^T - F_{2i}(\hat{A}_i(\theta) + \hat{B}_i(\theta) K_i(\gamma)) & P_i(\theta) + F_{2i} + F_{2i}^T \end{bmatrix} < 0 \tag{23}$$

To obtain LMI conditions [38,39], let

$$F_{1i} = a_i R_i, \quad F_{2i} = -b_i R_i \tag{24}$$

where $a_i \neq 0$ and $b_i \neq 0$. Then, by applying a congruence transformations by $diag\{F_{1i}^{-1}, F_{2i}^{-1}\}$ to (23) and denoting $R_i^{-T} = H_i$, $R_i^{-T} P_i(\theta)^{-1} R_i^{-1} = X_i(\theta)$, $K_i(\gamma) R_i^{-T} = Y_i(\gamma)$, $\alpha_i = 1/a_i$, and $\beta_i = 1/b_i$, we arrive at the condition in Theorem 1. □

Theorem 2. Given scalars α_i and β_i, if there exist matrices $X_{i,j} > 0$, $Y_{i,d}$, and H_i such that:

$$\Pi^i_{j,d} < 0 i, j, d : i \in \{1,2,3,\cdots,q\}, j, d \in \{1,2,3,\cdots,s\} \tag{25}$$

then System (21) is robustly stabilizable via (20), and the control input is given by

$$\Delta u_i(k) = K_i(\gamma)\hat{x}_i(k) = \sum_{d=1}^{s} \gamma_d Y_{i,d} H_i^{-1} \hat{x}_i(k) \tag{26}$$

In (25),

$$\Pi^i_{j,d} = \begin{bmatrix} -\alpha_i^2 X_{i,j} - sym(\alpha_i \hat{A}_{i,j} H_i + \alpha_i \hat{B}_{i,j} Y_{i,d}) & * \\ -\beta_i H_i^T - \alpha_i (\hat{A}_{i,j} H_i + \hat{B}_{i,j} Y_{i,d}) & \beta_i^2 X_{i,j} - 2\beta_i H_i \end{bmatrix}$$

Proof. Multiplying (25) by $\theta_j \gamma_d$ for $1 \leq j \leq s$ and $1 \leq d \leq s$ and summing them, according (14) and (15), we obtain

$$\Pi_i(\theta, \gamma) = \sum_{j=1}^{s} \sum_{d=1}^{s} \theta_j \gamma_d \Pi^i_{j,d} \tag{27}$$

and, thus, (25) can imply $\Pi_i(\theta, \gamma) < 0$. From (22), Theorem 2 holds. □

If the system model parameter can be available, the state feedback for System (20) to be designed

$$\Delta u_i(k) = \left(\sum_{j=1}^{s} \theta_j K_{i,j}\right) \hat{x}_i(k) \tag{28}$$

The matrices $K_{i,j}$ ($j = 1, 2, \cdots, s$) are gain matrices, and we let $K_i(\theta) = \sum_{j=1}^{s} \theta_j K_{i,j}$.

Applying (28) to System (13) yields

$$\hat{x}_i(k+1) = [\hat{A}_i(\theta) + \hat{B}_i(\theta) K_i(\theta)] \hat{x}_i(k) \tag{29}$$

Based on Theorems 1 and 2, the following corollaries are presented.

Corollary 1. The System (29) is asymptotically stable if there exist matrices $X_i(\theta) > 0$ and $Y_i(\theta)$ and scalars α_i and $\beta_i \in (0, 2)$, such that:

$$\Pi_i(\theta) = \begin{bmatrix} -\alpha_i^2 X_i(\theta) - sym(\alpha_i \hat{A}_i(\theta) X_i(\theta) + \alpha_i \hat{B}_i(\theta) Y_i(\theta)) & * \\ -\beta_i X_i(\theta) - \alpha_i(\hat{A}_i(\theta) X_i(\theta) + \hat{B}_i(\theta) Y_i(\theta)) & (\beta_i^2 - 2\beta_i) X_i(\theta) \end{bmatrix} < 0, \tag{30}$$

$$(i = 1, 2, \cdots, q)$$

Proof. In Theorem 1, let $F_{1i}(\theta) = a_i P_i(\theta)$, $F_{2i}(\theta) = b_i P_i(\theta)$, $P_i(\theta)^{-1} = X_i(\theta)$, $K_i(\theta) X_i(\theta) = Y_i(\theta)$, $\alpha_i = \frac{1}{a_i}, \beta_i = \frac{1}{b_i}$, then (30) can be obtained. □

Corollary 2. For known scalars $\beta_i \in (0, 2)$ and α_i, if there exist matrices $X_{i,d} > 0$ and $Y_{i,d}$ such that

$$\Pi^i_{j,d} + \Pi^i_{d,j} < 0, \; j \leq d : j, d \in \{1,2,3,\cdots,s\}, i \in \{1,2,3,\cdots,q\} \tag{31}$$

then the System (29) is asymptotically stable, and the control input is given by

$$\Delta u_i(k) = \left(\sum_{d=1}^{s} \theta_d Y_{i,d}\right) \left(\sum_{d=1}^{s} \theta_d X_{i,d}\right)^{-1} \hat{x}_i(k) \tag{32}$$

In (31),
$$\Pi^i_{j,d} = \begin{bmatrix} -\alpha_i^2 X_{i,d} - sym(\alpha_i \hat{A}_{i,j} X_{i,d} + \alpha_i \hat{B}_{i,j} Y_{i,d}) & * \\ -\beta_i X_{i,d} - \alpha_i(\hat{A}_{i,j} X_{i,d} + \hat{B}_{i,j} Y_{i,d}) & (\beta_i^2 - 2\beta_i) X_{i,d} \end{bmatrix}$$

The gain matrix $K_{i,j}$ in (20) is divided as follows:

$$K_{i,j} = \begin{bmatrix} K^i_{ej} & K^i_{xj} & K^i_{Rj}(0) & K^i_{Rj}(1) & \cdots & K^i_{Rj}(h_i) \end{bmatrix} \quad (33)$$

Equation (20) is then written as

$$\Delta u_i(k) = \sum_{j=1}^{s} \gamma_j \left[K^i_{ej} e_i(k) + K^i_{xj} \Delta x(k) + \sum_{d=0}^{h_i} K^i_{Rj}(d) \Delta r_i(k+d) \right]$$

Therefore, the control input of System (1) is given by

$$u_i(k) = K^i_e \sum_{h=0}^{k-1} e_i(h) + K^i_x x(k) + \sum_{d=0}^{h_i} K^i_R(d) r_i(k+d) \quad (34)$$

where $K^i_e = \sum_{j=1}^{s} \gamma_j K^i_{ej}$, $K^i_x = \sum_{j=1}^{s} \gamma_j K^i_{xj}$, and $K^i_R(d) = \sum_{j=1}^{s} \gamma_j K^i_{Rj}(d)$.

4.2. Static Output Feedback PC

To obtain the control law with preview compensation, for System (13), the output equation is modified as

$$z_i(k) = C_{Zi}(\theta) \hat{x}_i(k) \quad (35)$$

where

$$C_{Zi}(\theta) = \begin{bmatrix} I_{q_i} & & \\ & \sum_{j=1}^{s} C^i_j & \\ & & I_{(M_{R,i}+1)} \end{bmatrix} = \sum_{j=1}^{s} \theta_j C_{Zi,j} \quad (36)$$

We consider a output feedback controller

$$\Delta u_i(k) = \left(\sum_{j=1}^{s} \gamma_j K_{i,j} \right) z_i(k), \ (i = 1, 2, \cdots, q) \quad (37)$$

Based on (13), (35), and (37), we obtain the following system:

$$\hat{x}_i(k+1) = \left[\hat{A}_i(\theta) + \hat{B}_i(\theta) K_i(\gamma) C_{Zi}(\theta) \right] \hat{x}_i(k) \quad (38)$$

Lemma 2. [40]: *For appropriately dimensioned matrices F, R, S, and N and scalar β, $F + S^T R^T + RS < 0$ is fulfilled if the following condition holds:*

$$\begin{bmatrix} F & * \\ \beta R^T + NS & -\beta N - \beta N^T \end{bmatrix} < 0$$

Theorem 3. For given α_i, β_i, and ρ_i, the System (38) is asymptotically stable if there exist matrices $X_i(\theta) > 0$ and matrices Q_i, $L_i(\gamma)$, U_i, and H_i, such that:

$$\Pi_i(\theta,\gamma) = \begin{bmatrix} -\alpha_i^2 X_i(\theta) - sym(\alpha_i \hat{A}_i(\theta)H_i + \hat{B}_i(\theta)L_i(\gamma)Q_i) & * & * \\ -\beta_i H_i^T - \alpha_i(\hat{A}_i(\theta)H_i + \hat{B}_i(\theta)L_i(\gamma)Q_i) & \beta_i^2 X_i(\theta) - 2\beta_i H_i & * \\ -\rho_i \alpha_i L_i(\gamma)^T \hat{B}_i(\theta)^T + C_{Zi}(\theta)H_i - U_i Q_i & -\rho_i \alpha_i L_i(\gamma)^T \hat{B}_i(\theta)^T & -\rho_i sym(U_i) \end{bmatrix} < 0, \quad (39)$$

$(i = 1, 2, \cdots, q)$

Proof. Equation (39) is written as

$$\begin{bmatrix} \underbrace{\begin{bmatrix} -\alpha_i^2 X_i(\theta) - sym(\alpha_i \hat{A}_i(\theta)H_i + \hat{B}_i(\theta)L_i(\gamma)Q_i) & * \\ -\beta_i H_i^T - \alpha_i(\hat{A}_i(\theta)H_i + \hat{B}_i(\theta)L_i(\gamma)Q_i) & \beta_i^2 X_i(\theta) - 2\beta_i H_i \end{bmatrix}}_{F} & * \\ \underbrace{-\rho_i \alpha_i L_i(\gamma)^T \hat{B}_i(\theta)^T \begin{bmatrix} I & I \end{bmatrix}}_{\rho_i R^T} + \underbrace{U_i}_{N} \underbrace{U_i^{-1}(C_{Zi}(\theta)H_i - U_i Q_i)\begin{bmatrix} I & 0 \end{bmatrix}}_{S} & \underbrace{-\rho_i sym(U_i)}_{-\rho_i N - \rho_i N^T} \end{bmatrix} < 0. \quad (40)$$

According to Lemma 2, (40) can guarantee

$$\begin{aligned}&\begin{bmatrix} -\alpha_i^2 X_i(\theta) - \alpha_i sym(\hat{A}_i(\theta)H_i + \hat{B}_i(\theta)L_i(\gamma)Q_i) & * \\ -\beta_i H_i^T - \alpha_i(\hat{A}_i(\theta)H_i + \hat{B}_i(\theta)L_i(\gamma)Q_i) & \beta_i^2 X_i(\theta) - 2\beta_i H_i \end{bmatrix} \\ &- sym\left(\begin{bmatrix} I \\ I \end{bmatrix} \alpha_i \hat{B}_i(\theta)L_i(\gamma)U_i^{-1}(C_{Zi}(\theta)H_i - U_i Q_i)\begin{bmatrix} I & 0 \end{bmatrix}\right) \\ &= \begin{bmatrix} -\alpha_i^2 X_i(\theta) - \alpha_i sym(\hat{A}_i(\theta)H_i) & * \\ -\beta_i H_i^T - \alpha_i(\hat{A}_i(\theta)H_i) & \beta_i^2 X_i(\theta) - 2\beta_i H_i \end{bmatrix} \\ &- sym\left(\begin{bmatrix} I \\ I \end{bmatrix} \alpha_i \hat{B}_i(\theta)L_i(\gamma)U_i^{-1}(C_{Zi}(\theta)H_i - U_i Q_i + U_i Q_i)\begin{bmatrix} I & 0 \end{bmatrix}\right) \\ &< 0. \end{aligned} \quad (41)$$

Letting $K_i(\gamma) = L_i(\gamma)U_i^{-1}$, we have

$$\begin{bmatrix} -\alpha_i^2 X_i(\theta) - sym(\alpha_i \hat{A}_i(\theta)H_i) & * \\ -\beta_i H_i^T - \alpha_i(\hat{A}_i(\theta)H_i) & \beta_i^2 X_i(\theta) - 2\beta_i H_i \end{bmatrix} - \alpha_i sym\left(\begin{bmatrix} I \\ I \end{bmatrix} \hat{B}_i(\theta)K_i(\gamma)C_{Zi}(\theta)H_i \begin{bmatrix} I & 0 \end{bmatrix}\right) < 0,$$

and therefore

$$\begin{bmatrix} -\alpha_i^2 X_i(\theta) - \alpha_i sym((\hat{A}_i(\theta) + \hat{B}_i(\theta)K_i(\gamma)C_{Zi}(\theta))H_i) & * \\ -\beta_i H_i^T - \alpha_i((\hat{A}_i(\theta) + \hat{B}_i(\theta)K_i(\gamma)C_{Zi}(\theta))H_i) & \beta_i^2 X_i(\theta) - 2\beta_i H_i \end{bmatrix} < 0$$

From Theorem 1, Theorem 3 holds. □

Theorem 4. For given scalars α_i, β_i, and ρ_i and matrix Q_i, if there exist $X_{i,j} > 0$, $L_{i,d}$, H_i, and U_i such that

$$\Pi_{j,d}^i < 0 \ (i, j, d : i \in \{1, 2, 3, \cdots, q\}, j, d \in \{1, 2, 3, \cdots, s\}) \quad (42)$$

then the System (38) is robust asymptotically stable. The controller is given by

$$\Delta u_i(k) = K_i(\gamma)Z_i(k) = \sum_{d=1}^{s} \gamma_d L_{i,d} U_i^{-1} Z_i(k) \quad (43)$$

In (42),

$$\Pi^i_{j,d} = \begin{bmatrix} -\alpha_i^2 X_{i,d} - \alpha_i sym(\hat{A}_{i,j}H_i + \hat{B}_{i,j}L_{i,d}Q_i) & * & * \\ -\beta_i H_i^T - \alpha_i(\hat{A}_{i,j}H_i + \hat{B}_{i,j}L_{i,d}Q_i) & \beta_i^2 X_{i,d} - 2\beta_i H_i & * \\ -\rho_i\alpha_i L_{i,d}^T \hat{B}_{i,j}^T + C_{Zi,j}H_i - U_i Q_i & -\rho_i\alpha_i L_{i,d}^T \hat{B}_{i,j}^T & -\rho_i sym(U_i) \end{bmatrix}$$

Similarly, if the uncertain parameters of the system model are known, we consider the following form of the parameter-dependent output controller:

$$\Delta u_i(k) = \left(\sum_{d=1}^s \theta_d K_{i,d}\right) z_i(k) \tag{44}$$

where $K_{i,d}$ ($d = 1, 2, \cdots, s$) are gain matrices, and $K_i(\theta) = \sum_{d=1}^s \theta_d K_{i,d}$.

Based on (13) and (44), we obtain

$$\hat{x}_i(k+1) = \left[\hat{A}_i(\theta) + \hat{B}_i(\theta)K_i(\theta)C_{Zi}(\theta)\right]\hat{x}_i(k) \tag{45}$$

According to Theorem 3 and 4, Corollary 3 and 4 are given as follows:

Corollary 3. *For given scalars α_i, ρ_i and $\beta_i \in (0, 2)$, a sufficient condition for the proposed controller (44) that ensures the uncertain discrete-time closed system (45) to be asymptotically stable, if there exist matrices $X_i(\theta) > 0$, $L_i(\theta)$, Q_i, and $U_i(\theta)$ such that Equation (46) hold:*

$$\Pi_i(\theta) = \begin{bmatrix} -\alpha_i^2 X_i(\theta) - \alpha_i sym(\hat{A}_i(\theta)X_i(\theta) + \hat{B}_i(\theta)L_i(\theta)Q_i) & * & * \\ -\beta_i X_i(\theta) - \alpha_i(\hat{A}_i(\theta)X_i(\theta) + \hat{B}_i(\theta)L_i(\theta)Q_i) & (\beta_i^2 - 2\beta_i)X_i(\theta) & * \\ -\rho_i\alpha_i L_i(\theta)^T \hat{B}_i(\theta)^T + C_{Zi}(\theta)X_i(\theta) - U_i Q_i & -\rho_i\alpha_i L_i(\theta)^T \hat{B}_i(\theta)^T & -\rho_i sym(U_i) \end{bmatrix} < 0, \tag{46}$$

$$(i = 1, 2, \cdots, q)$$

Corollary 4. *For given $\beta_i \in (0, 2)$, α_i, ρ_i, and matrix Q_i, if there exist matrices $X_{i,d} > 0$, $L_{i,d}$ and U_i such that*

$$\Pi^i_{j,d} + \Pi^i_{d,j} < 0, \ (j \leq d : j, d \in \{1, 2, 3, \cdots, s\}, i \in \{1, 2, 3, \cdots, q\}) \tag{47}$$

hold, then the closed-loop System (45) is robustly asymptotically stable, and the controller is given by

$$\Delta u_i(k) = \sum_{d=1}^s \theta_d L_{i,d} U_i^{-1} Z_i(k) \tag{48}$$

In (47),

$$\Pi^i_{jd} = \begin{bmatrix} -\alpha_i^2 X_{i,d} - \alpha_i sym(\hat{A}_{i,j}X_{i,d} + \hat{B}_{i,j}L_{i,d}Q_i) & * & * \\ -\beta_i X_{i,d} - \alpha_i(\hat{A}_{i,j}X_{i,d} + \hat{B}_{i,j}L_{i,d}Q_i) & \beta_i^2 X_{i,j} - 2\beta_i X_{i,j} & * \\ -\rho_i\alpha_i L_{i,d}^T \hat{B}_{i,j}^T + C_{Zi,j}X_{i,d} - U_i Q_i & -\rho_i\alpha_i L_{i,d}^T \hat{B}_{i,j}^T & -\rho_i sym(U_i) \end{bmatrix}$$

We decompose the gain matrix $K_{i,j}$ as

$$K_{i,j} = \begin{bmatrix} K^i_{ej} & K^i_{yj} & K^i_{Rj}(0) & K^i_{Rj}(1) & \cdots & K^i_{Rj}(h_i) \end{bmatrix} \tag{49}$$

and then (37) is

$$\Delta u_i(k) = \sum_{j=1}^s \gamma_j \left[K^i_{ej} e_i(k) + K^i_{yj}\Delta y(k) + \sum_{d=0}^{h_i} K^i_R(d)\Delta r_i(k+d)\right]$$

The controller of System (1) can be taken as

$$u_i(k) = K_e^i \sum_{h=0}^{k-1} e_i(h) + K_y^i y_i(k) + \sum_{d=0}^{h_i} K_R^i(d) r_i(k+d) \qquad (50)$$

where

$$K_e^i = \sum_{j=1}^{s} \gamma_j K_{ej}^i, \quad K_y^i = \sum_{j=1}^{s} \gamma_j K_{yj}^i, \quad K_R^i(d) = \sum_{j=1}^{s} \gamma_j K_{Rj}^i(d)$$

Remark 3. *In light of (34) and (50), it is clear that the preview controller of System (1) consists of three terms. The first term is the integral action on the tracking error, the second term represents the state feedback or output feedback, the third term represents the feedforward or preview action based on the future information on $r_i(k)$.*

Remark 4. *If the construction method of AES proposed by [11,13,14,26] is used in this paper. In the other word, the future information of the reference signal $r(k)$ has been added to augmented state vector. The preview compensation term in PC will be the form of*

$$\sum_{d=0}^{h} K_R(d) r(k+d) = \sum_{d=0}^{h} K_R(d) \begin{bmatrix} r_1(k+d)^T & r_2(k+d)^T & \cdots & r_q(k+d)^T \end{bmatrix}^T \qquad (51)$$

It follows from the theoretical analysis and numerical simulations that the future information of $r_1(k)$, $r_2(k) \cdots, r_q(k)$ interacts with each other. This may lead to poor tracking performance.

5. Numerical Example

In (1), let

$$A(\theta) = \begin{bmatrix} 1 & -0.6 & -0.8 & -1 \\ 0 & 0 & -0.1 & 0.5 \\ 0.2 & 0 & 0.9 & -0.3 \\ 0.1 & -0.3 & -0.3 & 0.1 \end{bmatrix} \theta_1 + \begin{bmatrix} 0.9 & 1.2 & 0.4 & -0.3 \\ 0 & 1 & 0 & 0.2 \\ -0.6 & 0.3 & 1 & 0 \\ 0.3 & -0.5 & 0 & 1 \end{bmatrix} \theta_2$$

$$B(\theta) = \begin{bmatrix} -0.5 & 0.1 \\ -0.2 & 0.1 \\ 0.5 & 0 \\ 0 & 0.5 \end{bmatrix} \theta_1 + \begin{bmatrix} -0.3 & 0.2 \\ -0.1 & 0 \\ -0.6 & 0.2 \\ 0.2 & 0.5 \end{bmatrix} \theta_2$$

$$C(\theta) = \theta_1 \begin{bmatrix} 0.2 & 1.2 & 0.3 & 0 \\ -0.1 & 1.5 & 0.2 & 0.4 \end{bmatrix} + \theta_2 \begin{bmatrix} 0.3 & 0.8 & 0 & 0 \\ -0.7 & -2 & 0.5 & -0.3 \end{bmatrix}, \quad D(\theta) = 0.$$

For $s = 2$, the scalars are taken as $\alpha_1 = 4$, $\beta_1 = 0.6$, $\alpha_2 = 0.8$, and $\beta_2 = 0.5$ and $\gamma_1 = 0.3$ and $\gamma_2 = 0.7$. In this example, we selected the preview lengths as ① $h_1 = 6$, $(h_2 = 5)$, ② $h_1 = 2$, $(h_2 = 1)$, and ③ $h_1 = 0$, $(h_2 = 0)$. By solving the LMIs (25) using the MatLab LMI control toolbox, the gains were obtained as follows.

When $h_1 = 2$, we had

$$K_1 = \begin{bmatrix} 0.31429 & 0.94275 & 2.01847 & -0.33257 & -0.82234 & -0.31382 & -0.31125 & -0.29639 \\ -0.36601 & 1.14616 & -1.09108 & -1.71517 & -3.31321 & 0.36385 & 0.34914 & 0.28267 \end{bmatrix},$$

When $h_1 = 6$, we obtained

$$K_1 = \begin{bmatrix} 0.30753 & 0.95324 & 1.98948 & -0.34762 & -0.82702 & -0.30735 \\ -0.45000 & 1.08942 & -1.29829 & -1.74390 & -3.308732 & 0.4487631 \\ -0.30500 & -0.29540 & -0.28696 & -0.26726 & -0.24118 & -0.20619 \\ 0.43397 & 0.36963 & 0.27278 & 0.22070 & 0.18295 & 0.16303 \end{bmatrix}.$$

When $h_1 = 0$, we had

$$K_1 = \begin{bmatrix} 0.29017 & 0.95022 & 1.99563 & -0.37000 & -0.83099 \\ -0.37170 & 1.20180 & -1.19541 & -1.80608 & -3.39788 \end{bmatrix}.$$

When $h_2 = 1$, we had

$$K_2 = \begin{bmatrix} -0.11796 & 0.80069 & 1.46557 & -0.53132 & -0.62061 & 0.11759 & 0.11951 \\ -0.12550 & 0.91854 & -0.11027 & -1.29944 & -2.73462 & 0.11732 & 0.12856 \end{bmatrix}.$$

When $h_2 = 5$, we obtained

$$K_2 = \begin{bmatrix} -0.11978 & 0.79657 & 1.46443 & -0.53304 & -0.61610 & 0.11975 \\ -0.12802 & 0.91029 & -0.11878 & -1.29739 & -2.73190 & 0.12520 \\ 0.11903 & 0.11962 & 0.11649 & 0.11441 & 0.10747 \\ 0.13164 & 0.13769 & 0.12484 & 0.12282 & 0.11164 \end{bmatrix},$$

When $h_2 = 0$, we had

$$K_2 = \begin{bmatrix} -0.11994 & 0.81063 & 1.46822 & -0.53765 & -0.62579 \\ -0.13216 & 0.94764 & -0.09604 & -1.31084 & -2.74898 \end{bmatrix}.$$

The reference signal was selected as

$$r_1(k) = \begin{cases} 0, & k \leq 10, \\ 0.05(k-10), & 10 < k < 50, \\ 2, & k \geq 50. \end{cases} \quad (52)$$

$$r_2(k) = \begin{cases} 0, & k \leq 40, \\ 0.0375(k-40), & 40 < k < 80, \\ 1.5, & k \geq 80. \end{cases} \quad (53)$$

The outputs and the reference signals are depicted in Figure 1. Figure 2 plots the control input. As can be seen in Figures 1 and 2, the existence of the preview compensation accelerated the response speed, which reduced the tracking error.

To consider the robustness of the proposed PC, the simulations were completed with different θ_1 and θ_2 as long as they met A1. Here, the simulation results about $\theta_1 = 1$ and $\theta_1 = 0$ would be given separately. We depicted the output and control input of system (1) with $\theta_1 = 1$ and $\theta_2 = 0$ in Figures 3 and 4. Figure 5 plotted the output of System (1) with $\theta_1 = 0$ and $\theta_2 = 1$. The corresponding input control is shown in Figure 6. One can see from Figures 3–6 that the PC made the closed-loop system have a faster dynamic response speed compared with no preview.

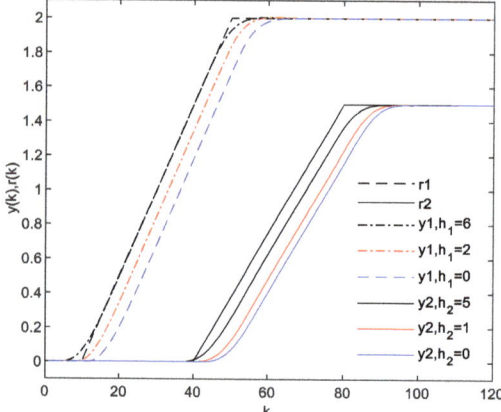

Figure 1. The output response and the reference signals.

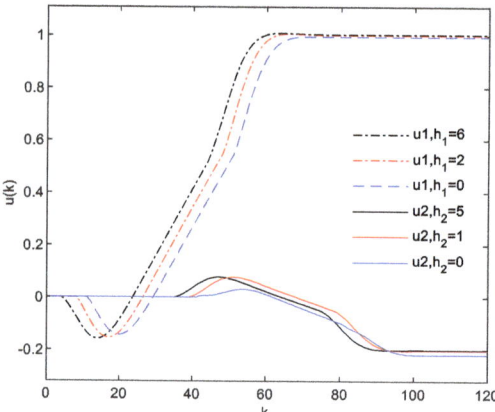

Figure 2. The control input.

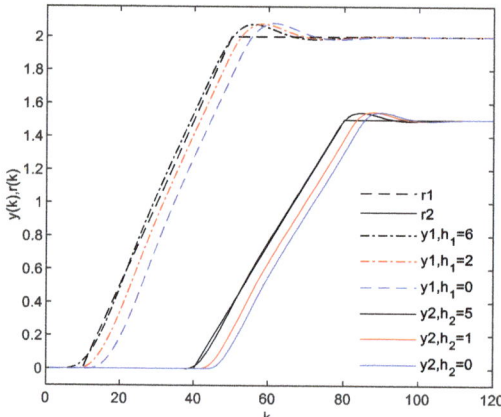

Figure 3. The output response of System (1) with $\theta_1 = 0$.

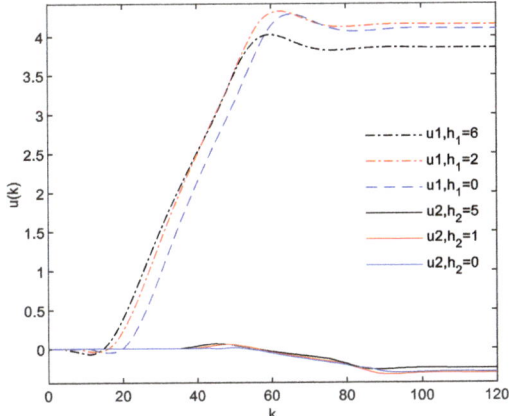

Figure 4. The control input of System (1) with $\theta_1 = 0$

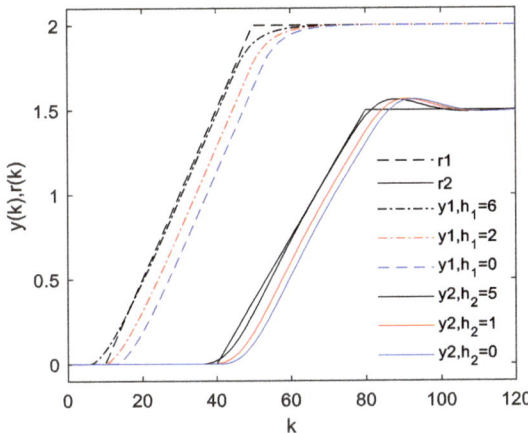

Figure 5. The output response of System (1) $\theta_1 = 1$.

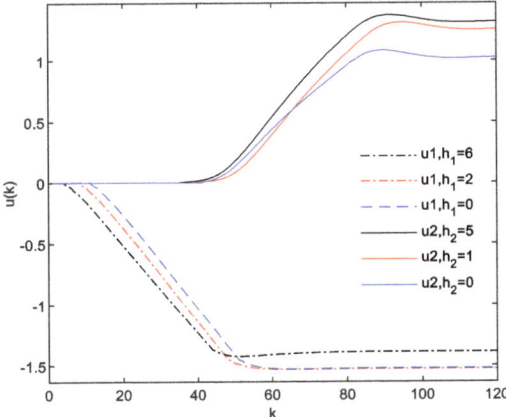

Figure 6. The control input of System (1) with $\theta_1 = 1$.

The construction methods of AES in [11,13,15,26] were employed, or, equivalently, the future information of $r(k)$ was added to the augmented state vector to derive the AES. For comparison, we performed simulations for this case in [11,13,15,26] by using the same example. From Figures 1 and 7, it can be seen that the future information of the signal components $r_1(k)$ and $r_2(k)$ interacted with each other. This led to poor tracking performance of System (1). In addition, From Figures 1, 2, 7 and 8, we could easily see that our proposed PC provided better tracking performance than those in [11,13,15,26].

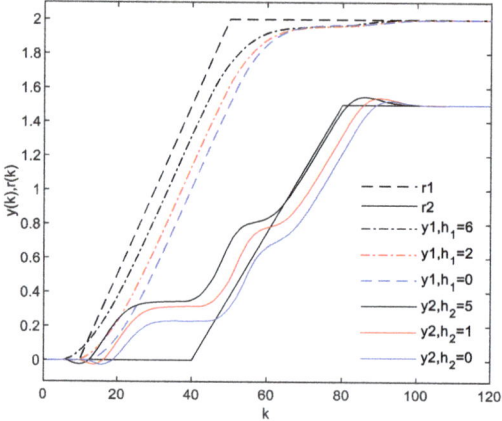

Figure 7. The output response.

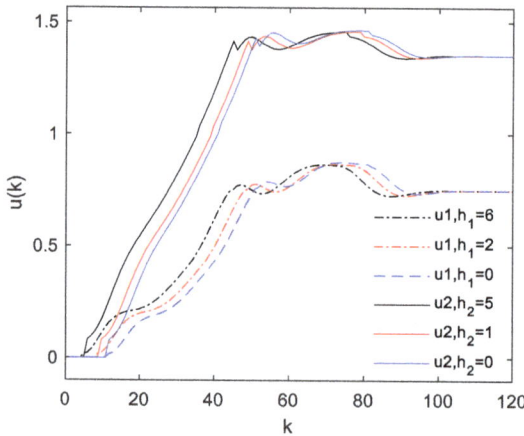

Figure 8. The control input.

Output Feedback Case

In System (1), we let

$$A(\theta) = \begin{bmatrix} 1 & -0.4 & 0.8 \\ 1 & 0 & 0 \\ 0 & 1 & 0 \end{bmatrix} \theta_1 + \begin{bmatrix} 1.2 & -0.6 & 0.7 \\ 1 & 0 & 0 \\ 0 & 1 & 0 \end{bmatrix} \theta_2,$$

$$B(\theta) = \begin{bmatrix} 1 & 1 \\ 0.3 & 0.3 \\ 0 & 0 \end{bmatrix} \theta_1 + \begin{bmatrix} 1 & 1 \\ 1.1 & 1 \\ 0 & 0 \end{bmatrix} \theta_2, \; C(\theta) = \theta_1 \begin{bmatrix} 1 & 0 & 0 \\ 1 & 0 & 0 \end{bmatrix} + \theta_2 \begin{bmatrix} 1 & 0 & 0 \\ 1 & 0 & 0 \end{bmatrix},$$

$$D(\theta) = 0$$

Letting $\alpha_1 = \alpha_2 = 4$, $\beta_1 = \beta_2 = 0.6$, and $\rho_1 = \rho_2 = 1$ and $\gamma_1 = 0.3$ and $\gamma_2 = 0.7$, we had matrices $Q_1 = 6(C_{Z1,1} + C_{Z2,1})$ and $Q_2 = 6(C_{Z1,2} + C_{Z2,2})$. According to Theorem 4, the static output feedback gain matrices were obtained as follows.

When $h_1 = h_2 = 2$, we obtained

$$K_1 = \begin{bmatrix} 1.26358 & -0.40042 & -1.26358 & -1.26358 & -1.26358 \\ -1.32911 & -0.14526 & 1.32911 & 1.32911 & 1.32911 \end{bmatrix}$$

$$K_2 = \begin{bmatrix} 1.26358 & -0.40042 & -1.26358 & -1.26358 & -1.26358 \\ -1.32911 & -0.14526 & 1.32911 & 1.32911 & 1.32911 \end{bmatrix}$$

When $h_1 = h_2 = 6$, K_1 and K_2 are given, respectively, by

$$K_1 = \begin{bmatrix} 1.31567 & -0.30661 & -1.31567 & -1.31567 & -1.31567 & -1.31567 \\ -1.38506 & -0.24404 & 1.38506 & 1.38506 & 1.38506 & 1.38506 \\ -1.31567 & -1.31567 & -1.31567 \\ 1.38506 & 1.38506 & 1.38506 \end{bmatrix},$$

$$K_2 = \begin{bmatrix} 1.31567 & -0.30661 & -1.31567 & -1.31567 & -1.31567 & -1.31567 \\ -1.38506 & -0.24404 & 1.38506 & 1.38506 & 1.38506 & 1.38506 \\ -1.31567 & -1.31567 & -1.31567 \\ 1.38506 & 1.38506 & 1.38506 \end{bmatrix},$$

When $h_1 = h_2 = 0$, we obtained

$$K_1 = \begin{bmatrix} 1.18156 & -0.45238 \\ -1.24364 & -0.09158 \end{bmatrix}$$

$$K_2 = \begin{bmatrix} 1.18156 & -0.45238 \\ -1.24364 & -0.09158 \end{bmatrix}$$

For the Signal (52) and (53), Figure 9 depicts the output and the reference Signals (52) and (53). Figure 10 indicates the control input for different preview lengths. From Figures 9 and 10, we found that the output response could reach a steady state faster when using the output controller with preview compensation.

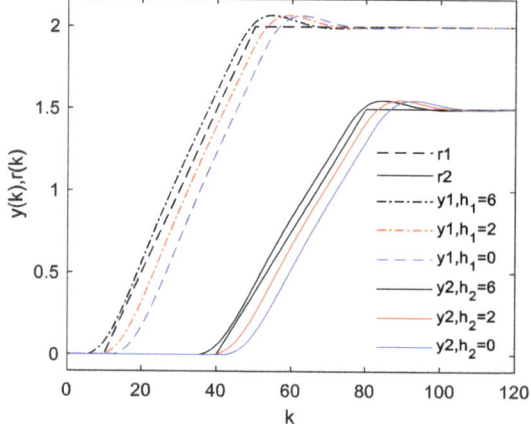

Figure 9. The output of System (1) with different M_R.

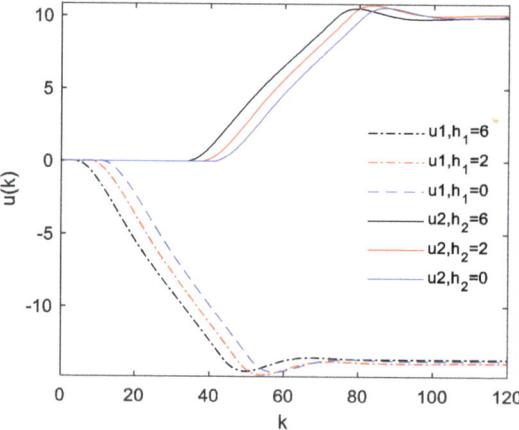

Figure 10. The control input of System (1) with different M_R.

For the static output feedback case, two extreme cases, namely, $\theta_1 = 1$ and $\theta_1 = 0$ have also been considered. Figures 11 and 12, respectively, show the output response and control input of System (1) by static output controller under $\theta_1 = 0$. When $\theta_1 = 1$, Figures 13 and 14 show the response and the control input curves, respectively. It is evident from Figures 11–14 that the tracking effect was still remarkable under the reference input preview compensation.

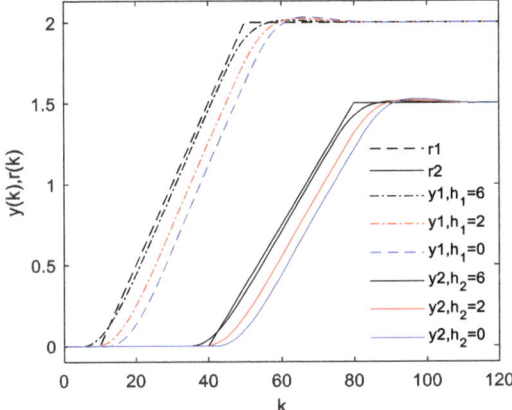

Figure 11. $\theta_1 = 0, \theta_2 = 1$, output response of system (1) with different M_R.

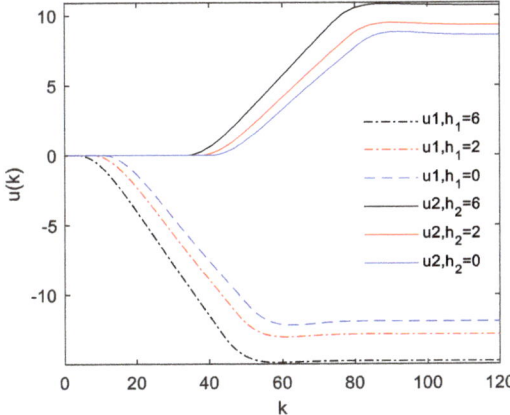

Figure 12. $\theta_1 = 0, \theta_2 = 1$, control of system (1) with different M_R.

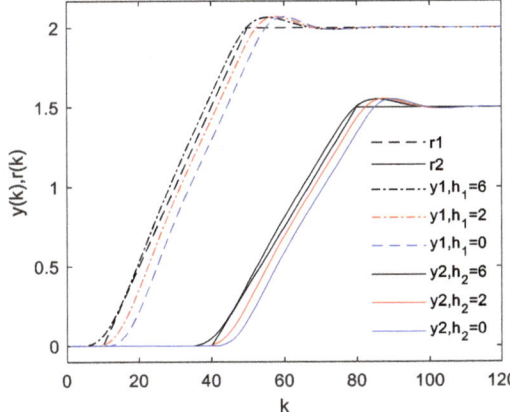

Figure 13. $\theta_1 = 1, \theta_2 = 0$, output response of system (1) with different M_R.

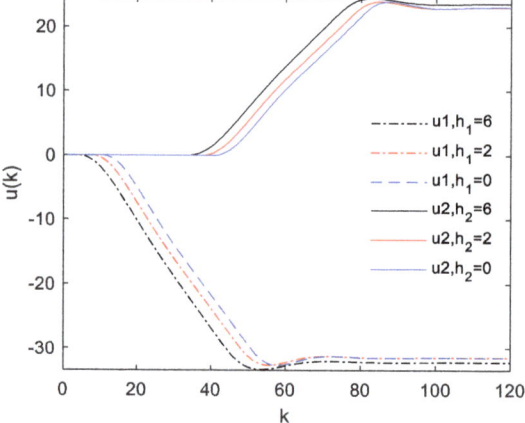

Figure 14. $\theta_1 = 1, \theta_2 = 0$, control input of system (1) with different M_R.

Similarly, for the output feedback case, the simulations were completed when the design methods in [11,13,15,26] were used. From these simulation results, we could find that the proposed output feedback PC had more advantages. Simulation and analysis were made separately under different situations of parameters θ_1 and θ_2. Considering length limitations, the figures for these results would not be provided here.

6. Conclusions

The PC problem for MIMO discrete-time systems with polytopic uncertainties was discussed in this paper. We derived the AES including previewed information on $r_i(k)$ by using classical difference method. The parameter-dependent state feedback and output feedback were proposed and the conditions of the design methods of PCs were given by using parameter-dependent quadratic Lyaounov functions and LMI approach. The robust controllers with preview actions using LMIs were presented.

Author Contributions: Supervision, F.L.; Writing—review and editing, L.L. and F.L. All authors have read and agreed to the published version of the manuscript.

Funding: National Natural Science Foundation of China [61903130] and the Hubei Provincial Natural Science Foundation of China [2019CFB227]. Hubei Provincial Department of Education [18G046 and B2018129].

Conflicts of Interest: The authors declare no conflict of interest.

References

1. Zheng, D.Z. *Linear System Theory*; Tsinghua University Press: Beijing, China, 2012.
2. Tan, K.K.; Zhao, S.; Xu, J.X. Online automatic tuning of a proportional integral derivative controller based on an iterative learning control approach. *IET Control Theory A* **2007**, *1*, 90–96. [CrossRef]
3. Li, Y.; Zhao, S.; He, W.; Lu, R. Adaptive finite-time tracking control of full state constrained nonlinear systems with dead-zone. *Automatica* **2019**, *100*, 99–107. [CrossRef]
4. Wang, Y.; Wang, R.; Xie, X.; Zhang, H. Observer-based H∞ fuzzy control for modified repetitive control. *Neurocomputing* **2018**, *286*, 141–149. [CrossRef]
5. Birla, N.; Swarup, A. Optimal preview control: A review. *Optim. Control Appl. Methods* **2015**, *36*, 241–268. [CrossRef]
6. Zhen, Z.Y. Research development in preview control theory and applications. *Acta Autom. Sin.* **2016**, *42*, 172–188.
7. Sheridan, T.B. Three models of preview control. *IEEE Trans. Hum. Factors Electron.* **1996**, *7*, 91–102. [CrossRef]

8. Bender, E.K. Optimum linear preview control with application to vehicle suspension. *J. Basic Eng.* **1968**, *90*, 213–221. [CrossRef]
9. Tomizuka, M. Optimal continuous finite preview problem. *IEEE Trans. Autom. Control* **1975**, *20*, 362–365. [CrossRef]
10. Tomizuka, M. Optimal discrete finite preview problem (Why and how is future information important?). *J. Dyn. Syst. ASME* **1975**, *97*, 319–325. [CrossRef]
11. Katayama, T.; Ohki, T.; Inoue, T.; Kato, T. Design of an optimal controller for a discrete-time system subject to previewable demand. *Int. J. Control* **1985**, *41*, 677–699. [CrossRef]
12. Katayama, T.; Hirono, T. Design of an optimal servomechanism with preview action and its dual problem. *Int. J. Control* **1987**, *45*, 407–420. [CrossRef]
13. Tsuchiya, T.; Egami, T. *Digital Preview and Predictive Control*; Beijing Science and Technology Press: Beijing, China, 1994.
14. Wu, J.; Liao, F.; Tomizuka, M. Optimal preview control for a linear continuous-time stochastic control system in finite-time horizon. *Int. J. Syst. Sci.* **2017**, *48*, 129–137. [CrossRef]
15. Wang, D.; Liao, F.; Tomizuka, M. Adaptive preview control for piecewise discrete-time systems using multiple models. *Appl. Math. Model* **2016**, *40*, 9932–9946. [CrossRef]
16. Lu, Y.; Liao, F.; Deng, J.; Pattinson, C. Cooperative optimal preview tracking for linear descriptor multi-agent systems. *J. Frankl. Inst.* **2019**, *356*, 908–934. [CrossRef]
17. Lu, Y.; Liao, F.; Deng, J.; Liu, H. Cooperative global optimal preview tracking control of linear multi-agent systems: An internal model approach. *Int. J. Syst. Sci.* **2017**, *48*, 2451–2462. [CrossRef]
18. Running, K.D.; Martins, N.C. Optimal preview control of Markovian jump linear systems. *IEEE Trans. Autom. Control* **2009**, *54*, 2260–2266. [CrossRef]
19. Liao, F.; Wang, Y.; Lu, Y.; Deng, J. Optimal preview control for a class of linear continuous-time large-scale systems. *Trans. Inst. Meas. Control* **2018**, *40*, 4004–4013. [CrossRef]
20. Bidyadhar, S.; Ogeti, P.S. Optimal preview stator voltage-oriented control of DFIG WECS. *IET Gener. Transm. Distrib.* **2018**, *12*, 1004–1013.
21. Kojima, A. H∞ controller design for preview and delayed systems. *IEEE Trans. Autom. Control* **2015**, *60*, 404–419. [CrossRef]
22. Gershon, E.; Shaked, U. H∞ preview tracking control of retarded state- multiplicative stochastic systems. *Int. J. Robust Nonlinear Control* **2014**, *24*, 2119–2135. [CrossRef]
23. Kristalny, M.; Mirkin, L. On the H2 two-sided model matching problem with preview. *IEEE Trans. Autom. Control* **2012**, *57*, 207–212. [CrossRef]
24. Hamada, Y. Preview feedforward compensation: LMI synthesis and flight simulation. *IFAC-Pap.* **2016**, *49*, 397–402. [CrossRef]
25. Li, L.; Liao, F. Robust preview control for a class of uncertain discrete-time systems with time-varying delay. *ISA Trans.* **2018**, *73*, 11–21. [CrossRef] [PubMed]
26. Li, L.; Yuan, Y. Output feedback preview control for polytopic uncertain discrete-time systems with time-varying delay. *Int. J. Robust Nonlinear Control* **2019**, *29*, 2619–2638. [CrossRef]
27. Shao, Y.-F.; Gao, S.-J. Robust preview control of uncertain discrete systems based on an internal model approach. *Sci. Technol. Vis.* **2018**, 1–3. [CrossRef]
28. Lan, Y.; Xia, J. Observer based design of preview repetitive control for linear discrete systems. *Comput. Integr. Manuf. Syst.* **2019**, 1–18.
29. Lan, Y.; Xia, J.; Shi, Y. Robust guaranteed-cost preview repetitive control for polytopic uncertain discrete-time systems. *Algorithms* **2019**, *12*, 20. [CrossRef]
30. Han, K.; Feng, J.; Li, Y.; Li, S. Reduced-order simultaneous state and fault estimator based fault tolerant preview control for discrete-time linear time-invariant systems. *IET Control Theory A* **2018**, *12*, 1601–1610. [CrossRef]
31. Han, K.; Feng, J. Data-driven robust fault tolerant linear quadratic preview control of discrete-time linear systems with completely unknown dynamics. *Int. J. Control* **2019**, 1–11. [CrossRef]
32. Yu, X.; Liao, F. Preview tracking control for a class of discrete-time Lipschitz non-linear time-delay systems. *IMA J. Math. Control Inf.* **2019**, *36*, 849–867. [CrossRef]

33. Lio, W.H.; Jones, B.L.; Rossiter, J.A. Preview predictive control layer design based upon known wind turbine blade-pitch controllers: MPC layer design based upon known blade-pitch controllers. *Wind Energy* **2017**, *20*, 1207–1226. [CrossRef]
34. Zhao, Y.; Cai, Y.; Song, Q. Energy control of plug-in hybrid electric vehicles using model predictive control with route preview. *IEEE/CAA J. Autom. Sin.* **2018**, 1–8. [CrossRef]
35. Al Khudir, K.; Halvorsen, G.; Lanari, L.; De Luca, A. Stable torque optimization for redundant robots using a short preview. *IEEE Robot. Autom. Lett.* **2019**, *4*, 2046–2053. [CrossRef]
36. Pak, H.A.; Shieh, R. On mimo optimal preview tracking control for known trajectory models. *Optim. Control Appl. Methods* **1991**, *12*, 119–130. [CrossRef]
37. Li, L.; Liao, F. Parameter-dependent preview control with robust tracking performance. *IET Control Theory Appl.* **2017**, *11*, 38–46. [CrossRef]
38. Chen, Y.; Fei, S.; Li, Y. Stabilization of neutral time-delay systems with actuator saturation via auxiliary time-delay feedback. *Automatic* **2015**, *52*, 242–247. [CrossRef]
39. He, Y.; Wu, M.; She, J.-H. Improved bounded-real-lemma representation and H∞ control of systems with polytopic uncertainties. *IEEE Trans. Circuits Syst. II Express Briefs* **2005**, *52*, 380–383.
40. Chang, X.H.; Zhang, L.; Park, H.P. Robust static output feedback H∞ control for uncertain fuzzy systems. *Fuzzy Sets Syst.* **2015**, *273*, 87–104. [CrossRef]

© 2020 by the authors. Licensee MDPI, Basel, Switzerland. This article is an open access article distributed under the terms and conditions of the Creative Commons Attribution (CC BY) license (http://creativecommons.org/licenses/by/4.0/).

Article

A Model for Determining Weight Coefficients by Forming a Non-Decreasing Series at Criteria Significance Levels (NDSL)

Mališa Žižović [1], Dragan Pamučar [2,*], Goran Ćirović [3], Miodrag M. Žižović [4] and Boža D. Miljković [5]

1. Faculty of Technical Sciences in Cacak, University of Kragujevac, Svetog Save 65, 32102 Cacak, Serbia; zizovic@gmail.com
2. Department of Logistics, Military Academy, University of Defence, Pavla Jurisica Sturma 33, 11000 Belgrade, Serbia
3. Faculty of Technical Sciences, University of Novi Sad, Trg Dositeja Obradovica 6, 21000 Novi Sad, Serbia; cirovic@sezampro.rs
4. AXIS Translations and Technical Services, 11000 Belgrade, Serbia; miodragz@gmail.com
5. Faculty of Education Sombor, University of Novi Sad, 21000 Novi Sad, Serbia; bole@ravangrad.net
* Correspondence: dragan.pamucar@va.mod.gov.rs

Received: 8 April 2020; Accepted: 6 May 2020; Published: 8 May 2020

Abstract: In this paper, a new method for determining weight coefficients by forming a non-decreasing series at criteria significance levels (the NDSL method) is presented. The NDLS method includes the identification of the best criterion (i.e., the most significant and most influential criterion) and the ranking of criteria in a decreasing series from the most significant to the least significant criterion. Criteria are then grouped as per the levels of significance within the framework of which experts express their preferences in compliance with the significance of such criteria. By employing this procedure, fully consistent results are obtained. In this paper, the advantages of the NDSL model are singled out through a comparison with the Best Worst Method (BWM) and Analytic Hierarchy Process (AHP) models. The advantages include the following: (1) the NDSL model requires a significantly smaller number of pairwise comparisons of criteria, only involving an $n - 1$ comparison, whereas the AHP requires an $n(n - 1)/2$ comparison and the BWM a $2n - 3$ comparison; (2) it enables us to obtain reliable (consistent) results, even in the case of a larger number of criteria (more than nine criteria); (3) the NDSL model applies an original algorithm for grouping criteria according to the levels of significance, through which the deficiencies of the 9-degree scale applied in the BWM and AHP models are eliminated. By doing so, the small range and inconsistency of the 9-degree scale are eliminated; (4) while the BWM includes the defining of one unique best/worst criterion, the NDSL model eliminates this limitation and gives decision-makers the freedom to express the relationships between criteria in accordance with their preferences. In order to demonstrate the performance of the developed model, it was tested on a real-world problem and the results were validated through a comparison with the BWM and AHP models.

Keywords: NDSL model; AHP; criteria weights; pairwise comparisons

1. Introduction

The determination of the relative weights of criteria in multi-criteria decision-making models represents a specific problem that is inevitably accompanied by subjectivities. This procedure is very significant, since it exerts a great influence on the final decision in the decision-making process [1]. Multi-criteria optimization methods use normalized values of weights, which meet the condition that $\sum_{i=1}^{n} w_i = 1$, $w_i \geq 0$. In many models for perceiving the relative ratios of weights, however, non-normalized values are used in the form of whole numbers or amounts in percentages [2]. The percentage value of the weight of one criterion denotes a part of the overall preference attributed to that criterion.

The determination of the values of criteria weights is a special problem in multi-criteria optimization, so numerous models have been developed to solve it. Multi-criteria optimization models are well-known for their sensitivity to change in the vector of weight coefficients, so minor modifications in the values of the mentioned vector can cause a major change in the order of the significance of alternatives in the model. Therefore, special attention has been devoted to studying these models in the literature dealing with multi-criteria optimization [3–6].

Studying the available literature allows us to notice that there is no unique classification of methods used for the determination of criteria weights, and their classification was, for the most part, performed in compliance with the author's understanding of and needs regarding the solving of a concrete practical problem. Therefore, in [7], the classification of criteria weight determination methods is given, and groups them into objective and subjective approaches. Objective models imply the calculation of criteria weight coefficients based on the value(s) of the criterion/criteria in the initial decision-making matrix. The most well-known objective models include the Entropy method [8], the CRiteria Importance Through Intercriteria Correlation (CRITIC) method [9], and the FANMA method (named after the authors Fan and Ma) [10].

On the other hand, subjective models include the application of a methodology implying the direct participation of decision-makers, who express their preferences according to the significance of criteria. There are several ways in which weights of criteria are obtained through the subjective approach, which may differ from each other in terms of the number of participants in the process of the determination of weights, the methods applied, and the manner in which the final criteria weights are formed. The group of subjective models used to aggregate partial values in multi-attribute analysis methods includes the trade-off method [11], which enables identification of the decision-maker's dilemmas through pairwise comparisons; the swing weight method [12], which involves the construction of two extreme hypothetical scenarios; the worst (W) and the best (B) method, in which the first scenario (W) is constructed based on the worst values of all criteria, and the second scenario (B) corresponds to the best values; the Simple Multi-Attribute Rating Technique (SMART) method [13], which includes a procedure for the determination of criteria weights based on comparing criteria with the best and the criteria from within the defined set of criteria; and SMART Exploiting Ranks (SMARTER), which was developed by [13] and which represents a new version of the SMART method. SMARTER uses the centroid method for ranking the criteria for the determination of weight coefficients.

Apart from the above-mentioned subjective approaches, there are also approaches exclusively based on criteria pairwise comparisons, and such approaches are referred to as pairwise comparison methods. The pairwise comparison method was first introduced by Thurstone [14], and it represents a structured way of producing a decision matrix. Pairwise comparisons (performed by an expert or a team of experts) are used to demonstrate the relative significance of m actions in situations in which it is impossible or senseless to assign marks to actions in relation to criteria. In pairwise comparison methods, the decision-maker compares the observed criterion/action with other criteria/actions, and determines the level of significance of the observed criterion/action. An ordinal scale is used to help determine the magnitude of the preference for one criterion over another. One of the most frequently used methods based on pairwise comparisons is the method of the Analytic Hierarchy Process (AHP) [15]. Apart from the AHP, the pairwise comparison methods include the Decision-Making Trial and Evaluation Laboratory (DEMATEL) method [16]; the Best Worst Method (BWM) [17]; the resistance to change method [18], which has elements of the swing method and pairwise comparison methods; and the Step-Wise Weight Assessment Ratio Analysis (SWARA) method [19]. In pairwise comparison methods, for example, in the AHP, weights are determined based on pairwise comparisons of criteria, and the results are generated from pairwise comparisons of alternatives with criteria. After that, by means of the usefulness function, the final values of alternatives are calculated. A very significant challenge in pairwise comparison methods arises from a lack of consistency of comparison matrices, which is frequently the case in practice [20]. Each of these methods has a wide application in the various areas of science and technology, as well as in solving real-life problems. The AHP method is used in [21] to make a strategic decision in a transport system. In [22], this method is employed to determine the significance of criteria in evaluating different transitivity alternatives in transport in Catania. In [23], the AHP method is using to identify and evaluate defects in the passenger transport system, whereas in [24], it is applied to select an alternative to the electronic payment system. Stević et al. [25] carried out site selection of a logistics center by applying the AHP method. In [26], the DEMATEL method is employed to analyze the risk in mutual relations in logistics outsourcing. Additionally, in [27], the authors proposed a two-phase model which aims to evaluate and select suppliers using an integrated Fuzzy AHP and Fuzzy Technique for Ordering Preference by Similarity to Ideal Solution (FTOPSIS) methods. Integration of the DEMATEL method is not rare, so in [27], along with the Analytic Network Process (ANP) and Data Envelopment Analysis (DEA), a decision is made on the choice of the 3PL logistics provider. The SWARA method is used in [28] to select the 3PL in the sustainable network of reverse logistics and a rough form [29] for the purpose of determining the significance of criteria to the procurement of railroad wagons. Moreover, the application of the SWARA method can be seen in [30–46]. BWM is a method that has increasingly been applied in a short period of time [47–70]. Some authors [55–57,61,67,71–73] see this method as an adequate substitute for the AHP. Its major advantage is the smaller number of pairwise comparisons ($2n - 3$) involved compared to the AHP.

Weight coefficients represent a means calibrating decision-making models and the quality of a decision made directly depends on the quality of their definition. The reason for studying this problem lies in the fact that each subjective method used for the determination of criteria weights has both advantages and disadvantages. In this research study, subjective methods based on pairwise comparisons of criteria, more precisely, the BWM and AHP models, as the highest-sounding representatives of this group of methods, are analyzed. Their advantages and disadvantages are analyzed. Based on the identification of the weaknesses of these models, a new approach to the determination of weight coefficients that involves forming a non-decreasing series at criteria significance levels (the NDSL model) is proposed. The NDSL model includes the application of an original algorithm to the grouping of criteria according to significance levels, through which the need to predefine the ordinal scale for the pairwise comparison of criteria is eliminated. Criteria are grouped according to significance levels in relation to the most significant criterion. After their grouping according to significance levels, the numerical values of the significance of the criteria are determined in accordance with the decision-maker's preferences. By employing this procedure, results which are fully consistent and also represent the real relationships defined by experts' preferences are obtained. The proposed model eliminates the deviations from experts' preferences that appear in the AHP model, since the NDSL's results are always consistent. We highlight this since an increase in the consistency ratio in the AHP leads to the distortion of experts' preferences and the values of weight coefficients deviate from the optimal values. This is what frequently appears in the mentioned models and most often, it is a consequence of using the 9-degree scale characterized by limited possibilities of expressing experts' preferences [74].

This paper has several goals. The first goal of the paper is to present a new model for the determination of criteria weight coefficients which enables a rational expression of the decision-maker's preferences with a minimal number of comparisons—$n - 1$. The second goal of the paper is to develop a model for the determination of criteria weight coefficients which always generates consistent results. The third goal of the paper is to eliminate the 9-degree scale for the expression of experts' preferences in pairwise comparison models through defining an original algorithm for comparing criteria according to the levels of significance. By forming significance levels, the shortcomings of the 9-degree scale, which include (1) its limited flexibility while expressing experts' preferences and (2) inconsistencies during criteria pairwise comparisons, are eliminated [74].

The rest of the paper is organized in the following manner: in the next section (Section 2), the mathematical bases of the NDSL model are presented, and the algorithm demonstrating the performance of the seven steps for defining criteria weight coefficients is presented; in Section 3, the NDSL model is tested on a real-world problem, and a comparison of the results with those of the BWM and AHP models is made; conclusive considerations and directions for future research studies are given in Section 4.

2. Model for Determining Weight Coefficients by Forming a Non-Decreasing Series at Criteria Significance Levels

Allow us to assume that, in a multi-criteria model, there is a set S containing n evaluation criteria $S = \{C_1, C_2, \ldots, C_n\}$, and that the weight coefficients of the criteria have not been predefined, i.e., that weight coefficients need to be determined. Allow us also to assume that, in that multi-criteria problem, the criteria $C_1, C_2, \ldots, C_n$ are ordered according to their significance (strength). Therefore, the weight coefficients of the criteria satisfy the relationships in which $w_1 \geq w_2 \geq \ldots \geq w_n \geq 0$, with the condition that the criteria weights are normalized and meet the condition stipulating that $\sum_{i=1}^{n} w_i = 1$.

Theorem 1. *For a randomly chosen real (natural) number N, which is such that $N > n$ (where n represents the number of criteria in the multi-criteria model), and if the criterion C_1 and the criterion C_x, $x \in \{1, 2, \ldots, n\}$, are assigned the sum of 2N, then it is possible to determine the number α_x, which is such that it fulfils the ratio between the criteria:*

$$C_1 : C_x = (N + \alpha_x) : (N - \alpha_x). \tag{1}$$

Proof. The proof of this ratio is obvious, since, for $x = 1$, we evidently obtain $C_1 : C_1 = (N + \alpha_1) : (N - \alpha_1)$, i.e., we obtain $\alpha_1 = 0$, i.e., we obtain $C_1 : C_1 = N : N$, i.e., the ratio $C_1 : C_1 = 1$.

If we assume that the ratio $C_1 : C_x = t_x$, then we also obtain $\frac{N+\alpha_x}{N-\alpha_x} = t_x \geq 1$, from which it follows that $N + \alpha_x = Nt_x - \alpha_x t_x$, i.e.,

$$\alpha_x = N \cdot \frac{t_x - 1}{t_x + 1}, \tag{2}$$

where α_x represents a non-negative number for the given $x \in \{1, 2, \ldots, n\}$. □

Corollary 1. *If the criterion C_x has a greater or equal significance (weight) for the criterion C_y, then the condition $t_x \geq t_y$ is met, from which it follows that $\alpha_x \geq \alpha_y$.*

Proof. The proof for Corollary 1 is evident, since it arises from Theorem 1:

If $C_x \geq C_y$, then we have $C_1 : C_x \geq C_1 : C_y$. Since $C_1 : C_x = t_x$ and $C_1 : C_y = t_y$, then we have $t_x \geq t_y$ and $\alpha_x \geq \alpha_y$. □

It follows from Corollary 1 that a non-decreasing series of numbers can be attributed to the series of the criteria ordered according to significance, i.e.,

$$\alpha_1, \alpha_2, \alpha_3, \ldots, \alpha_n. \tag{3}$$

Based on Theorem 1, it is possible to conclude that $\alpha_1 = 0$. Since we have

$$C_1 : C_1 = (N + \alpha_1) : (N - \alpha_1) \rightarrow C_1(N - \alpha_1) = C_1(N + \alpha_1),$$

then $N - \alpha_1 = N + \alpha_1$ and we have $\alpha_1 = 0$.

Additionally, based on Theorem 1, a new series (4) can be formed from the already formed series of elements (3), i.e.,

$$\frac{N+\alpha_1}{N-\alpha_1}, \frac{N+\alpha_2}{N-\alpha_2}, \ldots, \frac{N+\alpha_n}{N-\alpha_n}. \tag{4}$$

The non-decreasing series of elements that is presented by the expression (4) represents a series of ratios of the significance (strength) of the criterion C_1 against the other criteria from within the S set of criteria. Based on the condition (1), the series of elements (4) can be represented as a non-decreasing series of weight coefficients of the criteria of the multi-criteria model, which is such that

$$w_1 = w_1, \; w_2 = \frac{N-\alpha_2}{N+\alpha_2} \cdot w_1, \; w_3 = \frac{N-\alpha_3}{N+\alpha_3} \cdot w_1, \ldots, w_n = \frac{N-\alpha_n}{N+\alpha_n} \cdot w_1. \tag{5}$$

Based on the expression (5) and the condition that the sum of all weight coefficients of criteria of the multi-criteria model is equal to one, i.e., $\sum_{j=1}^{n} w_j = 1$, the following is obtained:

$$w_1 \cdot \left(1 + \sum_{j=2}^{n} \frac{N-\alpha_j}{N+\alpha_j}\right) = 1. \tag{6}$$

Therefore, it follows from this that the weight coefficient of the most influential (best) criterion is obtained as

$$w_1 = \frac{1}{1 + \sum_{j=2}^{n} \frac{N-\alpha_j}{N+\alpha_j}}. \tag{7}$$

It follows from the condition (1) that $w_1 : w_i = (N + \alpha_i) : (N - \alpha_i)$, i.e., $w_i = w_1 \cdot (N - \alpha_i)/(N + \alpha_i)$, from which the weight coefficients of the remaining criteria are obtained:

$$w_i = \frac{\frac{N-\alpha_i}{N+\alpha_i}}{1 + \sum_{j=2}^{n} \frac{N-\alpha_j}{N+\alpha_j}}; \; i = 2, 3, \ldots, n. \tag{8}$$

2.1. Forming a Non-Decreasing Series at Criteria Significance Levels

The basic idea of forming a criteria classification level precisely reflects the need to determine the significance of criteria and eliminate the limitations of using predefined scales for expressing experts' preferences. The basic limitation of using scales for expressing experts' preferences in subjective models, such as the AHP, BWM, and DEMATEL, relates to the small range of values of such scales, as well as the nonlinearity of the scale (in the AHP). The insufficient range of values makes the development of an objective expression of experts' preferences more difficult, which is particularly pronounced when comparing a larger number of criteria. Therefore, for example, the range of values for the scale employed in the AHP and BWM is from 1 to 9. Should there be a larger number of criteria (for example, seven) in the considered problem, experts' comparisons are made more difficult due to the small number of values in the scales. The 9-degree scale also implies that the greatest ratio between the weights of the best (C_B) and worst (C_W) criteria is limited to 9, i.e., $C_B:C_W = 9:1$. If, however, an expert considers the ratio $C_B:C_W$ to be greater than 9:1 and the $C_B:C_W = 15:1$, then such a preference cannot be presented. In order for experts to express preferences of this kind by applying the 9-degree scale, they are forced to distort their preferences, which leads to the deviation of weight values from the optimal values.

By introducing the level of criteria significance, experts are given a possibility to form as many criteria significance levels L_j, $j \in \{1, 2, \ldots, k\}$ as they need for expressing their preferences. Within the framework of significance levels, criteria are roughly classified according to experts' preferences.

Forming significance levels, i.e., grouping criteria according to levels, is performed by adhering to the following rules:

- Level L_1: At the L_1 level, the criteria from within the set S whose significance is equal to the significance of the criterion C_1 or up to two times as small as the significance of the criterion C_1 should be grouped. The criterion C_i belonging to the L_1 level will be presented as $C_i \in [1,2)$, $i \in \{1,2,\ldots,n\}$;
- Level L_2: At the L_2 level, the criteria from within the set S whose significance is exactly two times as small as the significance of the criterion C_1 or up to three times as small as the significance of the criterion C_1 should be grouped. The criterion C_i belonging to the L_2 level will be presented as $C_i \in [2,3)$, $i \in \{1,2,\ldots,n\}$;
- Level L_3: At the L_3 level, the criteria from within the set S whose significance is exactly three times as small as the significance of the criterion C_1 or up to four times as small as the significance of the criterion C_1 should be grouped. The criterion C_i belonging to the L_3 level will be presented as $C_i \in [3,4)$, $i \in \{1,2,\ldots,n\}$;
- Level L_k: At the L_k level, the criteria from within the set S whose significance is exactly k times as small as the significance of the criterion C_1 or up to $k+1$ times as small as the significance of the criterion C_1 should be grouped. The criterion C_i belonging to the L_k level will be presented as $C_i \in [k, k+1)$, $i \in \{1,2,\ldots,n\}$.

After grouping criteria as per the levels L_j, $j \in \{1,2,\ldots,k\}$, experts express their preferences through a numerical comparison of the criteria by means of the significance of the criteria (α_i). Therefore, based on the value α_i, a fine classification of the criteria is conducted within the observed level. The values of the significance of the criteria (α_i) within every level L_j, $j \in \{1,2,\ldots,k\}$, are defined based on experts' preferences; the final values α_i within every level L_j need to be defined. In the following part, the boundary values of the significance of the criteria (α_i) within the level L_j, $j \in \{1,2,\ldots,k\}$ are defined.

If the significance of the criterion C_i is expressed as α_i, where $i \in \{1,2,\ldots,n\}$, then subset of the criteria is formed for each criteria level, which together make the criteria set S. Then, it follows that $L_j = L_1 \cup L_2 \cup \cdots \cup L_k$, and for every level $j \in \{1,2,\ldots,k\}$,

$$L_j = \{C_{j_1}, C_{j_2}, \ldots, C_{j_s}\} = \{C_i \in S : j \leq \alpha_i < j+1\}. \tag{9}$$

Based on the previously defined relations, it is possible to define the boundaries within which the values of the significance of the criteria (α_i) move for each observed level L_j, $j \in \{1,2,\ldots,k\}$. If the criterion C_i belongs to the level L_j, $j \in \{1,2,\ldots,k\}$ is presented as $C_i \in [t_j, t_j + 1)$, $i \in \{1,2,\ldots,n\}$, $j \in \{1,2,\ldots,k\}$, and then, based on the relation (2), we can obtain the following:

- Level L_1: For $C_i \in [1,2)$, i.e., for $t_1 = 1$, it follows that $\alpha_i = 0$, whereas for $t_1 = 2$, we obtain $\alpha_i = N/3$. Therefore, it follows that the values of the significance of the criteria (α_i) at the L_1 level range in the interval $0 \leq \alpha_i < N/3$, i.e., $C_i \in [1,2) \Rightarrow 0 \leq \alpha_i < N/3$;
- Level L_2: For $C_i \in [2,3)$, i.e., for $t_2 = 2$, it follows that $\alpha_i = N/3$, whereas for $t_1 = 3$, we obtain $\alpha_i = N/2$. The values of the significance of the criteria (α_i) at the L_2 level range in the interval $N/3 \leq \alpha_i < N/2$, i.e., $C_i \in [2,3) \Rightarrow N/3 \leq \alpha_i < N/2$;
- Level L_k: For $C_i \in [k, k+1)$, i.e., for $t_k = k$, it follows that $\alpha_i = N \cdot (k-1)/(k+1)$, whereas for $t_k = k+1$, we obtain $\alpha_i = N \cdot k/(k+2)$. The values of the significance of the criteria (α_i) at the L_k level range in the interval $N \cdot (k-1)/(k+1) \leq \alpha_i < N \cdot k/(k+2)$, i.e., $C_i \in [k, k+1) \Rightarrow N \cdot (k-1)/(k+1) \leq \alpha_x < N \cdot k/(k+2)$.

Example 1. *If we assume that the criteria are grouped at three levels L_j, $j \in \{1,2,3\}$, and if we take that $N = 50$, then we can define the interval in which the values of the significance of the criterion C_i within the level L_j should range. By applying the previously defined relationships, we obtain the result that the values α_i range within the level L_j, $j \in \{1,2,3\}$, in the following intervals:*

1. Level L_1: $C_i \in [1, 2) \Rightarrow 0 \le \alpha_i < N/3$, then we have $C_i \in [1, 2) \Rightarrow 0 \le \alpha_x < 50/3$;
2. Level L_2: $C_i \in [2, 3) \Rightarrow N/3 \le \alpha_i < N/2$, then we have $C_i \in [2, 3) \Rightarrow 50/3 \le \alpha_x < 25$;
3. Level L_3: $C_i \in [3, 4) \Rightarrow N \cdot 2/4 \le \alpha_x < N \cdot 3/5$, then we have $C_i \in [3, 4) \Rightarrow 25 \le \alpha_x < 30$.

From the relations presented for the determination of the boundary values of the significance of the criteria (α_i), i.e., from experts' preferences within the level L_j, $j \in \{1, 2, \ldots, k\}$, we may perceive that the breadth of the interval $N \cdot (k-1)/(k+1) \le \alpha_x < N \cdot k/(k+2)$ depends on the value of the real (natural) number N. A broader interval and, simultaneously, a more comfortable scale with fewer decimal values for expressing experts' preferences, are obtained for greater values of the number N, such as $N \ge n^2$; vice versa, a scale with a larger number of decimal values for expressing experts' preferences is obtained for smaller values of the number N, such as $n < N < n^2$.

Based on Theorem 1, while performing a comparison of any criterion C_i with the criterion C_1 (where C_1 is the most influential criterion), the NDSL model ensures that the number $2N$ is added to the criteria. Simultaneously, a part greater than or equal to $2N$ belongs to the criterion C_1, as the most significant criterion, whereas a smaller or equal part belongs to the criterion C_i. If the problem of defining the number N is observed from an economic standpoint, and if we take $N = 50$, then this problem can be observed in ordinary economic terms, i.e., in percentages ($p\%$). If $p \ge 50$, then it belongs to the criterion C_1, while $(1-p)\%$ belongs to the criterion C_i. Since expressing in percentages is a normal thing to do during a pairwise comparison, the authors propose that $N = 50$ should be taken for the values of the number N for solving real problems.

2.2. Steps of the NDSL Model

Based on the previously demonstrated mathematical bases of the NDSL model, the steps that should be taken in order to obtain the weight coefficients of criteria are systematized in this section. In Phase One, a set of evaluation criteria is formed, and the criteria are further ranked in accordance with experts' preferences. In Phase Two, the levels of significance of the criteria are formed and the criteria significance level is determined within each level. Finally, the weight coefficients of the criteria are calculated in Phase Three. Figure 1 schematically presents the phases through which the NDSL model is implemented.

The NDSL model includes the calculation of the weight coefficients of criteria through the seven steps presented in the next part of the paper.

Step 1: Determining the most significant criterion from within the set of criteria $S = \{C_1, C_2, \ldots, C_n\}$. Allow us to assume that the decision-maker has chosen the criterion C_1 as the most significant, and allow us to assume that C_1 is a criterion from within the set $S = \{C_1, C_2, \ldots, C_n\}$, which is the most significant in the decision-making process.

Step 2: Ranking the criteria from within the defined set of evaluation criteria $S = \{C_1, C_2, \ldots, C_n\}$. Ranking is performed according to the significance of the criteria, i.e., from the most significant criterion to the criterion of the least significance. In that manner, we obtain the criteria ranked according to the expected values of weight coefficients:

$$C_1 > C_2 > \ldots > C_n, \tag{10}$$

where n represents the total number of the criteria. If it is estimated that there are two or several criteria with the same significance, instead of the sign ">", the sign "=" is placed in-between those criteria in the expression (10).

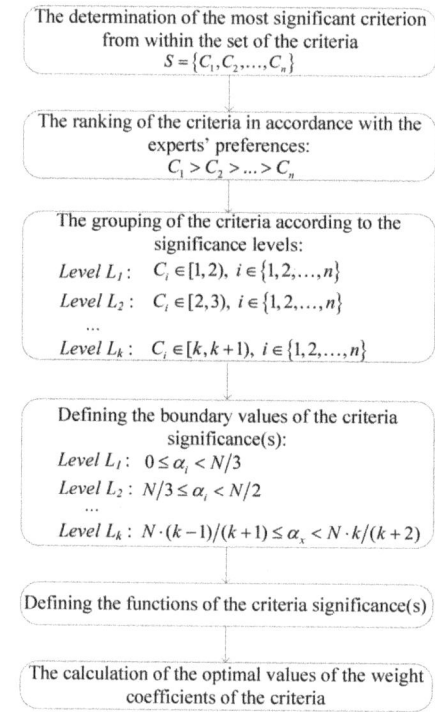

Figure 1. The non-decreasing series at criteria significance levels (NDSL) model.

Step 3: Grouping the criteria according to the significance levels. Allow us to assume that experts have grouped the criteria as per levels in accordance with their preferences, depending on the significance of the criteria. Grouping criteria as per levels is performed according to the rules defined in the previous section of the paper, namely:

- Level L_1: At the L_1 level, the criteria from within the set S whose significance is equal to the significance of the criterion C_1 or up to two times as small as the significance of the criterion C_1 should be grouped. The criterion C_i belonging to the L_1 level will be presented as $C_i \in [1,2)$, $i \in \{1,2,\ldots,n\}$;
- Level L_2: At the L_2 level, the criteria from within the set S whose significance is exactly two times as small as the significance of the criterion C_1 or up to three times as small as the significance of the criterion C_1 should be grouped. The criterion C_i belonging to the L_2 level will be presented as $C_i \in [2,3)$, $i \in \{1,2,\ldots,n\}$;
- Level L_k: At the L_k level, the criteria from within the set S whose significance is exactly k times as small as the significance of the criterion C_1 or up to $k+1$ times as small as the significance of the criterion C_1 should be grouped. The criterion C_i belonging to the L_k level will be presented as $C_i \in [k, k+1)$, $i \in \{1,2,\ldots,n\}$.

By grouping criteria as per levels, rough expert preferences for the criteria from within the set $S = \{C_1, C_2, \ldots, C_n\}$ are expressed. The precise definition of experts' preferences is expressed via the significance of the criteria (α_i). The boundary values of α_i as per levels are presented in the next step.

Step 4: Defining the boundary values of the significance of criteria (α_i) as per levels. When defining the boundary values of the significance of criteria, the following relations should be adhered to:

- Level L_1: For $C_i \in [1,2)$, the values of the significance of criteria (α_i) range in the interval $0 \le \alpha_i < N/3$, i.e., $C_i \in [1,2) \Rightarrow 0 \le \alpha_i < N/3$;

- Level L_2: For $C_i \in [2,3)$, the values of the significance of criteria (α_i) range in the interval $N/3 \leq \alpha_x < N/2$, i.e., $C_i \in [2,3) \Rightarrow N/3 \leq \alpha_i < N/2$;
- Level L_k: For $C_i \in [k, k+1)$, the values of the significance of criteria (α_i) range in the interval $N \cdot (k-1)/(k+1) \leq \alpha_i < N \cdot k/(k+2)$, i.e., $C_i \in [k, k+1) \Rightarrow N \cdot (k-1)/(k+1) \leq \alpha_x < N \cdot k/(k+2)$.

Step 5: Presenting experts' preferences as per levels. Based on the defined boundary values α_i, experts express their preferences in accordance with the significance of the criteria. Every criterion $C_i \in S$ within the level L_j, $j \in \{1, 2, \ldots, k\}$ is assigned the value α_i. Therefore, since it is the most significant criterion, the criterion C_1 is assigned the value $\alpha_1 = 0$. The rest of the criteria are assigned appropriate values α_i in compliance with the significances of the criteria. If the criterion C_i has a greater significance than the criterion C_{i+1}, then it is considered that $\alpha_i < \alpha_{i+1}$, or if the criterion C_i has a significance equal to that of the criterion C_{i+1}, then it is considered that $\alpha_i = \alpha_{i+1}$.

Step 6: Defining the $f(C_i)$ criteria significance functions. The $f : S \to R$ criteria significance function is defined in that manner. For each criterion $C_i \in S$, it is possible to define a criteria significance function by applying the following expression:

$$f(C_i) = \frac{N - \alpha_i}{N + \alpha_i}, \tag{11}$$

where $i \in \{1, 2, \ldots, n\}$, α_i represents the significance of the criterion assigned to the criterion C_i within the observed level, whereas N represents a real (natural) number.

Step 7: Calculating the optimal values of criteria weight coefficients. If the most influential criterion is marked as C_1, then, by applying the expression (12), it is possible for us to calculate the weight coefficient of the criterion C_1, i.e.,

$$w_1 = \frac{1}{1 + \sum_{j=2}^{n} f(C_j)}, \tag{12}$$

where $f(C_j)$ represents the criteria significance function.

The weight coefficients of the remaining criteria from within the set S are obtained by applying the following expression (13):

$$w_i = \frac{f(C_i)}{1 + \sum_{j=2}^{n} f(C_j)}, \tag{13}$$

where $f(C_i)$ represents the function of the significance of criteria whose weight coefficient is being calculated, whereas $f(C_j)$ represents the functions of the significance of all criteria (without the function of the significance of the most significant criterion).

The application of all multi-criteria models is aimed at selecting an alternative with the best final value of the criteria function. The total value of the criteria function f_l ($l = 1, 2, \ldots, m$) alternative l can be obtained through the transformation of the NDSL model into a classical multi-criteria model by the application of the expression (14). By applying the simple additive weighted value function (14), which is the basic model for the majority of MCDM methods, the algorithm of the NDSL model transforms into a classical multi-criteria model, which can be used to evaluate m alternative solutions as per n optimization criteria.

$$f_l = \sum_{i=1}^{n} w_i x_{ij}, \tag{14}$$

where w_i represents the values of the weight coefficients, whereas x_{ij} represents the values of the alternatives as per the optimization criteria in the decision-making initial matrix $X = [x_{ij}]_{m \times n}$.

3. Application of the NDSL Model

This section is a demonstration of the application of the presented model for solving a real-world problem. With the aim of understanding the presented algorithm as easily as possible, the application of the NDSL model for solving the simple problem of evaluating a car, which a large number of people are faced with every day, is presented. The subject matter of consideration was the problem of selecting an optimal car from a set of cars by applying a larger number of criteria. For the purpose of this study, the criteria defined in the study [74] were considered.

The subject matter of consideration was the example in which the car buyer is evaluating the alternatives by observing the following five criteria: The quality (C1), the price (C2), convenience/comfort (C3), the safety level (C4), and the interior (C5). If we accept the condition that $N \geq n^2$, i.e., $N = 25$, then we can determine the weight coefficients of the criteria by the NDSL model as follows:

Step 1: Determining the most significant criterion from within the set of criteria $S = \{C_1, C_2, \ldots, C_5\}$. Allow C1 to be selected as the most significant criterion;

Step 2: The criteria from within the set of criteria $S = \{C_1, C_2, \ldots, C_5\}$ are ranked as follows: C2 > C1 = C4 > C3 > C5;

Step 3: Grouping the criteria as per significance levels. The criteria are grouped into sets at four levels, as follows:

- Level L_1: {C2};
- Level L_2: {C1, C4};
- Level L_3: {C3};
- Level L_4, L_5, L_6, L_7: ∅;
- Level L_8: {C5}.

At the first level, the criterion C2 is positioned as the most significant criterion, i.e., $C_2 \in [1, 2)$. Since it has been estimated that the significance of the remaining criteria is more than two times as small as that of the criterion C2, they are classified as the other significance levels. At the second level, there are the criteria C1 and C4, because they have been estimated to have a weight coefficient which is two to three times as small as that of the criterion C2, i.e., $C_1, C_4 \in [2, 3)$. The criterion C3 is at the third level, since its weight coefficient is three to four times as small as that of the criterion C2, i.e., $C_3 \in [3, 4)$. The criterion C5 is at the eighth level, since its weight coefficient has been estimated to be between eight and nine times as small as the weight coefficient of the most significant criterion (C2), i.e., $C_5 \in [8, 9)$;

Step 4: Based on the relations for defining the boundary values of the criteria significance (α_i), we can determine the intervals for α_i at every significance level, as follows:

$$\text{Level } L_1 : \alpha_i \in [0.00, 8.33);$$
$$\text{Level } L_2 : \alpha_i \in [8.33, 12.5);$$
$$\text{Level } L_3 : \alpha_i \in [12.5, 15.0);$$
$$\text{Level } L_8 : \alpha_i \in [19.44, 20.0).$$

Step 5: Based on the defined intervals of the criteria significance (α_i), the experts' preferences as per levels are presented:

$$\text{Level } L_1 : \alpha_2 = 0$$
$$\text{Level } L_2 : \alpha_1 = \alpha_4 = 8.33$$
$$\text{Level } L_3 : \alpha_3 = 14.9$$
$$\text{Level } L_8 : \alpha_5 = 19.5$$

Based on the presented values of α_i, it is possible to conclude the following:

(1) For Level One: Since the criterion C2 is the most significant criterion, it has been assigned the value $\alpha_1 = 0$.;

(2) For Level Two: The criteria C1 and C4 have been estimated to have the same significance, which is exactly twice as small as the significance of the criterion C2, so they have been assigned the value $\alpha_1 = \alpha_4 = 8.33$;

(3) For Level Three: The significance of the criterion C3 has been estimated to be slightly less than four times as small as the significance of the criterion C2, so it has been assigned the value $\alpha_4 = 14.9$;

(4) For Level Eight: The significance of the criterion C5 has been estimated to be slightly more than eight times as small as the significance of the criterion C2, so it has been assigned the value $\alpha_4 = 19.5$;

Step 6: By applying the expression (11), the functions of the significance of the criteria $f(C_i)$, $i = 1, 2, \ldots, 5$, were defined as follows:

$$f(C_2) = 1.000$$
$$f(C_1) = 0.500$$
$$f(C_4) = 0.500$$
$$f(C_3) = 0.253$$
$$f(C_5) = 0.124$$

Step 7: Since the criterion C2 is defined as the most influential criterion, by applying the expression (12), it is possible to calculate the weight coefficient of the most significant criterion:

$$w_2 = \frac{1}{1 + \sum_{j=2}^{5} f(C_j)} = \frac{1}{1 + 0.500 + 0.500 + 0.253 + 0.124} = 0.421.$$

The weight coefficients of the remaining criteria are obtained by applying the following expression (13):

$$w_1 = \frac{0.500}{1 + 0.500 + 0.500 + 0.253 + 0.124} = 0.210$$
$$w_4 = \frac{0.500}{1 + 0.500 + 0.500 + 0.253 + 0.124} = 0.210$$
$$w_3 = \frac{0.253}{1 + 0.500 + 0.500 + 0.253 + 0.124} = 0.106$$
$$w_5 = \frac{0.124}{1 + 0.500 + 0.500 + 0.253 + 0.124} = 0.052$$

In that way, the vector of the weight coefficients $w_i = (0.210, 0.421, 0.106, 0.210, 0.052)^T$ is obtained.

4. Comparison and Discussion

In this section, based on the presented methodology, the advantages of the NDSL model that make the model a reliable and interesting multi-criteria model are singled out. The advantages of the NDSL model are presented through a comparison with known methodologies employed for the determination of criteria weight coefficients. The BWM and AHP methods were singled out for the purpose of the comparison, since the validity of both methodologies is based on the satisfaction of the condition of the transitivity of relations and a pairwise comparison. Additionally, other reasons for comparing the model with the BWM and AHP methods are the quality of the results and the widespread use of the BWM and AHP models by the scientific community for successfully solving numerous real world problems. Bearing in mind the fact that the NDSL model is methodologically based on an assessment of the comparative significance of criteria and satisfaction of the condition of transitivity, a comparison with the BWM and AHP models is a logical step for conducting a comparison of the results and validation of the model. In the following part, the application of the BWM and AHP methods is presented for the same example in which the NDSL model was tested in the previous chapter.

The algorithm of the BWM implies the formation of the Best-to-Others (BO) and the Others-to-Worst (OW) vector [75]: $A_B = (2, 1, 4, 2, 8)^T$ and $A_W = (4, 8, 2, 4, 1)^T$, respectively. By applying the BWM, the optimal values of the weight coefficients were obtained, namely,

$w_1 = 0.2105$, $w_2 = 0.4211$, $w_3 = 0.1053$, $w_4 = 0.2105$, $w_5 = 0.0526$, and a consistency ratio (CR) $CR = 0.00$.

Based on the data from [75], a pairwise comparison matrix of the AHP model (Table 1) was formed, and the values of the weight coefficients of criteria, with a consistency ratio $CR = 0.029$, were obtained.

Table 1. Criteria pairwise comparison—the Analytic Hierarchy Process (AHP) method.

Criteria	C1	C2	C3	C4	C5	Wj
C1	1.000	0.333	3.000	1.000	5.00	0.202
C2	3.000	1.000	5.000	3.000	7.00	0.464
C3	0.333	0.200	1.000	0.333	3.00	0.089
C4	1.000	0.333	3.000	1.000	5.00	0.202
C5	0.200	0.143	0.333	0.200	1.00	0.044

By applying the AHP method, the values of the weight coefficients of criteria similar to those in the BWM were obtained, but with a significantly larger number of pairwise comparisons. The differences in the values of the weight coefficients between the AHP and BWM are a consequence of the incomplete consistency of the results in the AHP model ($CR_{AHP} = 0.029$ and $CR_{BWM} = 0.000$). A comparative presentation of the results of all three approaches is shown in Table 2.

Table 2. A comparative presentation of the results obtained by applying the NDSL, Best Worst Method (BWM), and AHP methods.

Criteria	AHP (wi)	BWM (wi)	NDSL (wj)
C1	0.202	0.210	0.210
C2	0.464	0.421	0.421
C3	0.089	0.106	0.106
C4	0.202	0.210	0.210
C5	0.044	0.052	0.052
CR	0.029	0.000	-

Table 2 allows us to notice that identical values of the weight coefficients of criteria were obtained by applying the BWM and NDSL models. By applying the AHP, the values obtained deviate to a certain extent from the weights of the BWM and NDSL models. The solution obtained by the AHP model is also acceptable, since the values of the consistency ratio are within the permitted boundaries, i.e., $CR \leq 0.1$. We need to emphasize the fact that, by applying the BWM and NDSL models to this example, completely consistent results were obtained, which was also confirmed by the calculation made, i.e., $CR_{BWM} = 0.00$. Comparing criteria by applying a 9-degree scale (in the BWM), however, often leads to inconsistent results. Different from the BWM and AHP models, consistent results are always obtained when using the NDSL model because it applies an original methodology for grouping criteria as per significance, within which transitivity relations between criteria are retained. In the next part of the paper, a discussion is presented through a comparison of the NDSL model with the BWM and AHP models. The discussion aims to point to the limitations of the BWM and AHP models, which are eliminated by the application of the NDSL model. The discussion is organized through the following: (1) a comparative presentation of the number of criteria pairwise comparisons needed in the analyzed models; (2) the impact of the measuring scale on the results of the BWM, AHP, and NDSL models; (3) the consistency of the results of the analyzed models; (4) the problem of defining the best and worst criteria in the BWM and NDSL models; and (5) the problem of multi-optimality in the BWM.

In the AHP method, $n(n-1)/2$ pairwise comparisons need to be made, whereas the algorithm of the BWM implies $2n - 3$ comparisons. An increase in the number of criteria in the BWM and AHP models leads to a significant increase in the number of pairwise comparisons, through which the mathematical formulation of the mentioned models is, to a great extent, made more complex.

This makes the validation of the results and the impossibility of obtaining satisfactory values of the CR more complex. On the other hand, in relation to the presented subjective models (the AHP method and BWM), the NDSL only requires an $n-1$ comparison in pairs of criteria, so the mathematical formulation of the model is made more complex as the number of criteria increases. Apart from that, the presented methodology enables us to transfer mathematical transitivity as per significance levels, which produces maximally consistent results for the comparison.

In the case of a larger number of criteria (more than eight), it is difficult to obtain fully consistent results in the BWM and AHP models. That is a consequence of the small range of the 9-degree scale used in these models. The 9-degree scale limits the expression of experts' preferences to a maximum ratio of 9:1. This limitation further imposes an inconsistency in comparisons. This assertion will be illustrated by the example of an evaluation of suppliers A, B, and C. If suppliers B and C differ from each other a little in terms of the quality of the delivery, the company has a possibility to assign them the values 9 and 8 when comparing them with supplier A. Now, given the fact that there is a small difference between suppliers B and C, that difference cannot consistently be expressed by means of the 9-degree scale. In that situation, there is no other possibility but to assign the value 1, through which the same significance is assigned to suppliers B and C [76]. Another example is as follows: should alternative A be preferable to B, and should B be better than C (mark: 7), once A is compared with C, the highest available result is 9, which creates an inconsistency. Similar inconsistencies caused by the 9-degree scale also appear in the BWM, but can be eliminated by the implementation of different scales.

These inconsistencies in comparisons are eliminated in the NDSL model. The NDSL model applies a different logic for criteria comparison, which is performed in two steps. The first step involves grouping criteria according to the significance levels, whereas in the second step, an expert evaluation of criteria is carried out through the scale defined for every level individually. By forming a criteria significance level, the shortcoming of the predefined scale of values is eliminated. The NDSL model enables us to form the needed number of such levels, which implies that experts have a sufficient freedom to express the realistic advantages of the most significant criterion in relation to other criteria.

The results of the NDSL model do not require the consistency of the results to be checked because, in the first step of the model, weight coefficients are ranked in relation to the most significant criterion. Therefore, transitivity relations between criteria are formed in the first step. Those relations are retained throughout the model by forming a non-decreasing series as per significance levels, so the results of the model are simultaneously also always consistent. On the other hand, the BWM and AHP models require the consistency of solution(s) to be checked and validation of the results obtained. The 9-degree scale and a large number of comparisons frequently undermine the transitivity between criteria in both models, which leads to an increase in the CR and the boundary values being exceeded.

5. Conclusions

In this paper, a new model for determining the weight coefficients of criteria in multi-criteria models by forming a non-decreasing series at criteria significance levels (NDSL) is presented. The NDSL model involves forming a non-decreasing series based on criteria significance levels. The mathematical formulation of the NDSL model is systematized in the second section of the paper, and an algorithm, which is implemented through seven steps, is proposed. With the aim of presenting the applicability of the new model, its application in decision-making in a real-world problem is demonstrated. A comparison of the results of the NDSL model and the results of the BWM and AHP models is also presented in the paper. It was demonstrated through a comparison with the mentioned models that the NDSL model generates the same results as the existing models and enables elimination of the weaknesses that exist in the BWM and AHP models.

The NDSL model has several interesting characteristics that make it a robust and interesting model to apply in multi-criteria decision-making, namely due to the following facts: (1) the NDSL model requires a significantly smaller number of comparisons in pairs of criteria, only needing an $n-1$ comparison, whereas the AHP requires an $n(n-1)/2$ comparison and the BWM requires a $2n-3$

comparison; (2) the model enables us to obtain consistent results, even in the case of a larger number of criteria (more than nine criteria); (3) the NDSL model applies an original algorithm for grouping criteria as per significance levels, through which the shortcomings of the 9-degree scale applied in the BWM and AHP models are eliminated. In that way, the small range and inconsistency of the 9-degree scale are eliminated; (4) while the BWM includes defining a unique best/worst criterion, the NDSL model eliminates this limitation and gives decision-makers the freedom to express relationships between criteria in accordance with their preferences, irrespective of the number of best/worst criteria in the model.

The NDSL model represents a tool which helps managers cope with their own subjectivity when prioritizing criteria through a simple and logical algorithm. By employing the presented model, the appearance of the inconsistency of experts' preferences is eliminated through an original algorithm requiring a small number of comparisons ($n - 1$). The authors believe that this approach gives experts the opportunity to express their preferences in a natural way, by forming the level of significance of criteria. Accordingly, it is expected that by forming the criteria significance level, the shortcomings and limitations that exist in predefined assessment scales are eliminated. For example, when comparing the best (C_B) criterion with the C_x criterion, an expert knows that the C_B criterion is 2.5 times more significant than the C_x criterion. In pairwise comparison methods that use the Saaty scale, such a relationship cannot be represented directly, since the Saaty scale involves only integer values. Through the formation of significance levels, the expert is given the opportunity to classify the C_x criterion as belonging to another level in a logical manner, or based on their preferences, since they already know that the C_B criterion is 2.5 times more important than the C_x criterion. From this, we can conclude that the experts indirectly form the significance levels of the criteria. However, the mathematical formulation of existing models for pairwise comparisons requires experts to represent the significance of criteria by defining relationships over a numerical scale. In this way, criteria are indirectly grouped into levels of significance. However, such a procedure can lead to a misrepresentation of the significance of the criterion, which may be due to a misunderstanding of the mathematical apparatus of the method. Bearing all of the above in mind, the authors believe that this formulation of the interrelation between criteria enables the rational and logical expression of expert preferences, which further contributes to objective decision making.

Bearing in mind the mentioned advantages of the NDSL, there is a need for the development and implementation of software for real-world applications. Through such work, the model will be brought significantly closer to users and will enable the exploitation of all of the advantages mentioned in the paper. We also propose the application of the model in other real-world applications in which the NDSL model would be used with other developed MCDM tools. This limitation has already been eliminated. The authors developed a software solution in Microsoft Excel software while working on this study. One of the directions of future research studies should be working towards the extension of this model through the application of different theories of uncertainty, such as neutrosophic sets, fuzzy sets, rough numbers, grey theory, and so forth. The extension of the NDSL through the application of theories of uncertainty will enable the processing of experts' preferences, even when comparisons are made based on partly known or even very little-known data. This would enable an easier expression of the decision-maker's preferences, simultaneously respecting the subjectivities and shortcomings of information about certain phenomena.

Author Contributions: Conceptualization, M.Ž. and D.P.; methodology, M.Ž., D.P., and G.Ć.; validation, B.D.M. and M.M.Ž.; writing—original draft preparation, D.P.; writing—review and editing, M.Ž. and D.P.; supervision, D.P. All authors have read and agreed to the published version of the manuscript.

Funding: This research received no external funding.

Conflicts of Interest: The authors declare no conflict of interest.

References

1. Valipour, A.; Yahaya, N.; Md Noor, N.; Antuchevičienė, J.; Tamošaitienė, J. Hybrid SWARA-COPRAS method for risk assessment in deep foundation excavation project: An Iranian case study. *J. Civ. Eng. Manag.* **2017**, *23*, 524–532. [CrossRef]
2. Milicevic, M.; Zupac, G. Subjective Approach to the Determination of Criteria Weights. *Mil. Tec. Cour.* **2017**, *60*, 48–70.
3. Belton, V. A comparison of the analytic hierarchy process and a simple multiattribute value function. *Eur. J. Oper. Res.* **1986**, *26*, 7–21. [CrossRef]
4. Zanakis, S.H.; Solomon, A.; Wishart, N.; Dublish, S. Multi-attribute decision making: A simulation comparison of select methods. *Eur. J. Oper. Res.* **1998**, *107*, 507–529. [CrossRef]
5. Triantaphyllou, E. *Multi-Criteria Decision Making Methods: A Comparative Study*; Springer: New York, NY, USA, 2000.
6. Opricovic, S.; Tzeng, G.-H. Extended VIKOR method in comparison with outranking methods. *Eur. J. Oper. Res.* **2007**, *178*, 514–529. [CrossRef]
7. Tzeng, G.-H.; Chen, T.-Y.; Wang, J.C. A weight-assessing method with habitual domains. *Eur. J. Oper. Res.* **1998**, *110*, 342–367. [CrossRef]
8. Shannon, C.E.; Weaver, W. *The Mathematical Theory of Communication*; The University of Illinois Press: Urbana, IL, USA, 1947.
9. Diakoulaki, D.; Mavrotas, G.; Papayannakis, L. Determining objective weights in multiple criteria problems: The CRITIC method. *Comput. Oper. Res.* **1995**, *22*, 763–770. [CrossRef]
10. Srdjevic, B.; Medeiros, Y.D.P.; Faria, A.S.; Schaer, M. Objektivno vrednovanje kriterijuma performanse sistema akumulacija. *Vodoprivreda* **2003**, *35*, 163–176, 0350–0519. (In Serbian)
11. Keeney, R.L.; Raiffa, H. *Decisions with Multiple Objectives*; Wiley: New York, NY, USA, 1976.
12. Von Winterfeldt, D.; Edwards, W. *Decision Analysis and Behavioral Research*; Cambridge University Press: Cambridge, UK, 1986.
13. Edwards, W.; Barron, H. SMARTS and SMARTER: Improved Simple Methods for Multiattribute Utility Measurement. *Organ. Behav. Hum. Decis. Process.* **1994**, *60*, 306–325. [CrossRef]
14. Thurstone, L.L. A law of comparative judgment. *Psychol. Rev.* **1927**, *34*, 273. [CrossRef]
15. Saaty, T.L. *Analytic Hierarchy Process*; McGraw-Hill: New York, NY, USA, 1980.
16. Gabus, A.; Fontela, E. *World Problems an Invitation to Further Thought within the Framework of DEMATEL*; Battelle Geneva Research Centre: Geneva, Switzerland, 1972.
17. Rezaei, J. Best-worst multi-criteria decision-making method. *Omega* **2015**, *53*, 49–57. [CrossRef]
18. Roberts, R.; Goodwin, P. Weight approximations in multi-attribute decision models. *J. Multi. Criteria Decis. Anal.* **2002**, *11*, 291–303. [CrossRef]
19. Keršuliene, V.; Zavadskas, E.K.; Turskis, Z. Selection of rational dispute resolution method by applying new step-wise weight assessment ratio analysis (SWARA). *J. Bus. Econ. Manag.* **2010**, *11*, 243–258. [CrossRef]
20. Herman, M.W.; Koczkodaj, W.W. A Monte Carlo study of pairwise comparison. *Inf. Process. Lett.* **1996**, *57*, 25–29. [CrossRef]
21. Chatterjee, P.; Stević, Ž. A Two-Phase Fuzzy AHP - Fuzzy TOPSIS Model for Supplier Evaluation in Manufacturing Environment. *Oper. Res. Eng. Sci. Theor. Appl.* **2019**, *2*, 72–90. [CrossRef]
22. Ignaccolo, M.; Inturri, G.; García-Melón, M.; Giuffrida, N.; Le Pira, M.; Torrisi, V. Combining Analytic Hierarchy Process (AHP) with role-playing games for stakeholder engagement in complex transport decisions. *Transp. Res. Procedia* **2017**, *27*, 500–507. [CrossRef]
23. Raymundo, H.; Reis, J.G.M. Passenger Transport Drawbacks: An Analysis of Its "Disutilities" Applying the AHP Approach in a Case Study in Tokyo, Japan. In Proceedings of the IFIP International Conference on Advances in Production Management Systems, Hamburg, Germany, 3–7 September 2017; Springer: Cham, Switzerland, 2017; pp. 545–552.
24. Olivková, I. Methodology for Assessment of Electronic Payment Systems in Transport Using AHP Method. In Proceedings of the International Conference on Reliability and Statistics in Transportation and Communication, Riga, Latvia, 18–21 October 2017; Springer: Cham, Switzerland, 2017; pp. 290–299.

25. Stević, Ž.; Vesković, S.; Vasiljević, M.; Tepić, G. The selection of the logistics center location using AHP method. In Proceedings of the 2nd Logistics International Conference, Belgrade, Serbia, 21–23 May 2015; pp. 86–91.
26. Pamucar, D.; Bozanic, D.; Lukovac, V.; Komazec, N. Normalized weighted geometric bonferroni mean operator of interval rough numbers – application in interval rough DEMATEL-COPRAS. *Facta Univ. Ser. Mech. Eng.* **2018**, *16*, 171–191. [CrossRef]
27. Adalı, E.; Işık, A. Integration of DEMATEL, ANP and DEA methods for third party logistics providers' selection. *Manag. Sci. Lett.* **2016**, *6*, 325–340. [CrossRef]
28. Zarbakhshnia, N.; Soleimani, H.; Ghaderi, H. Sustainable third-party reverse logistics provider evaluation and selection using fuzzy SWARA and developed fuzzy COPRAS in the presence of risk criteria. *Appl. Soft Comput.* **2018**, *65*, 307–319. [CrossRef]
29. Zavadskas, E.K.; Stević, Ž.; Tanackov, I.; Prentkovskis, O. A Novel Multicriteria Approach-Rough Step-WiseWeight Assessment Ratio Analysis Method (R-SWARA) and Its Application in Logistics. *Stud. Inf. Control.* **2018**, *27*, 97–106. [CrossRef]
30. Nezhad, M.R.G.; Zolfani, S.H.; Moztarzadeh, F.; Zavadskas, E.K.; Bahrami, M. Planning the priority of high tech industries based on SWARA-WASPAS methodology: The case of the nanotechnology industry in Iran. *Econ. Res.-Ekon. Istraž.* **2015**, *28*, 1111–1137. [CrossRef]
31. Kouchaksaraei, R.H.; Zolfani, S.H.; Golabchi, M. Glasshouse locating based on SWARA-COPRAS approach. *International Int. J. Strat. Prop. Manag.* **2015**, *19*, 111–122. [CrossRef]
32. Karabasevic, D.; Paunkovic, J.; Stanujkic, D. Ranking of companies according to the indicators of corporate social responsibility based on SWARA and ARAS methods. *Serbian J. Manag.* **2016**, *11*, 43–53. [CrossRef]
33. Işık, A.T.; Adalı, E.A. A new integrated decision making approach based on SWARA and OCRA methods for the hotel selection problem. *Int. J. Adv. Oper. Manag.* **2016**, *8*, 140–151. [CrossRef]
34. Nakhaei, J.; Arefi, S.L.; Bitarafan, M.; Kildienė, S. Evaluation of light supply in the public underground safe spaces by using of COPRAS-SWARA methods. *Int. J. Strat. Prop. Manag.* **2016**, *20*, 198–206. [CrossRef]
35. Shukla, S.; Mishra, P.K.; Jain, R.; Yadav, H.C. An integrated decision making approach for ERP system selection using SWARA and PROMETHEE method. *Int. J. Intell. Enterp.* **2016**, *3*, 120–147. [CrossRef]
36. Vujić, D.; Stanujkić, D.; Urošević, S.; Karabašević, D. An approach to leader selection in the mining industry based on the use of weighted sum preferred levels of the performances method. *Min. Met. Eng. Bor.* **2016**, 53–62. [CrossRef]
37. Vesković, S.; Stević, Ž.; Stojić, G.; Vasiljević, M.; Milinković, S. Evaluation of the railway management model by using a new integrated model DELPHI-SWARA-MABAC. *Decis. Making Appl. Manag. Eng.* **2018**, *1*. [CrossRef]
38. Hong, H.; Panahi, M.; Shirzadi, A.; Ma, T.; Liu, J.; Zhu, A.X.; Kazakis, N. Flood susceptibility assessment in Hengfeng area coupling adaptive neuro-fuzzy inference system with genetic algorithm and differential evolution. *Sci. Total. Environ.* **2017**, *621*, 1124–1141. [CrossRef]
39. Juodagalvienė, B.; Turskis, Z.; Šaparauskas, J.; Endriukaitytė, A. Integrated multi-criteria evaluation of house's plan shape based on the EDAS and SWARA methods. *Eng. Struct. Technol.* **2017**, *9*, 117–125. [CrossRef]
40. Jain, N.; Singh, A.R. Fuzzy Kano Integrated MCDM Approach for Supplier Selection Based on Must Be Criteria. *Int. J. Supply Chain Manag.* **2017**, *6*, 49–59.
41. Urosevic, S.; Karabasevic, D.; Stanujkic, D.; Maksimovic, M. An approach to personnel selection in the tourism industry based on the SWARA and the WASPAS methods. *Econ. Comput. Econ. Cybern. Stud. Res.* **2017**, *51*, 75–88.
42. Panahi, S.; Khakzad, A.; Afzal, P. Application of stepwise weight assessment ratio analysis (SWARA) for copper prospectivity mapping in the Anarak region, central Iran. *Arab. J. Geosci.* **2017**, *10*, 484. [CrossRef]
43. Ighravwe, D.E.; Oke, S.A. Sustenance of zero-loss on production lines using Kobetsu Kaizen of TPM with hybrid models. *Total Qual. Manag. Bus. Excel.* **2017**, 1–25. [CrossRef]
44. Dahooie, J.H.; Abadi, E.B.J.; Vanaki, A.S.; Firoozfar, H.R. Competency-based IT personnel selection using a hybrid SWARA and ARAS-G methodology. *Hum. Factors Ergon. Manuf. Serv. Ind.* **2018**, *28*, 5–16. [CrossRef]
45. Ghorabaee, M.K.; Amiri, M.; Zavadskas, E.K.; Antucheviciene, J. A new hybrid fuzzy MCDM approach for evaluation of construction equipment with sustainability considerations. *Arch. Civ. Mech. Eng.* **2018**, *18*, 32–49. [CrossRef]

46. Fazli, M.; Afshari, A.J.; Hajiaghaei-Keshteli, M. Identification and ranking of risks in Green Building projects using the hybrid SWARA-COPRAS method. *Int. Conf. Iranian Oper. Res. Soc.* **2018**, *2*, 1–5.
47. Rezaei, J.; Wang, J.; Tavasszy, L. Linking supplier development to supplier segmentation using Best Worst Method. *Expert Syst. Appl.* **2015**, *42*, 9152–9164. [CrossRef]
48. Sadaghiani, S.; Ahmad, K.W.; Rezaei, J.; Tavasszy, L. Evaluation of external forces affecting supply chain sustainability in oil and gas industry using Best Worst Method. In Proceedings of the 2015 International Mediterranean Gas and Oil Conference (MedGO), Mechref, Lebanon, 16–18 April 2015; IEEE: Piscataway, NJ, USA, 2015; pp. 1–4.
49. Salimi, N.; Rezaei, J. Measuring efficiency of university-industry Ph. D. projects using best worst method. *Scientometrics* **2016**, *109*, 1911–1938. [CrossRef]
50. Gupta, H.; Barua, M.K. Identifying enablers of technological innovation for Indian MSMEs using best–worst multi criteria decision making method. *Technol. Forecast. Soc. Chang.* **2016**, *107*, 69–79. [CrossRef]
51. Rezaei, J. Best-worst multi-criteria decision-making method: Some properties and a linear model. *Omega* **2016**, *64*, 126–130. [CrossRef]
52. Rezaei, J.; Nispeling, T.; Sarkis, J.; Tavasszy, L. A supplier selection life cycle approach integrating traditional and environmental criteria using the best worst method. *J. Clean. Prod.* **2016**, *135*, 577–588. [CrossRef]
53. You, X.; Chen, T.; Yang, Q. Approach to multi-criteria group decision-making problems based on the best-worst-method and electre method. *Symmetry* **2016**, *8*, 95. [CrossRef]
54. Van de Kaa, G.; Kamp, L.; Rezaei, J. Selection of biomass thermochemical conversion technology in the Netherlands: A best worst method approach. *J. Clean. Prod.* **2017**, *166*, 32–39. [CrossRef]
55. Van de Kaa, G.; Scholten, D.; Rezaei, J.; Milchram, C. The Battle between Battery and Fuel Cell Powered Electric Vehicles: A BWM Approach. *Energies* **2017**, *10*, 1707. [CrossRef]
56. Hassanpour, M.; Pamucar, D. Evaluation of Iranian Household Appliance Industries Using MCDM Models. *Oper. Res. Eng. Sci. Theor. Appl.* **2019**, *2*, 1–25. [CrossRef]
57. Gupta, H.; Barua, M.K. Supplier selection among SMEs on the basis of their green innovation ability using BWM and fuzzy TOPSIS. *J. Clean. Prod.* **2017**, *152*, 242–258. [CrossRef]
58. Petrovic, G.; Mihajlovic, J.; Cojbasic, Z.; Madic, M.; Marinkovic, D. Comparison of three fuzzy MCDM methods for solving the supplier selection problem. *Facta Univ. Ser. Mech. Eng.* **2019**, *17*, 455–469. [CrossRef]
59. Salimi, N. Quality assessment of scientific outputs using the BWM. *Scientometrics* **2017**, *112*, 1–19. [CrossRef]
60. Gupta, P.; Anand, S.; Gupta, H. Developing a roadmap to overcome barriers to energy efficiency in buildings using best worst method. *Sustain. Cities Soc.* **2017**, *31*, 244–259. [CrossRef]
61. You, P.; Guo, S.; Zhao, H.; Zhao, H. Operation Performance Evaluation of Power Grid Enterprise Using a Hybrid BWM-TOPSIS Method. *Sustainability* **2017**, *9*, 2329. [CrossRef]
62. Rezaei, J.; Hemmes, A.; Tavasszy, L. Multi-criteria decision-making for complex bundling configurations in surface transportation of air freight. *J. Air Transp. Manag.* **2017**, *61*, 95–105. [CrossRef]
63. Ren, J.; Liang, H.; Chan, F.T. Urban sewage sludge, sustainability, and transition for Eco-City: Multi-criteria sustainability assessment of technologies based on best-worst method. *Technol. Forecast. Soc. Chang.* **2017**, *116*, 29–39. [CrossRef]
64. Pradityá, D.; Janssen, M. Assessment of Factors Influencing Information Sharing Arrangements Using the Best-Worst Method. In Proceedings of the Conference on e-Business, e-Services and e-Society, Delhi, India, 21–23 November 2017; Springer: Cham, Switzerland, 2017; pp. 94–106.
65. Salimi, N.; Rezaei, J. Evaluating firms' R&D performance using best worst method. *Evaluation Program Plan.* **2018**, *66*, 147–155. [CrossRef]
66. Askarifar, K.; Motaffef, Z.; Aazaami, S. An investment development framework in Iran's seashores using TOPSIS and best-worst multi-criteria decision making methods. *Decis. Sci. Lett.* **2018**, *7*, 55–64. [CrossRef]
67. Rezaei, J.; Kothadiya, O.; Tavasszy, L.; Kroesen, M. Quality assessment of airline baggage handling systems using SERVQUAL and BWM. *Tour. Manag.* **2018**, *66*, 85–93. [CrossRef]
68. Kara, M.E.; Fırat, S.; Ümit, O. Supplier Risk Assessment Based on Best-Worst Method and K-Means Clustering: A Case Study. *Sustainability* **2018**, *10*, 1066. [CrossRef]
69. Abadi, F.; Sahebi, I.; Arab, A.; Alavi, A.; Karachi, H. Application of best-worst method in evaluation of medical tourism development strategy. *Decis. Sci. Lett.* **2018**, *7*, 77–86. [CrossRef]
70. Yadollahi, S.; Kazemi, A.; Ranjbarian, B. Identifying and prioritizing the factors of service experience in banks: A Best-Worst method. *Decis. Sci. Lett.* **2018**, *7*, 455–464. [CrossRef]

71. Badi, I.; Ballem, M. Supplier Selection using rough BWM-MAIRCA model: A case study in pharmaceutical supplying in Libya. *Decis. Making Appl. Manag. Eng.* **2018**, *1*, 15–32. [CrossRef]
72. Pamučar, D.; Petrović, I.; Ćirović, G. Modification of the Best-Worst and MABAC methods: A novel approach based on interval-valued fuzzy-rough numbers. *Expert Syst. Appl.* **2018**, *91*, 89–106. [CrossRef]
73. Pamučar, D.; Gigović, L.; Bajić, Z.; Janošević, M. Location selection for wind farms using GIS multi-criteria hybrid model: An approach based on fuzzy and rough numbers. *Sustainability* **2017**, *9*, 1315. [CrossRef]
74. Asadabadi, M.R.; Chang, E.; Saberi, M. Are MCDM methods useful? A critical review of Analytic Hierarchy Process (AHP) and Analytic Network Process (ANP). *Cogent Eng.* **2019**, *6*, 1–11. [CrossRef]
75. Pamucar, D.; Stevic, Z.; Sremac, S. A New Model for Determining Weight Coefficients of Criteria in MCDM Models: Full Consistency Method (FUCOM). *Symmetry* **2018**, *10*, 393. [CrossRef]
76. Zizovic, M.; Damljanovic, N.; Nikolic, R.; Vujicic, M. Multi-criteria decision making method of minimal suitable values. *Math. Moravica* **2016**, *20*, 99–107. [CrossRef]

© 2020 by the authors. Licensee MDPI, Basel, Switzerland. This article is an open access article distributed under the terms and conditions of the Creative Commons Attribution (CC BY) license (http://creativecommons.org/licenses/by/4.0/).

Article

Predicting the Dynamic Response of Dual-Rotor System Subject to Interval Parametric Uncertainties Based on the Non-Intrusive Metamodel

Chao Fu [1,2], Guojin Feng [2], Jiaojiao Ma [2,3], Kuan Lu [1,*], Yongfeng Yang [1] and Fengshou Gu [2]

1. Institute of Vibration Engineering, Northwestern Polytechnical University, Xi'an 710072, China; fuchao0606@mail.nwpu.edu.cn (C.F.); yyf@nwpu.edu.cn (Y.Y.)
2. Centre for Efficiency and Performance Engineering, University of Huddersfield, Queensgate, Huddersfield HD1 3DH, UK; G.Feng@hud.ac.uk (G.F.); J.Ma@hud.ac.uk (J.M.); F.Gu@hud.ac.uk (F.G.)
3. School of Mechanical Engineering, Hebei University of Technology, Tianjin 300401, China
* Correspondence: lukuan@nwpu.edu.cn

Received: 12 April 2020; Accepted: 3 May 2020; Published: 7 May 2020

Abstract: In this paper, the non-probabilistic steady-state dynamics of a dual-rotor system with parametric uncertainties under two-frequency excitations are investigated using the non-intrusive simplex form mathematical metamodel. The Lagrangian formulation is employed to derive the equations of motion (EOM) of the system. The simplex form metamodel without the distribution functions of the interval uncertainties is formulated in a non-intrusive way. In the multi-uncertain cases, strategies aimed at reducing the computational cost are incorporated. In numerical simulations for different interval parametric uncertainties, the special propagation mechanism is observed, which cannot be found in single rotor systems. Validations of the metamodel in terms of efficiency and accuracy are also carried out by comparisons with the scanning method. The results will be helpful to understand the dynamic behaviors of dual-rotor systems subject to uncertainties and provide guidance for robust design and analysis.

Keywords: dual-rotor; multi-frequency excitation; non-intrusive calculation; metamodel

1. Introduction

Risk analyses and optimization of engineering mechanical systems always play an important role in the design and maintenance [1,2]. To optimize and improve the dynamic performance, a dual-rotor system is widely employed in modern aero-engines for large surge margin. It is more complicated than single rotor systems in both the structural and dynamical regimes. Researchers have paid attention to the vibrations of dual-rotors under faults, such as the imbalance and rub-impact [3–5]. The design and modeling of dual-rotors were also intensively studied over the past few decades [6–9]. The application of rotor-bearing structures in the dual-rotor systems were investigated both theoretically and experimentally [10]. To improve the fidelity, the differences between 1D and 3D models of dual-rotor systems were studied [11].

The reported contributions provide guidance for the dynamical assessments of dual-rotor systems. However, an important feature of practical engineering mechanical systems has been ignored, which is that the physical parameters of the models and working conditions will behave in an uncertain way inherently [12–15]. For a complex engineering dual-rotor system, this problem will be more prominent. In recent literature [16–19], the sources and causes of parametric uncertainties in rotor systems were explained in detail, especially the complex stiffness of the connecting structures. It is gradually recognized that the inherent uncertainty should not be overlooked for robust design and dynamic behaviors prediction. Efforts have already been made to investigate the effects of uncertainties in rotor dynamical systems. The polynomial chaos expansion in combination of the harmonic balance method was used to quantify the effects of different random parametric uncertainties on the linear and non-linear dynamical characteristics [20–22]. More recently, the Kriging metamodeling was applied to the prediction of uncertain behaviors of flexible rotor systems [17]. The nonparametric modeling [14] was also introduced into the uncertainty quantification for a Jeffcott rotor [23] as well as analyses in terms of the balancing and unbalancing [24]. Considering the random excitations, the power spectral density of the unbalance response of an aero-engine dual-rotor was analyzed in [25]. The modeling and stochastic frequency response functions of rotors subject to random uncertainties were studied by using the Karhunen–Loève decomposition [26].

As can be observed, the widely adopted and employed uncertainty analysis methods mostly belong to the probabilistic domain. In practical situations, it is generally difficult or too expensive to gather enough prior data for the uncertain parameters. The interval analysis procedures are more versatile and easier to implement due to their non-probabilistic characteristics [13]. The Chebyshev inclusion function proposed by Wu et al. [27] has attracted wide attention in the past few years due to its simplicity in concept and non-intrusiveness. Several improved forms have been developed and applied to uncertain mechanical systems [28,29]. Although the interval analysis has been widely used in structural dynamics of the truss and multibody systems, it has not been applied to the uncertain rotor dynamics until recent years [30,31]. Some meaningful results have been obtained in these contributions using the interval models. However, formulations and applications of metamodeling methodologies based on non-probabilistic descriptions have not attracted sufficient attention. The computational burden needs also to be reduced. The vibration characteristics of dual-rotor systems subject to multi-frequency excitation and interval variables remain to be revealed.

This paper presents the non-intrusive metamodeling for the uncertainty quantification of a dual-rotor system. The major purposes are to calculate the steady-state dynamic responses of such a system under interval uncertainties and illustrate the effectiveness of the metamodel. First, the dual-rotor model and its motion equations will be described in Section 2. Then, in Section 3, the formulation of the metamodel for single and multi-uncertain variables is explained. Next, propagations of uncertainties of different physical parameters are studied and discussed in Section 4. Finally, the concluding remarks are drawn in Section 5.

2. Model Description and Motion Equations

A dual-rotor system often consists of a higher pressure (HP) rotor and a lower pressure (LP) rotor, which are connected by the inter-shaft bearing and rotate at different angular speeds. They can also be referred to as the inner and outer rotors [8,32]. Figure 1 shows the schematic diagram of a typical dual-rotor system. The rotors are mounted on massless shafts and supported by three rigid isotropic bearings with stiffness and damping k_1, c_1 k_2, c_2 and k_3, c_3. The m_1, J_{d1}, J_{p1} and m_2, J_{d2}, J_{p2} are the mass, diameter moment of inertia and polar moment of inertia of the HP and LP rotors, respectively. There are mass imbalances on both of the rotors, denoted by e_1 and e_2. The angular rotating speeds of the LP and HP rotors are ω_1 and ω_2. The span of the system is L and the other locations are measured by their corresponding distances from the left end $L_i, i = 1, 2, 3, 4$, as shown in Figure 1.

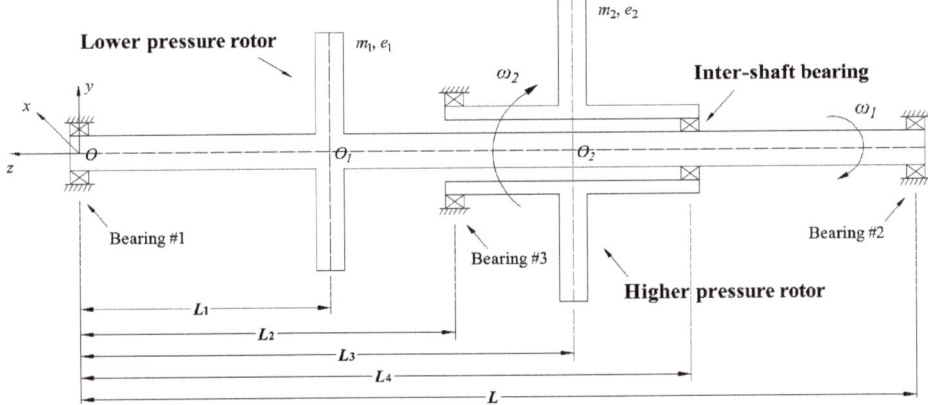

Figure 1. Configuration of a typical dual-rotor system.

The system can be described by eight degrees-of-freedom (DOFs) and four for each rotor, i.e., two lateral displacements and two rotational angles [33,34]. It is obtained as

$$\mathbf{q} = [x_1, y_1, \theta_{y1}, \theta_{x1}, x_2, y_2, \theta_{y2}, \theta_{x2}]^T \tag{1}$$

where subscripts 1 and 2 correspond to the LP and HP rotors. After this, the coordinates of the three bearing centers can be derived using the eight basic DOFs

$$\begin{cases} x_{b1} = x_1 - L_1 \theta_{y1} \\ y_{b1} = y_1 + L_1 \theta_{x1} \end{cases}, \begin{cases} x_{b2} = x_1 + (L - L_1)\theta_{y1} \\ y_{b2} = y_1 - (L - L_1)\theta_{x1} \end{cases}, \begin{cases} x_{b3} = x_2 - (L_3 - L_2)\theta_{y2} \\ y_{b3} = y_2 + (L_3 - L_2)\theta_{x2} \end{cases} \tag{2}$$

Modeling rotating systems based on the energy analyses is widely employed in the community of rotor dynamics [34]. For the system under study, the kinetic energy can be calculated as

$$\begin{cases} T = T_1 + T_2 \\ T_i = \tfrac{1}{2} m_i (\dot{x}_i^2 + \dot{y}_i^2) + \tfrac{1}{2} J_{di} (\dot{\theta}_{xi}^2 + \dot{\theta}_{yi}^2) + J_{pi} \omega_i^2 - J_{pi} \omega_i \dot{\theta}_{yi} \theta_{xi}, \; i = 1, 2 \end{cases} \tag{3}$$

The potential energy is contributed by the three bearings and can be denoted by

$$\begin{cases} V = V_1 + V_2 + V_3 \\ V_i = \tfrac{1}{2} k_i (x_{bi}^2 + y_{bi}^2), \; i = 1, 2, 3 \end{cases} \tag{4}$$

Accordingly, the dissipation energy can be expressed as

$$\begin{cases} D = D_1 + D_2 + D_3 \\ D_i = \tfrac{1}{2} c_i (\dot{x}_{bi}^2 + \dot{y}_{bi}^2), \; i = 1, 2, 3 \end{cases} \tag{5}$$

If the connection of the inner and outer rotors are modeled as a linear spring and its stiffness is k_c, the reacting forces of the inter-shaft bearing are as follows

$$\begin{cases} F_x = k_c [x_1 + (L_4 - L_1)\theta_{y1} - x_2 - (L_4 - L_3)\theta_{y2}] \\ F_y = k_c [y_1 - (L_4 - L_1)\theta_{x1} - y_2 + (L_4 - L_3)\theta_{x2}] \end{cases} \tag{6}$$

When rotating, the unbalance forces on the two rotors are obtained by

$$\begin{cases} \mathbf{F}_{u1}(t) = [m_1 e_1 \omega_1^2 \cos(\omega_1 t),\ m_1 e_1 \omega_1^2 \sin(\omega_1 t),\ 0,\ 0,\ 0,\ 0,\ 0,\ 0]^T \\ \mathbf{F}_{u2}(t) = [0,\ 0,\ 0,\ 0,\ m_2 e_2 \omega_2^2 \cos(\omega_2 t),\ m_2 e_2 \omega_2^2 \sin(\omega_2 t),\ 0,\ 0]^T \end{cases} \quad (7)$$

The Lagrangian equation considering dissipation effects can be applied to the system as

$$\frac{d}{dt}\left(\frac{\partial T}{\partial \dot{q}_j}\right) + \frac{\partial D}{\partial \dot{q}_j} - \frac{\partial T}{\partial q_j} + \frac{\partial V}{\partial q_j} = Q_j,\ j = 1,\ 2,\ \ldots,\ 8 \quad (8)$$

Submitting Equations (1)–(7) into Equation (8) and rearranging the results into matrix form, the motion equations of the dual-rotor system can be obtained as

$$\mathbf{M}\ddot{\mathbf{q}}(t) + \widetilde{\mathbf{C}}\dot{\mathbf{q}}(t) + \mathbf{K}\mathbf{q}(t) = \mathbf{F}(t) \quad (9)$$

where $\mathbf{M}$ and $\mathbf{K}$ are the mass and stiffness matrices of the system, $\widetilde{\mathbf{C}}$ includes the damping and gyroscopic effects, $\mathbf{F}(t)$ integrates the unbalance forces and the reacting forces in the inter-shaft bearing. A dot over the displacement vector $\mathbf{q}$ denotes derivation with respect to time. The rotational speeds or frequencies of the inner and outer rotors are incommensurable, making Equation (9) a system excited by two frequencies. Its solution can be obtained by numerical methods and the fourth order Runge–Kutta method with variable steps, which will be used in this paper.

3. Non-Intrusive Interval Analysis of the System Based on Meta-Modeling

As a practical problem, the accurate distribution model of the uncertainty is difficult to establish. In other words, the problem is small sample-sized. Therefore, the interval methods may be more suitable to implement. However, the intrusive interval methods need to modify the deterministic solution packages and are complicated in mathematical formulation. The surrogate methods [17,28,30] popular nowadays should be a good choice. These methodologies are simple in deduction and they work in a non-intrusive way because the deterministic dynamic problem can be used as a black box. Importantly, the computational cost of them should be carefully managed to ensure economic and feasible analyses. In this paper, we establish a simplex metamodel for the dynamic responses of the dual-rotor system considering non-probabilistic interval uncertainties. The small-range constraint in the conventional perturbation method is released. Moreover, the surrogates need not to find the gradient direction of parametric uncertainties to track their propagations, which is essential in the Taylor-based interval methods. In the latter, the difficulties in obtaining the high order derivative information will also limit the applications. Without loss of generality, we firstly consider the case where only one interval parameter is included. The interval parameter can be expressed as

$$a^I = [\underline{a},\ \bar{a}] = [a^c - \beta a^c,\ a^c + \beta a^c] \quad (10)$$

where superscript I designates an interval variable, the bars over and under a quantity denote its upper and lower limits. Notations a^c and β are the mid-value and uncertain degree of a^I. An interval character can be completely defined when the lower and upper bounds are given, which are much easier to obtain than the precise probability model. The following relationships can be further obtained

$$\begin{cases} a^c = (\underline{a} + \bar{a})/2 \\ \Delta a = (\bar{a} - \underline{a})/2 \\ \beta = \Delta a / a^c \end{cases} \quad (11)$$

Taking the interval uncertainty into consideration, the motion equations of the dual-rotor system evolve to interval ordinary differential equations (IODEs). Due to the interval input, the system outputs should also be interval quantities. Consequently, we can rewrite the displacement vector of the dual-rotor system in interval form

$$\mathbf{q}^I(t) = [\underline{\mathbf{q}}(t), \overline{\mathbf{q}}(t)] = \{\mathbf{q}(a, t) | a \in a^I\} \quad (12)$$

Efforts should be taken to find the distribution limits of the uncertain displacements. Direct interval arithmetic will introduce enormous errors which make the results meaningless. Here, we consider Equation (12) as a constraint to the system given in Equation (9) and formulate the metamodel based on the approximation theories. Equation (10) can be written in another form using the standard interval

$$a^I = a^c + \Delta a[-1, 1] \quad (13)$$

It is clear that for any possible value of the uncertain parameter $a \in a^I$, we can find an alternative variable $\xi \in [-1, 1]$ which is equivalent to it with linear projection. Therefore, this can be used to handle the uncertain problem on the standard interval. The actual value of the uncertain parameter can be obtained using a reverse projection. Therefore, a simplex radial basis is established

$$\Xi = [1, \xi, \xi_2, \cdots, \xi_n, \cdots]^T \quad (14)$$

Based on the polynomial basis, a simplex form metamodel of the uncertain responses of the dual-rotor can be constructed as

$$S(\xi) = \sum_{i}^{\infty} \Upsilon_i \xi^i = \Upsilon \Xi, i = 0, 1, 2, \ldots \quad (15)$$

Equation (15) attempts to approximate the actual uncertain system with the weighted sum of a series of simplex. In practical calculation, it is only possible to consider finite number of terms and we truncate it to k herein. The weight coefficient vector $\Upsilon = \{\Upsilon_i, i = 0, 1, 2, \ldots\}$ needs to be determined to fully formulate the metamodel. To this end, samples of the responses of the dual-rotor should be drawn. The roots of orthogonal polynomials are effective sample candidates in the parameter space and they are widely adopted in stochastic and non-probabilistic computations [29,35]. Here, the Chebyshev roots will be used, which can be calculated as

$$\vartheta_i = \cos[\frac{2i-1}{2(k+1)}\pi], i = 1, 2, \cdots, k+1 \quad (16)$$

Subsequently, the sampled responses from the deterministic system can be obtained by simulations of the model with the uncertain parameter specified to the samples and others kept to their mid-values.

$$\widetilde{a}_i = a^c + \beta a^c \vartheta_i, i = 1, 2, \cdots, k+1 \quad (17)$$

$$\widetilde{\mathbf{q}}_i(t) = \{\mathbf{q}(a, t) | a = \widetilde{a}_i \in a^I\}, i = 1, 2, \cdots, k+1 \quad (18)$$

Subsequently, Equation (15) evolves to

$$\widetilde{\mathbf{q}}(\vartheta) = \Upsilon \widetilde{\Xi}(\vartheta) \quad (19)$$

where $\widetilde{q}$ and $\widetilde{\Xi}$ are the sample response vector from the dual-rotor and the value matrix of the radius basis vector at uncertainty sample series $\vartheta = \{\vartheta_i\}, i = 1, 2, \cdots, k+1$. The $\widetilde{\Xi}$ is expressed as

$$\widetilde{\Xi} = \begin{bmatrix} 1 & \vartheta_1 & \vartheta_1^2 & \cdots & \vartheta_1^k \\ 1 & \vartheta_2 & \vartheta_2^2 & \cdots & \vartheta_2^k \\ \vdots & \vdots & \ddots & \vdots & \vdots \\ 1 & \vartheta_{k+1} & \vartheta_{k+1}^2 & \cdots & \vartheta_{k+1}^k \end{bmatrix} \quad (20)$$

In Equation (19), there are $k + 1$ unknown weight coefficients and the number of equations is the same. Thus, the coefficient vector can be directly solved

$$\Upsilon = \widetilde{q}(\vartheta)[\widetilde{\Xi}(\vartheta)]^{-1} \quad (21)$$

Once the coefficient vector is obtained, the metamodel is fully determined. It is a simplex form function aimed to represent the actual distribution model of the uncertain dynamic response, which has unknown mathematical descriptions. As the lower and upper bounds of the system responses are of interest, the metamodel can be used to derive these values, which should be simple.

For multi uncertain variables, the basic idea is the same but some strategies to reduce the computation cost should be incorporated. For example, in the case that the dual-rotor contains n interval uncertainties, the radius basis vector can be rewritten in ascending order as

$$\Xi = [1, \xi_1, \cdots, \xi_n, \xi_1^2, \xi_1\xi_2, \cdots, \xi_n^2, \cdots, \xi_1^k, \xi_1^{k-1}\xi_2, \cdots, \xi_n^k]^T \quad (22)$$

The number of elements in Ξ is

$$N = \frac{(n+k)!}{n!k!} \quad (23)$$

The metamodel is expressed by the weighted sum of terms whose order is no greater than k

$$S(\xi) = \sum_{0 \le i_1 + \cdots + i_n \le k} \Upsilon_{i_1, \cdots, i_n} \xi_1^{i_1} \xi_2^{i_2} \cdots \xi_n^{i_n} = \Upsilon \Xi, i_1, \cdots, i_n = 0, 1, \ldots, k \quad (24)$$

where $\Upsilon_{i_1, \cdots, i_n}$ is the multi-dimensional coefficient. There will be $(k+1)^n$ samples based on Equation (16) when all the sample candidates are chosen for every uncertain dimension.

In problems with relatively large number of interval parameters, the computation cost will be high. It is demonstrated that when the used samples are twice of the unknowns in the metamodel, the model will be robust and the efficiency is enhanced [36]. In such way, the number of samples kept will be $2N$. The number of unknown coefficients is not the same as that of equations, the least square method can be introduced to evaluate the regression coefficients

$$\Upsilon = \widetilde{q}(\widetilde{\vartheta})\widetilde{\Xi}(\widetilde{\Xi}^T\widetilde{\Xi})^{-1} \quad (25)$$

where $\widetilde{q}(\widetilde{\vartheta})$ is the $8 \times 2N$ matrix for the deterministic sample response drawn from the dual-rotor system based on the uncertain parameter sample sets

$$\begin{cases} \widetilde{\vartheta} = [\vartheta_1, \vartheta_2, \cdots, \vartheta_{2N}] \\ \vartheta_j = \{\vartheta_{i,j}\}, i = 1, 2, \cdots, n \end{cases} \quad (26)$$

In Equation (26), there are 2N sets of samples and each set contains n elements. The matrix $\widetilde{\Xi}$ in Equation (25) represents the values of the radius basis vector calculated at the parameter sample sets

$$\widetilde{\Xi} = \begin{bmatrix} 1 & \vartheta_{1,1} & \cdots & \vartheta_{n,1} & \vartheta_{1,1}^2 & \vartheta_{1,1}\vartheta_{2,1} & \cdots & \vartheta_{n,1}^2 & \cdots & \vartheta_{1,1}^k & \vartheta_{1,1}^{k-1}\vartheta_{2,1} & \cdots & \vartheta_{n,1}^k \\ 1 & \vartheta_{1,2} & \cdots & \vartheta_{n,2} & \vartheta_{1,2}^2 & \vartheta_{1,2}\vartheta_{2,2} & \cdots & \vartheta_{n,2}^2 & \cdots & \vartheta_{1,2}^k & \vartheta_{1,2}^{k-1}\vartheta_{2,2} & \cdots & \vartheta_{n,2}^k \\ \vdots & \vdots & \ddots & \vdots & \vdots & \vdots & \ddots & \vdots & \ddots & \vdots & \vdots & \ddots & \vdots \\ 1 & \vartheta_{1,N} & \cdots & \vartheta_{n,N} & \vartheta_{1,N}^2 & \vartheta_{1,N}\vartheta_{2,N} & \cdots & \vartheta_{n,N}^2 & \cdots & \vartheta_{1,N}^k & \vartheta_{1,N}^{k-1}\vartheta_{2,N} & \cdots & \vartheta_{n,N}^k \end{bmatrix}_{2N \times N} \quad (27)$$

in which the first sub index refers to different uncertain variables and the second to the sample sets expressed in Equation (26). The above deduction is for interval problems involving multiple parametric uncertainties embedded with computational burden alleviation strategies.

When the explicit meta-model is constructed, the bounds of the dynamic response or the extreme values of the meta-model can be easily solved. Since it is in simplex form, the scanning method can be applied to the meta-model to find the bounds efficiently when the dimension of uncertainties is not too high (no greater than three, for example). It can be expressed as

$$\begin{cases} s_i = S(\hat{\xi}_i), i = 1, 2, \ldots, p \\ \underline{q}(t) = \min([s_1, \ldots, s_p]), \overline{q}(t) = \max([s_1, \ldots, s_p]) \end{cases} \quad (28)$$

where $\hat{\xi}_i$ represents the grid parametric points produced in the scanning and p is the total number of them. If many uncertainties are involved (greater than three), the max/min values of the meta-function should be evaluated by the optimization methods, such as the genetic algorithm [28].

4. Results and Discussions

In this section, numerical simulations of the dual-rotor system based on the previous approaches will be presented. The model has the following values of the physical parameters: $m_1 = 16.25$ kg, $J_{p1} = 0.134$ kg·m^2, $J_{d1} = 0.0698$ kg·m^2; $m_2 = 8.4$ kg, $J_{p2} = 0.0793$ kg·m^2, $J_{d2} = 0.0405$ kg·m^2; $e_1 = 3 \times 10^{-5}$ m, $e_1 = 8 \times 10^{-5}$ m; $L_1 = 0.2$ m, $L_2 = 0.24$ m, $L_3 = 0.44$ m, $L_4 = 0.54$ m, $L = 0.62$ m; $c_1 = c_2 = c_3 = 14.69$ N·s/m, $k_1 = k_2 = k_3 = 5 \times 10^6$ N/m, $k_b = 8 \times 10^7$ N/m. The rotation speed ratio between the HP and LP rotors is 1.2. In this paper, we use the maximum vibration deflections of the two rotors at every rotating speed for demonstration, which can be calculated as $\max(\sqrt{x_i^2 + y_i^2})$, $i = 1, 2$. The deterministic steady-state dynamic responses of the HP and LP rotors excluding uncertainty are given in Figure 2. It is observed that the first two peaks appear at 738.4 rad/s and 886.1 rad/s for both of the rotors and the amplitudes of the LP rotor are higher than the HP rotor. It should be noted that the simplified model used in the currently study is sufficient for uncertainty propagation analysis and excludes irrelevant factors that may cause response variability. In order to capture detailed natural characteristics, however, sophisticated physical models should be developed for the comprehensive modal analysis of engineering dual-rotor systems. We refer interested readers to [37] for more information. In the next few sections, different physical parameters are considered uncertain and their effects are investigated based on the three-order metamodel.

4.1. Effect of Interval Mass Eccentricity

Firstly, we treat the uncertainties in the two eccentricities on the rotors. In an engineering context, the balancing status often gets worse after assembling the well-balanced rotors. The reason may be the assembly errors and hardness to measure. Moreover, the imbalance can be influenced by material degradation and wear. Therefore, the imbalance or mass eccentricity should be considered uncertain in analysis. We take the uncertain degree to be $\beta = 10\%$. If $e_1 = [2.7, 3.3] \times 10^{-5}$ m, the interval response can be analyzed using the metamodel established in Section 3 and the results for the LP rotor are plotted in Figure 3. For comparison, the results for uncertain imbalances on the HP rotor are given in Figure 4 when $e_2 = [7.2, \ 8.8] \times 10^{-5}$ m. To provide a reference for the uncertain effects, the deterministic curves shown in Figure 2 will be added in all the uncertain cases.

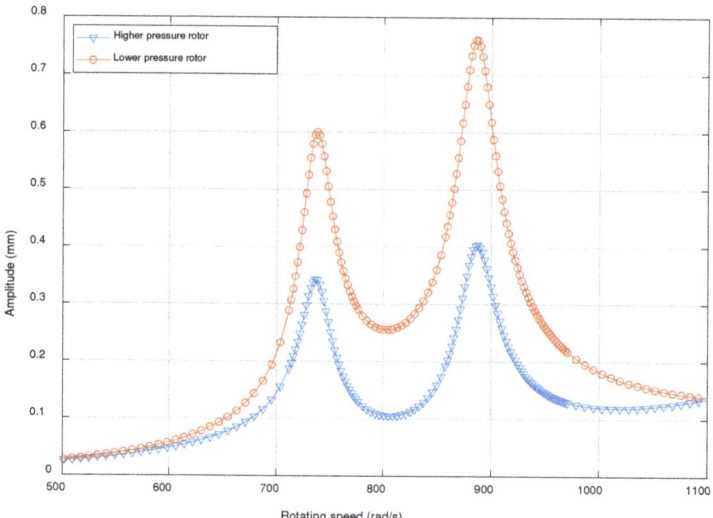

Figure 2. Deterministic steady-state responses of the dual-rotor system.

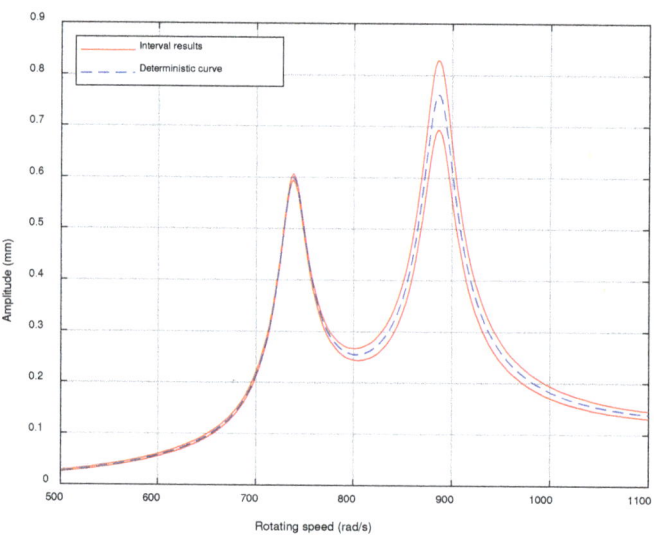

Figure 3. Dynamic response of the Lower Pressure (LP) rotor with uncertain imbalance on the LP rotor.

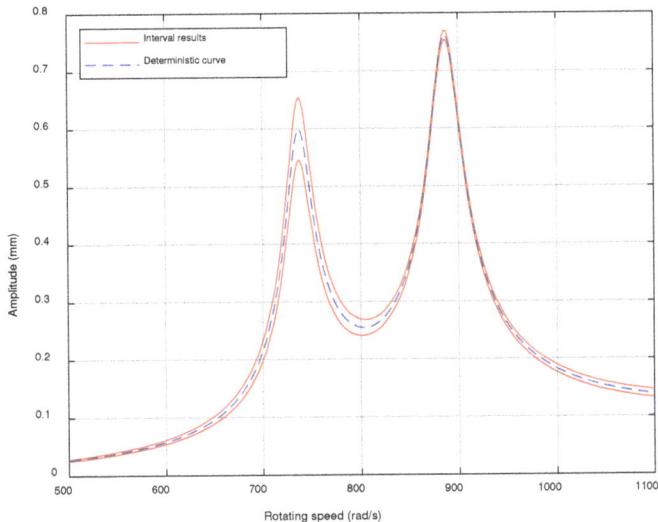

Figure 4. Dynamic response of the LP rotor with uncertain imbalance on the Higher Pressure (HP) rotor.

A major difference between Figures 3 and 4 is that the response interval occurs at different rotation speed bands. Uncertainty in either of the two imbalances will not cause significant deviations of the system responses in the whole speed range. More specifically, the uncertainty in the imbalance on the LP rotor has effects mainly in the speed range around the second peak, while interval imbalance on the HP rotor will influence the first resonance area. That is because the mass imbalances on the two rotors correspond to their respective vibration peaks. Similar characteristics are also found in the parametric investigations of the dual-rotor systems [8]. This phenomenon indicates the different sensitivities of the system in different speed ranges to the two imbalances, which is not observed in single rotor systems. In the respective effective ranges of the two uncertainties, the deterministic response is symmetrically deviated and the enveloped ranges are related to the magnitude of the uncertain degree. Due to the presence of uncertainties, the dynamic response of the system can be any possible values in the response interval.

4.2. Effect of Interval Bearing Stiffness

The stiffness of bearing #1 is taken as an interval quantity to cover its variability [15–18]. Generally, it is difficult to define the accurate value of the stiffness of a support. In this case, the uncertain degree of the interval uncertainty is 5%. Subsequently, the stiffness can be expressed as $k_1 = [4.75, 5.25] \times 10^6$ N/m. The response range of the HP rotor is shown in Figure 5.

As can been seen from Figure 5, the uncertain behaviors of the dual-rotor are totally different from the cases with uncertain imbalances. The deterministic response curve is significantly deviated and the lower bound and upper bound are asymmetric. Near the first peak, a slope peak in the upper bound and a sharp one in the lower bound are found. In addition, the positions of the peaks are shifted compared with the deterministic one with the lower to the left and the upper to the right. There is an observable flat band in the upper bound around the second peak. These features are introduced by the alterations in the intrinsic characteristics caused by the uncertainty. The results also prove that the dual-rotor is sensitive to the support stiffness of bearing #1. It may be considered a key factor for design and maintenance of such engineering systems.

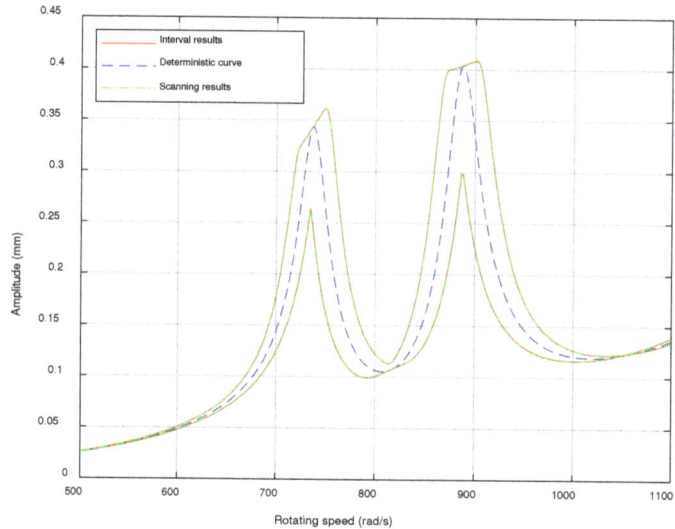

Figure 5. Dynamic response of the HP rotor with uncertain bearing stiffness.

In Figure 5, the reference solutions obtained from the conventional scanning method are also provided to verify the accuracy of the interval results. The scanning procedure generates evenly scattered samples in the uncertain parameter interval and then searches for the bounds of all the response samples. It serves as references similar to the Monte Carlo simulation in the probabilistic frame [38,39]. The 50-points reference solutions (green dotted line) plotted in Figure 5 agree well with the results obtained by the metamodel. Subsequently, the accuracy of the metamodel is validated. To obtain insight, comparisons of the vibration time histogram of the LP rotor at rotation speed 768.7 rad/s obtained from the two methods are illustrated in Figure 6. It is further demonstrated that the bounds calculated from the metamodel are in accordance with the scanning method in different time stamps. The peak shifts are observable as well. From the vibration pattern in Figure 6, we can also identify that the dynamical responses have multiple frequencies which is introduced by the multi-frequency excitations. It should be noted that, in the metamodel, only order three is used, which suggests that the deterministic model runs four times. The underlying computational cost is much lower than the scanning method. The simulations were carried out within MATLAB R2019b on a computer equipped with 16 GB RAM and Inter® Core™ i7-8550U@1.8GHz. It should be noted that the actual speed interval calculated is 0–1400 rad/s and only a part of the results are presented in Figure 5. Moreover, the increment for two consecutive speed steps is small and the initial 300 periods of the vibration are skipped for every rotational speed to eliminate the transient effects. The above conditions will cause the calculation time in a single deterministic simulation to be relatively long. However, the difference of computation time between the two methods can still show their efficiency. For the steady-state dynamical response calculations, the average CPU time elapsed in the metamodel was 28.23 min, while it was 351.87 min in the scanning method. It is shown that the computational cost needed is significantly reduced in the metamodel. The above analyses verify the accuracy and efficiency of the developed interval method in the uncertain responses prediction of the dual-rotor system.

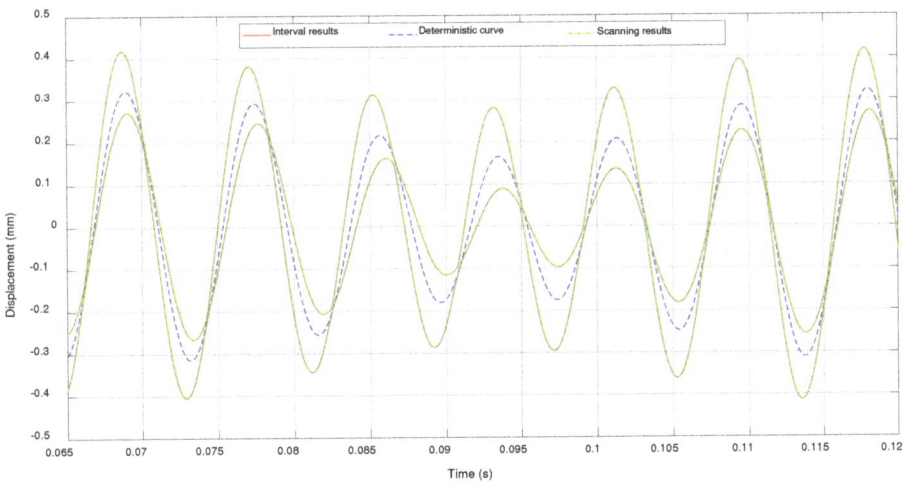

Figure 6. Time histogram of the LP rotor with uncertain bearing stiffness.

4.3. Effect of Interval Geometric Length

In this subsection, we assume the geometric length of shaft L_1 to be uncertain as a result of different assemble conditions. The uncertain degree is chosen as 10%. Figure 7 presents the interval responses of the HP rotor under uncertain shaft length. We can find that the uncertainty has influences on the whole speed range though the physical parameter is related to the inner rotor. There are trivial peak shifts as well in both resonance peaks. However, the impacts of the uncertain length are weaker than the bearing stiffness which suggests that the dual-rotor is insensitive to the length. In the speed range right after the first peak, the bounds of the response and the deterministic curve overlapped with each other. This further proves the ability of the metamodel in the prediction of the interval response of the system evidenced by the fact that the deterministic curve is rigorously enclosed in the narrow range.

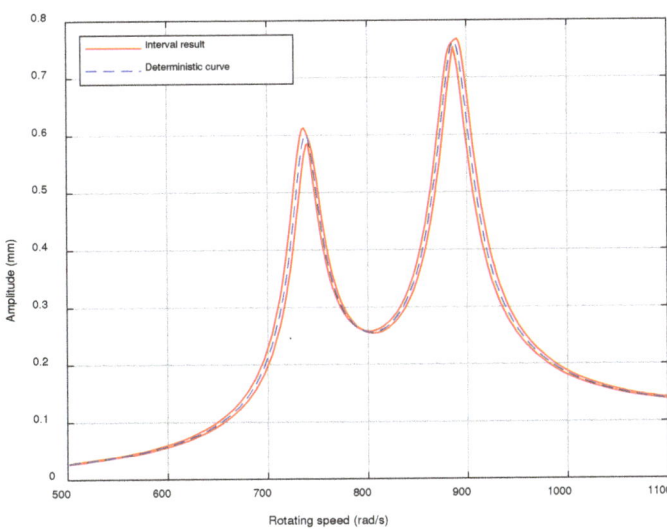

Figure 7. Dynamic response of the HP rotor with uncertain geometric length.

4.4. Effect of Multi Interval Parameters

This subsection pays attention to the influences of multi uncertain parameters [40,41] on the dynamic behaviors of the dual-rotor. Consider the uncertainties in the two imbalances and the bearing stiffness as studied in the previous subsections. The first set of uncertain degrees are 5% for the two imbalances and 2.5% for the stiffness of bearing #1. We then double their respective uncertain degrees for the second case. Figure 8 shows the results for the two cases with (a) for the HP rotor and (b) for the LP rotor. The dynamic response is significantly affected by the multiple uncertain parameters and larger uncertain degrees lead to wider response ranges. The peak shifts are observed. In the upper bounds for the HP and LP rotors, there is both a slope peak and a high-amplitude band, but the locations are switched. The slopes are also in opposite directions. These features correspond to the influence mechanism of the bearing stiffness on the two rotors since imbalances affect the vibration amplitudes linearly. We can observe a few trivial instable estimations in the upper bounds of Figure 8, which are caused by the minor errors of the metamodel as only order three is used.

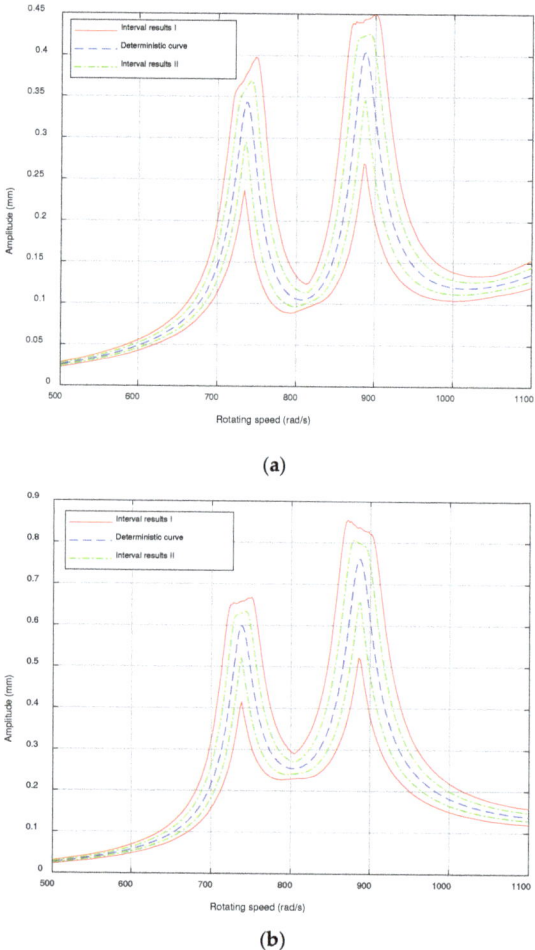

Figure 8. Dynamic responses of the dual-rotor with multi uncertain parameters: (a) Interval responses of the HP rotor; (b) Interval responses of the LP rotor.

In large-scale dual-rotor systems, the number of uncertain parameters that should be considered simultaneously may occasionally be very large. Although cost alleviating strategies are already incorporated, the non-intrusive metamodel used in the current research needs further improvement to cope with the exponentially growing computation burden. Alternatively, one can undertake sensitivity analyses using dedicated algorithms or investigations with individual interval parameters based on the metamodel to capture their respective contributions to the dynamical response variability and then discard those of trivial importance. Moreover, the dual-rotor system analyzed in this paper is linear. The nonlinear vibrational responses of such systems under multi interval uncertainties are much more complicated and difficult to predict, which can occur in the dual-rotors undergoing rub-impact [42], or the rotating shaft is cracked. The established method is capable of estimating the interval time history of such nonlinear vibrations. Further evaluation should be completed to verify the effectiveness of the metamodel when the steady-state frequency response has turning points.

5. Conclusions

The uncertain dynamics of a dual-rotor system under interval uncertainties are studied via non-intrusive computations. The governing motion equations are established by using the Lagrangian method. A simplex form metamodel for problems subject to single and multi-uncertain variables is constructed without modification to the deterministic solver. The calculation accuracy and efficiency are verified by the scanning method. It is found that the imbalances on the inner and outer rotors only affect speed ranges near one vibration peak. Peak shifts are observed when the bearing stiffness is considered an uncertain quantity. Moreover, the response interval of the dual-rotor is relatively small for the uncertain geometric length. These characteristics also indicate the sensitivities of the dual-rotor to the physical parameters. The multi-uncertain-variable simulations suggest that the cumulative uncertainties propagation will significantly influence the dynamics of the dual-rotor system. The main findings of this paper show some insights into the vibration characteristics of dual-rotor systems considering the non-probabilistic uncertainties.

Author Contributions: Conceptualization, C.F. and K.L.; Methodology, C.F. and J.M.; Software, G.F. and K.L.; Validation, Y.Y. and K.L.; Formal analysis, J.M. and G.F.; Investigation, K.L. and F.G.; Writing—Original draft preparation, C.F. and J.M.; Writing—Review and editing, K.L. and G.F.; Project administration, Y.Y. and F.G.; Funding acquisition, K.L. All authors have read and agreed to the published version of the manuscript.

Funding: This research was funded by National Natural Science Foundation of China, grant number 11802235 and 11972295, and Joint Doctoral Training Foundation of HEBUT, grant number 2018HW0005.

Conflicts of Interest: The authors declare no conflict of interest.

References

1. Stanković, M.; Stević, Ž.; Das, D.K.; Subotić, M.; Pamučar, D. A new fuzzy MARCOS method for road traffic risk analysis. *Mathematics* **2020**, *8*, 457. [CrossRef]
2. Roy, J.; Das, S.; Kar, S.; Pamučar, D. An extension of the CODAS approach using interval-valued intuitionistic fuzzy set for sustainable material selection in construction projects with incomplete weight information. *Symmetry* **2019**, *11*, 393. [CrossRef]
3. Gupta, K.; Gupta, K.D.; Athre, K. Unbalance response of a dual rotor system: Theory and experiment. *J. Vib. Acoust.* **1993**, *115*, 427–435. [CrossRef]
4. Yang, Y.; Cao, D.; Wang, D.; Jiang, G. Fixed-point rubbing characteristic analysis of a dual-rotor system based on the Lankarani-Nikravesh model. *Mech. Mach. Theory* **2016**, *103*, 202–221. [CrossRef]
5. Wang, N.; Jiang, D.; Behdinan, K. Vibration response analysis of rubbing faults on a dual-rotor bearing system. *Arch. Appl. Mech.* **2017**, *87*, 1–17. [CrossRef]
6. Childs, D.W. A modal transient rotordynamic model for dual-rotor jet engine systems. *J. Eng. Ind.* **1976**, *98*, 876–882. [CrossRef]
7. Zhou, H.; Chen, G. Dynamic response analysis of dual rotor-ball bearing-stator coupling system for aero-engine. *J. Aerosp. Power* **2009**, *24*, 1284–1291.

8. Hou, L.; Chen, Y.; Fu, Y.; Chen, H.; Lu, Z.; Liu, Z. Application of the HB–AFT method to the primary resonance analysis of a dual-rotor system. *Nonlinear Dynam.* **2017**, *88*, 2531–2551. [CrossRef]
9. Luo, G.; Hu, X.; Yang, X. Nonlinear dynamic performance analysis of counter-rotating dual-rotor system. *J. Vib. Eng.* **2009**, *22*, 268–273.
10. Chiang, H.W.D.; Hsu, C.N.; Tu, S.H. Rotor-bearing analysis for turbomachinery single- and dual-rotor systems. *J. Propul. Power* **2012**, *20*, 1096–1104. [CrossRef]
11. Miao, H.; Zang, C.; Friswell, M. Model updating and validation of a dual-rotor system. In Proceedings of the 26th International Conference on Noise and Vibration Engineering, KU Leuven, Leuven, Belgium, 15–17 September 2014.
12. Fu, C.; Ren, X.; Yang, Y. Vibration analysis of rotors under uncertainty based on Legendre series. *J. Vib. Eng. Technol.* **2019**, *7*, 43–51. [CrossRef]
13. Elishakoff, I.; Sarlin, N. Uncertainty quantification based on pillars of experiment, theory, and computation. Part II: Theory and computation. *Mech. Syst. Signal Process.* **2016**, *74*, 54–72. [CrossRef]
14. Soize, C. Maximum entropy approach for modeling random uncertainties in transient elastodynamics. *J. Acoust. Soc. Amer.* **2001**, *109*, 1979–1996. [CrossRef] [PubMed]
15. Fu, C.; Ren, X.; Yang, Y.; Lu, K.; Wang, Y. Nonlinear response analysis of a rotor system with a transverse breathing crack under interval uncertainties. *Int. J. Nonlin. Mech.* **2018**, *105*, 77–87. [CrossRef]
16. Ma, Y.; Wang, Y.; Wang, C.; Hong, J. Nonlinear interval analysis of rotor response with joints under uncertainties. *Chin. J. Aeronaut.* **2020**, *33*, 205–218. [CrossRef]
17. Sinou, J.J.; Nechak, L.; Besset, S. Kriging metamodeling in rotordynamics: Application for predicting critical speeds and vibrations of a flexible rotor. *Complexity* **2018**, 1264619. [CrossRef]
18. Fu, C.; Xu, Y.; Yang, Y.; Lu, K.; Gu, F.; Ball, A. Response analysis of an accelerating unbalanced rotating system with both random and interval variables. *J. Sound Vib.* **2020**, *466*, 115047. [CrossRef]
19. Yang, Y.; Wu, Q.; Wang, Y.; Qin, W.; Lu, K. Dynamic characteristics of cracked uncertain hollow-shaft. *Mech. Syst. Signal Process.* **2019**, *124*, 36–48.
20. Didier, J.; Faverjon, B.; Sinou, J.-J. Analysing the dynamic response of a rotor system under uncertain parameters by polynomial chaos expansion. *J. Vib. Control* **2012**, *18*, 712–732. [CrossRef]
21. Sinou, J.J.; Didier, J.; Faverjon, B. Stochastic non-linear response of a flexible rotor with local non-linearities. *Int. J. Nonlin. Mech.* **2015**, *74*, 92–99. [CrossRef]
22. Sinou, J.-J.; Jacquelin, E. Influence of Polynomial Chaos expansion order on an uncertain asymmetric rotor system response. *Mech. Syst. Signal Process.* **2015**, *50*, 718–731. [CrossRef]
23. Gan, C.; Wang, Y.; Yang, S.; Cao, Y. Nonparametric modeling and vibration analysis of uncertain Jeffcott rotor with disc offset. *Int. J. Mech. Sci.* **2014**, *78*, 126–134. [CrossRef]
24. Murthy, R.; Tomei, J.C.; Wang, X.Q.; Mignolet, M.P.; El-Shafei, A. Nonparametric stochastic modeling of structural uncertainty in rotordynamics: Unbalance and balancing aspects. *J. Eng. Gas Turb. Power* **2014**, *136*, 062506. [CrossRef]
25. Liu, X.; Gu, Z.; Wang, Z. Response analysis on aero-engine dual-rotor system under random excitation. *J. Propul. Tech.* **2012**, *33*, 43–46.
26. Koroishi, E.H.; Cavalini, A.A., Jr.; de Lima, A.M.; Steffen, V., Jr. Stochastic modeling of flexible rotors. *J. Braz. Soc. Mech. Sci. Eng.* **2012**, *34*, 574–583. [CrossRef]
27. Wu, J.; Zhang, Y.; Chen, L.; Luo, Z. A Chebyshev interval method for nonlinear dynamic systems under uncertainty. *Appl. Math. Model.* **2013**, *37*, 4578–4591. [CrossRef]
28. Wu, J.; Luo, Z.; Zhang, N.; Zhang, Y. A new interval uncertain optimization method for structures using Chebyshev surrogate models. *Comput. Struct.* **2015**, *146*, 185–196. [CrossRef]
29. Wu, J.; Luo, Z.; Zhang, Y.; Zhang, N.; Chen, L. Interval uncertain method for multibody mechanical systems using Chebyshev inclusion functions. *Int. J. Numer. Methods Engin.* **2013**, *95*, 608–630. [CrossRef]
30. Fu, C.; Ren, X.; Yang, Y.; Lu, K.; Qin, W. Steady-state response analysis of cracked rotors with uncertain-but-bounded parameters using a polynomial surrogate method. *Commun. Nonlinear Sci. Numer. Simulat.* **2019**, *68*, 240–256. [CrossRef]
31. Fu, C.; Ren, X.; Yang, Y.; Xia, Y.; Deng, W. An interval precise integration method for transient unbalance response analysis of rotor system with uncertainty. *Mech. Syst. Signal Process.* **2018**, *107*, 137–148. [CrossRef]
32. Hu, Q.; Deng, S.; Teng, H. A 5-DOF model for aeroengine spindle dual-rotor system analysis. *Chin. J. Aeronaut.* **2011**, *24*, 224–234. [CrossRef]

33. Sun, C.; Chen, Y.; Hou, L. Steady-state response characteristics of a dual-rotor system induced by rub-impact. *Nonlinear Dynam.* **2016**, *86*, 1–15. [CrossRef]
34. Qin, Z.; Chu, F.; Zu, J. Free vibrations of cylindrical shells with arbitrary boundary conditions: A comparison study. *Int. J. Mech. Sci.* **2017**, *133*, 91–99. [CrossRef]
35. Jacquelin, E.; Adhikari, S.; Friswell, M.; Sinou, J.-J. Role of roots of orthogonal polynomials in the dynamic response of stochastic systems. *J. Eng. Mech.* **2016**, *142*, 06016004. [CrossRef]
36. Isukapalli, S.S. Uncertainty Analysis of Transport-Transformation Models. *Diss. Theses Gradworks* **1999**, *57*, 31–32.
37. Lu, Z.; Zhong, S.; Chen, H.; Chen, Y.; Han, J.; Wang, C. Modeling and dynamic characteristics analysis of blade-disk dual-rotor system. *Complexity* **2020**, 2493169. [CrossRef]
38. Lu, K.; Jin, Y.; Chen, Y.; Yang, Y.; Hou, L.; Zhang, Z.; Li, Z.; Fu, C. Review for order reduction based on proper orthogonal decomposition and outlooks of applications in mechanical systems. *Mech. Syst. Signal Process.* **2019**, *123*, 264–297. [CrossRef]
39. Guo, X.; Ma, H.; Zhang, X.; Ye, Z.; Fu, Q.; Liu, Z.; Han, Q. Uncertain frequency responses of clamp-pipeline systems using an interval-based method. *IEEE Access* **2020**, *8*, 29370–29384. [CrossRef]
40. Zheng, Z.; Xie, Y.; Zhang, D. Numerical investigation on the gravity response of a two-pole generator rotor system with interval uncertainties. *Appl. Sci.* **2019**, *9*, 3036. [CrossRef]
41. Liu, B.; Yin, X.; Jian, K.; Wu, Y. Perturbation transfer matrix method for eigendata of one-dimensional structural system with parameter uncertainties. *Appl. Math. Mech.* **2003**, *24*, 801–807.
42. Ma, X.; Ma, H.; Zeng, J.; Piao, Y. Rubbing-induced vibration response analysis of dual-rotor-casing system. *Trans. Nanjing Univ. Aero. Astro.* **2018**, *35*, 101–108.

© 2020 by the authors. Licensee MDPI, Basel, Switzerland. This article is an open access article distributed under the terms and conditions of the Creative Commons Attribution (CC BY) license (http://creativecommons.org/licenses/by/4.0/).

Article

A New Fuzzy MARCOS Method for Road Traffic Risk Analysis

Miomir Stanković [1], Željko Stević [2,*], Dillip Kumar Das [3], Marko Subotić [2] and Dragan Pamučar [4]

1. Mathematical Institute of the Serbian Academy of Sciences and Arts, 11001 Belgrade, Serbia; miomir.stankovic@mi.sanu.ac.rs
2. Faculty of Transport and Traffic Engineering, University of East Sarajevo, 74000 Doboj, Bosnia and Herzegovina; marko.subotic@sf.ues.rs.ba
3. Civil Engineering, School of Engineering, University of Kwazulu Natal, Durban 4041, South Africa; dasd@ukzn.ac.za
4. Department of Logistics, University of Defence in Belgrade, 11000 Belgrade, Serbia; dragan.pamucar@va.mod.gov.rs
* Correspondence: zeljkostevic88@yahoo.com or zeljko.stevic@sf.ues.rs.ba

Received: 20 February 2020; Accepted: 20 March 2020; Published: 24 March 2020

Abstract: In this paper, a new fuzzy multi-criteria decision-making model for traffic risk assessment was developed. A part of a main road network of 7.4 km with a total of 38 Sections was analyzed with the aim of determining the degree of risk on them. For that purpose, a fuzzy Measurement Alternatives and Ranking according to the COmpromise Solution (fuzzy MARCOS) method was developed. In addition, a new fuzzy linguistic scale quantified into triangular fuzzy numbers (TFNs) was developed. The fuzzy PIvot Pairwise RElative Criteria Importance Assessment—fuzzy PIPRECIA method—was used to determine the criteria weights on the basis of which the road network sections were evaluated. The results clearly show that there is a dominant section with the highest risk for all road participants, which requires corrective actions. In order to validate the results, a comprehensive validity test was created consisting of variations in the significance of model input parameters, testing the influence of dynamic factors—of reverse rank, and applying the fuzzy Simple Additive Weighing (fuzzy SAW) method and the fuzzy Technique for Order of Preference by Similarity to Ideal Solution (fuzzy TOPSIS). The validation test show the stability of the results obtained and the justification for the development of the proposed model.

Keywords: Fuzzy MARCOS; Fuzzy PIPRECIA; traffic risk; TFN; MCDM

1. Introduction

Multi-criteria decision-making (MCDM) methods, [1–4] especially in integration with fuzzy theory [5–7], are a very powerful and useful tool for reliable decision-making in different fields of decision-making. The decision-making process, according to Stojić et al. [8], requires the prior definition and fulfillment of certain factors, especially when it comes to solving problems in complex areas. The theory of multi-criteria decision-making according to Zavadskas et al. [9] holds a special place in the field of science. The application of fuzzy MCDM methods contributes to a more precise determination of an acceptable solution, especially since considering them with respect to different factors is a very demanding and difficult task. Moreover, this was expressed in group decision-making processes [10]. The main motivation of this study can be considered in the following way: determining of risk level at road sections requires the inclusion of a lot of different variables. After experimental data collection, variables must be assessed in a clear and precise way. For this purpose, a new fuzzy linguistic scale was developed with quantification in TFNs. Moreover, a new fuzzy Measurement Alternatives and Ranking according to COmpromise Solution (Fuzzy MARCOS) was developed in this paper to evaluate sections of road infrastructure with the aim of determining the degree of risk on them. The development of new fuzzy MARCOS method and defining a new linguistic scale based on TFNs represent the main contributions of this paper. The advantages of the Fuzzy MARCOS method are as follows: consideration of fuzzy reference points through the fuzzy ideal and fuzzy anti-ideal solution at the very beginning of model formation, more precise determination of the degree of utility with respect to both set solutions, proposal of a new way of determining utility functions and its aggregation, possibility to consider a large set of criteria and alternatives, as demonstrated through a realistic example, too. This paper considers one of four the most important factors that affect traffic accidents and lead to hazardous situations, and it relates to the road. There are frequent situations where geometric characteristics can negatively affect the creation of potential situations and increase the risk for each traffic participant. The geometric characteristics of the road on particular sections have a major impact on increasing the risk of traffic accidents. Morency et al. [11] analyzed the extent to which road geometry and traffic volume influence social inequalities in pedestrian, cyclist and motorcyclist injuries in wealthy and poor urban areas. Based on their observational study, it was concluded that there were more injured pedestrians, cyclists and motorcyclists at intersections in poorer areas than in wealthier areas. Nevertheless, studies have shown that the two most important road factors affecting accident rates are the pavement condition and the geometric characteristics of the road [12]. Therefore, in this paper, on the basis of causal factors, the degree of risk was determined on sections of 200 m. In her research, Nenadić [13] carried out the evaluation of sections, i.e., three locations, based on seven criteria. In contrast to this research, the optimality criterion was set in such a way that the safest section was considered instead of the one with the highest risk. In the study performed by Bao et al. [14], the fuzzy methodology was used for similar purposes. An Improved hierarchical fuzzy TOPSIS model has been defined for evaluating road safety performance. The evaluation of safety performance indicators (SPIs) was performed by Khorasani et al. [15] as an MCDM problem in a methodological sense. The TOPSIS method in combination with other techniques was also used in Haghighat's research [16] for determining the safety position of the roads of the Bushehr province.

The rest of the paper is organized as follows. Section 2 provides the preliminaries necessary to develop the fuzzy MARCOS method. They refer to displaying basic operations with fuzzy numbers and presenting the steps of the crisp MARCOS method. Section 3 presents the development of the fuzzy MARCOS method algorithm (Figure 1), which consists of a total of 10 steps. In Section 4 of the paper, the MCDM model is formed and a detailed calculation of each step of the developed fuzzy MARCOS method is presented. The calculation of the criterion weight using the fuzzy PIPRECIA method is also summarized. The following Section 5 presents an overview of validation tests to verify the stability of the proposed model. Finally, Section 6 provides a brief overview of the most important tasks accomplished and the contributions of the paper along with future research guidelines.

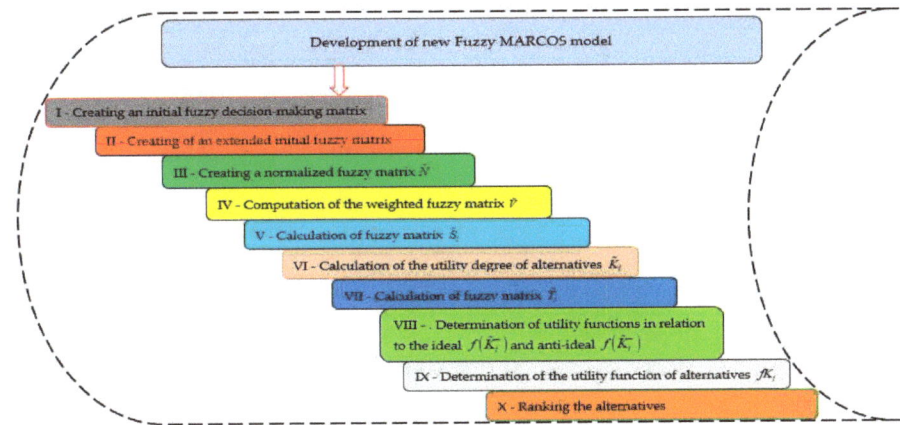

Figure 1. Algorithm of new developed fuzzy MARCOS method.

2. Preliminaries

A fuzzy number $\tilde{A}$ on R to be a TFN if its membership function $\mu_{\tilde{A}}(x)$: R→[0,1] is equal to Equation (1):

$$\mu_{\tilde{A}}(x) = \begin{cases} \frac{x-l}{m-l} & l \leq x \leq m \\ \frac{u-x}{u-m} & m \leq x \leq u \\ 0 & otherwise \end{cases} \quad (1)$$

where l represents the lower and u upper bounds of the fuzzy number $\tilde{A}$ and m is the modal value. The TFN can be marked as $\tilde{A} = (l, m, u)$.

The operations of TFN $\tilde{A}_1 = (l_1, m_1, u_1)$ and $\tilde{A}_2 = (l_2, m_2, u_2)$ are as follow [17,18]

Addition: $\tilde{A} = (l_1, m_1, u_1)$

$$\tilde{A}_1 \oplus \tilde{A}_2 = (l_1, m_1, u_1) + (l_2, m_2, u_2) = (l_1 + l_2, m_1 + m_2, u_1 + u_2). \quad (2)$$

Multiplication:

$$\tilde{A}_1 \otimes \tilde{A}_2 = (l_1, m_1, u_1) \otimes (l_2, m_2, u_2) = (l_1 \times l_2, m_1 \times m_2, u_1 \times u_2). \quad (3)$$

Subtraction:

$$\tilde{A}_1 - \tilde{A}_2 = (l_1, m_1, u_1) - (l_2, m_2, u_2) = (l_1 - u_2, m_1 - m_2, u_1 - l_2). \quad (4)$$

Division:

$$\frac{\tilde{A}_1}{\tilde{A}_2} = \frac{(l_1, m_1, u_1)}{(l_2, m_2, u_2)} = \left(\frac{l_1}{u_2}, \frac{m_1}{m_2}, \frac{u_1}{l_2}\right). \quad (5)$$

Reciprocal:

$$\tilde{A}_1^{-1} = (l_1, m_1, u_1)^{-1} = \left(\frac{1}{u_1}, \frac{1}{m_1}, \frac{1}{l_1}\right). \quad (6)$$

The following section provides a brief overview of the crisp MARCOS method defined by Stević et al. [19]:

Step 1: Designing of an initial decision-making matrix.

Step 2: Designing of an *extended* initial matrix, performed by defining the anti-ideal (AAI) and ideal (AI) solution.

$$X = \begin{array}{c} AAI \\ A_1 \\ A_2 \\ \vdots \\ A_m \\ AI \end{array} \begin{bmatrix} C_1 & C_2 & \cdots & C_n \\ x_{aa1} & x_{aa2} & \cdots & x_{aan} \\ x_{11} & x_{12} & \cdots & x_{1n} \\ x_{21} & x_{22} & \cdots & x_{2n} \\ \vdots & \vdots & \cdots & \vdots \\ x_{m1} & x_{22} & \cdots & x_{mn} \\ x_{ai1} & x_{ai2} & \cdots & x_{ain} \end{bmatrix} \quad (7)$$

(AAI) is the worst alternative, while (AI) is best alternative. Depending on type of the criteria, AAI and AI are defined by applying Equations (8) and (9):

$$AAI = \min_i x_{ij} \; if \; j \in B \; and \; \max_i x_{ij} \; if \; j \in C \quad (8)$$

$$AI = \max_i x_{ij} \; if \; j \in B \; and \; \min_i x_{ij} \; if \; j \in C \quad (9)$$

B belongs maximization group of criteria, while C belongs the minimization group of criteria.

Step 3: Normalization of previous matrix (X). $N = [n_{ij}]_{m \times n}$ are obtained using Equations (10) and (11):

$$n_{ij} = \frac{x_{ai}}{x_{ij}} \; if \; j \in C \quad (10)$$

$$n_{ij} = \frac{x_{ij}}{x_{ai}} \; if \; j \in B \quad (11)$$

where elements x_{ij} and x_{ai} represent the elements of the matrix X.

Step 4: Determination of the weighted matrix $V = [v_{ij}]_{m \times n}$ Equation (12).

$$v_{ij} = n_{ij} \times w_j \quad (12)$$

Step 5: Computation of the utility degree of alternatives K_i—Equations (13) and (14).

$$K_i^- = \frac{S_i}{S_{aai}} \quad (13)$$

$$K_i^+ = \frac{S_i}{S_{ai}} \quad (14)$$

where S_i ($I = 1, 2, \ldots, m$) represents the sum of the elements of matrix V, Equation (15).

$$S_i = \sum_{i=1}^{n} v_{ij} \quad (15)$$

Step 6: Determination of the utility function of alternatives $f(K_i)$ defined by Equation (16).

$$f(K_i) = \frac{K_i^+ + K_i^-}{1 + \frac{1-f(K_i^+)}{f(K_i^+)} + \frac{1-f(K_i^-)}{f(K_i^-)}}; \quad (16)$$

where $f(K_i^-)$ represents the utility function in relation to (AAI), while $f(K_i^+)$ represents the utility function in relation to the (AI).

Utility functions in relation to (AI), and (AAI), solution were determined using Equations (17) and (18).

$$f(K_i^-) = \frac{K_i^+}{K_i^+ + K_i^-} \tag{17}$$

$$f(K_i^+) = \frac{K_i^-}{K_i^+ + K_i^-} \tag{18}$$

Step 7: Ranking the alternatives.

3. A New Fuzzy MARCOS Method

Step 1: Creating an initial fuzzy decision-making matrix. MCDM models include the definition of a set of n criteria and m alternatives.

Step 2: Creating an *extended* initial fuzzy matrix. The extension is performed by determining the fuzzy anti-ideal $\tilde{A}(AI)$ and fuzzy ideal $\tilde{A}(ID)$ solution.

$$\tilde{X} = \begin{array}{c} \tilde{A}(AI) \\ \tilde{A}_1 \\ \tilde{A}_2 \\ \cdots \\ \tilde{A}_m \\ \tilde{A}(ID) \end{array} \begin{bmatrix} \tilde{C}_1 & \tilde{C}_2 & \cdots & \tilde{C}_n \\ \tilde{x}_{ai1} & \tilde{x}_{ai2} & \cdots & \tilde{x}_{ain} \\ \tilde{x}_{11} & \tilde{x}_{12} & \cdots & \tilde{x}_{1n} \\ \tilde{x}_{21} & \tilde{x}_{22} & \cdots & \tilde{x}_{2n} \\ \cdots & \cdots & \cdots & \cdots \\ \tilde{x}_{m1} & \tilde{x}_{22} & \cdots & \tilde{x}_{mn} \\ \tilde{x}_{id1} & \tilde{x}_{id2} & \cdots & \tilde{x}_{idn} \end{bmatrix} \tag{19}$$

The fuzzy $\tilde{A}(AI)$ is the worst alternative while the fuzzy $\tilde{A}(ID)$ is an alternative with the best performance. Depending on type of the criteria, $\tilde{A}(AI)$ and $\tilde{A}(ID)$ are defined by applying Equations (20) and (21):

$$\tilde{A}(AI) = \min_i \tilde{x}_{ij} \ if \ j \in B \ and \ \max_i \tilde{x}_{ij} \ if \ j \in C \tag{20}$$

$$\tilde{A}(ID) = \max_i \tilde{x}_{ij} \ if \ j \in B \ and \ \min_i \tilde{x}_{ij} \ if \ j \in C \tag{21}$$

B belongs to the maximization group of criteria while C belongs to the minimization group of criteria.

Step 3: Creating a normalized fuzzy matrix $\tilde{N} = [\tilde{n}_{ij}]_{m \times n}$ obtained by applying Equations (22) and (23):

$$\tilde{n}_{ij} = \left(n_{ij}^l, n_{ij}^m, n_{ij}^u\right) = \left(\frac{x_{id}^l}{x_{ij}^u}, \frac{x_{id}^l}{x_{ij}^m}, \frac{x_{id}^l}{x_{ij}^l}\right) if \ j \in C \tag{22}$$

$$\tilde{n}_{ij} = \left(n_{ij}^l, n_{ij}^m, n_{ij}^u\right) = \left(\frac{x_{ij}^l}{x_{id}^u}, \frac{x_{ij}^m}{x_{id}^u}, \frac{x_{ij}^u}{x_{id}^u}\right) if \ j \in B \tag{23}$$

where elements $x_{ij}^l, x_{ij}^m, x_{ij}^u$ and $x_{id}^l, x_{id}^m, x_{id}^u$ represent the elements of the matrix $\tilde{X}$.

Step 4: Computation of the weighted fuzzy matrix $\tilde{V} = [\tilde{v}_{ij}]_{m \times n}$. Matrix $\tilde{V}$ is calculated by multiplying matrix $\tilde{N}$ with the fuzzy weight coefficients of the criterion $\tilde{w}_j$, Equation (24).

$$\tilde{v}_{ij} = \left(v_{ij}^l, v_{ij}^m, v_{ij}^u\right) = \tilde{n}_{ij} \otimes \tilde{w}_j = \left(n_{ij}^l \times w_j^l, n_{ij}^m \times w_j^m, n_{ij}^u \times w_j^u\right) \tag{24}$$

Step 5: Calculation of $\tilde{S}_i$ fuzzy matrix using the following Equation (25):

$$\tilde{S}_i = \sum_{i=1}^{n} \tilde{v}_{ij} \qquad (25)$$

where $\tilde{S}_i(s_i^l, s_i^m, s_i^u)$ represents the sum of the elements of the weighted fuzzy matrix $\tilde{V}$.

Step 6: Calculation of the utility degree of alternatives $\tilde{K}_i$ by applying Equations (26) and (27).

$$\tilde{K}_i^- = \frac{\tilde{S}_i}{\tilde{S}_{ai}} = \left(\frac{s_i^l}{s_{ai}^u}, \frac{s_i^m}{s_{ai}^m}, \frac{s_i^u}{s_{ai}^l}\right) \qquad (26)$$

$$\tilde{K}_i^+ = \frac{\tilde{S}_i}{\tilde{S}_{id}} = \left(\frac{s_i^l}{s_{id}^u}, \frac{s_i^m}{s_{id}^m}, \frac{s_i^u}{s_{id}^l}\right) \qquad (27)$$

Step 7: Calculation of fuzzy matrix $\tilde{T}_i$ using Equation (28)

$$\tilde{T}_i = \tilde{t}_i = \left(t_i^l, t_i^m, t_i^u\right) = \tilde{K}_i^- \oplus \tilde{K}_i^+ = \left(k_i^{-l} + k_i^{+l}, k_i^{-m} + k_i^{+m}, k_i^{-u} + k_i^{+u}\right) \qquad (28)$$

Then, it is necessary to determine a new fuzzy number $\tilde{D}$ using Equation (29)

$$\tilde{D} = \left(d^l, d^m, d^u\right) = \max_i \tilde{t}_{ij} \qquad (29)$$

and then, it is necessary to de-fuzzify the number $\tilde{D}$ by using the expression $df_{crisp} = \frac{l+4m+u}{6}$ obtaining the number df_{crisp}.

Step 8. Determination of utility functions in relation to the ideal $f(\tilde{K}_i^+)$ and anti-ideal $f(\tilde{K}_i^-)$ solution by applying Equations (30) and (31).

$$f(\tilde{K}_i^+) = \frac{\tilde{K}_i^-}{df_{crisp}} = \left(\frac{k_i^{-l}}{df_{crisp}}, \frac{k_i^{-m}}{df_{crisp}}, \frac{k_i^{-u}}{df_{crisp}}\right) \qquad (30)$$

$$f(\tilde{K}_i^-) = \frac{\tilde{K}_i^+}{df_{crisp}} = \left(\frac{k_i^{+l}}{df_{crisp}}, \frac{k_i^{+m}}{df_{crisp}}, \frac{k_i^{+u}}{df_{crisp}}\right) \qquad (31)$$

After that, it is necessary to perform defuzzification for $\tilde{K}_i^-$, $\tilde{K}_i^+$, $f(\tilde{K}_i^+)$, $f(\tilde{K}_i^-)$ and apply the following step:

Step 9: Determination of the utility function of alternatives fK_i by Equation (32).

$$f(K_i) = \frac{K_i^+ + K_i^-}{1 + \frac{1-f(K_i^+)}{f(K_i^+)} + \frac{1-f(K_i^-)}{f(K_i^-)}}; \qquad (32)$$

Step 10: Ranking the alternatives based on the final values of utility functions. It is desirable that an alternative have the highest possible value of the utility function.

In addition to developing the new fuzzy MARCOS method, a new linguistic scale for evaluating alternatives has been defined, which is shown in Table 1. A total of nine linguistic terms are defined and for each term, its triangular fuzzy number.

Table 1. A newly defined scale for evaluating potential solutions.

Linguistic Term	Mark	TFN
Extremely poor	EP	(1,1,1)
Very poor	VP	(1,1,3)
Poor	P	(1,3,3)
Medium poor	MP	(3,3,5)
Medium	M	(3,5,5)
Medium good	MG	(5,5,7)
Good	G	(5,7,7)
Very good	VG	(7,7,9)
Extremely good	EG	(7,9,9)

4. Results

In order to determine the degree of risk on the roads in Bosnia and Herzegovina through the Rudanka-Doboj M-17 section (length 7.4 km), a list of six criteria was formed on the basis of which the evaluation was carried out. The analysis was conducted in 38 Sections of two-lane main roads of the first order in Bosnia and Herzegovina as potential alternatives. The following are the starting points for the potential criteria affecting traffic risk: a longitudinal gradient (upgrade/downgrade)—(C1), the number of access points on each section (left and right) (C2), the number of traffic accidents with fatalities (C3), the number of traffic accidents with slightly injured persons (C4), the number of traffic accidents with seriously injured persons (C5) and the number of traffic accidents with material damage (C6). The number of traffic accidents for all four classes was taken from the sample for the last four years.

As mentioned above, the Rudanka-Doboj M-17 section covers a total length of 7.4 km and was divided into 200-m sections that represent alternatives. After forming the MCDM model with 38 alternatives and six criteria in the first step, the fuzzy anti-ideal $\tilde{A}(AI)$ and fuzzy ideal $\tilde{A}(ID)$ solutions are defined in the second step on the basis of Equations (20) and (21). Thus, an extended fuzzy initial decision matrix is formed. Table 2 shows the extended initial fuzzy decision matrix with linguistic ratings, as well as quantified values in triangular fuzzy numbers.

Table 2. Extended initial fuzzy decision matrix.

	Linguistic Ratings						Ratings with TFNs					
	C1	C2	C3	C4	C5	C6	C1	C2	C3	C4	C5	C6
A1	EP	VP	EP	M	M	MP	(1,1,1)	(1,1,3)	(1,1,1)	(3,5,5)	(3,5,5)	(3,3,5)
A2	VP	VP	EP	EP	P	VP	(1,1,3)	(1,1,3)	(1,1,1)	(1,1,1)	(1,3,3)	(1,1,3)
A3	MP	VP	EP	EP	EP	VP	(3,3,5)	(1,1,3)	(1,1,1)	(1,1,1)	(1,1,1)	(1,1,3)
A4	M	EP	EP	M	EP	VP	(3,5,5)	(1,1,1)	(1,1,1)	(3,5,5)	(1,1,1)	(1,1,3)
A5	VP	VP	EG	EP	EP	EP	(1,1,3)	(1,1,3)	(7,9,9)	(1,1,1)	(1,1,1)	(1,1,1)
A6	MP	EP	EP	VP	P	VP	(3,3,5)	(1,1,1)	(1,1,1)	(1,1,3)	(1,3,3)	(1,1,3)
A7	P	VP	EP	MP	EP	MG	(1,3,3)	(1,1,3)	(1,1,1)	(3,3,5)	(1,1,1)	(5,5,7)
A8	MG	VP	EP	EP	P	P	(5,5,7)	(1,1,3)	(1,1,1)	(1,1,1)	(1,3,3)	(1,3,3)
A9	EP	VP	EP	EP	G	VP	(1,1,1)	(1,1,3)	(1,1,1)	(1,1,1)	(5,7,7)	(1,1,3)
A10	G	VP	EP	EP	EP	P	(5,7,7)	(1,1,3)	(1,1,1)	(1,1,1)	(1,1,1)	(1,3,3)
A11	VP	VP	EP	EP	EP	VP	(1,1,3)	(1,1,3)	(1,1,1)	(1,1,1)	(1,1,1)	(1,1,3)
A12	M	VP	EG	EP	EP	EP	(3,5,5)	(1,1,3)	(7,9,9)	(1,1,1)	(1,1,1)	(1,1,1)
A13	M	P	EP	VP	EP	VP	(3,5,5)	(1,3,3)	(1,1,1)	(1,1,3)	(1,1,1)	(1,1,3)
A14	MP	M	EP	VP	EP	P	(3,3,5)	(3,5,5)	(1,1,1)	(1,1,3)	(1,1,1)	(1,3,3)
A15	VP	MP	EP	VP	EP	P	(1,1,3)	(3,3,5)	(1,1,1)	(1,1,3)	(1,1,1)	(1,3,3)
A16	VP	VG	EP	VP	EP	EP	(1,1,3)	(7,7,9)	(1,1,1)	(1,1,3)	(1,1,1)	(1,1,1)
A17	MP	EG	EP	P	EP	P	(3,3,5)	(7,9,9)	(1,1,1)	(1,3,3)	(1,1,1)	(1,3,3)
A18	MP	VG	EG	EP	EP	P	(3,3,5)	(7,7,9)	(7,9,9)	(1,1,1)	(1,1,1)	(1,3,3)
A19	MP	G	EP	MP	EP	MP	(3,3,5)	(5,7,7)	(1,1,1)	(3,3,5)	(1,1,1)	(3,3,5)
A20	VP	VG	EP	MG	P	EG	(1,1,3)	(7,7,9)	(1,1,1)	(5,5,7)	(1,3,3)	(7,9,9)
A21	EG	G	EP	EP	P	VP	(7,9,9)	(5,7,7)	(1,1,1)	(1,1,1)	(1,3,3)	(1,1,3)
A22	MG	MP	EP	VP	EP	EP	(5,5,7)	(3,3,5)	(1,1,1)	(1,1,3)	(1,1,1)	(1,1,1)

Table 2. Cont.

	Linguistic Ratings						Ratings with TFNs					
	C1	C2	C3	C4	C5	C6	C1	C2	C3	C4	C5	C6
A23	MP	M	EG	VG	M	EG	(3,3,5)	(3,5,5)	(7,9,9)	(7,7,9)	(3,5,5)	(7,9,9)
A24	VP	MP	EP	EP	EP	VP	(1,1,3)	(3,3,5)	(1,1,1)	(1,1,1)	(1,1,1)	(1,1,3)
A25	P	M	EP	VP	EP	EP	(1,3,3)	(3,5,5)	(1,1,1)	(1,1,3)	(1,1,1)	(1,1,1)
A26	MG	M	EP	EP	EP	VP	(5,5,7)	(3,5,5)	(1,1,1)	(1,1,1)	(1,1,1)	(1,1,3)
A27	M	P	EP	VP	EP	VP	(3,5,5)	(1,3,3)	(1,1,1)	(1,1,3)	(1,1,1)	(1,1,3)
A28	VP	EP	EP	G	M	MP	(1,1,3)	(1,1,1)	(1,1,1)	(5,7,7)	(3,5,5)	(3,3,5)
A29	P	VP	EP	VP	EP	EP	(1,3,3)	(1,1,3)	(1,1,1)	(1,1,3)	(1,1,1)	(1,1,1)
A30	P	VP	EP	VP	EP	VP	(1,3,3)	(1,1,3)	(1,1,1)	(1,1,3)	(1,1,1)	(1,1,3)
A31	EP	VP	EP	VP	EP	P	(1,1,1)	(1,1,3)	(1,1,1)	(1,1,3)	(1,1,1)	(1,3,3)
A32	VP	P	EP	M	P	VP	(1,1,3)	(1,3,3)	(1,1,1)	(3,5,5)	(1,3,3)	(1,1,3)
A33	P	P	EG	VP	EP	MG	(1,3,3)	(1,3,3)	(7,9,9)	(1,1,3)	(1,1,1)	(5,5,7)
A34	VP	EP	EP	EP	EP	VP	(1,1,3)	(1,1,1)	(1,1,1)	(1,1,1)	(1,1,1)	(1,1,3)
A35	P	EP	EP	EP	EP	EP	(1,3,3)	(1,1,1)	(1,1,1)	(1,1,1)	(1,1,1)	(1,1,1)
A36	VP	VP	EP	VP	P	VP	(1,1,3)	(1,1,3)	(1,1,1)	(1,1,3)	(1,3,3)	(1,1,3)
A37	MG	VP	EP	EP	P	MP	(5,5,7)	(1,1,3)	(1,1,1)	(1,1,1)	(1,3,3)	(3,3,5)
A38	MP	VP	EP	EP	EP	VP	(3,3,5)	(1,1,3)	(1,1,1)	(1,1,1)	(1,1,1)	(1,1,3)

The scope of values of the observed road sections according to each individual criterion are as follows. For the first criterion, the scope of the values ranges from 0% to 1.4%, which generally represents favorable topographic conditions. For the second criterion relating to the total number of access points, the values range from zero to 23. Considering that there are over 20 access points on particular sections, a potential danger to traffic participants and an impact on traffic flow complexity can be noticed. When considering alternatives in relation to the third criterion, it is important to note that there are a total of five sections, with one fatal accident each. For traffic accidents with minor traffic injuries, the values are in the range of 0–7, traffic accidents with serious injuries in the range of 0–3 and material damage in the range of 0–19.

After forming the fuzzy initial decision matrix, it is necessary to determine the significance of input parameters, i.e., their values. For this purpose, the fuzzy PIPRECIA method developed in [20] was applied. As this is an already exploited method, detailed procedures for calculating the values of criteria are not shown, but rather, the summarized results by each step (Table 3).

Table 3. Calculation and results of applying the fuzzy PIPRECIA method for determining the criterion values.

	sj	kj	qj	wj	DF
C1		(1,1,1)	(1,1,1)	(0.136,0.182,0.223)	0.181
C2	(1.2,1.3,1.35)	(0.65,0.7,0.8)	(1.25,1.429,1.538)	(0.17,0.261,0.343)	0.259
C3	(0.5,0.667,1)	(1,1.333,1.5)	(0.833,1.071,1.538)	(0.113,0.195,0.343)	0.206
C4	(0.333,0.4,0.5)	(1.5,1.6,1.667)	(0.5,0.67,1.026)	(0.068,0.122,0.229)	0.131
C5	(1.1,1.15,1.2)	(0.8,0.85,0.9)	(0.556,0.788,1.282)	(0.076,0.144,0.286)	0.156
C6	(0.4,0.5,0.667)	(1.333,1.5,1.6)	(0.347,0.525,0.962)	(0.047,0.096,0.214)	0.107
SUM			(4.486,5.483,7.346)		
	sj	kj	qj	wj	DF
C1	(0.4,0.5,0.667)	(1.333,1.5,1.6)	(0.827,1.528,2.885)	(0.06,0.165,0.449)	0.195
C2	(1.1,1.15,1.2)	(0.8,0.85,0.9)	(1.323,2.292,3.846)	(0.095,0.247,0.599)	0.281
C3	(1.3,1.45,1.5)	(0.5,0.55,0.7)	(1.19,1.948,3.077)	(0.086,0.21,0.479)	0.234
C4	(0.5,0.667,1)	(1,1.333,1.5)	(0.833,1.071,1.538)	(0.06,0.116,0.24)	0.127
C5	(1.2,1.3,1.35)	(0.65,0.7,0.8)	(1.25,1.429,1.538)	(0.09,0.154,0.24)	0.158
C6		(1,1,1)	(1,1,1)	(0.072,0.108,0.156)	0.110
SUM			(6.423,9.268,13.885)		

Based on the aggregation of the values wj shown in Table 3, the final criterion values are obtained: $\tilde{w}_1 = (0.098, 0.174, 0.336)$, $\tilde{w}_2 = (0.133, 0.254, 0.471)$, $\tilde{w}_3 = (0.100, 0.203, 0.411)$, $\tilde{w}_4 = (0.064, 0.119, 0.234)$, $\tilde{w}_5 = (0.083, 0.149, 0.263)$, $\tilde{w}_6 = (0.060, 0.102, 0.185)$.

The elements of the fuzzy normalized matrix (Table 4) were obtained by applying Equation (23) since all the criteria are of benefit type, i.e., they need to be maximized. An example of normalization is

$$\tilde{n}_{11} = \left(\frac{1.000}{9.000}, \frac{1.000}{9.000}, \frac{1.000}{9.000}\right) = (0.111, 0.111, 0.111),$$
$$\tilde{n}_{15} = \left(\frac{3.000}{7.000}, \frac{5.000}{7.000}, \frac{5.000}{7.000}\right) = (0.429, 0.714, 0.714)$$

Table 4. Fuzzy normalized decision matrix.

	C1	C2	C3	C4	C5	C6
AAI	(0.111,0.111,0.111)	(0.111,0.111,0.111)	(0.111,0.111,0.111)	(0.111,0.111,0.111)	(0.143,0.143,0.143)	(0.111,0.111,0.111)
A1	(0.111,0.111,0.111)	(0.111,0.111,0.333)	(0.111,0.111,0.111)	(0.333,0.556,0.556)	(0.429,0.714,0.714)	(0.333,0.333,0.556)
A2	(0.111,0.111,0.333)	(0.111,0.111,0.333)	(0.111,0.111,0.111)	(0.111,0.111,0.111)	(0.143,0.429,0.429)	(0.111,0.111,0.333)
A3	(0.333,0.333,0.556)	(0.111,0.111,0.333)	(0.111,0.111,0.111)	(0.111,0.111,0.111)	(0.143,0.143,0.143)	(0.111,0.111,0.333)
			...			
A23	(0.333,0.333,0.556)	(0.333,0.556,0.556)	(0.778,1,1)	(0.778,0.778,1)	(0.429,0.714,0.714)	(0.778,1,1)
A24	(0.111,0.111,0.333)	(0.333,0.333,0.556)	(0.111,0.111,0.111)	(0.111,0.111,0.111)	(0.143,0.143,0.143)	(0.111,0.111,0.333)
A25	(0.111,0.333,0.333)	(0.333,0.556,0.556)	(0.111,0.111,0.111)	(0.111,0.111,0.333)	(0.143,0.143,0.143)	(0.111,0.111,0.111)
			...			
A36	(0.111,0.111,0.333)	(0.111,0.111,0.333)	(0.111,0.111,0.111)	(0.111,0.111,0.333)	(0.143,0.429,0.429)	(0.111,0.111,0.333)
A37	(0.556,0.556,0.778)	(0.111,0.111,0.333)	(0.111,0.111,0.111)	(0.111,0.111,0.111)	(0.143,0.429,0.429)	(0.333,0.333,0.556)
A38	(0.333,0.333,0.556)	(0.111,0.111,0.333)	(0.111,0.111,0.111)	(0.111,0.111,0.111)	(0.143,0.143,0.143)	(0.111,0.111,0.333)
ID	(0.778,1,1)	(0.778,1,1)	(0.778,1,1)	(0.778,0.778,1)	(0.714,1,1)	(0.778,1,1)

The values of the weighted normalized matrix shown in Table 5 are obtained using Equation (24): $\tilde{v}_{11} = \left(n_{11}^l \times w_1^l, n_{11}^m \times w_1^m, n_{11}^u \times w_1^u\right) = (0.111 \times 0.098, 0.111 \times 0.174, 0.111 \times 0.336) = (0.011, 0.019, 0.037)$.

Table 5. Fuzzy weighted normalized decision matrix.

	C1	C2	C3	C4	C5	C6
AAI	(0.011,0.019,0.037)	(0.015,0.028,0.052)	(0.011,0.023,0.046)	(0.007,0.013,0.026)	(0.012,0.021,0.038)	(0.007,0.011,0.021)
A1	(0.011,0.019,0.037)	(0.015,0.028,0.157)	(0.011,0.023,0.046)	(0.021,0.066,0.13)	(0.035,0.106,0.188)	(0.02,0.034,0.103)
A2	(0.011,0.019,0.112)	(0.015,0.028,0.157)	(0.011,0.023,0.046)	(0.007,0.013,0.026)	(0.012,0.064,0.113)	(0.007,0.011,0.062)
A3	(0.033,0.058,0.187)	(0.015,0.028,0.157)	(0.011,0.023,0.046)	(0.007,0.013,0.026)	(0.012,0.021,0.038)	(0.007,0.011,0.062)
			...			
A23	(0.033,0.058,0.187)	(0.044,0.141,0.262)	(0.077,0.203,0.411)	(0.05,0.092,0.234)	(0.035,0.106,0.188)	(0.046,0.102,0.185)
A24	(0.011,0.019,0.112)	(0.044,0.085,0.262)	(0.011,0.023,0.046)	(0.007,0.013,0.026)	(0.012,0.021,0.038)	(0.007,0.011,0.062)
A25	(0.011,0.058,0.112)	(0.044,0.141,0.262)	(0.011,0.023,0.046)	(0.007,0.013,0.078)	(0.012,0.021,0.038)	(0.007,0.011,0.021)
			...			
A36	(0.011,0.019,0.112)	(0.015,0.028,0.157)	(0.011,0.023,0.046)	(0.007,0.013,0.078)	(0.012,0.064,0.113)	(0.007,0.011,0.062)
A37	(0.054,0.096,0.261)	(0.015,0.028,0.157)	(0.011,0.023,0.046)	(0.007,0.013,0.026)	(0.012,0.064,0.113)	(0.02,0.034,0.103)
A38	(0.033,0.058,0.187)	(0.015,0.028,0.157)	(0.011,0.023,0.046)	(0.007,0.013,0.026)	(0.012,0.021,0.038)	(0.007,0.011,0.062)
ID	(0.076,0.174,0.336)	(0.103,0.254,0.471)	(0.077,0.203,0.411)	(0.05,0.092,0.234)	(0.059,0.149,0.263)	(0.046,0.102,0.185)

The fuzzy matrix $\tilde{S}_i$ is obtained by applying Equation (25)

$$\tilde{S}_{ai} = (0.062, 0.116, 0.219) \quad \tilde{S}\ldots = , (\ldots,\ldots,\ldots) \quad \tilde{S}_{,36} = (0.062, 0.158, 0.567)$$
$$\tilde{S}_1 = (0.113, 0.276, 0.660) \quad \tilde{S}_{23} = (0.286, 0.702, 1.466) \quad \tilde{S}_{37} = (0.119, 0.258, 0.705)$$
$$\tilde{S}_2 = (0.062, 0.158, 0.515) \quad \tilde{S}_{24} = (0.092, 0.172, 0.544) \quad \tilde{S}_{38} = (0.084, 0.154, 0.514)$$
$$\tilde{S}_3 = (0.084, 0.154, 0.514) \quad \tilde{S}_{25} = (0.092, 0.267, 0.555) \quad \tilde{S}_{ID} = (0.412, 0.974, 1.900)$$

as follows:

$$\tilde{S}_1 = \begin{pmatrix} 0.111 + 0.015 + 0.011 + 0.021 + 0.035 + 0.020, \\ 0.019 + 0.028 + 0.023 + 0.066 + 0.106 + 0.034, \\ 0.037 + 0.157 + 0.046 + 0.130 + 0.188 + 0.103 \end{pmatrix} = (0.113, 0.276, 0.660)$$

Using Equation (26), the matrix $\tilde{K}_i^-$ is obtained:

$\tilde{k}_1^- = (0.517, 2.386, 10.607)$ $\tilde{k}_{23}^- = (1.304, 6.064, 23.546)$ $\tilde{k}_{36}^- = (0.284, 1.367, 9.105)$
$\tilde{k}_2^- = (0.284, 1.367, 8.270)$, $\tilde{k}_{24}^- = (0.418, 1.487, 8.745)$, $\tilde{k}_{37}^- = (0.542, 2.229, 11.329)$
$\tilde{k}_3^- = (0.383, 1.333, 8.264)$ $\tilde{k}_{25}^- = (0.418, 2.307, 8.920)$ $\tilde{k}_{38}^- = (0.383, 1.333, 8.264)$

as follows:

$$\tilde{k}_1^- = \frac{\tilde{S}_1}{\tilde{S}_{ai}} = \left(\frac{s_1^l}{s_{ai}^u}, \frac{s_1^m}{s_{ai}^m}, \frac{s_1^u}{s_{ai}^l} \right) = \left(\frac{0.113}{0.219}, \frac{0.276}{0.116}, \frac{0.660}{0.062} \right) = (0.517, 2.386, 10.607)$$

Using Equation (27), the matrix $\tilde{K}_i^+$ is obtained:

$\tilde{k}_1^+ = (0.060, 0.284, 1.602)$ $\tilde{k}_{23}^+ = (0.151, 0.721, 3.557)$ $\tilde{k}_{36}^+ = (0.033, 0.163, 1.375)$
$\tilde{k}_2^+ = (0.033, 0.163, 1.249)$, $\tilde{k}_{24}^+ = (0.048, 0.177, 1.321)$, $\tilde{k}_{37}^+ = (0.063, 0.265, 1.711)$
$\tilde{k}_3^+ = (0.044, 0.159, 1.248)$ $\tilde{k}_{25}^+ = (0.048, 0.275, 1.348)$ $\tilde{k}_{38}^+ = (0.044, 0.159, 1.248)$

as follows:

$$\tilde{k}_1^+ = \frac{\tilde{S}_1}{\tilde{S}_{id}} = \left(\frac{s_1^l}{s_{id}^u}, \frac{s_1^m}{s_{id}^m}, \frac{s_1^u}{s_{id}^l} \right) = \left(\frac{0.113}{1.900}, \frac{0.276}{0.974}, \frac{0.660}{0.412} \right) = (0.060, 0.284, 1.602)$$

In Step 7, the matrix $\tilde{T}_i$ is calculated using Equation (28):

$\tilde{t}_1 = (0.577, 2.670, 12.210)$, $\tilde{t}_{23} = (1.454, 6.785, 27.103)$, $\tilde{t}_{36} = (0.317, 1.530, 10.481)$,
$\tilde{t}_2 = (0.317, 1.530, 9.519)$, $\tilde{t}_{24} = (0.466, 1.664, 10.066)$, $\tilde{t}_{37} = (0.605, 2.494, 13.040)$,
$\tilde{t}_3 = (0.427, 1.492, 9.512)$, $\tilde{t}_{25} = (0.466, 2.582, 10.268)$, $\tilde{t}_{38} = (0.427, 1.492, 9.512)$,

The elements of the matrix $\tilde{T}_i$ are obtained as follows:

$$\tilde{t}_1 = (0.517 + 0.060, 2.386 + 0.284, 10.607 + 1.602) = (0.577, 2.670, 12.210)$$

Then, it is necessary to determine a new fuzzy number $\tilde{D}$ using Equation (29) $\tilde{D} = \left(d^l, d^m, d^u\right) = \max_i \tilde{t}_{ij}$ and $\tilde{D} = (1.454, 6.785, 27.103)$ is obtained, and then it is necessary to defuzzify the number $\tilde{D}$ by using the expression $df_{crisp} = \frac{l + 4m + u}{6}$ obtaining the number $df_{crisp} = 9.283$. The calculation of the last two steps and the final results obtained using the fuzzy MARCOS method are shown in Table 6.

Table 6. Calculation of the two last steps and results of applied fuzzy MARCOS.

	$f(\tilde{K}_i^-)$	$f(\tilde{K}_i^+)$	K-	K+	fK-	fK+	Ki	Rank
A1	(0.006,0.031,0.173)	(0.056,0.257,1.143)	3.445	0.466	0.050	0.371	0.181	15
A2	(0.004,0.018,0.135)	(0.031,0.147,0.891)	2.337	0.322	0.035	0.252	0.084	29
A3	(0.005,0.017,0.134)	(0.041,0.144,0.89)	2.330	0.321	0.035	0.251	0.083	30
	....							
A23	(0.016,0.078,0.383)	(0.14,0.653,2.536)	8.184	1.099	0.118	0.882	1.082	1
A24	(0.005,0.019,0.142)	(0.045,0.16,0.942)	2.519	0.346	0.037	0.271	0.097	27
A25	(0.005,0.03,0.145)	(0.045,0.249,0.961)	3.095	0.416	0.045	0.333	0.144	20
	...							
A36	(0.004,0.018,0.148)	(0.031,0.147,0.981)	2.476	0.343	0.037	0.267	0.095	28
A37	(0.007,0.029,0.184)	(0.058,0.24,1.22)	3.464	0.472	0.051	0.373	0.185	14
A38	(0.005,0.017,0.134)	(0.041,0.144,0.89)	2.330	0.321	0.035	0.251	0.083	30

Utility functions in relation to the ideal $f(\tilde{K}_i^+)$ and anti-ideal $f(\tilde{K}_i^-)$ solution are determined by applying Equations (30) and (31).

$$f(\tilde{K}_1^+) = \frac{\tilde{K}_1^-}{df_{crisp}} = \left(\frac{0.517}{9.283}, \frac{2.386}{9.283}, \frac{10.607}{9.283}\right)$$

$$f(\tilde{K}_1^-) = \frac{\tilde{K}_1^+}{df_{crisp}} = \left(\frac{0.060}{9.283}, \frac{0.284}{9.283}, \frac{1.602}{9.283}\right)$$

After that, it is necessary to perform defuzzification for $\tilde{K}_i^-$, $\tilde{K}_i^+$, $f(\tilde{K}_i^+)$, $f(\tilde{K}_i^-)$, which is given in Table 6.

Determination of the utility function of alternatives fK_i. The utility function of alternatives is defined by Equation (32).

$$f(K_1) = \frac{K_1^+ + K_1^-}{1 + \frac{1-f(K_1^+)}{f(K_1^+)} + \frac{1-f(K_1^-)}{f(K_1^-)}} = \frac{0.446 + 3.445}{1 + \frac{1-0.371}{0.371} + \frac{1-0.050}{0.050}} = 0.181$$

The ranking represents the sorting of obtained values in descending order, where A23 represents the most hazardous 200-m section and is dominant over the others.

5. Validation Tests

5.1. Changing the Significance of Input Parameters

In the first phase of validation test, the impact of changing the three most significant criteria C1, C2 and C3 on ranking results was analyzed. Using Equation (33), a total of 30 scenarios were created.

$$\tilde{W}_{n\beta} = \left(1 - \tilde{W}_{n\alpha}\right)\frac{\tilde{W}_\beta}{\left(1 - \tilde{W}_n\right)} \tag{33}$$

The scenarios were formed through three different groups of 10 sets each. In the first group of scenarios, the first criterion was changed, criterion C2 was changed in the second group and criterion C3 was changed in the third group. If Equation (33) is observed, $\tilde{W}_{n\beta}$ represents the fuzzy corrected value of the criteria C2, C3, C4, C5 and C6, then C1, C3, C4, C5 and C6, i.e., C1, C2, C4, C5 and C6, respectively by groups. $\tilde{W}_{n\alpha}$ represents the reduced fuzzy value of the criteria C1, C2, and C3 respectively by groups, $\tilde{W}_\beta$ represents the original fuzzy value of the criterion considered and $\tilde{W}_n$ represents the original fuzzy value of the criterion whose value is reduced, in this case, C1, C2 and C3.

In the first scenario, the fuzzy value of criterion C1 was reduced by 5% while the values of the remaining criteria were proportionally corrected by applying Equation (33). In each subsequent scenario, the value of criterion C1 was reduced by 10%, while the values of the remaining criteria were corrected, so they met the condition $\sum_{j=1}^{n} w_j^m = 1$. These changes, i.e., these 10 scenarios represent the first group. Scenarios 11–20 represent the second group in which criterion C2 was corrected. The third group consists of scenarios 21–30 with the change in the value of the third criterion. After forming 30 new vectors of the weight coefficients of the criteria (Table 7), new model results were obtained, as presented in Figures 1–3.

Table 7. New criterion values across 30 scenarios.

	w1	w2	w3	w4	w5	w6
S1	(0.093,0.165,0.319)	(0.133,0.257,0.483)	(0.1,0.205,0.421)	(0.064,0.12,0.24)	(0.083,0.15,0.269)	(0.06,0.103,0.19)
S2	(0.083,0.148,0.286)	(0.135,0.262,0.507)	(0.101,0.209,0.442)	(0.065,0.123,0.252)	(0.084,0.154,0.283)	(0.061,0.105,0.199)
S3	(0.073,0.13,0.252)	(0.136,0.267,0.53)	(0.102,0.213,0.463)	(0.066,0.125,0.264)	(0.085,0.157,0.296)	(0.061,0.107,0.208)
S4	(0.064,0.113,0.218)	(0.138,0.273,0.554)	(0.103,0.218,0.484)	(0.066,0.128,0.276)	(0.086,0.16,0.309)	(0.062,0.109,0.218)
S5	(0.054,0.095,0.185)	(0.139,0.278,0.578)	(0.104,0.222,0.505)	(0.067,0.13,0.287)	(0.087,0.163,0.322)	(0.063,0.111,0.227)
S6	(0.044,0.078,0.151)	(0.141,0.283,0.602)	(0.106,0.226,0.525)	(0.068,0.133,0.299)	(0.088,0.166,0.336)	(0.063,0.114,0.237)
S7	(0.034,0.061,0.118)	(0.142,0.289,0.626)	(0.107,0.231,0.546)	(0.069,0.135,0.311)	(0.089,0.169,0.349)	(0.064,0.116,0.246)
S8	(0.024,0.043,0.084)	(0.144,0.294,0.65)	(0.108,0.235,0.567)	(0.069,0.138,0.323)	(0.09,0.172,0.362)	(0.064,0.118,0.255)
S9	(0.015,0.026,0.05)	(0.145,0.299,0.673)	(0.109,0.239,0.588)	(0.07,0.14,0.335)	(0.09,0.176,0.376)	(0.065,0.12,0.265)
S10	(0.005,0.009,0.017)	(0.146,0.305,0.697)	(0.11,0.243,0.609)	(0.071,0.143,0.347)	(0.091,0.179,0.389)	(0.066,0.122,0.274)
S11	(0.099,0.177,0.351)	(0.126,0.241,0.447)	(0.1,0.206,0.429)	(0.065,0.121,0.244)	(0.083,0.151,0.274)	(0.06,0.104,0.193)
S12	(0.1,0.182,0.381)	(0.113,0.216,0.4)	(0.102,0.213,0.466)	(0.066,0.125,0.265)	(0.085,0.157,0.298)	(0.061,0.107,0.21)
S13	(0.102,0.188,0.411)	(0.1,0.19,0.353)	(0.103,0.22,0.502)	(0.066,0.129,0.286)	(0.086,0.162,0.321)	(0.062,0.111,0.226)
S14	(0.103,0.194,0.441)	(0.086,0.165,0.306)	(0.105,0.227,0.539)	(0.067,0.133,0.307)	(0.087,0.167,0.344)	(0.063,0.114,0.243)
S15	(0.105,0.2,0.471)	(0.073,0.14,0.259)	(0.106,0.234,0.576)	(0.068,0.137,0.328)	(0.089,0.172,0.368)	(0.064,0.117,0.259)
S16	(0.106,0.206,0.5)	(0.06,0.114,0.212)	(0.108,0.241,0.612)	(0.069,0.141,0.349)	(0.09,0.177,0.391)	(0.065,0.121,0.276)
S17	(0.108,0.212,0.53)	(0.046,0.089,0.165)	(0.109,0.248,0.649)	(0.07,0.145,0.369)	(0.091,0.182,0.415)	(0.066,0.124,0.292)
S18	(0.109,0.218,0.56)	(0.033,0.063,0.118)	(0.111,0.255,0.685)	(0.071,0.149,0.39)	(0.092,0.187,0.438)	(0.066,0.128,0.308)
S19	(0.111,0.224,0.59)	(0.02,0.038,0.071)	(0.113,0.261,0.722)	(0.072,0.153,0.411)	(0.094,0.192,0.461)	(0.067,0.131,0.325)
S20	(0.112,0.23,0.62)	(0.007,0.013,0.024)	(0.114,0.268,0.758)	(0.073,0.157,0.432)	(0.095,0.197,0.485)	(0.068,0.135,0.341)
S21	(0.098,0.176,0.348)	(0.133,0.257,0.487)	(0.095,0.193,0.39)	(0.064,0.12,0.242)	(0.083,0.151,0.272)	(0.06,0.103,0.191)
S22	(0.099,0.18,0.371)	(0.135,0.264,0.52)	(0.085,0.172,0.349)	(0.065,0.123,0.259)	(0.084,0.155,0.29)	(0.061,0.106,0.204)
S23	(0.101,0.185,0.395)	(0.136,0.27,0.553)	(0.075,0.152,0.308)	(0.066,0.126,0.275)	(0.085,0.158,0.308)	(0.061,0.108,0.217)
S24	(0.102,0.189,0.418)	(0.138,0.277,0.586)	(0.065,0.132,0.267)	(0.067,0.129,0.291)	(0.086,0.162,0.327)	(0.062,0.111,0.23)
S25	(0.103,0.194,0.441)	(0.139,0.283,0.619)	(0.055,0.112,0.226)	(0.067,0.132,0.308)	(0.087,0.166,0.345)	(0.063,0.114,0.243)
S26	(0.104,0.198,0.465)	(0.141,0.289,0.652)	(0.045,0.091,0.185)	(0.068,0.136,0.324)	(0.088,0.17,0.363)	(0.063,0.116,0.256)
S27	(0.105,0.202,0.488)	(0.142,0.296,0.684)	(0.035,0.071,0.144)	(0.069,0.139,0.34)	(0.089,0.174,0.382)	(0.064,0.119,0.269)
S28	(0.106,0.207,0.512)	(0.144,0.302,0.717)	(0.025,0.051,0.103)	(0.069,0.142,0.357)	(0.09,0.177,0.4)	(0.065,0.121,0.282)
S29	(0.107,0.211,0.535)	(0.145,0.309,0.75)	(0.015,0.03,0.062)	(0.07,0.145,0.373)	(0.091,0.181,0.418)	(0.065,0.124,0.295)
S30	(0.108,0.216,0.559)	(0.147,0.315,0.783)	(0.005,0.01,0.021)	(0.071,0.148,0.389)	(0.092,0.185,0.437)	(0.066,0.126,0.308)

After forming scenarios as described above, results were obtained for each of the groups. Figure 2 shows the obtained ranks of the alternatives and comparison of initial results with the results in the first group of scenarios, i.e., S1–S10.

The change in the significance of the first criterion affects the ranks of road network sections, which is, in a way, understandable since there is a large number of alternatives. It is important to note that alternatives A23, A18, A20, A12, A5 and A16, which take the first, second, third, eighth, ninth and tenth places, respectively, do not change their positions in any scenario. With the elimination of the significance of the first criterion, since its value is 0.05 in the tenth scenario, there is a change in ranks by five positions for some alternatives.

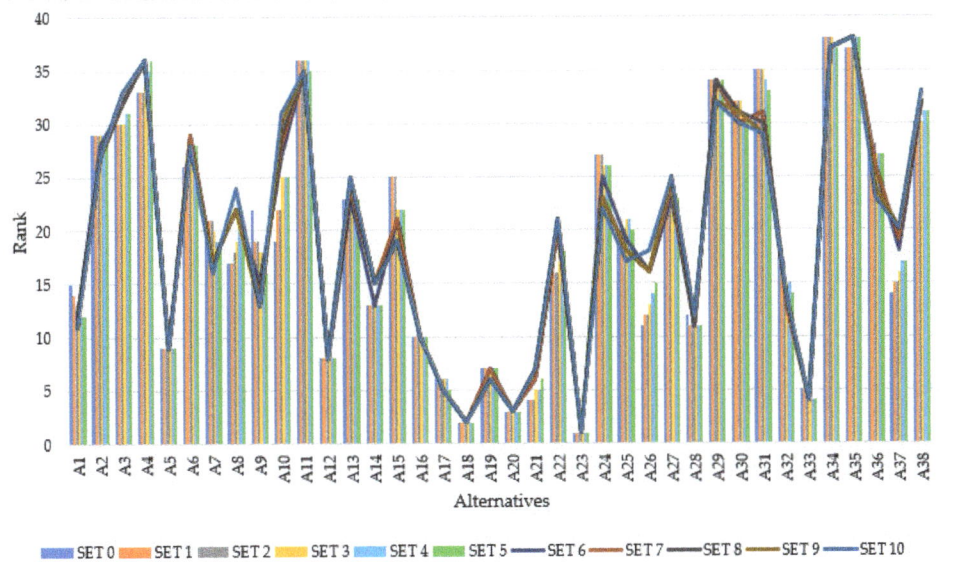

Figure 2. Comparison of initial results with scenarios S1–S10.

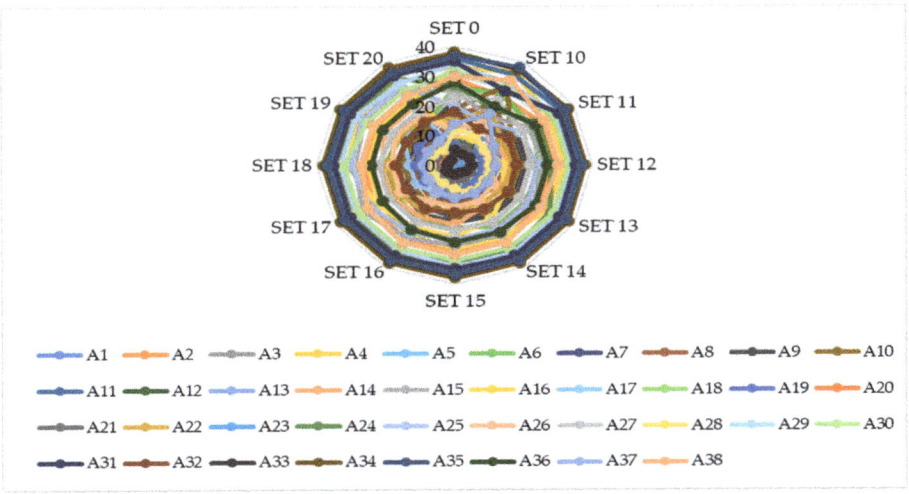

Figure 3. Comparison of initial results with the second group of scenarios, i.e., scenarios S11–S20.

Figure 3 shows the obtained ranks of the alternatives and comparison of initial results with the results in the second group of scenarios, i.e., S11–S20. In Figure 3, it can be noticed that there have been major changes in the ranks of alternatives across scenarios. The reason for this is the fact that the most significant criterion C2 has been changed, which has a significant impact on the output. However, alternative A23 remains in the first place, despite the fact that the influence of the most significant criterion is minimized. Additionally, alternatives A31 and A34 do not change their position and are ranked 35th and 38th, respectively. Alternative A18 in scenarios S11–S17 retains its second position, while in the remaining three scenarios (S18–S20), it is in the third place. Alternative A20 is in the third position in scenarios S11–S13, fourth in S14–S16 and fifth in S17–S20 scenarios. With the decrease in the impact of criterion C2, results and ranks change to a maximum of 37%.

Figure 4 shows the obtained ranks of the alternatives and a comparison of initial results with the results in the third group of scenarios, i.e., S21–S30.

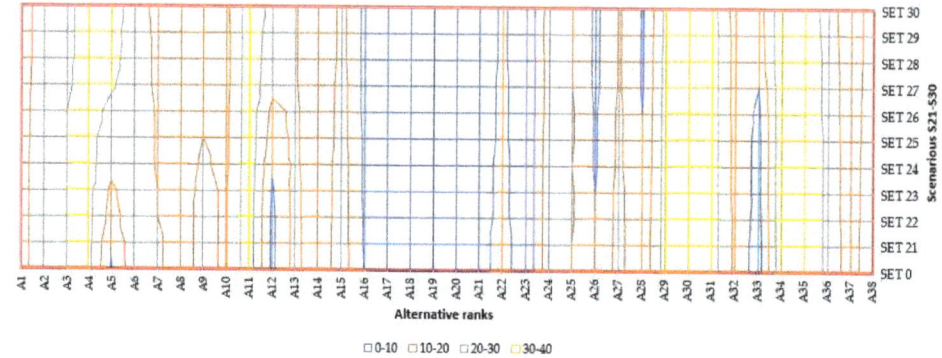

Figure 4. Comparison of initial results with third group of scenarios i.e., S21–S30.

In Figure 4, it can be noticed that there were also some changes in the ranks of the alternatives across the scenarios. The reason for this is the fact that the second most significant criterion C3 was changed, which has a slightly lower impact than C2, but is also very important in obtaining the output. However, alternatives A23, A34 and A35 do not change their ranks and they are still ranked as first, 38th and 37th, respectively. Alternative A20 retains its third position in scenarios S21 and S22, while holding second place in the remaining scenarios. Alternative A30 changes its position by one place only in the last S30 scenario.

5.2. Impact of Reverse Rank Matrices

One of the ways to test the validity of the obtained results of the model for decision-making is to construct dynamic matrices and then analyze the solutions that the model provides under newly formed conditions. If the solutions show some logical contradictions that are expressed in the form of undesirable changes in the ranks of alternatives, then one may express concern that there is a problem with the mathematical apparatus of the applied method. In line with this goal, a test in which the resistance of the model to the rank reversal problem is considered was conducted.

A change in the number of alternatives was made for each scenario, eliminating the worst alternative from further consideration. After defining a new set of alternatives, the ranking of the remaining alternatives is performed under newly formed conditions using the proposed model. In the test, 35 scenarios were formed in which the change in the elements of the decision matrix was simulated. As a rule, 37 scenarios should be formed (one less than the total number of alternatives). However, in this case, we had two newly formed scenarios in which two alternatives were eliminated. In scenario S7, there are two alternatives A3 and A38 that have the same position, and both alternatives were eliminated in the next eighth scenario. The same situation is with scenario S14 in which A13 and A27 were eliminated.

Based on the results obtained (Figure 5) and taking into account the complexity of the MCDM model, it can be concluded that the model is stable. In the first 14 scenarios, there is no change in ranks for any alternative. Only eight alternatives change their ranks after the fifteenth scenario has been formed when Alternative A9 is eliminated from the model. It is important to note that after obtaining the results in S15 when the change occurs, the alternatives retain their ranks until the last scenario.

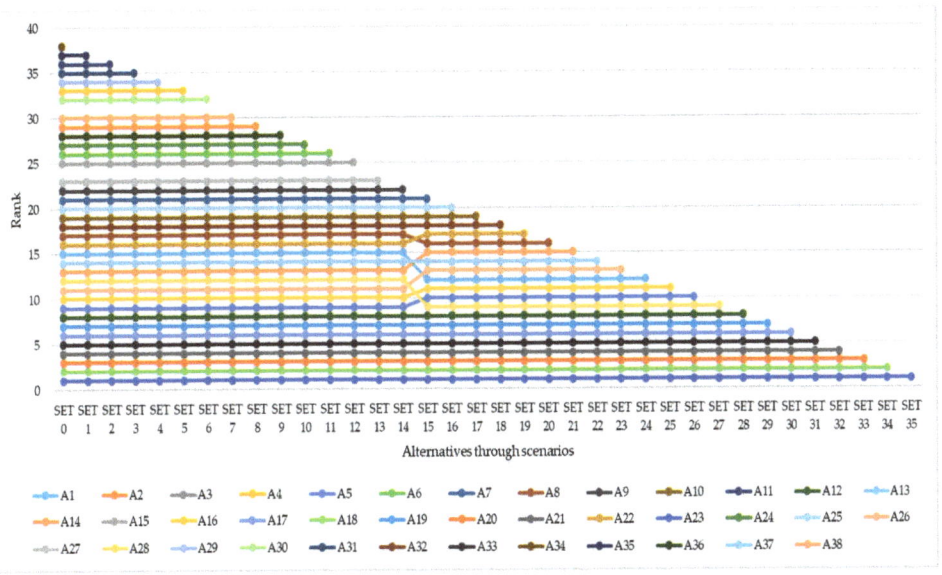

Figure 5. Results of the test of reverse rank matrix.

5.3. Comparison with Other Approaches

In this section, a validation test is performed involving comparison with two other methods in a fuzzy form: the Fuzzy SAW [21] and the fuzzy TOPSIS method [22], and the results are presented in Figure 6.

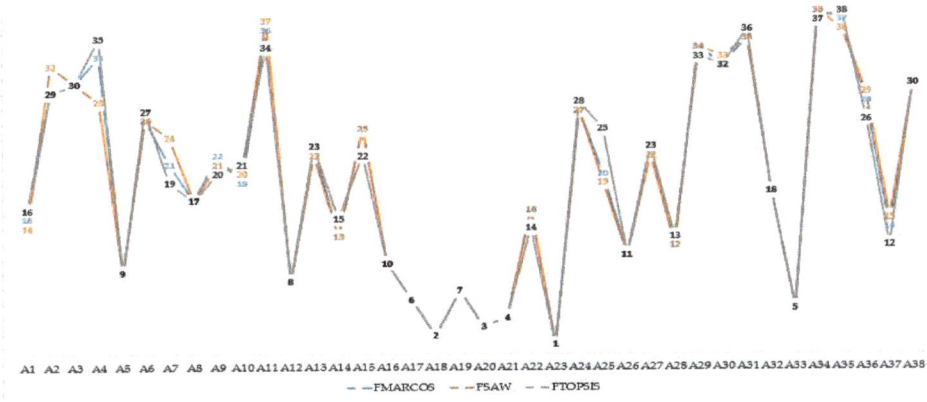

Figure 6. Results of comparison with Fuzzy SAW and fuzzy TOPSIS methods.

In this case study, we compared the fuzzy MARCOS technique with MCDM models that have a linear normalization. When observing the comparisons of the applied methods, it can be seen that in 15 cases, there is no change of ranks. It is of primary importance to note that the first 11 (A23, A18, A20, A21, A33, A17, A19, A12, A5, A16, and A26) alternatives do not change positions regardless of the approach taken. In addition, alternatives A8, A32, A3 and A38 do not change their ranks and are in 17th, 18th and 30th places, respectively. The last two mentioned alternatives share the 30th position. In addition, compared to the fuzzy SAW method, eight other alternatives do not change their ranks, while compared to the fuzzy TOPSIS method, three other alternatives do not change positions. The biggest difference is with alternative A25, which is ranked 20th applying the fuzzy MARCOS method and in the 25th position using the fuzzy TOPSIS method. The observed small differences in ranking of alternatives, between Fuzzy MARCOS results and Fuzzy SAW/Fuzzy TOPSIS results (see Figure 6) do not limit the usefulness of the study, as it is impossible to know in advance the possible outcomes of an applied methodology and the extent of possible deviation of the rankings, therefore making the process is significant for validation.

The advantages of the Fuzzy MARCOS method are as follows: consideration of fuzzy reference points through the fuzzy ideal and fuzzy anti-ideal solution at the very beginning of model formation, more precise determination of the degree of utility with respect to both set solutions, proposal of a new way of determining utility functions and its aggregation, possibility to consider a large set of criteria and alternatives, as demonstrated through a realistic example, too. Compared with other methods, this method is simple, effective, and easy to sort and optimize the process.

6. Conclusions

In this paper, a fuzzy MARCOS algorithm was developed to support multi-criteria decision-making, especially when considering parameters in an uncertain environment. Considering the relationships of indicators presented through TFNs between the ideal and the anti-ideal solution, it can positively affect making valid decisions. In addition, this paper defines a new fuzzy linguistic scale for parameter evaluation by decision-makers. The Fuzzy MARCOS model was tested using the example of determining the degree of risk on short sections of the first-order main road. A part of the road network with a length of 7.4 km divided into 38 short sections of 200 m each was analyzed. Thanks to the previously formed adequate database regarding all necessary parameters, the MCDM model was created. The results of the proposed model show that the 23rd section, i.e., the section between 4.2 and 4.4 km represents the most hazardous section since the value obtained is drastically higher than the others are. This result is caused by the fact that this section has an undesirable value considering almost all factors and an adequate reaction in terms of increasing surveillance and traffic safety on this section is required. The obtained results in terms of risk can be used for improving road safety. The results can help decision-makers take into account these indicators as an input parameter for all planning, design and operational analyzes, as well as indicators for the development of regulatory plans for a given area in local conditions. For the purpose of validation, an extensive analysis was carried out, which involves changing the significance of the input parameters, testing the factors of dynamic environment and comparing the results with two other methods in a fuzzy form. The validation tests support the development and application of the fuzzy MARCOS method. In order to improve the robustness of MCDM in fuzzy environment, a new fuzzy MARCOS method was developed in this study, which uses the ratio method and the reference point method to obtain a scheme of basic comprehensive decision information. The fuzzy MARCOS method is a powerful tool for optimizing multiple goals. Fuzzy MARCOS refreshes the MCDM domain by introducing an algorithm for analyzing the relationship between alternatives and reference points. The Fuzzy MARCOS method integrates the following points to provide a robust decision: defining reference points (fuzzy ideal and fuzzy anti-ideal values), determining the relationship between alternatives and fuzzy ideal/anti-ideal values, defining the utility degree of alternatives in relation to the fuzzy ideal and fuzzy anti-ideal solutions. The results obtained by the fuzzy MARCOS method are more reasonable due to the fusion of the results of the ratio approach and reference point sorting approach. The Fuzzy MARCOS method shows the significant stability and reliability of the results in a dynamic environment. Moreover, it is important to note that in numerous scenarios, the fuzzy MARCOS method shows stability in processing large data sets, which was proven in the performed research.

Future research may be based on the integration of particular short sections and their evaluation, and the development of the MARCOS method with other theories such as neutrophic [23], single-valued intuitionistic fuzzy numbers [24], grey theory [25] and others. Moreover, the approach of a building consensus in group decision making with information granularity [26] or the concept of a granular fuzzy preference relation where each pairwise comparison is formed as a certain information granule can be implemented [27].

Author Contributions: Conceptualization, M.S. (Miomir Stanković) and M.S. (Marko Subotić); methodology, Ž.S.; validation, D.K.D. and D.P.; investigation, M.S. (Marko Subotić); writing—original draft preparation, Ž.S.; writing—review and editing, D.K.D. and D.P.; supervision, M.S. (Miomir Stanković). All authors have read and agreed to the published version of the manuscript.

Funding: This research received no external funding.

Acknowledgments: The paper is a part of the research done within the project No. 19.032/961-58/19 "Influence of Geometric Elements of Two-lane Roads in Traffic Risk Analysis Models" supported by Ministry of Scientific and Technological Development, Higher Education and Information Society of the Republic of Srpska.

Conflicts of Interest: The authors declare no conflict of interest.

References

1. Zavadskas, E.K.; Turskis, Z. A new additive ratio assessment (ARAS) method in multicriteria decision-making. *Technol. Econ. Dev. Econ.* **2010**, *16*, 159–172. [CrossRef]
2. Keshavarz Ghorabaee, M.; Zavadskas, E.K.; Olfat, L.; Turskis, Z. Multi-criteria inventory classification using a new method of evaluation based on distance from average solution (EDAS). *Informatica* **2015**, *26*, 435–451. [CrossRef]
3. Pamučar, D.; Ćirović, G. The selection of transport and handling resources in logistics centers using Multi-Attributive Border Approximation area Comparison (MABAC). *Expert Syst. Appl.* **2015**, *42*, 3016–3028. [CrossRef]
4. Talevska, J.B.; Ristov, M.; Todorova, M.M. Development of methodology for the selection of the optimal type of pedestrian crossing. *Decis. Mak. Appl. Manag. Eng.* **2019**, *2*, 105–114. [CrossRef]
5. Baležentis, A.; Baležentis, T.; Misiunas, A. An integrated assessment of Lithuanian economic sectors based on financial ratios and fuzzy MCDM methods. *Technol. Econ. Dev. Econ.* **2012**, *18*, 34–53. [CrossRef]
6. Karaşan, A.; Kaya, İ.; Erdoğan, M. Location selection of electric vehicles charging stations by using a fuzzy MCDM method: A case study in Turkey. *Neural Comput. Appl.* **2018**, 1–22. [CrossRef]
7. Tripathy, P.; Khambete, A.K.; Chauhan, K.A. An Innovative Approach to Assess Sustainability of Urban Mobility—Using Fuzzy MCDM Method. In *Innovative Research in Transportation Infrastructure*; Springer: Singapore, 2019; pp. 55–63.
8. Stojić, G.; Stević, Ž.; Antuchevičienė, J.; Pamučar, D.; Vasiljević, M. A novel rough WASPAS approach for supplier selection in a company manufacturing PVC carpentry products. *Information* **2018**, *9*, 121. [CrossRef]
9. Zavadskas, E.K.; Stević, Ž.; Tanackov, I.; Prentkovskis, O. A novel multicriteria approach—Rough Step-Wise Weight Assessment Ratio Analysis method (R-SWARA) and its application in logistics. *Stud. Inform. Control* **2018**, *27*, 97–106. [CrossRef]
10. Morente-Molinera, J.A.; Kou, G.; Pérez, I.J.; Samuylov, K.; Selamat, A.; Herrera-Viedma, E. A group decision making support system for the Web: How to work in environments with a high number of participants and alternatives. *Appl. Soft Comput.* **2018**, *68*, 191–201. [CrossRef]
11. Morency, P.; Gauvin, L.; Plante, C.; Fournier, M.; Morency, C. Neighborhood Social Inequalities in Road Traffic Injuries: The Influence of Traffic Volume and Road Design. *Am. J. Public Health* **2012**, *102*, 1112–1119. [CrossRef]
12. Karlaftis, M.G.; Golias, I. Effects of road geometry and traffic volumes on rural roadway accident rates. *Accid. Anal. Prev.* **2002**, *34*, 357–365. [CrossRef]
13. Nenadić, D. Ranking dangerous sections of the road using MCDM model. *Decis. Mak. Appl. Manag. Eng.* **2019**, *2*, 115–131. [CrossRef]
14. Bao, Q.; Ruan, D.; Shen, Y.; Hermans, E.; Janssens, D. Improved hierarchical fuzzy TOPSIS for road safety performance evaluation. *Knowl. Based Syst.* **2012**, *32*, 84–90. [CrossRef]
15. Khorasani, G.; Yadollahi, A.; Rahimi, M.; Tatari, A. Implementation of MCDM methods in road safety management. In Proceedings of the International Conference on Transport, Civil, Architecture and Environment Engineering (ICTCAEE'2012), Dubai, UAE, 26–27 December 2012; pp. 26–27.

16. Haghighat, F. Application of a multi-criteria approach to road safety evaluation in the Bushehr Province, Iran. *Promet Traffic Transp.* **2011**, *23*, 341–352. [CrossRef]
17. Tzeng, G.H.; Huang, J.J. *Multiple Attribute Decision Making: Methods and Applications*; Chapman and Hall/CRC: Boca Raton, FL, USA, 2011.
18. Sun, C.C. A performance evaluation model by integrating fuzzy AHP and fuzzy TOPSIS methods. *Expert Syst. Appl.* **2010**, *37*, 7745–7754. [CrossRef]
19. Stević, Ž.; Pamučar, D.; Puška, A.; Chatterjee, P. Sustainable supplier selection in healthcare industries using a new MCDM method: Measurement of alternatives and ranking according to COmpromise solution (MARCOS). *Comput. Ind. Eng.* **2020**, *140*, 106231. [CrossRef]
20. Stević, Ž.; Stjepanović, Ž.; Božičković, Z.; Das, D.K.; Stanujkić, D. Assessment of conditions for implementing information technology in a warehouse system: A novel fuzzy piprecia method. *Symmetry* **2018**, *10*, 586. [CrossRef]
21. Fauzi, N.; Noviarti, T.; Muslihudin, M.; Irviani, R.; Maseleno, A.; Pringsewu, S.T.M.I.K. Optimal dengue endemic region prediction using fuzzy simple additive weighting based algorithm. *Int. J. Pure Appl. Math.* **2018**, *118*, 473–478.
22. Chatterjee, P.; Stević, Ž. A two-phase fuzzy AHP-fuzzy TOPSIS model for supplier evaluation in manufacturing environment. *Oper. Res. Eng. Sci. Theory Appl.* **2019**, *2*, 72–90. [CrossRef]
23. Pamučar, D.; Božanić, D. Selection of a location for the development of multimodal logistics center: Application of single-valued neutrosophic MABAC model. *Oper. Res. Eng. Sci. Theory Appl.* **2019**, *2*, 55–71. [CrossRef]
24. Karabašević, D.; Popović, G.; Stanujkić, D.; Maksimović, M.; Sava, C. An approach for hotel type selection based on the single-valued intuitionistic fuzzy numbers. *Int. Rev.* **2019**, *1–2*, 7–14. [CrossRef]
25. Badi, I.; Shetwan, A.; Hemeda, A. A grey-based assessment model to evaluate health-care waste treatment alternatives in Libya. *Oper. Res. Eng. Sci. Theory Appl.* **2019**, *2*, 92–106. [CrossRef]
26. Cabrerizo, F.J.; Morente-Molinera, J.A.; Pedrycz, W.; Taghavi, A.; Herrera-Viedma, E. Granulating linguistic information in decision making under consensus and consistency. *Expert Syst. Appl.* **2018**, *99*, 83–92. [CrossRef]
27. Cabrerizo, F.J.; Ureña, R.; Pedrycz, W.; Herrera-Viedma, E. Building consensus in group decision making with an allocation of information granularity. *Fuzzy Sets Syst.* **2014**, *255*, 115–127. [CrossRef]

© 2020 by the authors. Licensee MDPI, Basel, Switzerland. This article is an open access article distributed under the terms and conditions of the Creative Commons Attribution (CC BY) license (http://creativecommons.org/licenses/by/4.0/).

MDPI
St. Alban-Anlage 66
4052 Basel
Switzerland
Tel. +41 61 683 77 34
Fax +41 61 302 89 18
www.mdpi.com

Mathematics Editorial Office
E-mail: mathematics@mdpi.com
www.mdpi.com/journal/mathematics

www.ingramcontent.com/pod-product-compliance
Lightning Source LLC
LaVergne TN
LVHW070737100526
838202LV00013B/1256